The Making of the Modern Iranian Woman

Florida A&M University, Tallahassee
Florida Atlantic University, Boca Raton
Florida Gulf Coast University, Ft. Myers
Florida International University, Miami
Florida State University, Tallahassee
University of Central Florida, Orlando
University of Florida, Gainesville
University of North Florida, Jacksonville
University of South Florida, Tampa
University of West Florida, Pensacola

The Making of the Modern Iranian Woman

Gender, State Policy, and Popular Culture, 1865–1946

Camron Michael Amin

University Press of Florida

Gainesville · Tallahassee · Tampa · Boca Raton
Pensacola · Orlando · Miami · Jacksonville · Ft. Myers

07 06 05 04 03 02   6 5 4 3 2 1

Library of Congress Cataloging-in-Publication Data
Amin, Camron Michael.
The making of the modern Iranian woman: gender, state policy, and
popular culture, 1865–1946 / Camron Michael Amin.
p. cm.
Includes bibliographical references and index.
ISBN 0-8130-2471-4 (cloth)
1. Women—Iran—History. 2. Feminism—Iran—History. 3. Women's
rights—Iran—History. 4. Iran—Social policy—18th century. 5. Iran—
Social policy—19th century. I. Title.
HQ1735.2 .A75 2002
305.42'0955—dc21 2002016574

The University Press of Florida is the scholarly publishing agency
for the State University System of Florida, comprising Florida A&M
University, Florida Atlantic University, Florida Gulf Coast University,
Florida International University, Florida State University, University of
Central Florida, University of Florida, University of North Florida,
University of South Florida, and University of West Florida.

University Press of Florida
15 Northwest 15th Street
Gainesville, FL 32611–2079
http://www.upf.com

For my family, my friends, and all those who hope for freedom and equality for all Iranians

Contents

List of Illustrations and Tables   ix

Preface   xi

1. The "Women's Awakening" Reconsidered   1

2. Tradition and Renewal   16

3. Imagining the Modern Iranian Woman   48

4. Unveiling and Its Discontents   80

5. Renewal's Bride   114

6. The Capable Woman   142

7. The Limits of Emancipation   189

8. Breaking with Male Guardianship   215

9. The Legacy of the Women's Awakening   246

Notes   255

Bibliography   301

Index   313

Illustrations and Tables

Illustrations

2.1. Women in a Gilan shrine in 1861. 22
3.1. A leftist cartoon of Reza Shah, 1925. 75
3.2. Comparing Iranian and European Families I. 76
3.3. Comparing Iranian and European Families II. 77
5.1a. Women from around the world choose their ideal husbands, 1938. 133
5.1b. Iranian women choose their ideal husbands, 1939. 134
6.1. Ten women medical students at the University of Tehran in 1946. 143
6.2. Medical students protesting to increase the quota of students accepted into the University of Tehran Medical School, 1945. 143
6.3. University of Tehran medical students on an outing, ca. 1950. 144
6.4. Exercising for the nation-state in Germany and Iran. 173
6.5. Women students working in a lab alongside men, 1941. 174
6.6. Iranian women pilots, 1940. 175
6.7. The first woman pilot receives an award. 176
7.1. Young "educated housewives" in training, 1940. 203
7.2. The conflation of health and beauty, 1937. 209
7.3. The endurance of Western glamour, 1944. 211
8.1. Cover of *Women's World*, 1944. 216
8.2. "If a Woman Represented the Nation," 1946. 233
8.3. Princess Ashraf reclaims Zanjan, 1946. 235

Tables

1.1. Chronology of the "woman question" 8
6.1. Elementary school teachers in Iran, 1937–48 (1316–27) 185
6.2. Secondary school teachers in Iran, 1937–48 (1316–27) 186

Preface

A friend in graduate school told me a story that has stuck with me ever since. As I remember the story now, he had fallen asleep in an undergraduate history class. The professor called on him and asked him if a particular event (having been asleep, my friend could not tell me which event exactly) had changed anything or had merely preserved the status quo. My friend, exceptionally bright, quickly began, "Well, there was some continuity and some change." He survived the incident in good academic standing as the professor seized upon that tautology to elaborate upon ideas of his own for the class's benefit. Assessing the degrees of continuity and change in any given period is the essential burden of the historian, and, by that very simple measure, this is a study of an important change in the history of Iranian culture.

Most of the work on this manuscript was completed between 1997 and 2000. It was begun at an optimistic time in Iranian history and completed in a grim time of renewed crackdowns, intolerance, and uncertainty. As I argued for the emergence (and durability) of gender equality and an accompanying redefinition of gender hierarchy in Iranian public discourse in the first half of the twentieth century, I could not help but wonder about the durability of my thesis. Was I watching this slight (and, in my feminist perspective, positive) shift in Perso-Islamic culture crumble under the weight of more long-standing cultural history and the acute pressure of current political tensions? If I had been lulled into thinking otherwise, recent events in Iran have reminded me that history does not "progress" toward any particular end. That being said, the legacy of the Women's Awakening of the 1930s (in both its toxic and emancipatory aspects) has not yet played itself out. I hope my fellow students of Iranian history will appreciate the focus on the sociocultural aspects of a period that is often strictly defined in political terms. I hope the general reader will let go (just a little bit) of the urge to think of "the veil" as an unchanging symbol of tradition and women's oppression. Fortunately, traditions can change, and, unfortunately, oppression requires no distinctive costume or ideology.

My research for this manuscript began with my dissertation at the University of Chicago in 1996, and I would like to thank my committee members (Rashid Khalidi, John Woods, John Perry, and Richard Chambers) for their guidance and support over the years. I would also like to thank Afsaneh Najmabadi for indulging me in many discussions and debates about my research and Iranian history. If I have found my intellectual bearings, it is only due to her help. I could not have finished this manuscript without the support of all my wonderful colleagues at the University of Michigan–Dearborn, who gave me time to work and gave me their time as I worked. Here, in southeast Michigan, Linda Adler-Kassner, Don Anderson, Kathryn Babayan, Sid Bolkosky, Elaine Clark, Juan R. I. Cole, Greg Field, Brooks Hull, Maureen Linker, Joe Lunn, Marsha Richmond, Jonathan Smith, Pat Smith, and Wayne Woodward have all been kind enough to read parts of this work in various stages of development and offer their comments. I wish also to thank Lisa Pollard, Fatemeh Keshavarz, Mark Stein, Bruce Craig, Marlis Saleh, James Weinberger, Azadeh Ashraf, G. R. Afkhami, Mahnaz Afkhami, Hormoz Hekmat, Habib Ladjevardi, "Maryam Tusi," Sadiqeh Dowlatshahi, Carolyn Russ, Judy Goffman, Olaf Nelson, Betty Greco, Gerri Habitz, and Amy Gorelick for assistance in bringing this study to press. My research was supported by the Rackham Foundation at the University of Michigan and would not have been possible without the collections of the University of Chicago, Princeton University, the University of Michigan, the Foundation for Iranian Studies, and the Library of Congress. I need to offer special thanks to the Child Development Center at University of Michigan–Dearborn for granting me use of their scanner as I prepared images for publication. All mistakes are my own.

I could not have finished this work without the encouragement of my many nuclear families, all of whom I love dearly. Mohammad and Gloria Amin have put up with a lot from their son over the years, and I want my gratitude to them noted in print (as do they!). Sorry, I don't think the book will stay on the refrigerator door. Thank you to my sister, Melanie, and her husband, David, for always listening. My parents-in-law, Bob and Marie Harrell, have given me so much support and kindness over the years, and all I ever gave them was drafts of my manuscript for Bob to proof. Thank you for everything. For the forbearance and love of my brilliant wife, Amelia, and my thoughtful son, Caelin, I will be ever grateful—it all means nothing without you both.

The "Women's Awakening" Reconsidered

A major watershed in the making of modern Iranian society was the bold and controversial attempt of Reza Shah Pahlavi (reigned 1925–41) to radically transform Iranian womanhood. The Women's Awakening of 1936–41 was a state feminism project that offered new opportunities in employment and education for some Iranian women in exchange for the requirement that all Iranian women abandon their veils in public.[1] Drawing upon decades of debate on "the woman question" in the popular press, the regime of Reza Shah championed and enforced a particular vision of the modern Iranian woman. She was to be as educated as any European or American woman. She was to be integrated into the workforce in increasingly prestigious professions. Not just a supportive companion to her husband, she was also to complement the modern Iranian man in the civic arena—her unveiled entrance into society "chaperoned" by her modern male guardian. Yet the notion of the modern male guardian likewise reflected new social realities. He was no longer simply a woman's relative or husband, but also her classmate, her professor, her colleague, and, ultimately, her "great father," Reza Shah.

The policies and propaganda of the Women's Awakening of 1936–41 had a unique role in the history of the woman question in Iran. In attempting to strike a balance between emancipating and controlling women, the Pahlavi regime brought the long-standing tension between modern male guardianship and modern Iranian womanhood to a breaking point. It was only in the wake of the Women's Awakening in the 1940s that some Iranian feminists began to push for progress that was not linked to the service women provided men as wives and mothers; it was only after the Women's Awakening that public demands went up for true gender equality and a campaign for women's suffrage was undertaken. This is a study of the emergence of a concern for gender equality in Iranian public discourse—

the role of the Women's Awakening in provoking it and the memories of individuals who lived through it.

Reza Shah, Gender, and Iranian Historiography

It is natural and useful for historians to divide history into manageable periods for the purpose of analysis. Over time, early choices about periodization lead to the development of conventions regarding historical periods. The effort to legitimize conventions can lead whole generations of historians to ignore or dismiss certain historical processes because they are not seen as central characteristics of their period. Historians of modern Iran have fared no differently than others in this respect.

The political failure of the Qajar dynasty (1796–1925) cast it in the role of an ancien régime to be swept aside in two stages: first, by the sentiments of "liberty, equality, and fraternity" during the Constitutional Revolution of 1905–6 and then by the "Bonapartist" military adventurism of the founder of the Pahlavi dynasty, Reza Pahlavi. For decades following its fall, Qajar efforts at creating a modern state were minimized. The Qajar dynasty was the "feminine" decadent foil for the modernizing "manly" regime of Reza Shah Pahlavi, rather than the necessary foundation upon which Reza Shah built his fortune and the modern Iranian nation-state.[2] The Pahlavi regime's authoritarian rule eclipsed its ideological dependence upon the "constitutional period" (1906–25).[3] Similarly, the Pahlavi regime's antireligious policies obscured for many historians the dynamism of Iranian Islamic revivalism that overtook the Pahlavis at the end of their era (1925–79).[4]

One mode of historical analysis that has contributed to an increased awareness among historians of the limitations of conventional periodizations of modern Iranian history has been gender analysis. Afsaneh Najmabadi and Parvin Paidar have argued persuasively that considerations of gender and the role of women in society have been central to the construction of both nationalist and Islamic revivalist discourses.[5] Najmabadi and Janet Afary have rewritten the history of the Constitutional Revolution by factoring in the prevailing gender ideology of the time as well as the efforts of women activists.[6] Mohammad Tavakoli has illustrated the complexity of anti-imperialist sentiments by focusing on how men of the Iranian "East" fantasized about European women no less than European men dreamed about the pleasures of the Middle Eastern harem.[7] Shahla Haeri has advanced the debate about Islam and women by exposing the symbolic implications and practical complications of the Iranian/Twelver

Shi'ite institution of temporary marriage.[8] Eliz Sanasarian, Talat Basri, Pari Shaykh al-Eslami, Badr al-Moluk Saba, and all of the aforementioned historians and researchers have recovered much of the history of Iranian women and their contributions to the culture and politics of Iran, revising the male-centered view of Iranian history.[9]

All this was done, however, without completely abandoning the standard periodizations of Iranian history (the Qajar dynasty, 1796–1925; the "Constitutional Period," 1905–21; Reza Pahlavi's "Twenty Years," 1921–41; and the "Experiment with Democracy," 1941–53). The constitutional period was an ill-fated egalitarian gesture that paradoxically advanced the cause of women's progress while limiting or denying it. The dictatorial regime of Reza Shah is still mostly remembered for its oppression while its efforts at social reform are dismissed as ineffective, as illegitimate, or as intellectually and morally bankrupt renderings of the ideas of the reformers of the late nineteenth and early twentieth centuries. The period from 1941 to the 1953 Anglo-American-sponsored coup against Prime Minister Mohammad Mosaddeq is still considered a time in which progressive ideas struggled (and ultimately failed) to assert themselves in civic institutions, government policies, and popular culture. From such a perspective, Iranian society remains frozen in a frustrated attempt to liberate itself from sexism, despotism, and feudalism, beginning with the Constitutional Revolution of 1905–6 but denied success, first by the Pahlavi regime and then by the Islamic Republic. Nothing changes. As the sensational newspaperman and writer Mohammad Mas'ud, wrote in the 1940s, "Ours is a history of chaos after despotism, and despotism after chaos and nothing more."[10] Even Mohammad Khatami, the current president of the Islamic Republic and an optimist regarding the democratic potential of Iranian society, admitted that "Autocracy has become our second nature. We Iranians are all dictators, in a sense."[11] How, then, do we understand changes in modern Iranian culture? Were there any, and when might they have occurred? This work argues that a very basic change occurred in Iranian culture in the first half of the twentieth century. It became possible for Iranian women to imagine—publicly—a world in which they were not required to be obedient to the men in their lives. It became necessary for Iranian men and women to decide if they wanted to embrace, accommodate, or oppose this new possibility. In the end, they did all of these things and continue to do so. This change occurred after decades in which traditional notions of male guardianship had emerged to embrace (and to contain) new ideas of Iranian womanhood. There was a dynamic tension that culminated in Reza Shah's state feminism project called the Women's Awakening *(nahzat-e banovan)* in 1936. Yet only when this project was largely abandoned in the wake of the Allied invasion of August 1941 did its effects become visible for all to debate.

Writers of Iranian women's history, such as Parvin Paidar and Eliz Sanasarian, have critiqued the Women's Awakening project as just another rhetorically embellished opportunity for the Pahlavi state to build its power at the expense of true social progress by co-opting an independent women's movement and confirming the "patriarchal consensus."[12] It is perhaps ironic that secular humanist feminists like Paidar and Sanasarian would find some support for their critique from the historians of the Islamic Republic of Iran. Operating in the context of official Islamic revivalist revisionist historiography, these historians have systematically exposed and detailed the human-rights abuses and bureaucratic arrogance of the Pahlavi state in the 1930s as it sought to compel women to remove their traditional veils in public.[13] However, some of these historians would point to a different consensus at the time of the Women's Awakening: "The important thing to note here is the lack of belief at the time that the presence of women in society was compatible with maintaining the veil. Not clerics, not government men, and not even women believed that the social presence of women did not require the removal of the veil."[14]

In other words, both those for and against women's progress saw veiling as the pivotal issue. As we shall see, there was, in fact, no such consensus regarding the veil prior to the Women's Awakening. It was the policies of the Women's Awakening itself that reduced women's progress to the question of the veil, making it a necessary first step in an Iranian woman's journey toward modernity. Any traveler to Iran today can observe that the veil no longer signifies such a clear divide between public and private, office and home, or kitchen and school.[15] This is, in part, the unacknowledged legacy of the aggressive modernism of the Women's Awakening to the Islamic Republic of Iran. It is understandable that historians in Iran would want to downplay the common ground between the Islamic Republic and any aspect of the Pahlavi dynasty. But the tendency of historians to isolate the reign of Reza Shah from the rest of Iranian history predates the Islamic Republic.

The critical historiography of Reza Shah's period was first canonized by Hosayn Makki in his *Twenty Years of Iranian History*.[16] After Reza Shah's forced abdication, critics of various ideological casts found Reza Shah's brutal record of murder, torture, and theft an easy target, but their voices were eventually drowned out by the brutal regime of Reza Shah's son, Mohammad Reza Shah. From the late fifties until the eve of the Islamic Revolution in 1977, the Pahlavi regime's own laudatory histories of both father and son dominated classrooms and bookstores in Iran. Even insider accounts by Reza Shah's generals, often useful for their behind-the-scenes descriptions, were still histories written by devotees of the Pahlavi dynasty.[17] Western historians also were corralled into producing an unseemly tome in 1978, entitled *Iran under the Pahlavis*—a real coup for a dynasty that had protested even the slightest criticisms of its practices in foreign presses as far back as the early 1930s.[18]

Predictably, histories of Reza Shah's days upon the throne produced in the Islamic Republic of Iran have been, to say the least, critical—but often in quite useful ways. Never before have so many documents about the Pahlavis been published, albeit with predictable bias (Reza Shah was bad; press censorship in his time was particularly bad; the Women's Awakening was most certainly bad; etc.). Accompanying this scholarship is a cultural fascination with the Pahlavi mystique—plays about Reza Shah, television shows set in the 1930s, new memoirs, and a biography of the unhappy life of Mohammad Reza Shah's first wife, Egyptian princess Fowziyeh.[19] This nostalgic wave of scholarly and cultural output suggests a mix of confidence and dissatisfaction in contemporary Iranian society—confidence that the Pahlavis are, politically speaking, long dead and cannot reverse the effects of the Islamic Revolution and dissatisfaction with the apparent results of the revolution. Be that as it may, much of this scholarship and nostalgia tends to confirm Reza Shah's regime as a singular, despotic disruption of Iran's historical fabric. A recent exception is Cyrus Ghani's study of Reza Shah's rise to power and his success in negotiating the perilous political landscape of the late Qajar period. The concluding essay ties Reza Shah very firmly to progressive changes that underpin contemporary Iranian society.[20] Nonetheless, Ghani is at pains to soften Reza Shah's image as despot and leaves us with the question of how any emancipatory impulse, let alone gender equality, could emerge from "the Twenty Years."

I am committing to a different periodization of Iranian history: 1865 to 1946. The period begins with the rise of the woman question (as it was dubbed in the Iranian press) and ends with the rise of "equal rights" feminism (see table 1.1). In 1865, Mirza Fath 'Ali Akhundzadeh wrote his famous *Seh Maktub* (Three Letters). This was the first formal articulation of Iranian "renewalism" *(tajaddod-parvari)* and discussion of the woman question.[21] In 1946, the first aggressive attempt by women's groups and sympathetic male politicians to win suffrage for women came to an unsuccessful conclusion.

"Renewalism" was an amorphous cultural movement that began in the nineteenth century with thinkers like Akhundzadeh. It called for the moral and material rebirth of Iran, utilizing a mix of modern European technology and culture and a "renewed" awareness of the pre-Mongol, pre-Saljuq Turk, and pre-Islamic Iranian past. A central project of renewalism was improving the status of women in society (see chapters 2 and 3 of this work). *Three Letters* appeared well before any meaningful women's movement existed in Iran. The protofeminism of the Babi activist Qorrat al-'Ayn, who removed her Islamic veil to signal her break with Islamic traditions in 1850, did not result directly in a movement for women's emancipation.[22] In contrast, for a brief time in the 1940s, there was an independent women's political party supporting women's suffrage alongside women's groups that were auxiliaries of male-dominated political parties. The failed campaign for suffrage was accompanied by a press campaign on a scale unprecedented in the history of Iranian feminist activism. Modern Iranian womanhood was transformed from the pure fantasy of Iranian renewalist men into social and cultural reality for many Iranian women—one that was worth claiming, defending, and redefining.

The interplay between notions of male guardianship and modern Iranian womanhood in public debate, in state policy and propaganda, in popular culture (or, at least, the culture of educated city dwellers), and in the memories of individuals who experienced this period of history is the subject of this study.[23] Recent studies have suggested how understanding this interplay becomes essential to understanding political rhetoric and actions. Houchang Chehabi reminded us that it was men who first felt the oppression of "clothing reform" and that this led some in the city of Mashhad in the summer of 1935 to conclude that the unveiling of women was not far off and to preemptively challenge the Pahlavi state on the issue. Afsaneh Najmabadi has illustrated how discourses regarding male protection of women were crucial to interpretations of events at the time of Iran's Constitutional Revolution. By taking a longer view of the interplay between male guardianship and modern Iranian womanhood, I will show how a truly egalitarian view of modern Iranian womanhood developed in the wake of the Women's Awakening project. This egalitarian view affected the political rhetoric of the male-dominated political scene as ideologues of various stripes sought to put the genie of modern and independent Iranian womanhood back in her bottle or, at least, to co-opt her to their agenda. That some women felt freer to advocate true equality in the 1940s might, at first, seem unremarkable in a period characterized as Iran's "experiment with democracy." But one must remember that there were virtually no public advocates for true sexual equality in the "more liberal and democratic" constitutional period that preceded the reign of Reza Shah. One must at least be open to the possibility that a true emancipatory impulse was generated amid the empty rhetoric of the Women's Awakening and brutal oppression of the Reza Shah period. Did—to steal another image from Mohammad Mas'ud—a flower grow in hell?

Organizing this history around traditional political periods obscures the processes by which gender norms underwent change. For example, if one simply examined women's education during the regime of Reza Shah, one would fail to see how press discussions of women's education and women's professions in 1910 informed the regime's priorities. It would also obscure the regime's innovative efforts to celebrate Iranian women as educated professionals. Likewise, if one simply looked at the reappearance of independent women's organizations and women's political activity after the Allied invasion of 1941, and thought about it only in connection with Iran's political history from 1941 to 1953, one would fail to see how Iranian feminists in the 1940s were building on definitions of women's citizenship that were pioneered by the policies and propaganda of the Women's Awakening. These cultural changes were, of course, informed by the wider context of Iran's historical experiences, but their processes of development were not in absolute synchrony with political events and should not be studied as though they were.

From 1865 to 1946, one can observe a shift in Iranian popular culture and state policy with regard to gender, in processes that developed and came to fruition on a different schedule than major political events. For example, the Allied occupation of 1941–46 may have (quite unintentionally) ended the unveiling policies of the Women's Awakening, but it did not reverse the Marriage Laws of 1931 and 1937, the opening of higher education to women, or trends toward greater literacy and professional employment among urban women. It did not change the fact that the Iranian state—no matter who controlled it—now explicitly tied its legitimacy to efforts to improve the status of women in Iranian society. In 1865, Akhundzadeh was one Iranian man articulating what a few Iranian men felt about the role of women in Iranian society. In 1946, despite the failure of the women's suffrage campaign, there were different "facts on the ground." Some women, like Mehrangiz Dowlatshahi, had traveled abroad themselves and had already spent decades advocating for change in the pages of the Iranian press. Fatemeh Sayyah, who had been working as a university professor for over a decade, helped to found the Women's Party, and, at the time of her death, was supervising the work of Simin

Table 1.1. Chronology of the "woman question"

ca. 1850	Babi activist Qorrat al-ʿAyn unveils.
1865–1941	**"Complementary Rights" feminism enters public discourse.**
1865	"Woman question" raised by "renewalist" Akhundzadeh in *The Three Letters*.
1890	Mirza Malkam Khan addresses the woman question in the paper *Qanun*.
1894	Bibi Khanom Astarabadi publishes *The Vices of Men*.
1895	Opening of American missionary schools to Muslim girls in Iran.
1905	Muslim *Mokhadarat* School for Girls opened in Tehran.
1910	Patriotic Ladies Society formed; first Iranian women's magazine, *Danesh*.
1911	Women's suffrage discussed and rejected in Parliament.
1913	Nursing discussed in *Shokufeh* as a profession for women.
1914	Office work advocated for women in *Shokufeh*.
1919	Government Dar al-Moʿallamat school opened.
1920	Patriotic Women's League formed; Alumnae Society of the American School for Girls publishes *ʿAlam-e Nesvan* (Women's World)—lasts 13 years; expatriate periodical *Kaveh* advocates physical education for girls.
1921	Attempt to forcibly unveil women in Soviet Republic of Iran in Gilan.
1925	Mohtaram Eskandari, leader of the Patriotic Women's League, unveils in Tehran
1931	Marriage Reform Law of 1931; failed attempt of two women to seek employment at Ministry of Finance.
1932	Tehran hosts Second Congress of Eastern Women.
1933	Anglo-Persian Oil Company employs three Iranian women as clerks/translators.
1935	Government Women's Society formed; unveiling encouraged; Gowharshad massacre; decision to admit women to newly formed University of Tehran.
1936	Women's Awakening project launched.
1940	Women admitted to new flight school.
1941–present	**Equal rights feminism enters public discourse.**
1941	Women's Awakening project fades; beginning of male backlash against women working in offices.
1943	Religious extremists attack unveiled women in Tehran.
1943–46	Tudeh-affliated Women's Committee established; Women's Party established; first campaign for women's suffrage; first Iranian women high school graduates admitted to the University of Tehran Medical School.

Daneshvar who went on to become one Iran's most celebrated novelists. When the first women's suffrage campaign ended, it had been six years since Sadiqeh Dowlatshahi had flown her first solo flight and nearly twenty years since she had started her first job working in an office. And as we shall see, while the careers of the women did not begin (or end) with the Women's Awakening of 1936–41, key moments in their careers were tied directly to the state feminism project rather than to more celebrated political events like the Constitutional Revolution. The Women's Awakening project made it harder to "turn back the clock" on certain reforms and made the gender inequities that were, in fact, a part of the Women's Awakening project less tolerable.

A Note on Methodology, Sources, and Terminology

I have consulted archival material, the periodical press, literature, mem-oirs, and oral histories. The archival material is all from published sources—on microfilm in the cases of the proceedings of the Iranian Par-liament *(Majles)* and U.S. State Department records (1910–39, 1945–49) and in print in the cases of confidential Iranian government documents pertaining to the Women's Awakening project (1930s and 1940s) and British Foreign Office correspondence from Iran (1919–45). The archival sources have been invaluable in providing contemporary analysis of events from interested observers, insights into the workings of the Iranian bureaucracy and Parliament, and crucial glimpses into the social and eco-nomic structure of Iran at even the most humble levels. The archival ma-terial provides a depth and continuity of information that is essential for contextualizing information from literature, the press, and oral history. Archival material brought me closer to answering certain specific ques-tions, such as how good was a teaching career for women from an eco-nomic perspective or how the Marriage Law of 1931 affected members of different classes.

But it is the press and oral histories that inform the intellectual soul of this study and pose some of the greatest theoretical challenges. The pri-mary public forum for discussions of the woman question was the Iranian periodical press. Most studies of the Iranian press are captivated by the question of state censorship, placing the evolving institution of the press in conflict with evolving state mechanisms to control it once it had grown from its origins as an official gazette.[24] But the Iranian state was also a participant in the development of the periodical press. Official and semi-official newspapers helped shape the conventions and history of the press as much as "independent" publications.[25] Seen in this way, the state—even in its powerful and uncompromising incarnation during the regime of Reza Shah Pahlavi—was just another voice participating in national con-versations. There is no doubt that the regime of Reza Shah was committed to dominating the press (and other media as they became available) and other institutions with its messages—but what messages and what ideas?[26] Despite the political power of the Pahlavi state in the 1920s and 1930s, intellectually it was dependent on the weight of three decades of national discussions in the press on a variety of issues—especially the woman ques-tion. Similarly, discussions of the woman question that occurred in the 1940s could not ignore the effects of Women's Awakening policies upon society and Women's Awakening propaganda upon popular culture in the press.

If the press serves as a historical record of the shifts of publicly expressed opinions, oral history serves as an ahistorical record of the accumulated effects of historical experiences upon an individual psyche. It was in deciding to interview "Dr. Maryam Tusi" (a pseudonym) and her husband for an article on women's education in Iran (and in consulting oral history transcripts from the Iran Oral History Project at Harvard and the Foundation for Iranian Studies at Bethesda) that I entered the promising and problematic realm of oral history. Its potential and its frustrations were both movingly illustrated to me by the work of Sidney Bolkosky with Detroit-area Holocaust survivors.[27] The extreme trauma of survivor experiences threw into sharp relief the realities of all recollections that produce "answers [that] always seem incomplete, like shadows that are simultaneously real and unreal."[28] For many of its practitioners, oral history is a chance to capture the story of history's forgotten victims and recover lost voices—a powerful lure for students both of women's history and the Middle East.[29] In the field of Iranian studies, perhaps anthropologist Shahla Haeri has made the most of women's oral histories in examining the practice of temporary marriage in Iran. Although she spoke with many prominent individuals, most of her interview subjects were middle to very much lower class and quite marginalized by virtue of the culturally, if not legally, controversial practice in which they were engaged. This is not the case with the Tusis who are very successful doctors or with the women interviewed for the Iran Oral History Project. Habib Ladjevardi and his colleagues were looking for information about elite politics (from 1941 through the Revolution of 1978–79) from the perspective of "the actors involved."[30] It was fortunate that all subjects were asked to talk about their childhood and schooling before being grilled on the particulars of their political activity as adults, taking their recollections back as early as the 1920s and providing accounts of direct interest to this study.

Oral historians, like anthropologists, worry a great deal about the process by which they collect information and often explain their role in the interview process. But despite all the methodological rigor brought to bear on collecting oral histories, it remains true that oral histories are conversations. There is never a "pure" remembrance. In the words of Samuel Schrager, "[There] is no choice about being inside or outside the dialogue. Everyone is part of it, invested with a participant's responsibility for sifting through what he or she has lived."[31] Another common experience of oral historians, and mine also, is the realization that there is no way of controlling the interview process. Haeri would have preferred to talk to her subjects one-on-one, using a culturally familiar *dard-e del* (pain of the heart) style, but occasionally she had to make allowances for interruptions or the presence of others.[32] In addition to the unpredictability of the give-and-take in an interview, an interview subject might even disavow his or her statements when confronted with a transcript of them.[33]

At the same time, it was during my interview with Sadiqeh Dowlatshahi that I was reminded most clearly that the cultural attitudes and state policies I was describing did not simply wash over individual women and propel them into new situations. Before she became a pilot during the Women's Awakening, she had sought training as a typist and gone to work in the early 1930s—an act of assertiveness that she duplicated when she learned the latest office software working in Toronto in the 1980s. She was (and is) irrepressible in her desire to learn and achieve. Reflecting on the challenges in her life (she left Iran in the 1950s, was twice widowed, and worked many jobs to pay for all of her children to go to college), she told me, "If it weren't for some of those things, I think I would have been the first person on the moon." If she needed the government to allow her to fly an airplane in 1940, then the government also needed women like her to volunteer for such an experience.

Women's historians in a variety of fields have struggled with questions of terminology for describing the rise of feminist consciousness in the modern period (e.g., Joan Kelly's effort to distinguish modern feminists from "protofeminists" in the context of pre-modern European history). As Margot Badran has pointed out, the problem becomes additionally complicated when accounting for the rise of feminist consciousness outside of the Euro-American context because one must also wrangle with the complexities of, as Marshall Hodgson would say, "the great Western transmutation" of ideas. I will adopt Margot Badran's broad definition of feminism as an ideology that seeks to improve the status of women in society—a definition that regularly demands qualification for the sake of precision.[34]

Throughout this work I have translated *nahzat-e banovan* as "the Women's Awakening." A problem arises because the word *nahzat* can be correctly translated as "awakening" or, more actively, as "movement." In Persian and Arabic it implies both things simultaneously, allowing for a measure of tactical ambiguity. I will defend my choice of "awakening"—particularly in reference to the Pahlavi regime's project of 1936—by noting that in Persian, as in English, there were other words that could have been used to less ambiguous effect [*bidari* (awakening) or *jonbesh* (movement)]. Furthermore, other more active words of Arabic origin could have been selected to describe the feminist activism—by women's groups or by the Pahlavi regime—but were either not selected—*harakat* (movement), for example]—or were actively discouraged, as was the case when an activist named Zandokht Shirazi used the term *enqelab* (revolution) in the name of her organization in 1931. The Women's Awakening, as we shall see, was about containing and co-opting women's activism and also about promoting women's progress within a framework of male guardianship overseen by the state. Using a flexible term like *nahzat* allowed the Pahlavi regime to adjust the pitch of its rhetoric and policies during the Women's Awakening project without appearing to falter either in its conservatism or in its progressivism. I believe translating *nahzat* as "awakening" retains the deliberate ambiguity of the term better than translating it as "movement."

Finally, a phrase that I use often in this book is "male guardianship." I use it often in connection with the term "modern Iranian womanhood." I prefer the term male guardianship to patriarchy because it is an idea mentioned in the Koran (4:34–35, *The Women*) though not rooted there. Feminists and their opponents debated the limits and implications of Koran 4:34—"men are the guardians/protectors/sustainers/keepers of women"—throughout the history of the woman question in Iran and elsewhere in the Islamic world. Initial ideas about women's progress in Iranian society assumed some level of male guardianship, and so it is an idea that is always present, changing in reference to the idea of the "modern Iranian woman." I consider both terms to be dynamic, culturally conditioned ways of organizing experience that are found in the Iranian periodical press, intellectual treatises, archival records, and oral history narratives.[35]

The twin notions of male guardianship and modern Iranian womanhood framed the woman question even when not directly invoked. Perhaps because there was no formal or complete articulation of either idea independent of formal ideological contexts (e.g., renewalism, communism, or Islamic revivalism), they were subject to subtle and unconscious redefinition as often as they were directly challenged or negotiated. The definition of male guardianship could change in one context (say, in curriculum requirements for boys and girls attending government schools). Then, that change (or elements of it) could transmute into a different setting and ideological context (say, in an editorial in an Islamic revivalist newspaper—even as it criticized government policies toward women's education).

Outline of the Book

Chapter 2, "Tradition and Renewal," describes the rise of the woman question in nineteenth-century Iranian society and its perceived connection to the failures of Qajar society. Opponents of the Qajars used the woman question as part of a general critique of Iranian society in the spirit of an amorphous but potent cultural phenomenon known as "renewalism." Renewalist rhetoric set the agenda for the woman question and obscured the complexity of women's lives in the Qajar period and Qajar efforts to engage the woman question. It also obscured the fact that renewalist rhetoric assumed that men would guide and protect women in the transition from "backward tradition" to "enlightened modernity." While the Qajar state may have failed to address the woman question adequately, it was the Qajar cultural milieu (and all of its influences) that set the initial terms of male guardianship and modern Iranian womanhood in the public mind.

Chapter 3, "Imagining the Modern Iranian Woman," chronicles the development of an image of modern Iranian womanhood in the Iranian press—an image modeled on the modernity of Europe and America and set in contrast to a negative image of traditional womanhood. In the decades preceding the Women's Awakening of 1936, press discussions of the woman question went further in defining modern Iranian womanhood. Of course, the basic premise that the modern Iranian woman was to be an educated wife and mother was elaborated ad nauseam. But, more importantly, she was being imagined as a well-trained professional and a participant in national affairs (though not yet as a voter or an elected official). The modern Iranian woman was always a "possibility" patterned on the examples of European, American, Ottoman, Turkish Republican, and Japanese women. She did not "exist," and there was no consensus on what she would look like—veiled or unveiled. But the image of the unveiled modern Iranian woman was championed aggressively by some and, ultimately, by the Pahlavi regime itself.

Chapter 4, "Unveiling and Its Discontents," details the development of forced unveiling as a priority of the Women's Awakening project of 1936–41 (including regime attempts to encourage unveiling in the spring of 1935 and the massacre of conservative pro-veiling protesters in Mashhad in the summer of 1935). It explores the symbolism and mechanics of forced unveiling and argues that in forcing unveiling in 1936 the regime created the historiographical illusion that women's progress had always been synonymous with unveiling. Furthermore, unveiling became the chief symbol of Reza Shah's tyranny as much because of the way it trau-matized men as because of the way it controlled women. The violence and coercion of forced unveiling also obscured the fact that unveiling was *not* the main goal of the Women's Awakening. Rather, it was a means toward the end of fulfilling renewalist visions of the modern Iranian woman as a compatible spouse, an educated professional, and a visible participant in civic society.

Chapter 5, "Renewal's Bride," examines press discussions of marriage and courtship before and during the Women's Awakening, regime efforts to craft and enforce the Marriage Law of 1931 (among the lower classes), and the public symbolism and private realities of marriage among the elite classes in the 1930s. Indeed, it was the Marriage Law of 1931—not the Women's Awakening—that served as the regime's first major effort to re-cruit support from Iranian feminists. In establishing the law, the regime claimed to be answering the long-standing hope of Iranian feminists for companionate, secure, and monogamous marriages. After the onset of the Women's Awakening, the issue became less important to the regime as a matter of policy than as a matter of propaganda: the thoroughly arranged marriage of Crown Prince Mohammad Reza to Egyptian princess Fowzi-yeh serving as an ironic case in point.

Chapter 6, "The Capable Woman," analyzes the expansion of educa-tion and employment opportunities for women before, during, and after the Women's Awakening project. The reality of increased government sup-port for women's education and employment in the 1930s and 1940s is balanced against the recollections of women students and office workers. Using oral histories, memoirs, and an analysis of government propaganda and statistics, this chapter illustrates the ways in which even the women who benefited from the Women's Awakening felt the constraints (and oc-casional benefits) of male guardianship. This chapter also illustrates how male guardianship underwent a crucial redefinition in the public mind from referring to male family members (son, brother, father, and husband) to including other social relationships (mentor, teacher, supervisor, class-mate, coworker, and patient) in the first half of the twentieth century. Furthermore, the catalysts for this redefinition were the propaganda and policies of the Women's Awakening.

Chapter 7, "The Limits of Emancipation," describes the many ways in which male guardianship was asserted even in images of women's emanci-pation and "entrance into society." Starting with the regime's efforts to control coverage of the Eastern Women's Congress of 1932 in Tehran, this chapter looks at the way the regime sought to assure society that modern

Iranian womanhood would never be constructed independently from male guardianship. This was done by cultivating a negative version of modern Iranian womanhood as morally weak, seductive, and greedy—an image that shadowed the "capable" woman as if to warn of the risk of too much freedom and independence. Furthermore, it was during the Women's Awakening that women's health and athleticism became conflated with images of glamorous beauty generated in Hollywood and Europe. At the same time, the regime was clearly testing the limits of its own emancipatory rhetoric by flirting with the idea of women's political enfranchisement and creating a martial image for women to suggest the idea of full and equal citizenship. Again, oral histories and memoirs help to reveal some of the "staging" involved in Women's Awakening propaganda as well as the points of intersection between individual attitudes about gender roles and regime propaganda.

Chapter 8, "Breaking with Male Guardianship," explains the period between the early aftermath of the Women's Awakening project and the end of the first (and unsuccessful) women's suffrage campaign in 1946. It documents the emerging call for true gender equality by some Iranian feminists and simultaneous efforts by others to redefine (and thus sustain) male guardianship in politics, in the workplace, and in popular culture. The 1940s were the high-water mark of Communist efforts to reclaim the woman question from the Pahlavi state and the beginning of Islamic revivalist efforts to do so. Against these diverse efforts at co-option, some feminists attempted to create independent women's organizations or realign themselves with male-dominated organizations and factions that offered the best chance for progress on women's political enfranchisement (the defining issue for gender equality feminists at the time). Finally, chapter 9, a short, concluding essay, illustrates how the legacy of the Women's Awakening influences contemporary Iranian society. The stance of the Islamic Republic of Iran toward women can be better understood as an answer to the Women's Awakening of the 1930s than as a response to later changes in the Pahlavi era. For example, many of the activities that women are encouraged to engage in today in the Islamic Republic (receive an advanced education, enter certain professions, participate in athletic events) are simply "reveiled" versions of the things women were first encouraged to do during the Women's Awakening.

2

Tradition and Renewal

The woman question seemed to mark the frontier between the champions of tradition and the advocates of change. But what traditions were being defended and what changes were being comtemplated? In this chapter I will illustrate how tradition (championed by the Qajar dynasty) and change (championed by renewalist dissidents) were deployed along this frontier. As we shall see, the frontier was quite permeable and subject to shifts. Furthermore, it took some time for women themselves to articulate their stake in the woman question. Nonetheless, by the time of the Constitutional Revolution of 1905–6, women were challenging not only the durability of traditions but the possibilities of renewalist change.

Unlike students of Ottoman history who can follow a single narrative (albeit with multiple subplots) from 1280 to establishment of the Republic of Turkey in 1924, students of Iranian history need to account for a number of dynastic shifts from 1501 to the foundation of the Islamic Republic of Iran in 1979. Coming into their own as a royal house of Iran in 1501, the Safavid dynasty was shattered by an Afghan invasion in 1722, giving way to feuding successor states—the Afshars, the Zands, and the Qajars. From this fray, the Qajar dynasty emerged victorious in 1796. Before they were ousted in 1925, the Qajars were in the unenviable role of upholding traditions established by the Safavids while attempting to meet the challenges of modernization. The Safavid legacy was a complex one that the Qajars helped to forge as a *qezelbash* tribe (literally, "red heads," a reference to their distinctive headgear). The *qezelbash* tribal confederation formed the military backbone of the Safavids in the fifteenth century, when they made the transition from leaders of a radical mystical cult to dynastic contenders for the Iranian throne.[1] The Afshars, Zands, and Qajars had all initially bolstered their legitimacy by championing various Safavid puppets and pretenders. But in positioning themselves as the undisputed leaders of Iran, the Qajars appealed to the essence of the Safavid legacy for legitimacy rather than to the Safavids themselves. And there was nothing more "essential" than gender roles. When advocates of renewalism *(tajaddod-paravari)* took on the Qajars in the nineteenth century, they were also taking on the Safavid legacy in all its aspects.

The Historical Obligations of Qajar State and Society

The essence of the Safavid legacy was threefold: orthodox Twelver Shi'ism, sacral kingship, and an equating of the former Safavid realms with "the land of Iran." The Qajars assumed that, after they reestablished control of the central domains of the old Safavid dynasty in 1796, their next step would be to reestablish control over the Caucasus and to reassert sovereignty over Georgia.[2] Their assumptions proved wrong; in the intervening eighty-odd years since the Safavid defeat by the Afghans in 1722, the Russian Empire had modernized, expanded, and become a critical player not only in the balance of power of Europe but also in the Middle East and Central Asia. The Russo-Persian Treaty of Turcomanchai in 1813 marked the first loss of territory to Christian Europe by a power on the Iranian Plateau since the wars between the Sasanian and Byzantine Empires of the sixth and seventh centuries. This military defeat caught the attention of the Qajar aristocracy, whose unchallenged rule in Iran was only two decades old at the time of the treaty. Subsequent losses to Russia in Azerbaijan and to the British in southern Iran and Afghanistan blocked Qajar efforts to capture the territorial legacy of the Safavids.

As for the legacy of Twelver Shi'ism, the Qajars were more successful though no less embattled.[3] Their assumed role as the defenders of religion was severely tested by the rise of a new religion in the city of Shiraz in the mid-nineteenth century: Babism, the forerunner of modern Baha'ism. The *"Bab,"* or Gate (the facilitator for the return of the Twelfth and Hidden Imam), Sayyed Mohammad Shirazi, was judged to be a fraud and heretic by Twelver Shi'ite clerics, and the Qajars defended orthodox Twelver Shi'ism by crushing a Babi rebellion between 1848 and 1852 and executing its leaders. The fact that the rebellion occurred at all, combined with the fact that Iran was increasingly at the mercy of foreign (and non-Muslim) governments, discredited Qajar claims to sacral kinship as well. Of course, the notion that the king was "God's shadow upon the earth" was a pre-Islamic legacy that the Safavids had most recently formalized. The Qajar administration that supported "God's shadow" was largely Safavid in design, and it too fell into disrepute as the fortunes of the Qajar dynasty wobbled through the nineteenth century.[4]

Accompanying these Safavid legacies were traditions relating to gender roles. Divine sanction of male guardianship predated Islam, but Islam was deployed in support of male guardianship, an idea that had implications for both sexes.[5] As guardians, men not only had to control the affairs of the household but also the affairs of society as a whole. Women were their most precious symbols of personal and family honor *(namus)*. Women were never fully trusted and were seen as a continual threat to the moral order. There is a continuing debate regarding how much misogyny is inherent in religious texts and how much is the result of interpretation and historical context. Be that as it may, we certainly have evidence of misogynist readings of Islamic law that date from the Safavid period.

Respected works of Twelver Shi'ite religious jurisprudence, such as Mohammad Baqer Majlesi's (d. 1699) *hadith* collection *Helyat al-Mottaqin* (Ornament of the Pious), elaborated upon Koranic pronouncements regarding women.[6] A woman's value lay in her ability to produce children and to please her husband. Her inherent lack of honor and intelligence required that the man responsible for her shield her from strange men, from suggestive parts of the Koran, and even from her own sexual desires (via circumcision). Although she was supposed to be treated with patience, she was not to be consulted on any matter, and it was her obligation to obey her husband in virtually all respects. Another work attributed to a cleric of the Safavid period, Mohammad Ebn Hosayn Kh^wansari (ca. 1710), was a satirical treatise called *'Aqa'ed al-Nesa* (The Beliefs of Women). It was popularly referred to as *Kolsum Naneh* because the author attributed the text to "five of the most learned women clerics: Bibi Shah Zayneb, Kolsum Naneh, Khaleh Jan Aqa, Baji Yasaman, and Dedeh Bazm Ara."[7] It satirized the vanity, the superstitions, and the weak sense of religion assumed to be prevalent among women.

Together, *Ornament of the Pious* and *The Beliefs of Women* coincided with a time in Safavid history when a more conservative and "orthodox" brand of Twelver Shi'ism was being championed by the 'Olama (religious scholars), and this had implications for women. For example, the last Safavid monarch, Shah Soltan Hosayn (d. 1722), moved in 1695 to enforce both veiling and the seclusion of women from public places "contrary to past practice."[8] Furthermore, from the seventeenth century on, aristocratic women appear less frequently as significant political actors than they do in the sixteenth century.[9] But even in that first century of Safavid rule, before the fading of the Safavid cult and *qezelbash* political power, the participation of women in political matters (however frequent and significant, as in the case of Ottoman aristocratic women)[10] was a point of controversy.

On two occasions in the sixteenth century, women played leading roles in the politics of the Safavid court. Upon the death of Shah Tahmasb I on 14 May 1576, his daughter Pari Khanom championed the cause of his long-imprisoned son, Esma'il II. When the son was put to death by *qezel-bash* tribesmen on suspicion of favoring Sunnism, the enthronement of his blind brother, Soltan Mohammad, was supported by Soltan Mohammad's wife, Khayr al-Nesa Begom. Her rivalry with Pari Khanom, who had taken over the affairs of state after the murder of Esma'il II, resulted in Pari Khanom's strangulation on 11 February 1579.[11] Some *qezelbash* tribal leaders became wary of Khayr al-Nesa's influence over her husband, so later that year they had her strangled as well. The chronicler of these events, Eskandar Beg Monshi, bitterly condemned the murderers of Khayr al-Nesa, if for no other reason than he was preparing his chronicle for her son Shah 'Abbas I. As the mother of the future king, she held the title Mahd-e 'Olya (the Sublime Cradle). Nonetheless, Eskandar Beg included a letter from (or perhaps attributes a letter to) the conspirators warning of the danger to Mahd-e 'Olya if she did not remove herself from politics:

> Your Majesty well knows that women are notoriously lacking in intelligence, weak in judgment, and extremely obstinate. Mahd-e 'Olya has always opposed us, the loyal servants of the crown, and has never agreed with us on matters of state policy; she has acted contrary to the considered opinions of the *qezelbash* elders, and has constantly attempted to humiliate and degrade us. We have not been safe from her actions, even though up to the present time we have not been guilty of improper conduct, nor have we done anything to cause her alarm. . . . [We] do not consider it proper that word should spread among the neighboring rulers that no member of the royal family remains in the care of the *qezelbash* because a woman has taken charge of the affairs of state and is all-powerful. Mahd-e 'Olya's power and influence in the government of the realm is objectionable to all the *qezelbash* tribes, and it is impossible for us to reach a *modus vivendi* with her. If she is not removed from power, in all probability revolts will occur that will be to the detriment of both religion and state.[12]

In this account, the *qezelbash* clearly acted to preserve their role as the male guardians. The *qezelbash* had protected (and likely manipulated) young (or disabled) Safavids since the death of Esma'il I's father before the Safavid conquest in 1501. By interjecting herself as a de facto regent, Mahd-e 'Olya was not only violating a vaguely formulated norm for women in politics, but she was also assuming a role that the *qezelbash* tribes had depended upon to maintain their power within the Safavid state. Unlike her counterparts in the Ottoman Empire at this time, who also challenged male *lalas* (tutors) for access to princes of the line and young heirs to the Ottoman throne during the "sultanate of women," Mahd-e 'Olya was not able to develop her position as regent into an institution of Safavid politics.

In Qajar times, we also have accounts of royal women exercising their political muscle at court, but no woman in the nineteenth century seemed to subvert the moral order as much as Fatemah "Tahereh" Zarrin-Taj Baraghani, known by her *laqab* (title), Qorrat al-'Ayn (Solace of the Eye). Qorrat al-'Ayn was a highly controversial figure on a number of levels. She was an early adherent of the new religion Babism, which was considered heretical by Twelver Shi'ites. She became a figure of power within the movement, encouraging its full doctrinal break from Twelver Shi'ism. This was perhaps all the more shocking because she had been raised in a family of *osuli* Twelver Shi'ite scholars and had received a high level of religious scholarly training.[13] Her most controversial act was removing her veil in public. It has been interpreted variously as an act of sufi devotion, as a sign of commitment to a new religious order ushered in by the Bab, and as an act of protofeminist protest.[14] After the Babi movement was crushed in the late 1840s and the 1850s by forces under the command of the reforming Qajar prime minister Mirza Taqi Khan Amir Kabir, Qajar chronicler Mirza Mohammad Taqi Lesan al-Molk Sepehr seized on a pornographic characterization of Qorrat al-'Ayn in his history, *Nasekh al-Tavarikh-e Qajariyeh*. She appears as a seductive villain whose sexuality was as dangerous as her heresy: "She would decorate her assembly room like a bridal chamber and her body like a peacock of Paradise. Then she summoned the followers of the Bab and appeared unveiled in front of them. First she ascended a throne and like a pious preacher reminded them of Heaven and Hell and quoted amply from the Qur'an and the Traditions. She would then tell them: 'Who ever touches me, the intensity of Hell's fire would not affect him.' The audience would then rise and come to her throne and kiss those lips of hers which put to shame the ruby of Ramman, and rub their faces against her breasts, which chagrined the pomegranates of the garden."[15]

As we shall see, when Iranians began to imagine modern Iranian womanhood in the nineteenth century, the counterimage they constructed was of an uneducated, superstition-bound victim whose condition was brought about by the poor stewardship of the Qajars. But this image belied the complexity of women's relationship to the Qajar state. In contrast to Qorrat al-ʿAyn, whose assertion of power was an obvious threat to the Safavid underpinnings of the Qajar state, aristocratic Qajar women exercised power in the tradition of their Safavid foremothers. Boshra Delrish has demonstrated that aristocratic Qajar women were key players in the assignment of governorships and granting of foreign development concessions, especially during the long reigns of Fath ʿAli Shah (reg. 1797–1835) and Naser al-Din Shah (reg. 1848–96).[16]

Yet, the most noted episode of harem politics in Iranian historiography involves the downfall of Amir Kabir (after he had largely disposed of the threat posed by the Babis and Qorrat al-ʿAyn) at the hands of the queen mother, Malek Jahan Khanom, in 1852.[17] Told by Ann Lambton and recently retold by Abbas Amanat, the story casts the queen mother as a reactionary force who thwarted the actions of one of the few Qajar heroes in the saga of Iran's efforts to modernize itself. Indeed, the power of women at court was not cast by the early proponents of renewal as a positive thing but as further evidence of the corruption and ineffectiveness of the court. In criticizing the weakness of the court of Naser al-Din Shah, Mirza Malkam Khan wrote: "The spirit of Iranian partisanship has been so beaten that it cannot bear that one uneducated child of a slave come out of the mule stable and with the help of two or three women and children steal the intelligence and good intentions of the king, assume the throne of Iran, and in their rash impudence imagine the people of this kingdom to be their sacrificial lambs."[18]

Those "traditional women" who did not fit into the new order were both the victims and the collaborators of the Qajar order. Indeed, during the later days of the Qajar state, women were hired as undercover informants for the secret police.[19] On one occasion, women thugs (allegedly prostitutes hired by the Qajar secret police) violently disrupted a proconstitutionalist society meeting.[20] It is perhaps in this context that renewalist (and later Pahlavi) obsession with womanly virtue makes the most sense. Only ignorant women reduced to prostitution by a corrupt old order would act against progress. It was the liberation of these "traditional women" that ennobled the woman question.

There is evidence that the Qajar state took some interest in rebuffing renewalist use of the woman question. It is not that the Qajar state ever articulated a precise image of proper Qajar womanhood or made the same effort to propagate such an image as their renewalist detractors in the nineteenth century or Pahlavi successors in the twentieth century, but one can detect some movement in this direction well before the Constitutional

2.1. From *Vaqayeʿ-e Ettefaqiyeh* 485 (7 March 1861), 5. These women have awakened from a night's sleep in a shrine in Gilan in accordance with a local belief (a "miracle," according to the accompanying article) that the sight of a blind girl had been restored after doing so. This image of Iranian women from an Iranian periodical was produced before the woman question became a feature of the Iranian press. What in 1861 might have been presented as a religious and maternal image of Iranian womanhood would later be attacked as a symbol of superstition and ignorance and an obstacle to modern national progress. There were no female counterparts to the images of individual Iranian statesmen and notables who filled the pages of *Vaqayeʿ-e Ettefaqiyeh* at this time; those sorts of images would come to the Iranian press only with the Women's Awakening. By permission of MEDOC, University of Chicago.

Revolution of 1905–6. When the Qajars' official gazette, *Vaqaye'-e Ette-faqiyeh* (the Chronicle of Events), founded in 1851, began to publish illustrations in 1860, it mostly featured the king, court ceremonies, government officials (all men), and public buildings and palaces to help its subjects visualize their government. However, among the earliest images in *Vaqaye'-e Ettefaqiyeh* is that of a group of women visiting a shrine (see illustration 2.1).[21] Moved by the correct religious impulses, observed with children in their care, and covered by the *chador* (with faces visible, however), these women were more than loyal subjects—they were loyal dependents, as a group the antithesis of Qorrat al-'Ayn. From 1887 to 1890, twenty-two years after the appearance of Akhundzadeh's *The Three Letters*, the government-owned printing house at the Dar al-Fonun (a polytechnical institute established in 1851) published *Khayrat Hesan* (Excellent Women) in three volumes. A collection of biographies of prominent women in Perso-Islamic culture, it was a work relied upon even by women's historians writing in the context of Mohammad Reza Shah Pahlavi's White Revolution of the 1960s.[22] This Qajar-sponsored work inched closer to recognizing women as contributors to the traditional order, not merely its beneficiaries. While aristocratic Iranian women were not yet to be displayed for propaganda purposes, images of foreign women could be harnessed to support the cause of monarchy in the semiofficial periodicals of the Qajar state. For example, *Sharaf,* and its continuation, *Sharafat,* occasionally featured articles on famous women. Queen Victoria of England, during her fiftieth-anniversary jubilee,[23] and Queen Wilhelmina of Holland,[24] on the occasion of her coronation, were featured as symbols of popular and successful monarchies in Europe. Though tarnished by scheming her way to power rather than being born to it, the Chinese empress dowager Cixi was praised for opposing reformers in China and because she was "very intelligent, resolute, and autocratic (May God grant her a long reign)."[25]

As we shall see, the traditional Iranian woman was, by renewalist definition, trapped in poverty, ignorance, and superstition, and—rather importantly—she was a burden to her husband. She was not defined by the educated, aristocratic Qajar women of the imperial harem who were politically disenfranchised by the collapse of the Qajar regime. She was defined by the poorest of women, nineteenth-century embodiments of Kolsum Naneh. Lost in the construction of contrasting images of "modern" and "traditional" womanhood was the complexity of an individual life. As the following short biography of a Qajar aristocratic woman illus-

trates, the effort to describe an individual life blurs many categories, including that of male and female, modern and progressive:

Ashraf al-Saltaneh

The departed princess 'Ezzat al-Molk, granted the title Ashraf al-
Saltaneh, was the daughter of 'Emad al-Dowleh Emam Qoli Mirza
b. Mohammad 'Ali Mirza Dowlatshah b. Fath 'Ali Shah Qajar. She
was born in Kermanshah during her father's administration there.
As a young woman she was married to E'temad al-Saltaneh, who at
that time was [simply] Hasan Khan, attendant to the king, and came
to Tehran. Since she had no children, she spent most of her life studying books. She was partial to history and medicine. Owing to her
closeness with E'temad al-Saltaneh, she was well informed about the
politics of the Iranian court, national events, and foreign relations.
She was a master of the womanly arts and household crafts such as
cooking, sewing, baking, and *kamvaduzi* and other weaving, and
showed a special style and command. She had wide latitude in Naser
al-Din Shah's harem and in the service of the king. She had learned
some French from her husband. She did not care for poetry. She
completely disliked music and song. But, she played chess and back-
gammon very well. She took beautiful photographs. She learned
photography from my father, Prince Soltan Mohammad. She traveled to the holiest shrines twice. Toward the end of her life she traveled to Great Islambul [Istanbul] and spent 2,000 *tuman*s bringing a
group of people along. After the death of E'temad al-Saltaneh, she
married her cousin, the now-departed Sayyed Hasan 'Arab Na'eb al-
Tavileh. She then resided in the area of Sacred Mashhad. She granted
in perpetuity her estates located in the vicinity of the village of
Mayami, near Mashhad, for charitable purposes. In sum, she was a
manly woman who in all qualities—superficial and meaningful—
excelled over most other women, as well as her spouses. She passed
away in Mashhad in 1333 H.G. [1914/1915] at the age of 53. She is
buried in the Dar al-Sayyadeh cemetery.

(Yaman al-Dowleh—Mashhad)[26]

'Ezzat al-Molk, educated and prosperous, was able to benefit from the
position of her husband but was clearly not dependent upon him. She was
herself the patroness of others. And yet, the biography offers that she was
exceptional. Indeed, it goes further in marking her exceptional qualities as
"manly," as if her mastery of the "womanly" arts was not enough to

presage her competence in other endeavors. Many of the women who were to go on to be the pioneers of Iranian feminism likewise came from a background of privilege, if not to the same degree. Even those who did not at some point had to come to terms with the Qajars who would be their husbands, their censors, their mentors, or their detractors. Whether as loyal subjects or dissidents, there was no escaping the Qajar context— for men or women. The Qajar-era roots of the woman question will be apparent in our later discussions of marriage reform, women's education, the emergence of modern women professionals, and the increased civic presence of women during the reign of Reza Shah Pahlavi. Yet, in the middle of the nineteenthth century, some men began to define themselves in contrast to the Qajars and to the traditions they represented. As they presented an alternate vision of Iranian society, they also imagined themselves as new male guardians for Iranian women. Their creed was "renewal."

Modern Male Guardians and Calls for Renewal

Concern over the plight of women in Iran was adopted early on by the renewal movement in the nineteenth century. Renewal, or *tajaddod*, began as an amorphous cultural movement that questioned the traditions of Iranian society on a variety of levels. In regard to literature, it became entwined with the "literary return" or *bazgasht-e adabi*, that sought to purge Iranian poetry of Safavid-era poetic conventions in favor of reconstructed pre-Safavid sensibilities.[27] Renewalism sought the moral and material rebirth of Iran and liberation from superstition and tyranny. To some, superstition was an aspect of folk culture and, thus, considered separate from a true Islam. To others, superstition was Islam itself. Tyranny was closely associated with monarchy and thus with the Qajar dynasty. A desire to purify Iranian culture of Mongolian (code for non-Muslim) or Turkish (often code for non-Iranians generally and the Qajars specifically) elements was also a part of renewalism. One of the most enduring legacies of the renewal movement was the articulation of modern Iranian nationalism.

Scholars have emphasized the concern of several nineteenth-century Iranian thinkers with the emancipation of women, and all have rightly noted that men like Mirza Fath 'Ali Akhundzadeh, Mirza Aqa Khan, and Mirza Malkam Khan showed genuine sympathy for women and concern for their progress and envisioned a wider (or, at least, a more respected role) for women in Iranian society.[28] However, a close reading of their views on women shows them to have been primarily concerned with women's role in the domestic sphere and to have been the true architects of "the patriarchal consensus" that Paidar identifies with the building of the modern nation-state in the twentieth century.

Mirza Fath 'Ali Akhundzadeh, an intellectual who stood at the crossroads of Persian, Turkish, and Russian cultures and who was himself an avowed atheist, raised the woman question in 1865 in his famous treatise *Seh Maktub* (The Three Letters).[29] Akhundzadeh strongly criticized the ruling order in Iran as corrupt due to the despotic rule of the Qajar kings. In fact, his treatise is couched in the form of three letters of admonishment from a fictitious Indian prince, Kamal al-Dowleh, to a Qajar prince, Jalal al-Dowleh. As an example of capricious rule, Akhundzadeh referred to an incident guaranteed to incite the passions of sexual honor. An unnamed but "famous" Qajar prince took a fancy to his minister's wife, had him killed, and then confiscated both his wealth and his wife.[30] This reprehensible behavior was portrayed as resulting both from "turcoman rule" and from Islamic teaching, including the "exemplary" behavior of the prophet Muhammad. Akhundzadeh portrayed Muhammad as a lascivious old man who benefited from convenient Koranic revelations in his quest to amass many wives who were too young for him.[31]

Since the women were married to Muhammad against their will (according to Akhundzadeh), they naturally resorted to devious methods to secure other romantic liaisons or to avoid having to be with Muhammad. This in turn led to further Koranic strictures upon women, in the form of veiling and seclusion, that "in the passage of time tossed half of the tribe of Noah—women—into an eternal prison."[32] He praised the leadership of the Esma'ili Shi'ite sect, who (according to Akhundzadeh) broke with the Islamic teaching of their day and allowed their women to go out in public unveiled, until the sect was crushed by the "ignorant Saljuq" Turks in the eleventh century.[33]

Akhundzadeh also raised the woman question in his plays. In *Vazir Khan-e Lankoran* (The Great Minister of Lankoran), Sho'leh, the wife of a scheming minister, subverts her husband's attempt to marry off their daughter to an old man for social and political reasons. She does this by arranging secret liaisons between her daughter, Nesa, and the man of her dreams, the young and dashing Taymur Aqa.[34] In *Vokala-ye Morafe'eh* (The Quarreling Advocates), the sister and the temporary wife of a recently deceased man vie over his estate. In the course of events, the sister tries to marry off her niece, Shakiba, to a wealthy merchant. Shakiba protests, "Auntie! When did I give you permission to make Aqa Hasan my husband? From now on I have no father, and no brother! I will be my own representative."[35] But as Sho'leh Abadi has noted, the rights for which these bold female characters in Akhundzadeh's plays struggle are limited to rights within the context of the family and not broader civil rights.[36]

Indeed, Akhundzadeh's critique of the treatment of women in Iran was part of a larger attack on despotic government and the religious culture that helped perpetuate that government and prevented Iran from attaining greatness. The same forces that deprived Iranians of their freedom and humanity had a specific and shameful effect upon women. It was a sympathetic stance that saw women's moral faults as a reflection of their environment rather than their nature, but at the same time Akhundzadeh was not primarily concerned with how to improve the status of women. And although he clearly favored education for both men and women,[37] he did not articulate a specific role for women. The wretchedness of their condition was a minor symptom of a much larger problem, not in and of itself a justification for a call to arms.

A later but more influential voice on the woman question, was that of Mirza 'Abd al-Hosayn Khan Kermani, known as Mirza Aqa Khan, in his unfinished political treatise *Sad Khetabeh* (The Hundred Sermons).[38] Only forty-two of the seventy finished sermons were known to people in the late nineteenth century and survive to this day. In an obvious allusion to Akhundzadeh, the treatise was framed as a bit of advice from a fictitious Indian prince, Kamal al-Dowleh, to a fictitious Iranian prince, Jalal al-Dowleh.[39] Scholars discuss The Hundred Sermons simultaneously with a different and untitled treatise that Kermani also framed as a correspondence between Kamal al-Dowleh and Jalal al-Dowleh. Because it closely simulated the opening of the first of Akhundzadeh's The *Three Letters,* the unnamed treatise was dubbed *Seh Maktub-e Kermani.*[40] In any case, four of *The Hundred Sermons* addressed the woman question.[41]

Kermani called Iranian women "the living dead."[42] He saw them—as he did all of Iranian society—as victims of a social and political environment that deprived them of their natural and, implicitly, virtuous national attributes. Due to the corrupting moral environment, "The possibility of one truthful, pleasant, and beneficent woman in all of Iran does not exist."[43] For Kermani, there were two principal sources of corruption: the wealthy elites of the Qajar dynasty, whose Turkish ancestry was anathema to the national spirit he wished to foster, and Islam, which he often portrayed as a vehicle for the transmission of inferior Arab culture.

He was neither consistent nor careful with his rhetoric as he attacked polygyny, the seclusion of women, and the veil. For example, in the twenty-second sermon he attacked the hoarding of wives by the wealthy because it deprived the nation's young men of wives, and it deprived women of true marriage because the wealthy polygynists "gathered them [young girls and women] with neither the intent to be their husbands [in the full sense] nor the intent to do without them."[44] In the thirty-third sermon, he attacked polygyny for being the source of poverty.[45] However, he did not explain how polygyny would reduce its rich practitioners to a state of financial ruin. For Mirza Aqa Khan, marriage was for reproduction and the care of children. This required a happy household, an environment that could only result from the happy union of a man and woman in a monogamous marriage.[46] At the same time, Kermani believed that prostitution in the Ottoman Empire and Iran, "taking a mistress" in Europe, and "taking a friend" in India were acceptable avenues "to friendship and companionship" for men, as if such relationships would never result in children.[47]

In any case, he claimed that children needed five "schools" to obtain morality and to perfect their personalities and attributes: (1) the mother's womb in which they would somehow absorb morality and natural characteristics; (2) the family, in which the child would naturally incline to the mother; (3) religion; (4) the government, which if tyrannical would corrupt and if just would cultivate good character; and (5) the very air, land, and water of the country in which they were born.[48] Kermani's expectation that moral character would be osmotically transferred from mother to child is characteristic of Kermani's appreciation for the power of nature. The closer one was to the workings of nature, the better. For example, he believed that tribal women had a more fearless disposition than urban women because they were closer to nature.[49] Also, Kermani's reference to religion marks an important distinction between him and his apparent inspiration, the atheist Akhundzadeh.

Another distinction from Akhundzadeh on the woman question was Kermani's explicit appreciation of women in their roles as mothers and "the first teachers" of children. The critical role of the mother in the first two "schools" made her of prime importance to the future of the nation. A mother who was in a constant state of conflict with her husband and his other wives and their children could not help but become morally reprehensible and pass this on to her children both through her womb and by her example. Polygyny, in Kermani's view, caused a lack of love and friendship between husbands and wives and even promoted the spread of venereal disease. He called on Muslims to heed the word of God in the Koran, which forbade the taking of additional wives if they could not be treated justly.[50] He felt that the problem of polygyny in Iran was worse than elsewhere in the Islamic world because Twelver Shiʿism permitted temporary marriage, which he considered a particularly barbaric Arab custom from pre-Islamic days to which he referred, as Muslims do, as the age of ignorance (jaheliyat).[51]

In the thirty-fourth sermon, Kermani turned to the question of women's mixing with men in public. He insisted that the presence of women at concerts, balls, and state functions in Europe was not at all immoral. "Because it is not against nature, the order of the country, or the customs of the nation, it is [instead] the source of honor and pride, not the cause of obscenity and shame."[52] Kermani then digressed into a diatribe against customs observed in Iran. He railed against the Iranian prime minister for still wearing the Arab clothes of a thousand years ago and against Iran for still following the "savage" customs of the Arabs of the Arabian Peninsula that were "not only the cause of harsh behavior and the source of taunts and contempt but also the cause of accusations of heresy and bloodshed."[53] He rather oddly claimed that in Europe a drunk who went to see a prostitute could still trust that his "life, wealth, and honor" would be safe with the prostitute, whereas in Iran a drunk in the same situation would be at such risk that theft would be the least of his troubles.[54] Even Europe's vices were less savage than Iran's symbols of elite culture.

Against the backdrop of these damning digressions, Kermani returned to the woman question. He felt that the seclusion of Iranian women caused defects in their character and made them the agents as well as the victims of a corrupting environment:

But this phenomenon [i.e., women interacting in public] is prevalent in the worst way in Iran because it causes fear, passivity, and embarrassment in all respects, but nevertheless they [women] serve to advocate the spread of this baggage with complete courage and shamelessness and in the utmost state of chaos and disorder. For example, there is passivity in the laws of nature and in the council of government and the nation in regard to the prostitutes of Iran. Family embarrassment and fear of the day of judgment, terror of the government, the police chief, and his henchmen, trepidation and fear of one's father, mother, and people, strangers as well as foreigners—

with all these hardships and out of the severity of poverty and indigence they give in to any taunts and blame and become satisfied with this dishonor.[55]

The seclusion of women and its deleterious effects on society at large were reinforced by the practice of veiling. "For a thousand years Iranian women have been hidden behind the confining chastity of the veil and shrouded in seclusion at home like the blind, like the Arab dead, like the walking dead."[56] The veil deprived women of their education, their humanity, and the pleasures of life.[57] It reinforced the lack of natural social interaction between men and women, with adverse effects upon both sexes. Deprived of the company and beauty of women, men were driven to homosexuality and pedophilia, as evidenced in the poetry of Qa'ani and Sa'di.[58] Men and women could not get to know each other before marriage, and this encouraged enmity in Iranian marriages with consequent ill effects for society. For Kermani, all of these practices stood in sharp contrast to the European model in which men had "given the reins of freedom and choice to women."[59]

Kermani, like Akhundzadeh, was quite familiar with Islamic teachings and used Koranic passages to augment his critique of Muslim practices. But despite his respect for the value of religion in general, Kermani had absolutely no respect for Islam. His hostility could manifest itself in unseemly satire:

A "holy man" stands in prayer in a London hotel after ordering some coffee. When the waiter brings the coffee, he sees that this honored guest has left his normal, natural state—sometimes bent over, sometimes upright, and sometimes upon the floor with his ass in the air. [The waiter] raises his hands in complete fright and makes agitated inquiries in two or three languages about the health of the holy man. Because "sacrophile" is busy praying he doesn't answer, so the poor waiter runs frightened out of the room and tells the manager, who dutifully fetches the hotel doctor and enters the room of the "holy man" and sees him prostrated in ritual prayer and says, "This man is crazy."[60]

Kermani's Babism and Akhundzadeh's atheism imbued anything they might advocate with an overt hostility to Islam. Indeed, the next treatise in which Kermani addressed the woman question was *Hasht Behesht* (The Eight Heavens) in 1892. An explication of the Babi religion, it was coauthored by Shaykh Ahmad Ruhi and called for women to become "equal partners with men in all affairs and rights . . . including learning and education, government, inheritance, industries, and commerce."[61] In this view, Ruhi and Kermani were actually more progressive than the leaders of the emerging Baha'i movement. Both Mirza Hosayn 'Ali Nuri Baha'o'llah (d. 1892) and 'Abbas Nuri 'Abd al-Baha' retained male advantages in matters of inheritance and governance at the level of the "Universal House of Justice," the supreme ruling body of the Baha'i faith.[62] Nonetheless, from the standpoint of formal Islamic teaching in Iran in the nineteenth century, the woman question—especially in the rare equal-rights expression—was immediately a question of belief or unbelief. It was an antagonism that was nearly impossible to reconcile in the nineteenth century. Nonetheless, attempts to do so were undertaken very early.

Outside Iran, Muslim reformist thinkers like Rifa' Rifa'a al-Tahtawi (d. 1873) in Khedival Egypt and Namık Kemal (d. 1888) in the Ottoman Empire had already initiated "woman question" debates in those countries. The Iranian-born pan-Islamist Jamal al-Din Asadabadi "al-Afghani" (d. 1897) signaled his interest in women's education as early as 1879, while in Egypt.[63] Kermani and al-Afghani's paths crossed in Istanbul in the 1890s, and despite his hostility to Islam, Kermani was inclined to work with al-Afghani for the sake of advocating reform and perhaps due to a common dislike of the Qajar dynasty back in Iran.[64] Al-Afghani had a falling out with the Qajar monarch Naser al-Din Shah (d. 1896) because of al-Afghani's opposition to the Tobacco Concession of 1890. As a result of public pressure generated by al-Afghani and others, the trade concession to British interests was canceled at the Iranian government's expense in 1892. Moreover, opposition to the trade concession put al-Afghani and Kermani in touch with another key opponent of the Qajars, Mirza Malkam Khan (d. 1908). It was Mirza Malkam Khan's London-based newspaper *Qanun* (The Law) that began the transformation of the woman question from an elite discussion among exiled intellectuals into a matter of Iranian public discourse through the press.

Many of Kermani's treatises, including *The Hundred Sermons,* seem to have been circulated informally rather than published. But during his own time, Kermani had access to the popular press through two channels: the Istanbul-based *Akhtar* (The Star) and *Qanun.* In 1888, Mirza Aqa Khan left his native Kerman and settled in Istanbul. He visited Cyprus briefly to marry a daughter of the Babi leader Mirza Yahya Nuri Sobh-e Azal and remained in the Ottoman Empire until he was extradited in 1896 on suspicion of involvement in the assassination of Qajar monarch Naser al-Din Shah in that same year. In Istanbul, he worked for *Akhtar.*

Kermani was impressed with the efforts of Malkam Khan and *Qanun* and began a long correspondence with him starting on 18 November 1890.[65] Kermani saw in Malkam Khan a fellow traveler who, like himself, was disgusted with the corrupt environment of Iran and the tyranny of the Qajars. He even acted as an informal distributor of *Qanun* for other Iranians living in the Ottoman Empire.[66] None of the available letters from Kermani to Malkam Khan raise the woman question.

In fact, *Qanun* raised the woman question directly only five times in the course of forty issues and not at all after the twentieth issue (ca. 1892).[67] As Rowshanak Mansur has observed, the woman question was discussed in the context of Malkam Khan's notion that Iranian society needed to be reformed and brought under the rule of law. Taking his cue from Comte, Malkam Khan argued that a society would only respect laws when its members were fully aware of their humanity *(adamiyat)*. The spread of this "humanist" creed was argued as the key to Iran's future progress. As they constituted "one half of the nation," women were essential to the spread of the creed. A woman, fully aware of her humanity, would be worth "one hundred intelligent men."[68] Later, Malkam Khan listed the five means by which humanism would spread: (1) the distribution of *Qanun*, (2) instructing the learned in humanism, (3) using women as "instructors of their kind *[now'-e khud]*" and the "inflamers of public fervor," and (4) providing material support for those who make sacrifices for the cause of humanism.[69] He described women as "the best agents in any age for the spread of truths."[70]

Subsequently, Malkam Khan published letters that he claimed came from readers in Iran. A letter attributed to a "humanist brother" stated that women were awakening to the truth sooner than men and reported that at a secret meeting women had stood up and condemned the tyranny that squandered their taxes and bought and sold people like "slaves and concubines."[71] Two other letters played with gender categories more than they explicitly advocated an improvement in the lives of women. The first, attributed to a woman from a family of "unrivaled gentility and poetic [talent]," proclaimed: "Do not be disheartened by Iranian women. We have not become so unmanly as to confine the capital of life to profligacy like the husbands and young men of this time. In the concord of humanity, in the army for the salvation of Iran, we see quite well what our responsibilities are. Yes, it is up to us to destroy this bazaar of dishonor. Till now we did not know what to do. *Qanun* has opened our eyes and hearts all at once. The torch of humanity is now in our hands."[72]

The second letter, attributed to an unnamed cleric, stated: "What use is there to complain like women about the severity of the tyranny and the darkness of the days? If we have a little bit of insight, if we are really tired of this disaster of captivity, if we consider ourselves deserving of life, if we are men in the arena of truth we must all—men and women, big and small, cleric and soldier—join hands without delay."[73]

Up to this point, women appeared in *Qanun* as a force to be respected but not as full participants in whatever social change Malkam Khan was envisioning. They existed to inspire men to "humanism." In the letters to *Qanun*, they existed as symbols to rally around or as rhetorical devices to be manipulated to reach an implicitly male audience. Although his rhetoric was respectful toward women and could possibly have implied the same crucial role for women in Iran's renewal as was made explicit in Kermani's *The Hundred Sermons*, Malkam Khan was initially careful not to call for women's education, the unveiling of women, or any other change in their condition in Iranian society.

This changed in the nineteenth issue of *Qanun* (ca. early 1892). Malkam Khan produced an account of a meeting with a venerable, anonymous *sayyed* (descendant of the prophet). It was a clear allusion to al-Afghani. A number of unnamed individuals, as likely to be fictional representatives of various segments of Iranian society as to be actual people, asked the Sayyed about a number of issues connected by the overarching question "Is 'humanism' consistent with Islam?" It was at this moment, when Malkam Khan was being most specific about the woman question and its connection to his humanism movement, that he was also the most deferential toward Islam.

A cleric asked, "Mr. Sayyed, in the matter of women this group has heard many exaggerations. What is the truth of the matter?" The Sayyed responded that his opinion of women was so great that it could not be exaggerated: "We consider women to be the instructors of children, the authors of domestic tranquillity, and the instigators of progress in the world. In accordance with this observation, we consider the education of women to be the height of modesty and sacred innocence and to be among the duties of civilization. We respect and hold dear those women, who are humans, more than you can imagine."[74] A story was related that a colonel who had come from Istanbul noted that women's stature in society was related to their status in marriage and asked the Sayyed's opinion about the number of wives a man should take. The Sayyed answered that religion steered men to monogamy.[75] Contrived or not, this story explicitly stated the views of Malkam Khan on the woman question. It introduced the woman question to the moral proving ground of the press and attempted to reconcile it rhetorically with Islamic teaching, an effort neither Akhundzadeh nor Kermani felt obliged to make.

Nonetheless, it cannot be said that women's rights were the primary concern of Mirza Malkam Khan. From the twentieth issue of *Qanun* onward, Malkam Khan abandoned the woman question entirely, focusing instead upon imagining a new political system for Iran based on the rule of law, yet not quite democratic.[76] Nor was Malkam Khan immune from relying on rhetoric that made the feminine negative and the masculine positive. "Manliness is the very coin of humanism," he declared.[77]

Even Kermani, in his critique of veiling, could not escape the sexual objectification and exoticizing of women as he tried to move the relationship between the sexes to a higher moral plane. The beauty and charms of a woman were there for a man:

> Seeing their violet eyes, which are like [those of] a sacred gazelle resting in the shade of hyacinth ringlets above the grass and flowers and purple fields, awakens the claws of passion of strong lions hidden in the reedbeds of men's souls and excites them. Ruby lips like the life-giving Kauthar River, [bodies like] straight cypresses of the plain, goodness and spice making a halo around a spring of light and a ruby box full of jewels—all lead those thirsty in the valley of desire and rivalry to the spring of honor and manliness. Etiquette, maturity, and circumspection, mercy, manliness, moderation and generosity are perfected in the company of honorable women who are the teachers in the school of love. Alas, that Iranians have not savored the pleasure of this water of life that makes a nation alive with enthusiasm and zeal.[78]

Kermani's clumsy rhetoric betrays the struggle to reconcile the image of women as inciters of animal passion with that of women as a civilizing influence. Ultimately, both aspects of women are seen to be for the benefit of men. The idea that women are to be hunted and possessed by men survives in the notion that women's sexuality and virtue are to be put in the service of perfecting men and arousing the spirit of the Iranian nation. What did women make of this transition?

While the Qajar periodical press did not take up the woman question as such, handwritten books, which in their day circulated informally within Iran, suggest that discussions of the appropriate roles and morals of men and women were taking place. Sometime between 1882 and 1889, an anonymous and quite misogynous treatise entitled *Ta'dib al-Nesvan* (The Disciplining of Women) appeared. It addressed an explicitly male audience on how their women should mirror their moods, make themselves pleasing and inoffensive to them, and be ardently available for their sexual gratification. Islam was called upon to legitimize this dominance. In 1894, a woman's response appeared: *Ma'ayeb al-Rejal* (The Vices of Men), by Bibi Khanom Astarabadi.[79]

In contrast to Mirza Malkam Khan's finessing of Islam on the woman question and Kermani's unvarnished attack upon Islam, Bibi Khanom Astarabadi engaged in a true believer's critique of the interpretations of Islamic teaching found in *The Disciplining of Women*. While accepting the principle of male guardianship over women, Astarabadi argued that female submission to male authority would need to be conditioned on the piety of the male in question.[80] With this in mind, she then catalogued a list of typical male vices including infidelity, drinking, gambling, and sex with young boys. As Najmabadi has observed, this was a highly literate text firmly located in Perso-Islamic culture and addressed (ostensibly) to a female audience. But just as *The Disciplining of Women* clearly made its way to a female readership, eventually *The Vices of Men* found its way to a male readership—an eventuality that may have been anticipated. But here literature imitated life in that this dialogue was undertaken while maintaining the traditional ideal of keeping women secluded from strange men. In separate homosocial spheres, men spoke to men about women, and women spoke to women about men. Of course, once these "conversations" were written and distributed, the two spheres could intersect.

Astarabadi never challenged Islamic conventions such as veiling. She criticized the practice of polygyny and temporary marriage by calling upon the Koranic injunction that a man should take on additional wives only if he feels he can treat them all justly.[81] Unlike Kermani, there is some ambiguity as to whether or not she felt this "condition of justice" could ever be fulfilled. For example, she praised Naser al-Din Shah for treating all of his many wives well and wondered why monogamous men did not treat their wives as well.[82] But she also included a personal account of how her own security was threatened by her husband's taking of a temporary wife.[83] Thus, it is debatable as to whether or not *The Vices of Men* amounts to a self-conscious discussion of the woman question in the modern context of the renewal movement.

Regardless of such considerations, *The Vices of Men* was a clear reaction to male presumption of unbridled dominance over women and to some of the same social conditions that Kermani had condemned. Astarabadi took issue with the familial metaphor used by the author of *The Disciplining of Women* to justify male tyranny: "If the relationship between husband and wife is familiar like that of father and child, it must be complete love and friendship, not enmity . . . The author imagines all women as concubines and servants, and all men kings and lords."[84]

Despite the fact that *The Vices of Men* drew upon long-standing Perso-Islamic cultural traditions and that engagement of these traditions dominated the text, in a few passages there was also a very modern impression that women's lot in Europe was different and perhaps better. Astarabadi ridiculed the author of *The Disciplining of Women* for his claim to be familiar with the ways of Europe, arguing that "In contrast to the people of Europe, the author is terrible, fault-seeking, and insulting and is consumed with belittling women."[85] She also noted that, according to "histories and travelogues," all European women were noble, educated, and knowledgeable in several areas and that they dine and dance with "strange men." But because the "customs of Islam" were different, Iranian women were burdened with "housework and service [khedmatgozari], particularly peasant women."[86]

For Astarabadi, these images of Europe were images of emancipation. They were not threatening as they had been for some nineteenth-century Iranian visitors to Europe (see chapter 3). Neither were they images of women's obligations in the new order as envisioned by Kermani or, more especially, by Malkam Khan. Women's education is explicitly seen in contrast to domestic work. For Astarabadi, knowledge entitled women to enjoy food and dance as men did. Thus, her reaction to Europe differs from the reactions of men who reviled it in the name of tradition and men who admired it in the name of renewal. Astarabadi's rebellion against the misogyny of male guardianship and its traditional expressions in religion and culture suggests that there may have been a long-standing literary "battle of the sexes" before questions of modernity became relevant to the conduct of the rhetorical war.

There were other opportunities for Qajar society to address the woman question at the turn of the century. An adaptation of *Tahrir al-Mar'ah* (The Emancipation of Women), written by Egyptian judge Qasim Amin in 1899, was published in Tabriz by Yusef Ashtiani E'tesam al-Molk in 1900.[87] Amin's original work, along with his later *Al-Mar'ah Al-Jadidah* (The New Woman) advocated education for women, unveiling, and limits on polygyny and divorce. Although Amin seems to have been open to the idea of some professional training for "the new woman," like his Iranian male contemporaries "he favored a domestic vocation for her."[88] Nonetheless, Ashtiani was careful to edit out references to unveiling.[89] Also, sometime between 1898 and 1900, the Cairo-based Persian-language newspaper *Sorraya* (Pleiades) ran a five-piece series on the woman question.[90] It advocated education for Iranian women, claiming that the cultural forces prohibiting women's education were not properly Islamic but instead were the result of foreign values that accompanied the Mongol invasion.

Renewalist arguments for a redefinition and rebirth of Iranian society clashed with the historical obligations of Qajar state and society, but they were also part of them. It was one thing for political exiles to imagine a different society and quite another for their vision to be implemented. The Constitutional Revolution of 1905–6 would show how difficult it was to change the Qajar context. It would also show how the ideal of male guardianship was a bridge between the old order and the renewalist vision of society.

The Constitution and the Parliament: Gender and the Failures of the Last Qajar Institution

The Constitutional Revolution of 1905–6 provided an uneven transition for Iranian society. It began with the familiar ring of protest against monarchical excess and calls for justice by religious leaders and did not end until a constitution was granted. Early debates in Iran's Parliament revealed how unsure many deputies were about their precise function, namely, consideration of legislation. Champions—as well as opponents—of constitutional limits upon monarchical privilege and of freedom of the press and democracy came from all the traditional "estates" of Qajar society, including the Qajar aristocracy. What the Fundamental Laws and Supplementary Fundamental Laws (as the Constitution was called) could not resolve on paper was settled by violence.

The Qajar order was not eradicated by the Constitutional Revolution. The new constitutional monarchy was a blend of renewalist ambitions and Qajar institutional reform. The hostility that continued to build toward the Qajars and the Parliament itself in the years leading up to Reza Khan's coup was often expressed in terms of gender. Afsaneh Najmabadi has skillfully chronicled how the "Daughters of Quchan" incidents of 1906 helped to define Qajar impotence as Iranian Muslim peasant girls were carried off to the Russian Empire by Turcoman raiders, allegedly to be sold as slave girls to Armenians there.

The Iranian Constitution of 1906 banned women from voting or election to office. At no time during the First Parliament was this issue questioned or debated. Women's right of association was briefly discussed in 1908 but not resolved. Interestingly, representatives agreed that the matter should be debated not in the Parliament but in the press.[91] However, late in the tenure of the Second Parliament, which was again operating soon after the very principle of parliamentary rule had plunged Iran into a brief civil war, the representatives drafted and debated a new comprehensive electoral law. In the summer and fall of 1911, when this electoral law was being debated, issues of both principle and practical politics were at issue. Although the political enfranchisement of women could have had broad moral and political implications, debate on this point was tellingly brief.

On 4 August 1911, Article 4 of the proposed new electoral law was introduced for the first round of debate.[92] Article 4 specified who was ineligible to vote, and the first group on the list was women. The parliamentary commission that drafted the law was headed by Mohammad 'Ali Forughi Zoka al-Molk, and in the course of the debate questions were directed toward him. Only one representative, Hajj Shaykh Mohammad Taqi Vakil al-Ra'aya, questioned the ban:

> I will be bold and ask about that first part about forbidding women, who are part of God's creation, from voting. If we are going to bar them from the vote, what logical reasons do we have for barring them from the vote? I will dare to say—that regardless of what we want, and [even] if we are bound to act [in accordance] with the Koran in all cases, those who do not want to can go [sic]; [they] are not forced to obey. So we must know here what logical reasons we have to forbid them [from the vote]. If we have a logical reason for barring them, I will be the first person to pay deference to it. If we say they must be protected, and concede this point, it is not necessary that they enter among men [in order to vote (?)]. It is possible for them to have their own world, and have everything. How long should these creations of God be forbidden and how long must a group loved by God suffer because something that is a sign of their humanity is forcibly taken? We have gradually pulled back to the extent that we are hiding behind clouds.[93]

Zoka al-Molk responded:

> This is a very great dispute, but we did not anticipate that it would come up here. Perhaps I am, more than anyone, a partisan of women having their main rights, having a proper way of life, and having the basic, fixed rights they do have [sic]. I said this was a big dispute, and

I did not expect this discussion to come up now. I am also very eager that the situation of women in this country improve and progress, and that they come out of this life that is in fact a life of imprisonment. There is no one who is not sorry about the fact that their conditions of life are not good. That we negated their right [to vote] does not require reasons or demonstrations from me. Whenever it becomes possible for women to participate in the elections and to vote, we will immediately approve it.[94]

Shortly thereafter, the president of the Parliament, Hosayn Mo'tamen al-Molk Pirniya,[95] moved to close debate, but before doing so he deferred to a cleric known as Sayyed Hasan Modarres. Earlier accounts of this exchange assume that Modarres was an elected member of the Parliament in 1911. In fact, he was not, but his voice had more authority than an elected official at the time. Modarres was a respected cleric and teacher in Isfahan who had been sent by the religious establishment not as an elected deputy but to serve as a member of the Hayat-e 'Elmiyeh (Learned Council). The Iranian Constitution had provided for a council of religious scholars to ensure that the laws passed by Parliament conformed to the teaching of Twelver Shi'ite Islam. The only legislative session to take this provision seriously before the formation of the Islamic Republic in 1979 was the Second Parliament of 1909–11. Modarres was one of ten clerics sent to the Majles in this oversight capacity, half of whom resigned.[96] Modarres was later elected as a representative from Tehran, and as a member of Parliament he tried to block the removal of the Qajar dynasty in 1925. This opposition cost him dearly in the long run. In 1938, he was poisoned while under house arrest in Mashhad.

Modarres responded to several issues raised in the discussion of Article 4, but the first was the issue of women's suffrage:

First, women must not be named as those who have the right to vote, because they are women. The example of saying "they are not insane" and "they are not idiots"—that is a matter for the committee. But our answer must be out of reason. Courtesy and lack of courtesy are matters of friendship. We must have reasoned conversation and the reason is that today, no matter how much we deliberate, we will see that God has not given them the capacity so that they might merit the right to vote. They and the feeble minded are among those whose intellects are not capable. Never mind that, in truth, women in our religion of Islam are under guardianship. "Men manage the affairs of women."[97] They are under the guardianship of men. Our official religion is Islam. They are under guardianship. They will never have the right to vote. Others must protect the rights of women, because God has ordered in the Koran that they are under guardianship and will not have the right to vote.[98]

And with Modarres's comments, the issue of women's suffrage was effectively sealed for thirty-three years. This brief "debate" was all the discussion devoted to the question in the months of deliberation that surrounded the passage of the Electoral Law of 1911. *Iran-e Now* (New Iran), the most progressive paper in Iran at the time and the organ of the Social Democrat faction of the Parliament, regularly summarized parliamentary proceedings in such a way as to make its opinions clear. Of Modarres's "reasoned answer," it reported only that "in reference to the first proviso [denying women the vote] Mr. Modarres gave a useful explanation."[99] This ended any meaningful public discussion of women suffrage until after the Women's Awakening project of 1936–41.

If the Parliament was closed to women, the forum of the press was not. However, in 1910, the first Iranian women's magazine, *Danesh* (Knowledge), was careful to emphasize in its legend that it was "a paper about morality, and the domestic sciences and child-rearing—a useful magazine for girls and women, and it absolutely does not discuss politics and policies of the country."[100] But, of course, the issue of women's education was manifestly a matter of domestic policy, and there is a clear record of women voicing their opinions on political matters from their earliest days of participation in the press.[101] The line between acceptable and unacceptable political commentary, as far as the authorities were concerned, was open political partisanship and specific discussions of political institutions.

For example, the next major women's periodical, *Shokufeh* (Blossom), which appeared on the scene in 1913 (two years after *Danesh* stopped publishing), was more explicit in positioning itself outside politics while simultaneously including itself in the progressive and moral modern age. Like *Danesh*'s legend, *Shokufeh*'s legend promised, "*[Shokufeh]* is a moral and literary newspaper [concerned with] child hygiene, housekeeping, and child-rearing whose sound path is [advocating] the education of young women and the refinement of their morals in women's schools."[102] Its publisher and editor was Maryam 'Amid Mozayyen al-Saltaneh, the daughter of Aqa Mirza Sayyed Razi Ra'is al-Atebba, a ranking medical advisor to the Qajar court. "The director of the Blessed School for the Education of Young Women" wrote to *Shokufeh* to praise Mozayyen al-

Saltaneh for her patriotism and to encourage the public—especially women—to subscribe. In her response to the letter, Mozayyen al-Saltaneh took the opportunity to elaborate on the separation of male and female spheres of activity:

> The honor and superiority of humans over animals and things of this round earth is in possessing knowledge, praiseworthy morals, and approved habits, and what emanates from all learning is the knowledge of ethics. God Most High (exalted be His name) created everything in this world for a purpose or to suit a need. Humans' stature is adorned with the thought, "We created humans in a most noble image."[103] So, everyone must act in accordance with their position, and in accordance with their honor. For example, men, who are stronger and more muscular than women, must throw themselves in the path of various dangers and harm so as to manage the daily affairs of a few members of their family and children. After many injuries, punishments, and strains, a man cannot help but want to be comfortable in his house, and to have a few *shahi*s (for which he has toiled) with peace of mind, to have an orderly life, to have well-educated children, and to have a moral wife. This, so he can obtain the natural pleasure which God had bestowed. The duty of the woman is to establish the administration of the household.[104]

By using the letter of a supporter to solicit subscriptions, Mozayyen al-Saltaneh distanced herself from petty business concerns. The letter also affirmed her patriotic aims. Then the introductory article shared the common concern for education and morality while implicitly promising to stay clear of the "rough and tumble" male world of politics and business. It was not a promise that *Shokufeh* was able to keep, but it was the standard to which it was held by Qajar censors. When a list of recently elected parliamentary deputies was published on page four of issue 16 (published between 5 Shawwal and 9 Dhu'l-Hijjah 1331 A.H. [September 1913]), the Ministry of Education and Pious Endowments protested that this was "outside of the duty and purpose of the newspaper."[105] Mozayyen al-Saltaneh replied that the paid announcement had not been printed on her behalf or on behalf of anyone in her family. In addition, she claimed that it never occurred to her that this was a political announcement per se and that, therefore, it was not a violation of the newspaper's stated purpose.[106] It is remarkable that, even in a time of great political strife and disorder, the slightest transgression into the male world of politics by a women's magazine would be noticed.

But if the state was anxious about women's political aspirations, Iranian politicians were increasingly aware of the woman question as a matter of national progress. Prince Vosuq al-Dowleh, who served as prime minister in 1919,[107] made a point of opening up a government school for women, the Dar al-Mo'allamat, in 1919 as one of many reforms to revive Iran's (and the Qajar dynasty's) fortunes in the wake of the chaos of World War I. Unfortunately, his effort to seek British support for his regime via the Anglo-Persian Treaty of 1919, which would have made Iran a virtual protectorate of Great Britain, was too obvious and drew fire from all quarters of Iran's intelligentsia and fragmented elites. The first Iranian women's periodical to take an overtly political stand against the Qajar dynasty was Sadiqeh Dowlatabadi's *Zaban-e Zanan* (Women's Voice) in 1919. Her attack upon the Anglo-Persian Treaty caused her paper to be shut down. The modern Iranian woman, however she was to be defined and constructed, could not ally herself with the Qajars any further.

Women were denied political rights during the constitutional period; nonetheless, the first women's periodicals associated themselves with the progressive spirit of constitutionalism and tacitly accepted an unequal voice in the new order. The goals expressed in public by early women feminists were very much in line with nineteenth-century renewalism. In the following letter, published in *Danesh* on 27 May 1911—roughly three months before the question of political enfranchisement was sealed in the Parliament[108]—the explanation of the goals and benefits of women's education clearly demonstrated the way modern Iranian womanhood was simultaneously broadened and restrained:

> The Letter of One of the European-Educated Girls that Is Worthy of the Attention of [Our] Honorable Women [Readers]
>
> In this auspicious age in which ignorance has been overshadowed by science, all of the misfortune and hopelessness of us Iranian women was due to the lack of science and education. From this same cause, the destruction and wasting of all areas of the country increases daily. In previous ages women had absolutely no power or position at their husband's side except for a brief time—meaning that as long as she had, so to speak, "fruits and endowments" and youth, he would like her. As soon as her attractiveness was lost [the husband] would either divorce her or forsake her because in [the eyes of husbands] women and animals were no different. There was no science and knowledge so that a husband could desire her for that. Rather,

he was attracted to her beauty, and as soon as her beauty subsided he would select another wife.

Changing or adding wives was not a source of that man's contentment, rather it was the cause of his complete financial ruin and even criminality. This was because he spent most of his work and earnings on either many wives or children. He always had headaches and irritation and spent most of his time with them in bitterness, quarrels, and contempt. Everyone knows this and there is no need to cite chapter and verse.[109]

Women's welfare is linked to two things: the dawning of an age of renewal and the ability of women to please their husbands. The descriptions of the problems of domestic life before this age of renewal are reminiscent of those raised by Kermani, and they reiterate a link between the personal/domestic sphere and wider public and national interest. The consequences and benefits of this connection are made clear:

Praise God that today educated women display learning and knowledge. They will be at complete ease in their husband's home and will provide all the means of happiness and good fortune for [themselves and their husbands]. And if [a] woman does not have enough education, her husband prefers that she not leave her studies unfinished. He will finish her [education] himself or use another so that gradually she will progress, and this will be the cause of warmth and tenderness between them . . .

How unfortunate is the illiterate woman—especially if she has no preparation. Gradually she will disappoint her man. Honoring the happiness of adornment will not secure [one's] welfare. An educated woman will come to possess praiseworthy morals and approved qualities. One fruit of good morals is that a husband and wife will regard each other with affection as long as God wills and will not act against one another.

What a great mistake it was for the women of the age of honor and prettiness who thought they should continuously make themselves up and primp and prance and no longer pay any attention to raising children or housekeeping. They were completely obsessed with their fortunes and wealth. [But] because those wretches had no knowledge or awareness, they were not at fault. I wonder why it is that today some women who possess knowledge and accomplishment behave like those people of that base era. How they cheat themselves and their children! The result of devoting oneself to worship of the body, to laziness, and to prestige will be that a great injustice will be done to themselves and to their husbands.[110]

Education, the transmission mechanism of renewal, frees a woman from her own body. It frees her from her dependence on a part of herself that she cannot control but not from her obligation to see to the needs of her husband and household. She simply acquires a better, modern tool to perform that obligation. It is, in fact, the most basic benefit of modernity that she acquires. Just as a tractor makes a better farmer or a machine gun makes a more effective soldier, education makes a better wife. Modernity lies in activity, thrift, and industriousness, which are set against the laziness and ignorance of the time before the current age of renewal. The letter continues:

Many times such people, due to their husbands' lack of financial means and due to their own lack of the vocational skills needed to sustain income, will—for the sake of maintaining their prestige—have to resort to dishonorable and incorrect measures. A knowledgeable, educated woman, [on the other hand], will please and delight her husband because she possesses piety and correctness, which are the source of happiness.

Beauty and attractiveness or putting on airs will not be the cause of a woman's good fortune, rather, it is knowledge and accomplishment that ensure that a man will never tire of her. For an accomplished woman, ugliness and attractiveness, youth and age make no difference.

Dear sisters of mine who have husbands and who have had some education, always try to act in accordance with what you have learned. Do not allow all that suffering and toil you endured during your studies to go to waste. Act in accordance with what is good and the cause of happiness and good fortune. Continue to pursue your studies and increase your knowledge. Do not let your dear time and precious life go to waste. Endeavor at least so that your education and standing are not less than that of your husband. Do not think you will be loved by your husband because of superficial laughter and a pretty face.

A woman must be the friend and intimate of a man. That means that she must be the ally and aid of her husband in all affairs. How can she be of help to her husband, until she has had some education, of course. Such an [educated] woman makes the happiness of her husband her fascination and her need *[maftun va mohtaj-e khud misazad],* which all the while will transform him into such a tender companion. He will want her help in his profession and in his work. If he seeks pleasure, he will take pleasure in his own wife. If he wants to listen [to music ?] and wants amusement, he will benefit from his own wife. Men who, because of such a woman, are sufficiently at ease with life can better serve the people of the homeland and be the cause of their country's progress. The other request that I have of the dear brothers who have read this article carefully and who have correctly understood its content is that they understand that the education and training of unfortunate weak women will not be possible without the support and cooperation of men.

To the same extent that [men] show neglect and heedlessness toward the progress of women, they will be held answerable and responsible to God for the misfortune and ruin of the country. Also, the fathers and mothers who seek betrothal for their children should try to select moral, healthy girls from noble families so that the wife and husband will not have a contagious disease and will possess good morals. It is especially difficult for a woman with an unhealthy constitution and an absence of morals that her children be fortunate and serve their kind *[khadem-e now'-e khud bashand].* It is important to stress that [the parents] not always chase after wealthy and beautiful girls and understand that:

Good behavior is better than a pretty face,
There are thousands of points besides beauty,
A bad woman in a good man's house
Is always his torment in this world,
"Lord, save us from the torment of fire."[111]

Education would make possible a more secure, affectionate, and *monogamous* relationship with a man who is acknowledged as the ultimate guardian of the woman's interests as well as his own and, by extension, the interests of the nation. Even the earlier promise of freedom from the consequences of aging is belied in the connection made between physical and moral health. Bearing in mind that many of *Danesh*'s articles on health were no more than articles on beauty, this connection is all the more subversive of the freedom supposedly gained through education. Furthermore, "noble families" are portrayed as the final arbiters of who is healthy and moral. So, according to the terms of this letter, the modern criteria for evaluating women are still beauty, lineage, and morality—much as had been the case before.

In this construction, women's progress has nothing to do with independence from male authority. The appeals to men to guarantee their wives' educations are in the same spirit as Bibi Khanom Astarabadi's criticism of men in *The Vices of Men*. She encouraged men to act appropriately in their roles as guardians as ordained by religion. This letter portrayed male support of women's education as an extension of their duty to God and nation. Men are only answerable to God. Although the anonymous author is endowed with the modernity of Europe through education, tradition is upheld by closing the letter with metered verse (a classical Persian literary form) and a reference to the Koran.[112] As far as the relation between the sexes is concerned, the old order is comfortably transmuted into the new order. And yet, as we shall see, it is women's entry into public discussions of the woman question that begins the transformation of the modern Iranian woman from a renewalist, male fantasy to a complex reality.

It is perhaps an irony of history that the same gambit that tarnished Vosuq al-Dowleh and the Qajars in 1919 propelled the fortunes of their usurpers, the Pahlavi dynasty. Cossack brigade colonel Reza Khan also relied on British support to execute his coup d'état against the Qajars in February 1921. This association does not seem to have tarnished him as he seized the opportunity to reorganize the military, quell internal tribal rebellions, and ally himself with the heirs of nineteenth-century renewalism, the Renewal Party, and even, for a time, the Socialist Party. Once established in 1925, the Pahlavi dynasty identified itself with the renewalist ambitions that, as we have seen, used the Qajars to embody all that was backward, traditional, and corrupt in Iranian society. Although the Pahlavis did not immediately turn to the woman question in social policy, it became one of many point-for-point rebuttals of the Qajar legacy. While the Qajars had failed to develop Iran's infrastructure, the Pahlavis would build the railroad. While the Qajars had granted extraterritorial privileges to foreigners, the Pahlavis would revoke them. Whereas the Qajars had granted an oil development concession to the British, the Pahlavis would embarrass themselves trying to renegotiate it. As for the institution of the Parliament, the Pahlavi dynasty would co-opt it directly. The Qajar dynasty was voted out of existence by an Act of Parliament, albeit a Parliament controlled by then prime minister Reza Khan. However, while Parliament was chaotic and fractious under the Qajars, it would be decisive and harmonious under Reza Shah Pahlavi—at the cost of democratic legitimacy. Nonetheless, the Constitutional Revolution was celebrated in grand style in 1935 by the regime of Reza Shah. It was, after all, the first and most tangible symbol of renewalism.

In all these areas, the Pahlavis co-opted the Qajar legacy instead of replacing it. And, finally, while the Qajars had failed to improve the condition of women, the Pahlavis would implement the Women's Awakening and make it an integral part of their political legitimacy. The woman question, then, was one of many symbols of Qajar failure that the Pahlavi regime was to attempt to convert into its own successes. But the Pahlavi dynasty was to be no less bounded by the conception of modern Iranian womanhood and male guardianship than the Qajars or their renewalist opposition had been. The difference rested in their effort to realize a list of expectations generated by decades of debate on the woman question. It is to describing these expectations that we now turn.

3

Imagining the Modern Iranian Woman

Modern Iranian womanhood was an idea that changed over time in relation to four interrelated themes: marriage and motherhood, women's education, women's employment, and women's civic participation in society. With every change in the definition of modern Iranian womanhood, there was a change in the definition of male guardianship, sometimes anticipating and sometimes reacting to changes in modern Iranian womanhood. Weaving in among these themes, and also changing over time, were two tropes that I wish to highlight in the present chapter: the Euro-American example and the traditional woman. As much as modern Iranian womanhood was defined in relation to male guardianship, it was also defined in relation to these two images of womanhood.

The Euro-American example, as the name suggests, was an image of modern womanhood associated with Europe and America, not only in its positive aspects, and often mediated through images from other Near and Far Eastern countries. It is not that Europe and America were perceived as part of a cultural monolith—differences were noted and commented upon—but they did share common associations with both progress and moral laxity. The image of the traditional woman, on the other hand, was drawn from an Iranian society that renewalists were trying to change. Whether as a victim or collaborator, the traditional woman was mired in superstition and ignorance. She was an additional mouth to feed and not the loyal companion so craved by renewalist men to assist them in ushering in the moral and material rebirth of Iran. When imagined positively, the modern Iranian woman was defined against the ignorance and moral confusion of the traditional woman *and* against the seductive immorality of the Euro-American woman. At the same time, her progressive qualities were derived from successfully adapting Euro-American culture to an Iranian context. When defined negatively, the modern Iranian woman combined the vices of the Euro-American society with those of her own and was, conversely, ridiculed for not measuring up to the Euro-American example. There has never been a resolution of these competing images. Iranian society, however, did settle on a common frame of reference to mark the boundary between modernity and tradition, ignorance and enlightenment, morality and vice: the veil. While there was no consensus on what veiling and unveiling meant until Reza Shah moved to impose a definition (the subject of the next chapter), there was a tacit consensus that to talk about veiling or unveiling was to stake out one's position in the process of imagining modern Iranian womanhood.

From the late nineteenth century onward, imagining the modern Iranian woman was an increasingly public process undertaken in the pages of the periodical press. Indeed, the periodical press was a steadily expanding enterprise (both in terms of titles that appeared and circulation numbers) throughout the period covered by this book. While a full discussion of the history of the Iranian press is well beyond the scope of this study, it is appropriate to highlight a few aspects of its development through the 1940s.[1] First of all, the periodical press was introduced to Iranian culture as an instrument of state control by the Qajar dynasty in 1851. In 1876, the first expatriate newspaper, *Akhtar*, was published in Istanbul. From then until the Constitutional Revolution of 1905–6, the world of the Iranian press was filled with official and semi-official periodicals produced in Iran and expatriate newspapers produced in Cairo, Calcutta, Istanbul, and London by both supporters and detractors of the Qajar state. The Constitutional Revolution ushered in a period of great expansion in the periodical press and the appearance of ideological, domestically produced newspapers, with left-wing papers like *Sur-e Esrafil* (Esrafil's Trumpet), opening in 1907, and *Iran-e Now* (New Iran), opening in 1909, serving as models of journalistic activism for later generations of Iranian newspapermen and women. The first women's periodicals—*Danesh* (Knowledge), first published in 1910, and *Shokufeh* (Blossom), first published in 1913—also date from this period. Although the Pahlavi dynasty eventually ushered in more de facto and de jure press restrictions than the Qajars were able to impose (both before and after the Constitutional Revolution), the press actually became more diverse in the 1920s and much more commercially viable in the 1930s and 1940s. Iran's largest daily, *Ettela'at* (Information), began with a circulation of 2,000 in 1926 and was estimated to have a weekly circulation of 100,000 in the 1940s.

In 1931, the Pahlavi regime's banning of "collectivist" ideologies temporarily ended press debates between supporters of Reza Shah (organized into the Renewal Party) and Socialist and Communist detractors in Iran (although Iranian Communists published a paper in Berlin until 1933).[2]

But, as we shall see in this chapter, despite their political differences, leftists and supporters of the Pahlavi regime developed a common vision of modern womanhood in the pages of the periodical press. Furthermore, it was a vision developed by men and women feminists.

The Euro-American Example

Before Akhundzadeh and Kermani articulated the woman question in renewalist rhetoric, the discourse on modern Iranian womanhood was being defined by over a century of (primarily) male travelers to Europe and an increasing presence of Europeans and Americans in Iran throughout the nineteenth century. It is through the eyes of two travelers to Europe, Mirza Saleh Shirazi and Rezaqoli Mirza Hedayat, that we will come to appreciate the negative and positive dimensions of the Euro-American example as our two travelers encountered middle-and upper-class nineteenth-century English women.

In 1811, Qajar crown prince 'Abbas Mirza (d. 1833), who, as the governor of Azerbaijan province, represented the first line of defense against the Russians, decided to send student missions to Europe to acquire medical and technical knowledge that could aid in his attempt to develop a military force capable of handling the Russians. It was as one of those students that Shirazi set off for England in 1815. He wrote an extensive memoir of his travels in which he described not only technical wonders but also the particulars of English society and government as he saw them.[3] Among the skills he acquired was printing, and, in 1837, eighteen years after his return from Europe, he started Iran's very first newspaper.[4] There are few copies of this newspaper extant, and it apparently did not last very long. Indeed, there is even some question as to the extent to which Shirazi's travelogue was known in the Qajar Empire.

But Shirazi agonized about the relationship between modernization and Europeanization on a very personal level—as personal as the clothes on his back. It was suggested to him that he might have a more fruitful visit to England if he tried to blend in and look like an Englishman. The idea was not agreeable to him at first, but finally he acquiesced:

> Before this, Colonel d'Arcy had said that I should wear English clothing. I had not accepted this because you can study anywhere in Iranian clothing, and also the esteemed Prophet—may my soul be sacrificed for him—had commended in a blessed pronouncement, "Do not change your clothes." [But] because the dear colonel made

a big issue of my changing clothes, in Croydon I took people into account, shaved my beard, and put on English clothing, but I did not observe their habits or customs. Apart from customs and rules, what is a beard but a handful of wool? It will grow back after four months of not shaving. I acted in accordance with the poem of Shaykh Saʿdi: Do not exalt your neck with a turban and a beard, for the turban is cotton and your mustache weeds. Furthermore, it did not seem reasonable to be bound to wearing Iranian clothing. If the dear colonel is trying to get me to wear English clothing, then I will be understanding, and if the exigencies of the time are such that I wear English clothing, well, that is also easy. And actually being caught up with being this or that, and preferring a skin cap to a European beret, is also pleasing. Again, according to the poetry of Shaykh Saʿdi: It will never matter to limpid water whether its pitcher is of gold or clay.[5]

Shirazi justified compromising his own standards of appropriate clothing by clinging to an internal sense of his identity as an Iranian Muslim. For a man, adopting foreign clothing was both a trifling matter and an amusing diversion. But Shirazi was also to encounter a different model for women. Coming from a culture where unrelated men and women were separated as much as possible, he entered a culture where the formal rules of social interaction between the sexes were more permissive. He recorded, in some detail, his reaction to the modern European woman as she appeared in a well-to-do English household in 1815. He was, in a word, enchanted.[6]

He was taken with an English woman, Miss Haversham, whom he described as "a woman of the utmost insight, good behavior, and magnanimity."[7] She was also well versed in chess, and he played a few games with her. He traveled by rented coach with two unmarried women, Miss Sarah (though her brother was along for the ride as well) and Miss Goodwin, from Ashberton to Plymouth. He described his conversation with the women as "infinitely enchanting" and averred that he had never enjoyed a trip so much. He was quite taken with Miss Sarah, describing her as "a girl of the utmost virtue, sagacity, and gentleness, magnanimous and proud, with small gentle eyes and adorned with a variety of perfections."[8] As for Miss Goodwin, she was also an "intelligent, learned, smart, and genteel" girl.[9] Both showed him friendship, but Miss Sarah (not surprisingly, the one he seemed the most taken with) "lavished upon me a special sort of hospitality and affection."[10] He found Mr. Abraham's sister, Betty, quite knowledgeable and remarked, "Truthfully, I was able to further test the faculties of English girls on that day. In truth, on every topic that I raised, I found them accomplished and aware."[11]

As an outside observer, Shirazi witnessed a number of occasions when unrelated women and men mingled socially. In Ashberton, Shirazi attended a feast in which thirty men and women dined. After dinner, boys and girls sang and danced together.[12] Shirazi noted, without apparent rancor, men and women walking arm in arm at Vauxhall Gardens outside London.[13] In London, he observed how pastry shop owners made a point of hiring pretty girls to attract customers.[14]

Shirazi came away from his stay in England with specific impressions of the role of women in English society. Although his impressions may seem a bit naive and sanitized at times, there is a remarkable resonance between Shirazi's observations and the image of modern Iranian womanhood that was to dominate the Iranian press in the twentieth century. He wrote, "The affairs of the house and the managing of the house are absolutely up to women, and men have absolutely no information about the house or the expenses of the house."[15] To support his observation, Shirazi seems to take at face value the claim of Sir John Malcolm (the English ambassador to Iran) that at home he was subject to the orders of his wife. Malcolm told him, "I issue some money [at her request], and that's it."[16] Shirazi apparently saw no irony in the fact that Malcolm's self-deprecating description of his role actually confirmed his economic control over his household. However, Shirazi did note that English women received an extensive education in order to prepare for their roles as household managers, hostesses, wives, and mothers:

> And as for the education of girls, first they are sent to the household study (i.e., receiving tutoring in a room at home), and they immediately learn reading and writing in English. After they have mastered that, they are taught French and Italian. Although it is not the rule for girls to be taught Latin and Greek, some women have mastered Latin and Greek. All girls, or at least seven out of ten, can sing. As part of the education of girls they learn singing and *saz* playing—like the piano, which is a *saz* like our *santur*, except the *saz* has a big chest in which it is strung, high and low. They play it with their fingers outside the chest. There are also *chang*s, *seh-tar*s, and other kinds of *saz*es. Also, women are taught how to sew, how to run a household, and the etiquette of dealing with their husbands and relatives. This is so that, for example, when a fifteen-year-old girl leaves the boarding

school, she has mastered sewing, housekeeping, dealing with people and her husband, playing the *saz,* singing, dancing, reading French and Italian, and painting.[17]

All of this training was important because men and women selected each other after courting for about a year and half. And courtship was the ultimate end of socializing. "To sum up, in all English gatherings, men and women try to display their external and intellectual accomplishments. Each man and woman at the gathering tries to act so as to endear themselves to the hearts of everyone."[18] However, Shirazi insisted, this social order, in which men and women were groomed to select each other, and in which women were more educated and mixed with men in public, was not a breeding ground for vice or lewd behavior. Interestingly, his discussion of women, education, and morality led directly to a terse, almost defensive discussion of sexual immorality:

> Most men and women treat each other with the utmost affection, friendship, and loyalty. Just between God and me *[bayni wa bayn Allah],* few English women are guilty of obscene acts. If somebody defames or insults them, they may pay a fine to the man and woman. This is all the more strange because women do not cover their faces. [But] they never have the opportunity to commit inappropriate acts, because women and girls never leave the home alone. When staying at someone's house they cannot easily enter someone's quarters with the intent of doing obscene things. There is good and bad everywhere, but the education they give women does not solicit shameful acts. Further, the English never [have to] call any one a pederast. If anyone does this and it is proven, they execute him. Of course there are *ahl-e feyuj* in England,[19] and they practice it. That is enough of that.[20]

Our other traveler, Rezaqoli Mirza, a grandson of the Qajar king Fath 'Ali Shah, set out for England in 1835. The circumstances of his visit were quite different from Shirazi's a generation earlier. He was on the losing end of a brief war of succession following the death of Fath 'Ali Shah in 1834. The prince had backed his father, Hosayn 'Ali Mirza Farmanfarma, who controlled the southern province of Fars and who was supported in his bid for the throne by his brother Hasan 'Ali Mirza. Unfortunately for them, it was their nephew, Mohammad Mirza, who managed to secure the capital, Tehran. Ascending the throne as Mohammad Shah, he sent troops under the command of an English officer, Sir Henry Bethune Lindsay, who defeated and captured Hasan ʿAli Mirza and Hosayn ʿAli Mirza. Hasan ʿAli Mirza was blinded, and Hosayn ʿAli Mirza died of cholera while in prison in the northern town of Ardabil.[21] Rezaqoli Mirza and his two younger brothers managed to escape capture and were granted asylum in England.

Rezaqoli Mirza compiled a travelogue, and his accounts of English social customs and English women provide a quite different impression from Shirazi's travelogue. Rezaqoli Mirza seems to have been less interested than Shirazi in getting to know English women and less at ease with the mixing of men and women socially. One of his first recorded encounters with English women happened while admiring a building in London. Soon, he and his companions found themselves the object of attention of men and women in the street, so much so that they felt obliged to move on. Later, "groups of women came up to our home to look at us and we did the same, derisively."[22] One of his British liaisons, James Baille Fraser, reported Rezaqoli Mirza to be fascinated with women in attendance at a party, alternately staring at and dismissing them. "They are cheats," he would say upon seeing up close a woman who had caught his eye from a distance. Rezaqoli Mirza stated his preference for brunettes, and Fraser admitted that blond, fair-skinned women were considered more beautiful in England. Rezaqoli Mirza explained that Iranian men valued women with spice more than those with perfect features.[23] Nevertheless, when attending the theater in London, he was, according to his own pen, enchanted by the women he saw: "And in that house [i.e., the theater] there were more than fifty thousand moon-faced women and pretty young women in the room. The sight of each of them was a shining tower of beauty, like the sun. They had prepared themselves to pillage hearts and religion, all with uncovered heads, bared breasts, and with that makeup and those fine jewels: standing like cypresses with rope-like hair, their tongues daggers and their lips sugar."[24]

In this description we see the exotic West. To Rezaqoli Mirza, England was a land of available and beautiful women. However, he seems to have shrunk from the opportunity to actually touch these available women. One night he went to a "strange" and "amazing" party at an unnamed English nobleman's home:

> As many as a thousand men and women were thrown together. Anyone could take the hand of any woman and converse with her. If someone talks and socializes too much with his own wife, they find fault with him. As soon as the music starts, the notables and ministers and officers take the women by the hand and begin to dance. If

they have not danced they are considered deficient and are said to be unrefined—it is considered particularly bad among women that someone not dance. But with all of this, one of them grabbed us by the collar to dance. We swore that we had no acquaintance with dancing. They made several entreaties before they gave up on us. So far, praise God, we have not danced, and after this may God protect the world![25]

In the travelogues of Mirza Saleh Shirazi and Rezaqoli Mirza, we see the essential paradox of the example of the European woman. To Shirazi, the English woman was engaging, attractive, and morally sound. She was educated and capable of being both an ideal companion for a man and an ideal mother. On the other hand, to Rezaqoli Mirza, the English woman was at best an amusement and at worst a potent, available, and corrupting temptress. Mohamad Tavakoli-Targhi considers the misogynous combination of contempt and eroticization of European women to be characteristic of the process of defining the other,[26] and the admiration of the education of European women to be a function of admiration for nineteenth-century European hegemony.[27] But, ultimately, we have only to remember the bifurcated view of womanhood in Qajar society (as part of the Safavid legacy) to suspect that Shirazi and Rezaqoli Mirza were applying their own cultural scheme to European women—at least at first. Male guardianship formed a point of intersection between English society and Qajar society—a space in which individuals from the two societies might feel that they understood one another even though both they and their societies were changed once the space was entered. The good and bad seen in modern Euro-American womanhood would be applied to modern Iranian womanhood. In the eyes of Iranian feminists, as we shall see later, Euro-American womanhood was at once a symbol of liberation (recall Bibi Khanom's reading of social equality into the social mixing of sexes), oppression (in the form of "cultural imperialism"), and even competition (for the small supply of "modern" Iranian husbands).

Returning again to the uneasy synthesis of Qajar tradition and renewalism during the early constitutional period, some of these issues are readily apparent. For example, even as the politicians of the Second Parliament opted not to quarrel among themselves on the question of women's suffrage, the most progressive journalists marveled at the efforts of European suffragettes. On 27 February 1908 *Sur-e Esrafil* reprinted without commentary an article from the Ottoman newspaper *Irşad* about the activities of suffragettes in England.[28] Women and girls had tried to force an appointment with the prime minister at the same time that a meeting of ministers was discussing the matter of political rights for women. Two issues later, on 23 April 1908, satirist ʿAli Akbar Dehkhoda sarcastically contrasted the efforts of English women who had advocated their political rights in speeches, articles, and books with the efforts of the fictional Iranian "wife of Molla Mohammad Rowzeh-Khʷan" who spent all of her efforts arguing with her lazy husband about household chores.[29]

Iran-e Now acknowledged the issue of women's suffrage rather obliquely just as *Sur-e Esrafil* had done. Brief reports in the world news section occasionally covered the activities of European suffragettes. These reports were presented without comment and by themselves presented an ambivalent image of the political activities of European women. For example, a Danish woman was ejected from the Danish Parliament after charging up to the speaker's podium and boldly haranguing members about sacrificing the national interest for their own particular interest.[30] Rioting English suffragettes were arrested and imprisoned in Glasgow after smashing doors and windows with bricks.[31] Whatever the intentions behind these "trial balloons" for women's suffrage in Iran, these were perhaps unfortunate choices to represent the "European example." Were these reports about brave women fighting for their rights, or were they examples of how women were the cause of social chaos? Were the reports of the actions of the European women intended to inspire Iranian women—or merely to illustrate how proper (and passive) Iranian women were in comparison?

Iranian women themselves turned to the European example in a variety of ways in women's magazines. Most of the notable women featured in *Danesh* were European royalty: the queen of Belgium,[32] the queen of the Netherlands,[33] the German empress,[34] the English queen mother,[35] and the queen of Romania.[36] While there was a feature on the empress of Japan, her success was attributed to her embrace of European progress in general and to the example of Queen Victoria of England in particular.[37] They were educated, public figures who made conspicuous efforts to nurture and educate their subjects and to strive for the well-being of their nations. The Romanian queen wrote a book of ethics and supported hospitals and schools. So concerned was she for her country that, because "Romania—like Iran—was at the beginning of its progress and awakening, she thought it best to take a husband who would be able to accompany and to aid her in awakening this new country."[38] As female royal personages, queens embodied a blend of ideal motherhood and patriotism in the nations they represented. For example, during the Russo-Japanese War of

1905, the Japanese empress personally attended not only the Japanese wounded but also the captured Russians, saying, "Our two governments are enemies and at war, but what is the fault of [these] soldiers?"[39] Motherhood transcended (though did not conflict with) patriotism. In contrast, the Dutch queen was mindful of her patriotic duty to provide an heir (notably, perhaps, a daughter) so that a foreign-born prince would not have to be sought.[40]

Royal women were not the only ones who could be role models for Iranian women. To illustrate that the ideal public woman was an active partner for her husband, *Danesh* ran a feature on the wives of English members of Parliament that emphasized the administrative assets they were to their husbands.[41] Another article featured English women who "mothered" travelers—and as such, strangers—aboard passenger ships.[42] In fulfilling this public and nurturing role, the English women had managed the expansion of the charity from a two-room boarding house on the docks to five separate buildings with a number of related charities that welcomed "any group or nation that exists, and [the women published] a moral newspaper with useful news especially for the crews and dockworkers."[43] Of course, not only European women could serve as examples for Iranian women. *Danesh* also featured an article on Ottoman women and their desirable progress toward modernity through education.[44] Again, Ottoman modernity was patterned on the progress of Europe:

> For the past several years, taking more than one wife has met with the disapproval of some in the Ottoman Empire. In this constitutional era the whole situation and routine for Ottoman women is like that of the European women whom they imitate in all their business and affairs *[kar va omurat]*. For example, the veil *[neqab]* that women formerly covered their faces with in the street and in the bazaar is no longer customary. In place of a veil *[hejab]* they only have a thin face veil *[yashmaq]* upon their heads the corner of which they pull over their faces just below their eyes. But still half their faces are visible from under the head veil. [Indeed], all of their manners and ways except marriage are like the women of Europe.[45]

This passage is one of the earliest in the Iranian women's press that associates fashion with progress. The less "veiled" the Ottoman women were, the more they followed the European example and the more modern they were. The substance of this modernity was in Ottoman women's greater public visibility and fuller partnership with their husbands—but its symbol was clearly the veil. During World War I, *Shokufeh* could look to "the Ottoman example" as a counter to the European example as well, telling readers of the efforts of Ottoman women to support the empire's war effort against the Entente. It likened the sacrifices Ottoman women were making for their country to the efforts of the women who stood behind Arab Muslim warriors, exhorting them to show courage and nursing their wounded in the early days of the Islamic community. Expressing the hope that the Ottoman women would serve as examples for all women, *Shokufeh* boasted: "This support and sensitivity is not special to European women, rather, it is automatic for most Muslim women. . . . They make sacrifices in [all aspects of] their lives. They don't flinch at giving up wealth or the lives of their young to protect independence."[46]

Indeed, *Danesh*'s simple adoration of the West was replaced by something more complex in the pages of Mozzayen al-Saltaneh's *Shokufeh*. Two articles in *Shokufeh* illustrate both deference to Islam and the complex relationship with Europe. The first was a defense of veiling in which Islam was a progressive moral force, and it was Europe that lacked something:

> Our Prophet, blessings and peace be upon him and his family, in every single order and prohibition that are established in the esteemed path of Islam, was only concerned with the tranquillity, civilization, progress, and uplifting of the nation of Islam. When the firm command of *hejab* has been rightfully issued to us women, we think and then realize to what extent the most generous Prophet has prevented the corruption of morals . . . For example, in Germany 7 percent, in Belgium 6 percent, in England 5 percent, in Austria 4 percent and in the Ottoman Empire 1 percent of the women are unfaithful *[kha'eneh]*. In this survey it is clear what complete influence *hejab* has. Why, if there was no issue of *hejab,* at least 25 percent of the women of the vast Ottoman Empire would be unfaithful owing to its great size and population.[47]

There was also a defense of veiling along nationalist lines: "Leaving aside the question of religiosity, Iranian customs *[adab-e iraniyat]* have always maintained *hejab* as the primary basis of the honor of Iranian women. Even such that Zoroastrian, Jewish, and Armenian women whose religion does not have the order of *hejab* nevertheless have their faces covered in the street and bazaar and do not allow themselves to fall under the eyes of men at all. Ferdowsi, God's mercy upon him, when telling of the daughter of Afrasiyab, says that even Manijeh, Afrasiyab's daughter, was not seen uncovered."[48]

Rather than a sign of backwardness and oppression, the veil here is a symbol of a religion whose moral guidance is exemplary among progressive societies and a symbol of an Iranian national culture that transcends religious divisions. The reference to Afrasiyab is interesting because he appears in the "Iranian national epic" as the king of Turan, the land of non-Iranian Turks or Scythians. Also interesting is the pseudostatistical analysis of the effect of veiling on the morality of women in various countries and the speculation that Ottoman women's morality would surely be more lax than their European sisters without the help of Islam.[49] The article closed by praising the Muslim women of Bukhara and the Caucasus who clung to their veils despite impoverishment due to heavy taxation—an implicit condemnation of Russian rule in those areas.[50]

On the very same page as the article praising *hejab,* we find an article entitled "A Comparison between the Situations of European Women and Iranian Women." The article praised the "earnestness and struggles" of English women in pursuing the advancement of their political rights.[51] It also emphasized how frequently and aggressively English women lobbied their political leaders for the right to vote. In Iran, on the other hand, "Education [for women] is still considered blasphemy according to Koranic verses that are obligatory for each female Muslim. They [Iranian women] do not refrain in any way from wildness nor vile customs and morals. They never pursue education and duties that indeed are housekeeping, cooking, good morals, attracting their [husbands who are their] housemates and partners in life."[52]

Both European modernity and Iranian tradition beckoned—and both repelled. Islam, reduced to the veil in one article, was portrayed as an exemplary moral force in the modern world. Yet, in the next article Islam (in any event as practiced by Iranians) was portrayed as an obstacle to women's obtaining a modern "education" and therefore good morals. On the one hand, European women were morally lax when compared to observant Iranian Muslim women. On the other hand, European women were in a better position to secure their rights in a modern society.

Individual lives, of course, were not reducible to any particular vision of Iranian society—even in the words of those committed to realizing a particular vision. How much more chaotic must the situation be if one wishes to account for all the various opinions on modernity and the woman question. Yet, if one examines the press of the 1910s and 1920s, one cannot fail to be impressed by the ever increasing presence of women in this most public of forums as advocates for causes, as producers of goods, as professionals, and as consumers. *Danesh* covered events at girls' schools, such as graduation ceremonies and the taking of final exams, and featured an article on the history of women's education in Iran[53]—and efforts to raise money for women's education continued throughout the decade in the wider press as well.[54] By 1923, a woman doctor, Khanom Doktor Gowhar, was advertising her services in *Setareh-e Iran* (Iranian Star).[55] Also, in that year, the editors of *Setareh-e Iran* criticized the appointment of a male principal over a female candidate at the government's Dar al-Mo'allamat school for girls as illegal and in contradiction to the practice of civilized countries.[56] Iranian women organized to address issues of regional, not just national, importance. For example, an organization called the Society for the Guidance of Women (Jam'iyat-e Ershad al-Nesvan) used the press to publicize a conference protesting the British occupation of Iraq in solidarity with their "Iraqi sisters."[57] Along with the increased civic presence for Iranian women came more press advertisements for clothes, cosmetics, and medicine targeting women customers. Skinny women were enjoined to use "Source du Force" health drink.[58] "Creme Simon" was "very useful for the maintenance of beauty and softness of skin."[59]

In the field of journalism itself, the presence of women was increasingly felt. Let us consider the example of the longest running women's magazine in Iranian history, *'Alam-e Nesvan* (World of Women).[60] It provides a clear view of the ironic coupling of modern and traditional Iranian womanhood. The magazine's offices were located in the American Presbyterian Bethel School for Girls, and although the owner of the publishing license was an Iranian, the board of directors always included American women.[61] Also, a number of *'Alam-e Nesvan*'s subscription representatives throughout Iran were Americans or Europeans.[62] In contrast to *Shokufeh* and *Danesh*, *'Alam-e Nesvan* referred to its introductory article as a "platform" *(maramnameh)* and signaled a more assertive tone:

> In this new age [and] auspicious period when the fiery arrow of knowledge has alighted from the horizon of our Iran . . . , *'Alam-e Nesvan* has taken its first weak and shaky steps in the arena of periodicals and congratulates and greets its Iranian sisters. In civilized countries in which the press paves the road of improvement and progress, women's newspapers and magazines play an important part. In America a special monthly [women's] periodical is published, and its subscribers amount to half a million. The Society of Iranian Women Graduates of Bethel (the American School for Girls) has wanted to establish a magazine for Iranian ladies for a long time. Fortunately, it has arrived at that triumphant day and has success-

fully published *'Alam-e Nesvan*. In this *maramnameh* first the aims of this magazine are presented to the honored reader: The aim of founding *'Alam-e Nesvan* is to help in the rise and progress of women and to encourage them in service to the homeland, the family, and the sound administration of educational affairs.[63]

'Alam-e Nesvan's introductory article did not present women's contributions to society as solely restricted to assuring a man's comfort as *Shokufeh* had done explicitly. For the first two years, it sought to publish articles only by women.[64] It emphasized not only a general tradition of the press but also the role of women within that tradition. In addition to embracing the press as a symbol of progress and change, *'Alam-e Nesvan* retained a claim to special moral authority with respect to the nation's families as had *Danesh* and *Shokufeh*. Jane Doolittle, a longtime teacher at Bethel and a devoted missionary, recalled a much more humble agenda for both the founding of the Bethel alumnae society and the establishment of *'Alam-e Nesvan*:

Q. I mean, how did people go about their social life and socializing? What did they do? I mean, what were you doing there? For instance, you, as an American: were you accepted into society?

JD. Yes, very much so. In those days, the movies and the American Army and so forth had not come to Iran, and so they set the Americans on a pedestal, and they were always eager to have us visit them. Every afternoon after school, we would go to their homes. Of course, the women in those days had no recreation whatsoever. There was nothing for them: they just sat at home and took care of their children and their husbands. So they were always glad to have anybody from outside. One of our chores during the holidays (and in those days, we gave Jewish holidays and Armenian holidays and Moslem holidays)—and whenever holidays came up, the students would expect us to call on them. So we would set out at about nine o'clock in the morning and call on as many people as we could, and come back for lunch, and we'd start out at two o'clock in the afternoon and get back at six, calling in their homes. They were very eager to have us. As I said, they had very little to do, of interest. In 1919 or '20, Mrs. Boyce, who was head of the alumnae association of the girls' school, had the girls start a magazine: *'Alam-e Nesvan*. To give them something to do. That is, have the graduates do that, the alumnae association. For about thirteen years, they published this magazine and sent it all through Iran. They had a subscription, I think, of about—I'm afraid to say, whether it was four hundred or four thousand; anyway it was very few. But everybody liked that very much. They had a great time getting articles for it. . . . That gave these women something to do. As I say, they kept it up for about thirteen years, and it was—I don't know whether the first or the second women's magazine to be published in Iran. It was very well liked, but gradually they found it was too much hard work to get it out and supervise it and provide the finances for it and so forth, so they gave it up. But they really had no social life. For instance, in order to raise money to help this, they had to find various means. One idea was to have movie performances, because the women couldn't go to movies. Although by 1927 or '8 movies were in Tehran. But the women couldn't go to them; only the men went to them. So somebody had the bright idea of having a movie given at our school, and charge for it and so forth. But there was great excitement as to what they should do, because it would have to be a man who would run the movie, and he would hear the women's voices. That was not allowed [chuckles]. But they finally had it, and they earned quite a bit for their magazine. But their lives were very narrow; very uninteresting. But they had a good time in their own homes. It was always amazing to me, what good times they did make up and how the children of the second or third wife would associate with the other children and the wives all got along so well together; that was amazing.[65]

Perhaps because she felt she had few genuine converts to Christianity among her Iranian pupils or perhaps because of the rise of the Islamic Republic, Doolittle minimized the impact of American Bethel and the accomplishments of its graduates. If *'Alam-e Nesvan* enjoyed a circulation of 400 it would have been doing no worse than many other publications in Iran at the time, and if it had enjoyed a publication of 4,000, it would have been doing considerably better than most. As noted earlier, Iran's main daily, *Ettela 'at,* began in 1926 with a daily circulation of 2,000. One of the keys to *'Alam-e Nesvan*'s longevity in a very tight market for periodical publication might have been its roots as a social activity rather than a purely political or commercial enterprise. In her description of the Iranian women who made a success of *'Alam-e Nesvan,* Doolittle cannot seem to get past the fact that their lives were a mix of traditional and modern cultural impulses and obligations. In her recollections, that fact undermines the efforts of these women to improve their lives, but there is no reason for us to cling to her assessment.

In any case, *'Alam-e Nesvan* was not alone. Women's magazines in this period tried to embrace the wider world of both the press and politics. *Nameh-e Banovan* (The Ladies' Paper) carried domestic and foreign news.[66] In 1919, newspaperwoman Sadiqeh Dowlatabadi addressed political issues directly with articles entitled "Long Live the Pen!" and "Down with Tyranny" in her Isfahan-based paper *Zaban-e Zanan* (Women's Voice)—for which it was shut down by Qajar authorities.[67]

If the creation of modern Iranian womanhood was complicated by the Euro-American example, so too was the male-dominated project of renewalism that claimed the woman question as a central issue. By the time of the Fourth Parliament in 1919, the nineteenth-century renewal movement had crystallized into the statist, fascist-influenced Renewal Party on the right and the Socialists and Communists on the left. It was the Social Democrats who drove the woman question discussion (along largely nineteenth-century renewalist lines) in the press of the early constitutional period in newspapers like *Sur-e Esrafil* and *Iran-e Now*. They were also behind Azeri papers produced in Baku that reached Iran both through the immigrant Azeri-Iranian oil worker community and as a result of the high volume of trade between the Russia and Iran through Azerbaijan. But the Bolshevik Revolution of 1917 and attempts to create a Soviet Republic of Iran in Gilan in 1920–21 helped both to radicalize the left and to make the Iranian government increasingly wary of them. But even before the regime of Reza Shah moved against advocates of "collectivist ideologies" in the late 1920s and 1930s, the voices of the Renewal Party came to dominate the press through such periodicals as *Kaveh*, *Iranshahr*, *Setareh-e Iran*, *Shafaq-e Sorkh*, and others. When it came to the woman question and the image of modern Iranian womanhood, there was a good deal of common ground between the modernist Left and Right. As times seemed increasingly desperate in the wake of World War I, calls for Iranians—all Iranians—to play a part in defending and rebuilding Iran became more salient. The state needed to be transformed from its fractious and inefficient reality into a dream of efficiency and effectiveness. Politicians' speeches seemed poor substitutes for the decisive action of military men. In a parallel way, veiled and secluded women seemed to symbolize a backward country in need of rescue. Unveiling was fast becoming a symbol of national liberation from chaos and European colonialism, not just a symbol of women's liberation from ossified traditions.

Born in 1916 in Berlin during the tumult of World War I, Taqizadeh's

Kaveh had a rather inauspicious start as a showcase for German war pro-paganda. Named after the blacksmith who led a revolt against the mythi-cal tyrant Zahhak, the magazine was filled with pro-German accounts of battles, attacks upon Entente propaganda, and news of the ill-fated at-tempt of a group of Iranians to stir up tribes around Kermanshah in Iran to harass British and Russian troops in Iran. When the war was over, *Kaveh* reinvented itself as the very symbol of Iranian renewal and, in its thirty-sixth consecutive issue on 22 January 1920, announced its "new era."[68] It tried to change not only its future direction but also the images of its past. It disavowed its older incarnation as being the product of the strains of war, poor organization, and the absence of a managing editor.[69] From its older incarnation, it only offered reprints of articles on Iranian culture and history. Just as Malkam Khan had issued a blueprint for politi-cal reform in the later issues of *Qanun* in the 1890s, Taqizadeh made political recommendations in *Kaveh*'s last year of publication:

> This knowledgeable newspaper is at war with [the agents of] corrup-tion and is opposed to the achievement of aims that benefit and accord with the beliefs of old fogies and the misguided, and is op-posed to persons and classes that seek disruption. . . . [A] thousand times more important than political and governmental reforms are *national public education* for the young and old, male and female, doing away with opium, preventing disease, encouraging physical exercise, acquiring the protocols of civilization from Europe, and warding off groundless fears, superstitions, ignorance, and fanati-cism. The salvation of the nation depends on it (emphasis in the original).[70]

Kaveh was at once involved in politics and contemptuous of politics. It combined themes of morality and the need for education with bold politi-cal assertions. Education was to be academic, moral, and physical. This new call for physical education for men and women was echoed and am-plified in the press, and physical fitness was incorporated into modern Iranian womanhood.[71] As *Kaveh* elaborated upon modern Iranian wom-anhood, it also seized upon the woman question and integrated it into its fiery rhetoric:

> But we believe that the formation of various political constituencies and parties should not be about whether or not a ministry is con-trolled openly or covertly by this group of people or that group of people. Rather, if a faction or constituency is created and if it must

certainly do battle with another, then "Here is the ball, and here is the field!" We must fight against ignorance, and the honorable informed ones must fight against public illiteracy, against those who rioted to close girls' schools in Shiraz, against those who rioted against the children's clothes at the Zoroastrian School in Yazd. We must fight against illness and those who deny its spread, against filth and its obvious sources, and against the [virtual] imprisonment of women and their lack of rights.[72]

Kaveh outlined not one but two platforms containing a total of twenty-three items.[73] Simultaneously contradictory and far reaching, the platforms implied a level of state control that was completely unprecedented in 1921. On one hand, Iran was to accept unconditionally the "principles, customs, and protocols of Europe" and even adopt European sports. On the other hand, Iran was to maintain its independence and revive ancient customs and traditions. Freedom and political equality were to be established, and women were to be granted their rights. At the same time, national unity and serious-mindedness were to be promoted alongside campaigns against rebellious tribes, lying, facetiousness, joking around, and unnatural sexual acts. Education and resources were to be extended to all sectors of society, and the state's power was to be strengthened to maintain public order. At the same time "corrupt," "freeloading" public servants were to be purged.

This colossal and self-contradicting enterprise presupposed an interdependent moral and material order as powerful as any traditional cosmology it presumed to replace. Education of the masses, conditioning their bodies, and extending state control over them would inoculate the system against the dangers posed by democracy, freedom, and diversity. Right in the middle of this totalitarian vision sat women. Yet, as the editors of *Nimeh-e Digar* have noted, for all the bombast of this particular essay, *Kaveh* only devoted two articles exclusively to the woman question.[74] But they were important articles, and they offer tremendous insight into the contradictory and complementary issues that were entwined in any discussion of women.

The first article was written by author Mohammad 'Ali Jamalzadeh's wife Zhazi and appeared on 18 June 1920.[75] The first half of the article elaborated on the premise that "women, like men, have been brought into this world for a purpose, albeit a less brilliant purpose than men."[76] It advocated women's education with the primary beneficiaries of this education being husbands, families, and, by extension, the whole nation. The second half of the article elaborated on the premise that "women must not only be educated to benefit the country but also must be educated and knowledgeable for their own happiness and honor."[77] Here the emphasis was on the necessity for mixed schools or at least a complete abandonment of "ornamental education" for women, as was already beginning to happen in Europe. It was only in this way that educated women could support themselves with honorable work, and it was only by being able to support themselves that women could contain the "instincts of tyranny and oppression" that reside deep in the hearts of even the most enlightened men.[78] She closed her article with a list of women Nobel laureates and with the wish that her Iranian sisters could have been born and raised in Europe like her and wished them success in achieving progress.

The next article was anonymous and appeared on 13 December 1920.[79] It condemned the situation of women in Iran, even attributing the lack of success of the Iranian delegation at the peace conference in Paris with American president Wilson (who, after all, attended the conference arm-in-arm with his wife) to the poor social status of women in Iran.[80] The article then embarked on a bizarre and inconsistent argument that at once embraced the notion of "racial competition" and bemoaned it. The article argued that Iran would be ill equipped to compete in the world. With its women underutilized, it would be like a partially paralyzed man in a race. The article then sought to apply "scientific" reasoning to the issue. Apparently oblivious to the sexist and racist physiological "facts" it accepted as science, the article then challenged the misogynous and colonialist implications of its facts:

> For example, it is a fact that women have fewer red blood cells than men, lighter brains, less strength. The bone structure of ribs, spine, and pelvis of men and women differ; women's muscles tire more easily; the monthly habit, pregnancy and lactation, and even the absence of facial hair form the basis of difference between the sexes. [Opponents of women's rights] assume that these scientific results are justifications for taking two wives, divorcing, imprisoning, or beating a woman!! From this logic, if one of the European scientists argued for the complete rule of Europe over the East because of the blackness of the hair and eyes of Iranians, the shortness of the Japanese, the fast rate of maturation of the Arabs, the lightness of the brains of the Chinese, or the thinness and dark coloring of Indians, would we be ready to accept this?[81]

The article went on to argue that sexual prejudices (as opposed to the list of "scientific facts" offered above), like racial ones, are based in fanatical religious roots. The Jews were condemned by others because they killed Jesus. The Babis were persecuted by others because they killed Naser al-Din Shah. But, it cautioned, the improvement of the status of women in Iran was one of the keys to progress, and if Iranians continued on the same path they were on, they would not even be as well off as the Jews in two hundred years of trying.[82] This unhappy mix of pseudo-science, racism, and sexism is what passed for progressive thinking in the pages of *Kaveh*. What is important here is the extent to which the poor record of modern male guardians in supporting their "inferior" female charges was felt to risk the national goal of modernized prosperity. Another feature of this article—a feature shared with the article by Zhazhi Jamalzadeh—is that it located the progress of Iran and Iranian woman in relation to the progress of the rest of the world. In the global race of nations to develop and prosper, Iran lagged behind the example of Europe.

If the Euro-American example dangled in front of the modern Iranian woman like a prize just out of reach, the example of the traditional woman weighed on her like an anchor. But the superstitious ignorance of the traditional woman was less often portrayed as a burden upon women than as a burden upon renewalist men—be they devoted to the Renewal Party or the Socialist Party. And more than anything else, the veil came to represent the traditional woman in her seclusion, her ignorance, and, ultimately, her moral confusion. To renewalist sentiment, the traditional woman came to symbolize the very things that had to be rooted out of Iranian society, by persuasion and, ultimately, by force.

The Traditional Woman

In chapter 2, we saw examples of how "traditional women"—be they aristocratic Qajars, wretched collaborators with the Qajars, or Kermani's "living dead"—were the enemies of renewalist progress. In the wake of the Constitutional Revolution, the traditional woman could surface as a corrupted enemy of society, posing as an ally of progress to further her criminal intent. In 1909, *Iran-e Now* ran the story of a doctor, Aqa Mirza Sayyed Hosayn Khan, who took in a poverty-stricken woman who claimed to be the widow of a soldier in the Civil War of 1908–9. When the doctor and his family went out on a holiday, they returned to find their house ransacked: "After much investigation, a medical student named Nasrollah Khan finds the woman in front of the Hajeb al-Dowleh arcade. She is selling a night veil [*sic*] from among the stolen possessions. With a thousand hassles he brings her to the authorities, and after a great deal of interrogation she confesses to her theft and charlatanry, and they recovered the rest, which she has sold to Jews. We must [learn to] recognize these deceitful and sly women."[83]

Aside from her status as a petty criminal, what marks the woman as traditional is her shameless attempt to capitalize on sympathy for the constitutional movement. How else might she deceive a modern Muslim man of science? This didactic use of the press was very much in line with renewalist attitudes about culture. Mirza Aqa Khan Kermani had insisted that one needed to marshal the force of literature as well as science to demonstrate and propagate the morals of national salvation. In that spirit, Mohammad ʿAli Jamalzadeh, the venerated founder of modern Iranian prose, published one of his short stories, "Persian Is Sugar," in Taqizadeh's *Kaveh*. Short on character development but long on satire, Jamalzadeh's stories combined the folksy moral commentary of Dehkhoda with a concern for storytelling. Jamalzaldeh's stories were published in a collection in 1921. Among the social ills lampooned was the treatment of women. In the story "What's Sauce for the Goose . . ." Jamalzadeh creates a fictional report on Iranian society by a European observer:

> Another thing that is very strange about Iran is that a substantial part of the people, about half the population of the country, wrap themselves from head to foot in black sacks, not even leaving a place to breathe. And that's how they go about the alleyways, in that black sack. These people are never allowed to speak and have no right to enter a teahouse or any other place. Their baths are also separate, and at public gatherings like passion plays and mourning-fests, they have their own viewing sections. As long as they are alone, you never hear a peep from them, but as soon as they get together, they start cackling weirdly. I believe they are a form of Iranian priest, similar to the strange types we have back home from Europe. If they are indeed priests, the people do not seem to hold them in much respect, for they have dubbed them *zaʿifeh*, which means "weak" or "insignificant."[84]

In this passage, Jamalzadeh offers us the renewalists' construction of the traditional woman. She is the specter of not just Iranian women's abject state, but that of the whole country. Women are cackling "Iranian priests," rightfully separate from the rest of society, and yet proof of Iranian society's backwardness. A contemporary piece of literature—though in a more traditional form—was Iraj Mirza's (d. 1926) satirical *masnavi*, the *'Arefnameh*. The poem—which was directed against the anti-Qajar, popular bard of the Constitutional Revolution, 'Aref of Qazvin—soon expands its scope to Iranian society. Like Kermani, Iraj Mirza blamed the veil and the seclusion of Iran's women for a widespread lack of morality. After a lengthy and vulgar passage in which he successfully seduces a veiled woman, he offers this attack upon the veil:

Thus, ignorance, when maintained under wraps,
Make *chador* and *hejab* a woman's traps.
Her *kos* [vagina] she casually put up for sale,
For she was on better terms with her veil,
Yes, shame and virtue are both in the eyes,
When those are shut what remains are lies.
If they would teach a woman propriety,
She could parade unveiled in society.
Were she to learn what virtue really meant,
Unveiling would induce her betterment:
She'd go out and with men associate,
And try her nature to indoctrinate.
A woman schooled, who has been to college,
Illuminates her soul with knowledge.
Her purity's immune to any trick,
Were mud thrown at her it wouldn't stick.
Like sunlight her rays would light up the world,
Out of the fray and beyond insults hurled.
A colleged woman who's been to *la faculté*,
Who comes to you her neckline *décolleté*,
If you see that she's honest, pure, and wise,
You'd never view her with immodest eyes.
From her to expect sin and collusion?
To think her evil's just a delusion . . .
Where did the Prophet state in the Holy Writ
That women and ghouls must be one IT?
Show the *hadith*, report, what you can,
That says women must be the bogeyman . . .
Do what the Prophet said was commonplace;
And neither sell your charms, nor hide your face.
It's against the Holy Koran, I am certain,

To hide your hands and face behind a curtain . . .
Do rural women and tribal folks
Conceal their faces using veils and cloaks?
Why aren't they subject to filth and lust?
Why isn't their bazaar bereft of trust . . . .
In other parts women help the men;
In this unhappy place they hamper them.
There, men and women share one profession;
Here men must toil in lonely obsession.
You, who are the same stuff as musk and *fleurs,*
Don't [you] feel alone in that *chador* of yours?
A bud won't flower 'til it sheds its veil:
Is this not how it ought to end its trail?
Now raise your hand and draw the curtain wide
To show the world your own perfection's pride;
And keep the veil so far from your own face,
It lights up doors and walls around this place.
I'd give my life for breasts unveiled and that hair,
In which demur and loveliness are a pair.[85]

In this poem was the renewalist argument for unveiling with all its contradictions. It was about liberating women so they could help men rather than be a burden to them. It was about freeing women from religious traditions but principally by redefining those traditions rather than disavowing them. Clearly, Iraj Mirza imagines unveiling in the same fashion as did Qasim Amin and, ironically, as the Islamic Republic currently imagines *veiling*—all covered except the hands and the face.[86] The main indications that Iraj Mirza imagined modern Iranian womanhood in relation to Euro-American education and fashion comes from his use of the words, "college," "faculté" and "décolleté." Unveiling was about creating an internal sense of modesty for women that, as the last couplet indicates, is no less alluring to men, despite exhortations to men not to view the modern Iranian woman's neckline with "immodest eyes."[87] Earlier, the poet and military adventurer Lahuti wrote the poem "To the Girls of Iran" in January 1918 while residing in Istanbul.[88] In the first half of the poem, he elaborated upon his longing for the girls of his homeland; but then, the desire expressed, Lahuti warned them, "I will not buy beauty without knowledge; sell me beauty no more and bring on deeds."[89] He then devoted the rest of the poem to admonishing Iranian girls to remove their veils, to educate themselves, and to serve as mothers for their nation. The conception of women as peddling their talents—be they physical, moral, or intellectual—to a male admirer suggests that the role of women in the new order was not completely different from their role in the old order. To impress the poet, a new woman had to be accomplished and educated as well as beautiful. For modern male guardians, a clear benefit of unveiling was that women would become more available to them socially and that women would choose them as partners in marriage.

In modernist Persian prose, the traditional woman was left to the corrupting environment of child marriage, polygynous marriage, temporary marriage, and prostitution with only empty superstitions to console her. From the amoral ʿAlaviyeh Khanom, the murderous Aziz Agha, and envy-filled Abji Khanom in the short stories of Sadeq Hedayat in the 1930s and 1940s to the hapless ʿEsmat in the fiction of Ebrahim Golestan in the 1960s, the many manifestations of the traditional woman were an enduring target of modern social criticism in literature. The subject of the child bride continues in the fiction of the Islamic Republic as a lasting symbol of Iran's backwardness.[90] The Euro-American example, however, was never the simple "good" opposite of tradition. The closer some Iranian women came to embracing Euro-American-style social mixing, the more they came to represent Euro-American vice infiltrating and corrupting the lives of Iran's desperate youth. In 1932, well into the reign of Reza Shah Pahlavi, the first excerpt from a novel by Mohammad Masʿud—the future populist newspaperman and fiery critic of Reza Shah's regime—appeared in the newspaper *Shafaq-e Sorkh* (Red Aurora). The novel was entitled *Tafrihat-e Shab* (Night Amusements), and it criticized corrupt civil servants, the poor treatment of women, the education system, the absence of economic opportunity, and—as the following passage illustrates—the increasingly lax morals of Iran's urban youth:

> "We want a fox-trot! A band without old women! . . . Why don't you unkind women dance? Are the dancers crippled? The tango? Tango!"
>
> It is still the first round [of drinks] when drunkenness starts. Young men who are a composite of youthful energy, a vile environment, and the stupidity of the schools raise an odd uproar. Fists strike the table like sledgehammers—their thudding reverberates in the air. Feet are continually stomping the floor. Faces are alight. Eyebrows are bent into a scowl. Eyes are bloodshot, mouths foaming, hair disheveled, veins popping out, blood boiling. Drunken shouts are mixed with demands of "We want a fox-trot!" Bawdy ditties

rend the air of the nightclub, and drunken brawls rattle the windows. A girl who had drawn attention to herself [from amid] the momentary din with her seductive eyes now moves into gear and laughs, dances, and entices; now coiled upon her knees like a spring, spinning quickly, and standing again; now moving elegantly on the tips of her toes, now entwining her hands, bending and straightening her fingers. Her locks bounce on her shoulders, filling the air with a delicious and agreeable fragrance. Breasts slide under silk like swimming fish. Their rapturous trembling excites the atoms of my soul . . . This same filthy nightclub, which in my opinion represents the cesspool of society, seems to become a clear pond in which I want to mix and dissolve like a drop of rain . . . It is the band's fifth set. One person in the crowd shouts, "This song's grown whiskers and the band is only good for your granny's wedding." Another shouts, "They pulled this same stunt at the late Hajji Mirza Aqasi's circumcision party!" The bandleader gets angry and says, "Go complain to your fathers; nobody's put us in charge of your inheritance." The owner of the nightclub is at his wit's end and wants to calm them down. An ominous whispering and muttering starts. A short, stocky youth splits from the crowd and pipes up, "We pay good money. We want a good band. If you know how [to play], get on with it! If you don't, tighten your asses and get lost and go set monkeys dancing! Who let you scum in here?" The sound of a stinging slap rings out. At once there is a hubbub of curses, kicks, the tumbling of tables and seats.[91]

Perhaps the most interesting thing about Mas'ud's work is the language in which it was reportedly praised. A shrewd publicist, Mas'ud included in the 1940s seventh printing of *Tafrihat-e Shab* words of praise about his book from the father of modern Persian prose himself, Jamalzadeh. Mas'ud also included praise from Mohammad Hejazi, the editor of the regime's premier propaganda periodical in 1939, *Iran-e Emruz* (Today's Iran).[92] Among these early favorable reviews cited for *Tafrihat-e Shab* are the following passages:

Tafrihat-e Shab criticizes the lewd behavior of rootless youth and illuminates the dark corners and the regrettable results of nightlife. Mr. Mohammad Khan Mas'ud is a young and gifted writer who for the first time in Iran has succeeded in uncovering the ills of society and has thrown open to public view the cramped corners of nightclubs, and therefore it *[Tafrihat-e Shab)* is to be considered a valuable gift for the enlightened class and a guide for the common class. (Sayyed Kazem Khan Ettehad)[93]

And:

Let the efforts of the past master of science and learning [Mas'ud] . . . cast a shadow over the devotees of science and enlightenment and become the source of pride for his countrymen in the face of foreign scrutiny. (From an article in *Kushesh*)[94]

Sincerely or not, Mas'ud's literary effort was extolled on the basis of its "scientific" and "educational" value and on its value as a negative object lesson. It spoke to moral truths or, rather, their absence. The corrupting combination of youth, music, alcohol, and seductive women produced angry chaos among the men in the ballroom. Neither criticized for its awkward composition, nor praised for his nightmarish portrayals of nightspots or brashly titillating descriptions of the attractions of nightlife, *Tafrihat-e Shab* was praised in accordance with the cultural aesthetics of renewal—it was praised as valuable social and moral commentary. If "tradition" was corrupt by definition and Euro-American "modernity" was also morally perilous, then how might one assure a smooth transition to modernity? The answer, not surprisingly, was that modern male guardians would chaperone Iranian women into modernity. In political terms in the 1920s, however, there were two "modern" chaperones available: the Renewal Party and the Socialist Party.

Although it did not dominate the political and press landscape in the same way as the Renewal Party, the political left in Iran did speak on the woman question through its two primary outlets, *Nahid* (Venus) and *Tufan* (The Storm). The publisher and editor of *Nahid*, Mirza Ebrahim Khan Nahid, endured a number of government shutdowns and one fire during the life of the paper from 1921 to 1933 and resorted to publishing his paper under different names to frustrate government censors—*Aflak* (The Heavens), *Setareh-e Sobh* (The Morning Star), and *Khalq* (The People).[95] *Nahid* seems to have been more engaged with the woman question, printing articles on both the international women's movement and tried-and-true domestic woman-question issues, such as monogamy.[96] *Tufan* (1921–27) seems to have given less direct attention to the woman question as its editor, the poet and activist Mirza Mohammad Farrokhi Yazdi, was more single-mindedly focused on tangling with the regime of Reza Shah.[97] Of course, Farrokhi was quite willing to play upon the theme of men as the guardians of women, as an element in provocative rhetoric, as on one occasion in 1922 when he attacked the Parliament for not protecting civil liberties in Iran: "You were so traitorous and cowardly that when the military government was whipping women, not hesitating to imprison or exile, and threatening to cut tongues and break hands, not even once did the Parliament rise up to question and investigate to see how [the military government] would answer."[98]

Yet, when *Tufan* ran articles criticizing the noninclusive nature of the Parliament[99] or the poor condition of state-sponsored education in Iran[100] —perfect opportunities to advocate women's rights—it failed even to mention that women existed. Like the men of the modernist political right, Communist and Socialist men wanted women as part of their cause and wanted to serve as their protectors. When it was politically convenient, this shared vision of modern Iranian womanhood could illustrate (even fabricate) common ground between the modernist right and left and between the regime of Reza Shah and the Left (see illustration 3.1).[101] Furthermore, the Left provided graphic images of the benefits that would accrue to men if their households and their women would modernize (see illustrations 3.2 and 3.3).[102]

The political cartoons of the Left, like renewalist literature in general, provide us a glimpse of the cultural impulses that constructed modern Iranian womanhood and modern male guardianship on the eve of the Women's Awakening. The modern Iranian woman kept a clean household and contributed to the success of her male guardian (more often conceptualized as her husband rather than her father). The interesting point in the cartoons from *Nahid* is that children are not central to the mission of the modern Iranian woman. Though she would be repeatedly celebrated as a mother before, during, and after the Women's Awakening, the domestic efforts of the modern Iranian woman are clearly conceived of in relation to (almost as an extension of) her husband. She was to be educated for this purpose and have her education supported by her husband. Indeed, her husband was to guide her—chaperone her—to modernity. Prior to 1932, the political left had gone further than adherents of the Renewal Party in providing an organizational framework for their enlightened male guardianship. The Patriotic Women's League was organized by Mohtaram Eskandari—wife of the prominent socialist (and, later, founding member of the communist Tudeh Party in 1941) Solayman Eskandari—in 1919.[103] When its membership proved too bourgeois, the fledgling Iranian Communist Party (formed in 1920) authorized the formation of a splinter group called the Women's Awakening (Bidari-ye Zanan) and a provincial

3.1. *Khalq* 31 (18 December 1925), 4. This cartoon appeared in *Khalq* shortly after Reza Shah was constitutionally recognized as Iran's new king in December 1925. Captions *(clockwise from bottom):* (1) "The final death of feudalism"; (2) "Opening the doors of prosperity"; (3) "Complete centralization in the shadow of His Majesty Pahlavi"; and (4) "Freedom and progress remove the veil from the face." Unveiling, centralization, economic development, and even ending feudalism are bundled together as areas of agreement between the Left and Reza Shah. A feminine angel symbolizes both freedom and progress and is herself freed by the removal of her veil.

3.2. *Khalq* 29 (11 December 1925), 4. Comparing Iranian and European Families I. *Top caption:* "Scene of an Iranian family in a wealthy, flourishing country as a result of the nation's ignorance and the carelessness of thoughtless, corrupt rulers." *Bottom caption:* "The situation of European families due to having knowledge and the blessing of security [in a] wealthy country." Notice how the man in the European family is the center of attention (rather than the child) and is entertained by three women. By permission of MEDOC, University of Chicago.

3.3. *Khalq* 33 (25 December 1925), 4. Comparing Iranian and European Families II. *Top caption:* "Oh, Dad's back! One person whose beard is in the hands of seven people!" *Bottom caption:* "In a European family, his wife also works!" As in the previous comparison, women are valued on the basis of either the burden or the comfort they are to men. European attire for men and women symbolizes the gulf between modernity and tradition as much as it does the difference between European and Iranian. By permission of MEDOC, University of Chicago.

group in Enzeli called The Messenger of Women's Prosperity (Payk-e Sa'adat-e Nesvan).[104] It was political renewalism, however, that won the day with the coup of Reza Khan in 1921. Efforts of the Left to ally itself with Reza Shah after 1925 proved illusory, and it was shut down in 1931 with a law banning "collectivist ideologies." It was in 1931, also, that the renewalist Pahlavi state moved to ally itself with Iranian feminists— gradually replacing the Left's organizational links to the women's move- ment with its own (see chapters 5 and 7).

Renewalist men portrayed themselves as the vanguard of modernity for all of Iranian society—and, in some sense, this self-portrayal was not empty. Men like Shirazi traveled to the heart of European modernity first, men like Akhundzadeh and Kermani do seem to have given the woman question its initial trajectory, and men like Mirza Malkam Khan and Taqizadeh linked the woman question to broader issues of political and social reform. The idea of renewalist men paving the way for others was reinforced in literature—with Iraj Mirza and Jamalzadeh telling Iranian women how veiled they should be—and in portrayals of political action.

What is lost in some of these cultural artifacts is women's active in- volvement in defining modernity and tradition. The staff of 'Alam-e Nesvan struggled to balance the Euro-American example with traditional expectations every bit as much as Mirza Saleh Shirazi did when he donned English clothing. Their challenge was greater since they had to engage in their struggle while living in Iran with their families; Shirazi made choices contending only with his conscience. Women's political participation and commitment to renewalism occurred even in the face of expectations (and pressures) that they not be political. Of course, women did not necessarily bend to such pressures. In 1922, a woman signing her name "Tal'at Sh." wrote an expressly political letter and sent it both to the renewalist Setareh-e Iran and to Tufan, "the finest and most reasonable newspaper of the Left."[105] She warned readers of British influence at all levels of the government, from the king to the members of Parliament (it is not clear if she intended to include Reza Khan in this condemnation). Taking the stance of an independent and patriotic woman, she signaled her displea- sure with both wings of modernism, prefacing her letter sarcastically with the claim that she had refrained from political commentary up to that point because "women in Iranian society did not and do not have the right to interfere in politics."[106] To this she added that she felt compelled to write about political matters because of the dangers threatening her coun- try and also because she was tired of the empty discussions of love and morality that bounded any discussion in the press that involved women.[107]

As we shall see in chapter 4, these "empty" discussions ultimately led to the first efforts of the Pahlavi state to engage the woman question. Yet, Tal'at's complaint was a sign of how widely held notions of male guardianship limited the range of the woman question even in "revolutionary" public discourse. The fact of women's increasing civic presence and greater social and economic presence in this period was greeted with little celebration, and indeed, as we have seen in the example of Mohammad Mas'ud's literature, it could be met with condemnation. This neglect would be turned on its head during the Women's Awakening as Pahlavi propaganda obliterated traces of women's progress (even its own early efforts in this regard) prior to 1936.

Another illusion created by the Women's Awakening is that unveiling has always meant a very close approximation of the Euro-American fashion. Iraj Mirza's calls for unveiling, for example, clearly hovered closer to the Qasim Amin definition (namely removal of the face-veil only). As we can see in the political cartoons from *Nahid* in 1928, it is clear that some defined unveiling as the removal of any head covering and the adoption of European fashions. Thus, in addition to lack of consensus regarding the virtues of veiling, the very definition of veiling was in flux. The Women's Awakening attempted to realize two goals: the development of a consistent image of the modern Iranian woman (with a proper balance of native virtue and Euro-American appearance), and the enforcement of unveiling as a precondition to realizing renewalist expectations of modern Iranian womanhood (namely, that she be educated, that she have a greater civic and economic presence, and that she be a loyal companion). It was the Women's Awakening that was to define the traditional woman as veiled in modernist discourse (a definition now aggressively combated in the present-day Islamic Republic of Iran). Unveiling was to be a means to an end, but it was unveiling that became the area of greatest government effort and greatest resistance. It is to the history of unveiling and its consequences that we now turn.

4

Unveiling and Its Discontents

Arise from the sleep of shame and neglect!
Take your mind off superstitious thoughts!
Arise from neglect, and this ignorant sleep,
For it has come, the Seventeenth of Day!
Women's freedom is victorious
In the shadow of the King today!
The Seventeenth of Day celebration is afoot!
It is our day of happiness and freedom!
The King's favor has granted us freedom,
So that we may show pleasure and joy.
We too have been granted freedom;
Long live the freedom-granting King!
The Young Women's Anthem, 6 January 1939[1]

Out of fear for the country, we praised and saluted,
In reluctance, we praised and saluted.
However much we drew the curtain, sin tore it asunder;
It became clear that sin was a little girl, tearing her veil.
One cannot cover with silk brocade a burning flame,
For upon blinking, the brocade's curtain is aflame.
"In Memory of the 20 of Shahrivar 1320 [Reza Shah's abdication and exile]" (1944)[2]

Unveiling was both celebrated and minimized during the Women's Awakening project. While it was the essential symbol of Reza Shah's most audacious social policy, it was not the ultimate *goal* of that social policy. Women's bodies needed to be unveiled so that the regime could display and celebrate the progress of women in Iran—progress it initiated, progress it co-opted, and, most importantly as we shall see in later chapters, progress it controlled. The coercive power of the state operated on two levels: enforcing unveiling as a fact of life and defining the symbolism of unveiling in propaganda. In Pahlavi propaganda, unveiling was made to symbolize a blend of virtue, civilization, progress, Islam, and ancient Iranian custom rather than impiety, the corrupting influence of Euro-

American culture, and sexual vice. The state obsessively removed the veil while trying to empty it of its traditional symbolism. If virtue, religion, and culture were not located in the object of the veil, it was of no consequence to take it off. Leaving it on, however, perpetuated bankrupt traditions and signaled a disinterest in national or individual progress. Veiling was a selfish, foolish, and even treasonous act.

In this chapter we will focus not on ultimate ends of the Women's Awakening—the display of modern Iranian womanhood—but its widely executed means: unveiling. Once the mechanisms of implementing and justifying unveiling are chronicled, it will not take much imagination to appreciate the resentments of Iranian society with regard to the state's treatment of women. However, I wish also to bring into focus the effect of the Women's Awakening upon men and their sense of powerlessness and victimization. By extending the state's authority over the bodies of women, Reza Shah was also extending the state's authority over the men who would be their guardians. The goals of the Women's Awakening have been obscured in Iranian historiography, in part because most Iranians— men and women—could not get past the indignities of unveiling. Forced unveiling became, in the minds of many Iranians, the point of the Women's Awakening and the cause of their resentment toward Reza Shah.

State Coercion and Women's Bodies

When Reza Shah embarked on his Women's Awakening project in 1936, it was neither wholly unprecedented nor wholly predictable. A key feature of this project was the forced unveiling of women—an enterprise the Communists had attempted during their ill-fated effort to co-opt a rebellion in Gilan in 1920.[3] The Communists in Gilan simply did not have the state resources that Reza Shah applied to his project. Earlier in his political career, Prime Minister Reza Khan had trodden more carefully. He allowed writer Ebrahim Khʷajehnuri to be convicted for speaking against Islam when Khʷajehnuri advocated in an article that Iranian women merely replace the veil with a kerchief like women in the Republic of Turkey.[4] When Mohtaram Eskandari, a Qajar princess and founder of the Patriotic Women's League, acted on the substance of Khʷajehnuri's suggestion on 21 April 1925, she was escorted under guard to police headquarters.[5] On the other hand, there seems to have been no official reaction to the protests of Afzal Vaziri, the granddaughter of Bibi Khanom Astarabadi, in *Shafaq-e Sorkh* in 1930 as she complained about "harassment" by school officials of girls of seven or eight who came to school without veils.[6]

Indeed, Reza Shah first imposed a disciplined sartorial reform upon Iran's men. On 30 December 1928, he proclaimed and enforced the wearing of the "Pahlavi cap" by all Iranian men. This was surely an invasive and annoying display of state authority, and there are records of people resisting the change.[7] In that same year, the king of Afghanistan, Amanollah Khan, had attempted a state-sponsored unveiling effort that cost him his throne and perhaps provided an object lesson for any like-minded rulers in the neighborhood.

Far from being public policy in Iran in the early 1930s or a matter of popular consensus, unveiling was a rumor, a fear, and a hope. A few feminist women, like Sadiqeh Dowlatabadi, would venture forth unveiled in the northern, more affluent part of Tehran as early as 1927.[8] Among the upper classes, unveiling was a secret activity shared among like-minded peers and sympathetic foreigners. One "unveiled" in front of guests at a private home or a private school, not in the street. Charles C. Hart, the head of the American Legation in 1931, reported "an unveiling" as a rite of passage into modernity and freedom—a ceremony unto itself that required witnesses:

> Reverting to the subject of women's progress, one incident of interest which has taken place since previous dispatches on that subject were written, was an unveiling which Mrs. Hart and I attended as the honor guests. Madame Garighaozalou [sic], wife of Ebrahim Khan Garighozalou, decided with enthusiastic approval of her husband, whose father was once Persian Minister to Washington, to remove her *chadar* [sic]. A dinner was given at the Garighozalou home at which were several guests besides ourselves. While formal invitations were sent out for the dinner, Madame Naghi Khan Garighozalou, the former Miss Katherine Ladd of Washington, urged to accept because she said the dinner was to give encouragement to her sister-in-law on her new start in life. We found the hostess to be a most charming young woman, anxious to be hospitable on this first brave adventure into a new world [though] she was manifestly nervous and shy. Madame Gharighozalou was educated in France and speaks French quite as fluently as Persian. Having witnessed her nervousness in removing the chadar, I can readily sense the reluctance with which Persian women who have never been outside their own country move toward freedom from customs that are several centuries old.[9]

As we shall see in the next chapter, the Pahlavi regime decided to begin its engagement of the woman question with the Marriage Law of 1931 rather than with unveiling. As late as the Second Eastern Women's Congress in Tehran in 1932, the regime of Reza Shah sent strong signals against unveiling (see chapter 7). And when unveiling was discussed, it was not uniformly defined as the complete removal of the *chador* or uncovering of the head. To many, "unveiling" meant merely the removal of the face veil—as had been advocated by Qasim Amin in Egypt at the turn of the century and as had been exhibited by Egyptian feminists in the twenties. Nonetheless, the principle of unveiling had its advocates in the court of Reza Shah Pahlavi. As Mehrangiz Dowlatshahi, an activist and one of the young women in attendance at the Daneshsara (a training college for teachers) on the day unveiling was decreed in 1936, recalled:

> Of course, in this business one must not forget the role of some of Reza Shah's advisers. For the removal of the veil, Teymourtache was very influential—another was 'Ali Asghar Hekmat and another was my father. During the time my father was at court, he would often speak about this issue with Reza Shah. Once even, now I don't know who else was there [but] there were two or three people who were talking about the necessity of removing the veil and these things. The Shah said, "Well, if this is a change that really is necessary to be brought about, very well, let it come. It should not be an obstacle to the progress of the country. But, I think I will divorce both my wives at that time." But, later, he did not do this because he went to Turkey and changed his outlook. And when Reza Shah came back, he decided to remove the veil in Iran.[10]

That Teymourtache might still be an influence upon Reza Shah in 1935 is a very interesting possibility. He was Reza Shah's powerful minister of court until 1932, when he was dismissed and imprisoned on charges of treason—dying in prison in 1933. His daughter, Iran, had established a women's organization (the United Women's Organization). But Teymourtache, like Reza Shah himself, was no model of modern male guardianship, taking his third wife in 1931. Before his ouster and murder in prison, Teymourtache had been one of only a few men who might have been able to threaten Reza Shah's power—a true rival. From an aristocratic family of Khurasan, the product of Russian military training and a European education, Teymourtache was sophisticated and urbane where Reza Shah was not, as well as pedigreed and titled where Reza Shah was not. Not an early confidant of Reza Shah, Teymourtache had been made minister of court because of his familiarity with European diplomatic and royal protocol—his first major assignment being the coronation ceremony for Reza Shah in 1926.[11] His rise within the Pahlavi court was probably always shadowed by suspicions regarding his political motives. In forcing the issue of unveiling, Reza Shah could be as "progressive" as Teymourtache and could eclipse his memory. Mirza'Ali Asghar Khan Hekmat, as minister of education for key periods surrounding the Women's Awakening, did play an active role in the project. Dowlatshahi's father, Mohammad 'Ali Dowlatshahi Moshkat al-Dowleh, was one of the early supporters of Reza Shah who had the good fortune to retire and die in his sleep, never having the earned the ire of his king in any appreciable way. But, then, he was more than a political ally; he was family. When Reza Shah was still minister of war in 1923, Mohammad 'Ali Dowlatshahi brokered the marriage between Reza Shah and his fifteen-year-old niece, 'Esmat Taj al-Moluk, the daughter of Gholam 'Ali Dowlatshahi Mojallal al-Dowleh.[12] It was her first marriage and Reza Shah's third. This marriage turned out to be an important one as it resulted in the birth of Crown Prince Mohammad Reza. It was 'Esmat who appeared with her daughters unveiled on 7 January 1936 at the Daneshsara.

The trip to Turkey does seem to have played an important role in Reza Shah's thinking, but the fact that he embarked on a trip to Turkey in 1934 suggests a new level of confidence in his own command over Iran's political landscape. Indeed, in 1934 he was at the zenith of his power, and this seemed to inspire him to more audacious personal and state action. With the perilous negotiations with the Anglo-Persian Oil Company from 1931 to 1933 to improve Iran's share of oil profits behind him, he could (and did) present the outcome as a success. Tribal unrest being more or less quelled, he passed a law barring tribal representation in the Majles.[13] Proposed in late 1933, the trip to Turkey was undertaken in June and July of 1934 and was heavily publicized. Taken out of context, one might have inferred from the pictures of Reza Shah in Turkey that he had conquered the country rather than merely visited it![14]

Hasan Arfa', a career general and diplomat for both Pahlavi kings and who accompanied Reza Shah on his visit to Turkey, provides some interesting—though not conclusive—insight into the impact of Atatürk upon Reza Shah. Reza Shah was clearly charmed by Atatürk, who helped his Iranian guest win a hand of poker against, of all people, Percy Loraine one evening.[15] Reza Shah retired early in the evening and did not witness Atatürk's drinking binges, as Arfaʿ himself did, nor an incident in which an enraged Atatürk ordered the town of Ushak to be razed because a turbaned cleric had tried to shake his hand at the train station (luckily, Atatürk's retinue knew better than to implement a drunken order).[16] This episode suggests that Atatürk was concerned to present a "modern" face to his Iranian counterpart. When not being led through battlefield tours, military exercises, and other martial amusements, Reza Shah would have occasion to experience Turkish hospitality mediated by European manners. The shah's retinue was entertained at the home of İsmet İnönü where they were received by İnönü's "charming wife."[17] The link between military might and "modern" manners could not have been lost on the king. Though Reza Shah did not comment on any specific achievement by Atatürk, upon leaving Turkey he told his staff, "We have been privileged to see a very great man."[18] Interestingly, when Arfaʿ talks of Reza Shah's own efforts at sartorial discipline, he does so in the context of relations with Afghanistan rather than Turkey—the significance of this connection will be evident presently. When Reza Shah returned to Iran, the new imperial national anthem appeared in *Ettelaʿat* for the first time,[19] and preparations were underway for a gala celebration of the thousand-year anniversary of the birth of Iran's epic poet, Ferdowsi. The shah's visit to Turkey reportedly inspired him to remake the Persian language by establishing the Iranian Academy (Farhangestan) to purify Persian of foreign words and to remake Iranians as well by getting them to dress like modern Europeans.[20]

On the woman question, inklings of things to come were manifested in the early spring of 1935. The minister of education, Mirza ʿAli Asghar Khan Hekmat, threw a party in Shiraz; his guests were outraged when a group of women tore off their veils and began to sing and dance.[21] Protests over unveiling at a new girls' school in Shiraz in March went unanswered.[22] On 12 May, "women of culture" were invited by Hekmat to a gathering at the Daneshsara where they were informed of the new society they were to create under the auspices of the Ministry of Education: the Women's Society (*kanun-e banovan*).[23] Among the cultural trends the Women's Society was to promote was unveiling. Hekmat's official participation in a government-sponsored demonstration of unveiling no doubt fueled rumors that forced unveiling was at hand. Covered in the French-language *Journal de Teheran* (published by the brother of *Ettelaʿat*'s ʿAbbas Masʿudi), the parade on 24 May 1935 may have been as much for foreign consumption as for domestic display. The parade, seen in connection with the formation of the Women's Society twelve days earlier, was received glowingly by American diplomats:

> [For] the first time in the history of post-Islamic Iran, minor girl students paraded in public in bloomers, chanting the national anthem and performing athletic exercises and rhythmic dancing in the presence of a distinguished gathering. In addition to thousands of spectators, the Government was represented by the Prime Minister, members of the Cabinet, senior officers of the Army and many other high officials . . . These two developments, the parade and the formation of the women's society, constitute further steps in that gradual movement initiated by Reza Shah Pahlevi [sic] after coming to power looking to the breaking down of the barriers of prejudice and the institution of reforms in ancient habits imposed by the Islamic faith, making possible the steady march of Iran towards modernism.[24]

In June, the government announced that all men were to discard their paramilitary Pahlavi caps in favor of European brimmed hats. Reportedly, Reza Shah expressly linked this change in men's attire to the hope that women would gradually abandon the veil so as not to be "incongruous" with the appearance of their men—although no suggestion was made that women (especially the older ones) be *forced* to unveil.[25] Nonetheless, the prime minister planned a reception for members of the cabinet and their undersecretaries and their unveiled wives for 28 June.[26] As early as 2 July, American diplomats had begun to appreciate both the unpopularity of unveiling and Reza Shah's determination to implement it, going so far as to speculate that the policy could invite an assassination attempt.[27]

Indeed, political violence was not far off. In early July, a cleric from Mashhad, Ayatollah Hajj Aqa Hosayn Qommi, decided to make for Tehran and protest to the king about the European hats and unveiling of women.[28] He was arrested and deported to Iraq, but not before his presence at the shrine of Shah 'Abd al-Azim outside Tehran inspired sympathetic strikes in the Tehran bazaar from 4 to 6 July. Police threats squelched this defiant display in the capital, but disturbances broke out in Mashhad itself on 8 July.[29] The rioting evolved into the bloodiest urban confrontation of Reza Shah's reign, centering on the Gowharshad Mosque on Friday, 12 July 1935. The administrator of the main shrine at Mashhad, Mohammad Valikhan Asadi, wired the capital suggesting that the sacred city be exempted from the new dress code, but this suggestion was rejected. On Sunday, 14 July, the artillery and machine guns once used to enhance Reza Shah's popularity in the cities by quelling rural tribes now blasted Gowharshad and the protesters within.[30] Asadi was blamed for the whole affair and was executed after a military trial later that year.[31] This rare application of military firepower in a city made its point. The potential for brazen, organized, and public defiance of unveiling was crushed even before the Women's Awakening was inaugurated.

How might the supporters of the Pahlavi regime have rationalized the brutality at Gowharshad—an event Islamic Republican historiography has made synonymous with the excesses of westernizing modernism? The recollections of Mohammad Ebrahim Amirteymour, a tribal leader, landowner, and career politician during the reign of both Pahlavi shahs and present in Mashhad at the time of the massacre, provide us with some clues. At the time that Amirteymour was in Mashhad, he was "cooling his heels" after being forbidden by Reza Shah from running again for the parliamentary seat he had held from 1928 to 1934. He was a man of divided loyalties but ultimately loyal to the Pahlavi regime and its policies until 1963, when Mohammad Reza Shah's White Revolution removed the economic basis for his power through the redistribution of land to Iranian peasants. Exonerating his friend Asadi, Amirteymour blamed the Gowharshad incident on a foreign preacher. He confuses the order of things, erroneously remembering that Reza Shah unveiled his family before encouraging the nation to do so and before the massacre at Gowharshad.[32] He may also have confused the timing of the mixed social gatherings he was ordered to organize in Mashhad in relation to the massacre. But his memories of the social gatherings and the massacre as events are compelling for the themes they conjure. Interestingly, Amirteymour does not connect the disturbances with anything the Iranian government did or anything that any Iranian may have done. Rather, he blames the British acting through Afghan agents:

Q. Who all came [to the party] then? [Clerics] of the first rank?

A. [People] like Aghazadeh, you understand? Like Azadeh Moshraf. Aghazadeh did not come but the rest came. So, that night there were musicians at our house. It was in my father's home, which they have destroyed and turned into a street. It had two or three big halls—12 by 12 *zara* so that in the halls you could have seven to eight hundred people. Inside it was all beautiful and chic and furnished. In short .
. .

Q. Was there alcohol?

A. No. We entertained. After this happened [there was] some guy named Bahlul who came every day and went to the Gowharshad Mosque and spoke against [un]veiling. "People, don't be taken in. It is against the *shari'ah*. It is against the Prophet. It is against . . ." he said. Things like that.

Q. He was the father of this Mohandes Haqq Parast, right?

A. No. He was a sonofabitch *[mard-e pedar-sukhteh'i bud]*. Also there was a group of barbarians *[barbari]*. These barbarians lived ten to twelve *farsakh*s outside the city. Perhaps 1,700 barbarians had come to the pulpit that day at Gowharshad to listen. There were reports that some were armed . . . Amir 'Abd al-Rahman Khan [a former ruler of Afghanistan] had defeated these barbarians. He killed many and a number of them came to Iran. Nearly seventy or eighty thousand of them settled in the villages of Iran. Amir Abd al-Rahman Khan wrote in a book later that it will be remembered that people cursed twice: once when they heard that I killed so many of these people—they will say, "What a bloodthirsty tyrant man he was, may God curse him"—and again when they become involved with one of these men and they will curse me, [asking] why did I leave one of these people alive." Know this. Also, when World War I happened, some of these people—perhaps 2,000 of them—came to Khurasan as part of the English army. It was clear that they were still in the pay of the British . . . This the shah knew. He understood that they were coming to the foot of the pulpit and was certain this business was at the instigation of the British. It was for this that he gave an order to Iraj Khan—the poor guy who they just killed the year before last [1980].

Q. Iraj Matbu'i

A. Matbu'i. [The shah] said that if you don't put this disturbance down in twenty-four hours I will execute you. This Iraj Khan went and put the trouble down in twenty-four hours. No one was killed like—they say some thousand people—no sir, altogether sixty-three people died in the disturbance.[33]

Thus, in the mind of a supporter of the Pahlavi regime, a massacre of Iranian civilians at a shrine by their own military is transformed into a defense against nomadic barbarism and British imperialism. The urban victims become tribal raiders from Afghanistan. Religious functionaries become British agents. The army of the most authoritarian regime Iranians had known is reduced to one reluctant officer standing between a wrathful monarch and the threat of a new Golanabad (site of the routing of Safavid forces by Afghan invaders in 1722). In his account of the massacre at Gowharshad, Hasan Arfaʿ notes that "the ringleader" of the "revolt," Shaykh Bahlul, escaped to Afghanistan.[34]

A British dispatch filed on 15 July, the day after the massacre at Gowharshad, does register concern for one "British-protected person" and the loss of fifteen Afghan visitors to the shrine, as well as relief that Indian Muslim pilgrims to the shrine had departed Mashhad for Iraq before the disturbances broke out.[35] Otherwise, British interest in the matter seemed rather low. The dispatch does corroborate Amirteymour's memory that "a shrine pensioner" named Bahlul was the instigator of the disturbances at the shrine on the night of 10 July. He took advantage of the fact that the tenth was the anniversary of a Russian bombardment of the shrine twenty years earlier, and, hence, "attendance was larger than usual." The dispatch, however, talks of two massacres at the shrine. The first, on the morning of 11 July, was ordered in rage (or, perhaps, panic) by Gen. Iraj Matbuʿi after he was dumped into a water channel by protestors during his attempt to clear the shrine. "Sartip Iraj Khan, apparently overcome by the turn events had taken, and the fact that his orders had resulted in desecration of the shrine, withdrew the troops, and even failed to picket the shrine to prevent further ingress."[36]

Not only Iraj Matbuʿi was overcome. Contrary to Amirteymour's memory, Reza Shah seems to have ordered negotiations to clear the shrine and a ban on the use of firearms to clear the shrine. This order held until the night of the thirteenth, when it was clear that both the number and temper of the protestors at the shrine were on the rise. At 2:00 A.M. on the fourteenth, the shrine was cleared by a special detachment known as the *Marg* ("death" in Persian)—the local military unit had been disarmed, confined to barracks, and was guarded by machine gun nests. The hapless conscripts were safer in their barracks than either the civilians in the shrine or the forces sent to clear them. Civilian deaths in the second massacre were estimated at 128; military and police deaths were estimated at 22. After the second massacre, some 800 persons were arrested.[37] Subsequent reports were that the prisoners were routinely tortured, being "flogged daily in batches of thirty."[38]

Once the violence in Mashhad was over, the Pahlavi government renewed its efforts to encourage unveiling. Members of the Iranian Foreign Ministry began appearing at diplomatic functions in Iran with their unveiled wives in August.[39] The shah himself began to use public occasions to criticize veiling:

> The local press failed to quote the Shah, but according to confidential and reliable information which I have obtained from high Iranian sources, His Majesty served implicit notice on his audience that the *chador* must go. As the spokesman of the deputies, the President of the Majlis, a strict Moslem of considerable training in Islamic law, is said to have addressed the Shah in the following sense, "I have indeed the greatest pleasure to voice the congratulations of my colleagues on this greatest of Islamic feasts [Feast of Mab'as on 26 October] to the greatest of Islamic Kings." The Shah is reported to have replied in laudatory terms of Islam per se but defied the superstitions which have been imposed thereupon by the mullahs. "It was indeed for this reason that the mullahs are gone," remarked the Speaker of the Majlis. "But the West scorns Iran for existing superstitions," declared His Majesty. "True, Sire," retorted Mr. Esfandiary, "the West in fact ridicules the whole Moslem world!" It was then that His Majesty revealed his attitude towards the *chador* by contemptuously mimicking the Iranian women covering and uncovering their faces when meeting a man. "Either the women of Iran should abandon the *chador* or go to the sacks!" the Shah is reputed to have stated on the occasion.[40]

Recently published documents demonstrate, however, that the government did not act recklessly in the wake of Gowharshad. Coercion was always an available tool but not always the preferred one. Written after the violence of Gowharshad and shortly before the aggressive press campaign that accompanied forced unveiling, a memorandum from the Ministry of Education in Tehran to all provincial offices tells us a great deal about the regime's unease with using force and its preference for persuasion. Dated 16 December 1935, the memorandum charged provincial officials with creating mixed-sex kindergartens, issuing new (and veil-less) uniforms to girl students, and sponsoring mixed-sex adult gatherings at which women were to appear unveiled to mingle with men and listen to edifying lectures.[41] Although the memorandum suggested that the project enjoyed complete state support (including the police to ensure the smooth implementation of all aspects of the project), provincial officials were warned to go lightly:

> This has been a summary of the details of the program that has already commenced in the capital according to orders and must now be appropriately executed everywhere in the provinces [in accordance] with the exigencies of the moment and the environment, and in accordance with the specifications and clarifications of the officials in [the Ministry of] Education who are in charge of educating public morality. Of course, you must conduct yourself and operate with the utmost intelligence, composure, and organization in cooperation with government officials and officials within your jurisdiction.
>
> Minister of Pious Endowments.
>
> Related note: And it should be especially emphasized that in this important matter all sorts of harshness, posturing, and rudeness are to be avoided and that matters should not depart from planning and composure.[42]

For all of its confidentiality, the rationale for unveiling offered to provincial officials as inspiration and as "talking points" for dealing with unhappy citizens had already appeared in some form during the long and very public history of the woman question in the periodical press. The rhetoric about enlisting the hitherto-ignored female half of society to the goal of national renewal stretched back to the nineteenth century and to Akhundzadeh and Mirza Malkam Khan. In likening the condition of Iranian women to a "palsied limb," the memorandum recalled the link between physical and moral health that had figured so prominently in the pages of *Kaveh, Iranshahr,* and *Setareh-e Iran.* This same link had also found expression in the efforts of *Danesh* and *Shokufeh* to instill morality and hygiene in a generation of modern Iranian mothers. The memorandum conflated the Qasim Amin standard of unveiling (that is, the removal of the face veil) with contemporary Euro-American standards of public dress, with the hair completely uncovered. Unveiling was presented as a modernizing and "civilizing" act based on the European example but also as being in accord with "true" Islamic teaching and pre-Islamic Iranian practice. In such rhetoric, the act of unveiling was the perfect symbol for Iran's own renewal and means to include Iran among the modern community of civilized nations. Mixed-sex social gatherings were justified because they would reverse the effects of women's seclusion by placing them in the company of educated men. Men, in turn, would benefit from the polite company of women and would suppress rude and rough behavior (it is not hard to imagine Bibi Khanom Astarabadi nodding her head in agreement). The memorandum cautioned that women and men with bad reputations should be completely banned from mixed social gatherings. This way the moral integrity of the gatherings would mirror the moral character of the modern unveiled Iranian woman—whose genuine chastity was, as Iraj Mirza had argued fifteen years earlier in his ʿArefnameh, the only "strong veil" *(pardeh-'e mohkam)* that she would ever need. Indeed, the memorandum assured provincial officials that "the great father and crowned monarch of Iran has always preferred that the girls of Iran all wear simple clothing and be adorned with the ornaments of chastity, honor, and modesty."[43]

The general principle of male guardianship was preserved in the symbolic figure of Reza Shah as the great father. He could not be a stranger and remove the veil, and he could not be a sexual intimate like a husband. He could also not be a peer, and so he would be the supreme patriarch overseeing the moral guidance of his extended national *andarun* (the private space of a family home). One of the imperatives of male guardianship that was originally safeguarded by the veil—that women would keep themselves modest and sexually unavailable to strangers—was now to be preserved by an internalized sense of morality instilled through education. On the occasion of a well-publicized meeting of the Women's Society on 18 October 1935 at their headquarters building on Sepah Street, the president of the Parliament, Hajj Mohtashem al-Saltaneh Esfandyari, drew upon this paternal metaphor in his opening remarks: "Dear ladies to whom this talk is directed, you must not expect to hear a sermon from a preacher, but rather imagine [me] as a father among his dear children who is desirous of their true happiness and real well-being. I will offer a few words of advice and prompting. Since this is [my] intention [I] hope that [you] will overlook any faulty expressions or explanations and focus on the spirit of the matter with [your] keen intuition."[44]

In his speech, Esfandyari outlined the four "moral duties of women" to be (1) obtaining an education, (2) governing their entrance into society, housekeeping, "husbandkeeping" *(showhardari,* a new counterpart to the traditional *zandari,* "wifekeeping"), and child raising with utmost circumspection and attention to protocol, (3) work, and (4) simplicity.[45] In addition, the vast majority of Esfandyari's remarks emphasized the domestic applications of women's education and work. To underscore his paternalistic view of women's emancipation, he related a folksy anecdote about a doctor who was visited by a father and son. The old man appeared to be at death's door, and the doctor asked the young man what had happened to his father. The young man said that he himself was the father and that his son only looked old and sick because his wife did not do a good job taking care of him and the household.[46]

After Esfandyari, the director of the Women's Society, Mrs. Tarbiyat, addressed the gathering at length and with an earnestness that contrasted with the president's casual presentation.[47] She also stressed the importance of motherhood in the beginning of her speech but saw motherhood as part of a larger formula. *Ettela'at* highlighted the slogans "personal, motherly, and social duties" and "good housewife, good mother, and good individual."[48] The last phrase seemed to promise more to women than domestic bliss. For example, like men, Iranian women were encouraged to develop their bodies and characters through sports.[49] Tarbiyat elaborated on the moral duty of "work" that Esfandyari had raised in his talk. Women who were not solely committed to domestic duties could and should enter the workplace: "In the future, in order for our girls to be immune from the dangerous results of idleness, which is the very mother of evil, it is necessary that the high schools train them in skills and crafts such as painting, fretwork, tailoring, bookkeeping, typing, and so on. Or [the girls] could be admitted to college for medicine and its branches, especially dentistry, pharmacy, midwifery, and nursing. Of course, this way girls who have no life partner can, by working in these fields and crafts, personally and independently secure a living."[50]

In addition to these "womanly" occupations, Tarbiyat expressed the hope that women would involve themselves in all levels of education—including teaching as members of university faculties. She drew upon American labor statistics to support her vision.[51] Tarbiyat also drew upon the specifically American example of Harriet Beecher Stowe to make the case that women could and should influence important social issues. Noting that around the world women had proven themselves in government, in war, and in their willingness to address important social issues on the national and international level, she noted proudly that Iranian women had participated in the 1935 International Women's Congress in Istanbul and declared the twentieth century to be the "Century of the Woman."[52] The meeting of the society closed with a short speech by Batul Homayun regarding the need to help poor mothers and their children, and by Pari Khanom Hosam, the commanding officer of the newly formed Iranian Girl Scouts.[53]

Throughout the fall of 1935, the regime saturated *Ettela'at* with the images of unveiled Iranian women. But unveiling was still voluntary for the majority of Iranian women, and Reza Shah was soon dissatisfied with the results of these bureaucratic and propaganda efforts. Yet it was not until 7 January 1936 that Reza Shah unequivocally committed both the full resources of the state and the symbolism of the throne to the goal of unveiling. As the seventeenth approached, *Ettela'at* hinted at the changes to come. On 16 Day, articles advocating simplicity of dress for men and women proclaimed that one of the "natural duties" of humans was to reform past errors and argued that science and mysticism agreed on fundamental truths, and so all religions were of equal value.[54] Without directly raising the woman question, the article on science and mysticism opened with the provocative line, "How can a substance devoid of intelligence give rise to creatures with intelligence?" On 17 Day itself, news of the visit of the royal family to the Daneshsara had not yet made the papers, but again articles appeared, anticipating the coming propaganda blitz: "We have great responsibilities with respect to life and our advancement and good fortune. One of these responsibilities is to live simply—especially for women. This is special to women as a group, since they have been partners and participants in this movement and this progressive life. And, since they have entered into a life of change and improvement, and they also have been and are participants in performing these great duties also, then they must also show their worthiness for this progress and awakening. Their simplicity, chastity, and strength will be an example for others."[55]

Finally, after some discussion with his cabinet about the best way to publicize his Women's Awakening, Reza Shah attended a graduation ceremony at the Daneshsara in Tehran with his wives and daughters, all of whom were unveiled.[56] The Iranian date was 17 Day 1314, and the beginning of Reza Shah's unveiling policy was popularly celebrated (and vilified) as "the Seventeenth of Day."

Until 1936, the coverage of the progress of women in Iran during the Pahlavi regime (and elsewhere in the world) was a mere extension of the way in which modern Iranian womanhood had been framed in the Iranian press since the late nineteenth century. The achievements of Iranian women were not—and perhaps could not be—celebrated in writing and in pictures as those of foreign women could be. Until Iranian women could be celebrated (and pictured) in the pages of the Iranian press for their public service, their professionalism, their athleticism, and their overall ability, they would always appear to be standing still in comparison with their sisters around the world.

The staging of the Seventeenth of Day required the regime to recruit participants from outside of the Daneshsara. Jane Doolittle, the headmistress of the American Bethel Girls School, recalled that girls from the eleventh and twelfth grades (as well as graduates from the previous year) were recruited to participate in the ceremony on 7 January:

> [All] the girls had to be completely in white, and we were told what the principals should wear and so forth—I think it was to begin at two o'clock in the afternoon. We were fortunate in that we had the twelfth class. . . . [All] the girls who had received their diplomas the year before were on hand, so we could get hold of them and get them dressed in their white dresses and stockings and shoes and all the rest of it. Then we went to the teacher's training college [the Daneshsara], and the girls were all lined up in one room, a line side-by-side, with the principal at the head of each line, and the boys were in another room. We stood there waiting for a while—[interview interrupted] . . . Then Their Majesties—appeared in the room where the women were, and then, one by one, called up the school, and the school principal went and received the diplomas from Her Majesty, and took them back to the girls. When that was finally finished, then the girls were all told to go down and line up on both sides of the road out to the main road. It was winter, with the snow, but all the girls had to go there in their white clothes, no coats or anything. We lined up there for Their Majesties to leave. Then, the next morning, we had word from the Ministry of Education to come there for a meeting. We all got there, and then the Minister said, "Now that Her Majesty and her daughters appeared without chadors, but hats and proper clothes, it is unseemly that any woman in Iran should appear in anything but a hat." And we were to see to it in our schools that nobody came, except in modern European clothing. So that's what happened; we all went back. For me, it was easy, because I said, "Our girls have already started doing that." But as you probably know, no woman was allowed on the streets without any scarf of any sort over her head [before].[57]

The next day, 8 January, coverage of the Women's Awakening began in earnest. For more than three months, the pages of *Ettela'at* were filled with articles covering Women's Awakening ceremonies around the country, editorials, letters to the editor in support, and articles discussing women in a variety of contexts. Reza Shah's two rather short speeches at the Daneshsara were printed in their entirety on 8 January, and portions were reprinted repeatedly.[58] Although reports of the royal family's visit mentioned that the women participants were unveiled, Reza Shah's speeches made no mention of it or its significance. Certain portions of the speech were in boldfaced print:

> I am pleased to see that women have recognized their position through education and knowledge, and have pursued their rights and excellence . . . Half of our national workforce was idle. Censuses of women were never taken. . . . You my sisters and daughters, now that you have entered society and have taken steps for your country's and your own happiness, must know that it is your duty to work in the path of the homeland. . . . [My expectation of you is that] you will be satisfied with life, work at economizing, accustom yourselves to thrift in life, and refrain from luxury and extravagance. . . . The point is that you should respect yourselves, have self-esteem and reserved nature, not consider yourselves base or despicable, and think that you have always been great, that you are great, and that you are capable of possessing greatness. . . . To you, my own children, I say that you must show with the efforts and actions you perform for the freedom and independence of the country . . . that your honor and pride are linked to the freedom and independence of your country.[59]

Reza Shah embraced a familial metaphor with respect to his female subjects, finally resolving on the paternal image toward the end of his speech. *Qanun*'s call for the utilization of "the other half of society," *Kaveh*'s rhetorical support for women's pursuing their rights, and *Danesh*'s and *Shokufeh*'s and *'Alam-e Nesvan*'s advocacy of an educated, morally circumspect, and thrifty modern Iranian woman all figured in Reza Shah's speech. But he seemed to be speaking to something more—to the capability of Iranian women and to their potential for greatness. Without his specifying what "work" women were to do,[60] it was possible to imagine Iranian women filling in the same press reports that had been reserved for the achievements of European women. For the first time, the Iranian queen and princesses undertook public inspections of hospitals and orphanages on their own as European royal women had done (and as was reported in the pages of *Danesh*).[61] Just as Reza Shah was the "great father," the queen (as boldfaced print in the pages of *Ettela'at* would point out) could stroke the hair of orphans "like a beloved and loving mother."[62] Also, the members of the Iranian Parliament brought their wives to the reception there, emulating the "public wife" first exemplified by the wives of English members of Parliament in the pages of *Danesh*.[63]

As mention of unveiling was absent from Reza Shah's speech, so too was a mention of religion. But it would be wrong to conclude that there was a complete absence of concern about Islamic legitimacy. On the very day that the royal visit to the Daneshsara was publicized, the publication of a new two-volume commentary on the Koran was announced.[64] Of the many Women's Awakening celebrations covered, the one held in the religious city of Qomm received special attention with two articles and a photograph.[65] In addition, *Ettela'at* reported the attendance of clerics with their unveiled wives at a celebration in Kermanshah and printed a picture of clerics at a celebration in Qazvin.[66] In the closing days of the initial press campaign in late February and March 1936, *Ettela'at* ran the text of a series of lectures given by a Dr. Zanjani at the Daneshsara on the topic of women in Islam. Far from portraying Islam as a source of fanaticism, Zanjani spoke of Islam as a progressive[67] and civilizing force and as continuing a tradition of respect for women that was found among other religions (Confucianism, Hinduism, Judaism) and ancient civilizations (Greek, Roman, Egyptian, and Iranian).[68] If Islam was anything, it was a progressive reaction to barbaric practices against women in the Arabian peninsula by providing women personal, marital, and property rights—improvements that impressed the eighteenth-century French philosopher Voltaire.[69]

While the specific issue of unveiling was alluded to in religious terms in press propaganda, it was very directly advocated in pseudoscientific and nationalistic terms. Veils prevented physical exercise, induced laziness, and sapped the intellectual and moral strength of women by preventing them from "entering society," an article proclaimed.[70] For the same reason, veils prevented women from pursuing their legal rights.[71] The removal of the veil would allow women to reach their full potential and contribute to the progress of the nation.[72] Indeed, women were cautioned that unveiling was part of the greater national will that they dared not challenge: "Those women who still have not abandoned the *chador* must realize that when society has welcomed a national decision, and a great and sacred idea to grant half of society a new life, and [this idea] has progressed rapidly and has been accepted heart and soul by everyone, they must no longer give in to negligence and procrastination. That is because this negligence suggests that they do not want to show respect for society's decision."[73]

This was about as close as the Pahlavi propaganda came to admitting the coercive nature of their project of liberation. That the project was a matter of national pride was never in doubt, but occasionally this point was made out of a sense of inferiority. Shayesteh Sadeq gave a speech at the Women's Society comparing the position of women in Turkish and Iranian society. The comparison was a lopsided recounting of the successes of Turkish women, concluding with the rather meek observation that two Iranian women, Ms. Jurabchi and Ms. Asaf Barkhiya, had attended the women's conference in Istanbul in 1935 by imperial order.[74]

Such negative examples were the exceptions rather than the rule in the propaganda of the Women's Awakening. It was a time of great expectations. Women's entry into "society" was expected to raise its moral standards. The presence of women in society was even supposed to raise the moral standards of literature,[75] and Ettela'at was careful to advertise celebrated poetess Parvin E'tesami's collection of poetry.[76] Starting on 13 January 1936, the pictures of young women who delivered speeches at Women's Awakening events around the country began to be published along with (on occasion) the texts of their speeches.[77] Poems in praise of women and their newfound freedom also began to appear, including one by Iran's foremost neoclassical poet, Malek al-Sho'ara Bahar, that concluded with the couplet "Strive for knowledge, virtue, and strength today, / For you are the mother of the people of tomorrow, O Woman!"[78]

At a meeting of the Women's Society on 18 January 1936, attended by ministers, parliamentary officials, military officers, and the Pahlavi princesses, the regime trotted out Hasan Vosuq to deliver a speech.[79] As prime minister in 1919, Qajar prince Hasan Vosuq al-Dowleh had attempted to secure Iran's future—and his own—through a close alliance with Great Britain. Denounced in the press and around the country for agreeing to a virtual British protectorate over Iran, the alliance, and the prince with it, failed, and he was forced into temporary exile. But on that night of 18 January, he was a devoted supporter of the Women's Awakening as he spoke to the women of the audience about how "your loving, crowned father has taken the chains [of the veil] from your hands and feet."[80] But while he believed men and women were of equal value, he nonetheless believed they were fundamentally different and that women were "naturally" inclined to the duty of motherhood.[81] He conceded that women could be more than that, however, and proceeded briefly to discuss the literary talent of tenth- and eleventh-century Persian-speaking poetesses

Makhfi, Mehri, and Mahsati and a woman named Laleh Khatun who at some unspecified time had ruled in Kerman.[82] He then turned to the accomplishments of European women, including Joan of Arc.[83] Women were born to be mothers, but they could be and had been more. Thus, the emerging message of the Women's Awakening was mixed.

Majid Movaqqar's *Mehregan* embraced this new media project in its Now Ruz (Iranian new year) issue of 1936. It was the first day of the Iranian solar year 1315, three and half months after the Seventeenth of Day. *Mehregan* featured a photo spread of unveiled Iranian girls participating in a variety of activities under the banner "Examples of the Intellectual and Physical Progress of Iranian Young Women."[84] The top girl students in the country were pictured along with the top boys.[85] Of course, there were still many articles on the achievements of foreign women,[86] but at least Iranian women were now members of the "modern world." To this end, a regular feature was a section on the latest European and American fashions—the uniforms of modernity.

Mehregan was targeted at a younger readership, and it attempted to engage them with frequent essay contests. A few of the essay contests involved prompting the readers with a premise. One such premise was entitled "Innocent." Readers were presented with the situation of a young woman surprised in her bedroom by a strange man. They were asked to look past the violent and sexual potential of this situation and to complete it in such a way as to create a morally edifying story.[87]

With the veil removed, appearances were more important than ever. The Ministry of Education's directive that unveiled social gatherings exclude disreputable women and rowdy men found even stronger expression. A memorandum dated 18 December 1935 from Prime Minister Mahmud Jam, who acquired this position shortly after Gowharshad, specified that when unveiling was enforced known prostitutes were to be prohibited from removing their veils.[88] Later, in the spring of 1936 when unveiling was being strictly enforced everywhere, a question arose about the prostitutes of Hamadan.[89] Local authorities requested that they be allowed to force prostitutes to unveil as well because it was hard to restrict their movements and because their presence on the street undermined the overall project. Tehran replied that if the prostitutes would take husbands, they could then remove their veils like other respectable women. The act of unveiling required the imposition of intimate male guardians to ensure the prostitutes' transition to respectability.

State vigilance in the enforcement of the unveiling was far reaching and quick to react. Even the lowest state official in the provinces needed to be on guard. On 21 January 1936, security officials in Sabzavar noted that a local cleric named Shaykh Mahmud had made statements in opposition to unveiling, as had his cousin Ms. Shariʿati, who was also the principal of a local girl's school. He was banished, and she was to be dismissed. However, by 4 February, she had recanted, and the Ministry of Education had rescinded its order to remove her. The entire episode was resolved within two weeks.[90] Even after the collapse of the regime, orders were issued to enforce unveiling on trains.[91]

In Mashhad, the site of the massacre at Gowharshad months earlier, it was clear that enforcement of unveiling remained problematic. Parvin Moayyed-Sabeti married her husband at age seventeen and went with him to Mashhad shortly after their marriage—sometime around 1939–40. Her memories of unveiling in Mashhad continue into World War II, during which time she had formed a Nurbakhshiyan Society (a charitable society for alumnae of American Bethel).

Q. In those days women all wore *chadors*, [didn't they]?

A. Yes, yes. There was no veil when we married and went to Mashhad. I never wore the veil. No, what you are talking about has to do with 1314; I was born in 1301. Therefore, when I went to Mashhad the veil had been removed. There was no veil. Of course, those who went into the shrine wore the veil, and the fanatical classes. They had their veils and head coverings again.

Q. But the women who attended meetings [of the Nurbakhshiyan Society in the 1940s]?

A. No. Never.[92]

Although Moayyed-Sabeti was dismissive of veiled women as fanatics, other pro-unveiling women expressed real sympathy for older women who had grown up all their lives with the veil. This sympathy, however, did not change the opinion of some that unveiling was a necessary action and, ultimately, beneficial.[93]

State efforts at forming a single "modern Iranian womanhood" in the 1930s were complicated not only by "backsliding" among traditional women but also by confusion over how the unveiling was to be applied. For example, in the summer of 1936 officials in Khurasan asked about how they should treat Muslim women from India and Afghanistan.[94] It was decided that as long as they did not wear the black veils typical of Iran, they were to be left alone. Earlier, on 2 March 1936, the question arose in Mashhad as to whether or not women with hats or handkerchiefs used as scarves would be permitted to visit the shrines. It was decided that scarves were a violation of unveiling, but that hats were not.[95]

The Ministry of Education had urged in its late 1935 memorandum that cooler heads prevail and that persuasion be used over violence. But this went hand in hand with the understanding that the coercive arms of the government were at the disposal of local officials. And despite a sensitivity to Islam—perhaps made all the keener in the aftermath of Gowharshad—the implications of unveiling were explored and enforced by the state in even the most personal and religious circumstances. In Qa'enat, men and women who were forbidden by religious law to see each other were forced to sit together during religiously and emotionally charged *rowzeh-kh"ani* gatherings (which focus on the martyrdom of the third Shi'ite Iman Hosayn).[96] Poor attendance by the wives of local officials at the first-anniversary celebration of the Seventeenth of Day in 1937 in Maragheh triggered inquiries from Tehran.[97]

It is clear that early efforts to pair forced unveiling and elegant soirées were awkward and even painful for many unwilling participants. As N. M. Butler reported to the British Foreign Office from Tehran, "[Officials] and all persons upon whom pressure can easily be brought are being made to unveil their wives and take them to mixed parties compulsorily organised to enable their participants to express spontaneous joy at this new reform. Recently one such party was given by the Mayor of Gulhek for the leading inhabitants of the village, but I understand that it was a complete failure, as there was much undisguised weeping and the men and women kept strictly apart, the latter hiding their faces as much as possible with their hands or the lapels of their coats. As a result, it is believed that another party is to be organised."[98]

Reporting on another such "command performance" social event, the British consul in Tabriz wrote:

> The reception of the 6th of February was a pathetic affair. By common consent the women had covered their faces with scarves and turned up the collars of their coats, looking forth with one eye as of old; but with their *charshabs [sic]* had gone their assurance and dignity. Almost any European woman would have had sympathy and understanding for the panic-stricken, elderly creatures huddled together in groups, but no one present was sure enough of herself for that. Those who had passed the ordeal of arriving, of being presented, and of finding a seat tried to find some assurance for them-

selves by marking the poor performance of the men who came later. They did not all, as some did, kiss in return the hands of the men who, obeying orders, had greeted them in that fashion;[99] but few could have left the hall without feeling that they, too, had given cause for comment and mirth in some quarter, and judging by accounts, few have resisted the temptation to minimise their own shortcomings by exaggerating those of the others. It was a day of bitterness for many of these old ladies.[100]

By 1938, it was clear that the Imperial Court, at least, had smoothed out its Western look. On 26 October, crown prince Mohammad Reza's twentieth birthday was celebrated at a dinner party attended by seventy foreign ambassadors and ranking cabinet ministers and their wives. Except for the band playing through the prime minister's toast, the British consul, H. J. Seymour, found little in the event to criticize:

> The Shah took great pains to make a success of this "western" party, personally seeing to the requirements of his guests for cigarettes and so forth, and taking an evident pleasure in answering questions about the rare stones and marbles which have been used in the decoration of the palace. About an hour after dinner supper was served; and the Shah, after seeing his guests gathered in the supper-room, withdrew. The Crown Prince remained and took leave of the guests as they departed. This reception, which may perhaps be regarded as an experiment, was certainly successful. It is not yet three years since Iranian women were unveiled and, though many of them are still painfully shy in general company, they have on the whole—at least in Tehran—adapted themselves remarkably well to the new social requirement.[101]

In this diplomatic account of a dinner party we come full circle. The private "unveiling" attended by Charles C. Hart in April 1931, which took place on the eve of the regime's state feminism initiatives, became in the fall of 1938 an official, if not public, unveiling attended by many Western diplomats. This was not the sweeping change promised in Women's Awakening propaganda or even the change inferred from the event by Seymour, but it was a change. An unveiled image of modern Iranian womanhood had been realized. It was an elaborate and staged effort to be sure, but in staging unveiling, Reza Shah had forced into being a historical reality that had been only imagined by some less than a decade earlier. Whatever the legacy of that reality, however, it was not a construction that would survive Reza Shah's "twenty years."

The forced abdication of Reza Shah was taken by all as a sign that it might again be safe to petition against government policies. The forced unveiling of the Women's Awakening was indeed protested a mere two days after Reza Shah was deposed. On 18 September 1941, a cleric named Shaykh 'Abdollah Masih Tehrani wrote the prime minister (and apparently not for the first time) to protest the rough treatment of veiled women by police in the capital and received assurances on 23 September from the prime minister that there would be an investigation.[102] But the violence against women was not always initiated by the state, even in the 1930s. On 5 May 1936, memoranda were exchanged between the local administration of Najafabad and provincial administration in Isfahan regarding a man named Mas'ud Qane'. He made statements against unveiling and "even went to the gate of the women's public bath and shouted insults."[103] An apparently irritated official in Isfahan wanted to know, in view of all the efforts that had been made on this issue, why Qane''s activities had not been brought to his attention earlier.[104] As we shall see in chapter 7, a petty act of violence against *unveiled* women became the occasion for much press discussion in 1943. This petty and unofficial act of violence should be understood, in part, as an expression of resentment that had been brooding in Iranian men all during the Women's Awakening. The forced "emancipation" of Iranian women had been accompanied by an unprecedented emasculation of Iranian men.

The Emasculation of Men

> The prince must none the less make himself feared in such a way that, if he is not loved, at least he escapes being hated. For fear is quite compatible with an absense of hatred; and the prince can always avoid hatred if he abstains from the property of his subjects and citizens and from their women.
> **Niccolò Machiavelli, *The Prince***

In the case of a regime known for its oppression, it may seem redundant to explore how the Women's Awakening fit into the broader themes of oppression and control. Is it not obvious from the previous discussion how the Women's Awakening oppressed "the people"? But the project also, as Foucault might have noted, expanded the control of the state—the male-dominated state—over women's bodies. As we shall see in greater detail, the Women's Awakening was consumed with a vision of modern Iranian womanhood that was clearly subordinated to the needs of men. Could not men, at least men of a renewalist mind-set and supporters of the regime, be said to have gained power in society over women by having their vision of modern Iranian womanhood ratified by state policy and propaganda? The irony is that even male supporters of the regime of Reza Shah seem to have experienced a sense of powerlessness during the Women's Awakening. For this reason, it is worth considering the effect of the Women's Awakening upon men separately from its effect upon women—dispensing, for the moment, with the fact that men's and women's reactions to the Women's Awakening did not occur in isolation from one another.

We have seen how women's bodies were made expressions of the state's power, forced to conform to a standard (if occasionally self-contradictory) image of modern Iranian womanhood. Despite the state's strenuous efforts to frame unveiling in terms that were consistent with the renewalist notions of modern male guardianship, it is clear that if women's bodies had become expressions of the power of Reza Shah's state, they were also expressions of the powerlessness of other men in Iran. Creatures of Reza Shah's new military were no safer than anyone else. Hasan Arfaʿ, who accompanied Reza Shah to Turkey in 1934, found that he and his brother, Major Ibrahim Arfaʿ, were not immune to the king's caprice. Ibrahim was accused and convicted of negotiating kickbacks with an American armored-vehicle supplier, Marmon-Harrington Inc., and angling for a job with United Aircraft Exports Corporation while serving as a purchaser for the Iranian army.[105] Reza Arfaʿ, the former Prince Arfaʿ al-Dowleh, was lured back to Tehran from his residence in Monaco in an effort to "ransom" his son from the clutches of Reza Shah—to no avail.[106] United Aircraft Exports Corporation sent a notarized statement to the Iranian government, assuring them that they had no inappropriate dealings with Ibrahim Arfaʿ—again, to no avail.[107] His eventual release was secured only when he was made personally accountable both for recovering funds in a dispute with American La France and Foamite Corporation and covering losses incurred to overseas accounts resulting from the effects of the United States going off the gold standard.[108] The effect of this incident upon Hasan Arfaʿ was personal and professional. In his memoirs, he had this to say of the death of his father in 1937: "It was sad end for this loyal and devoted servant of his country and his Sovereign to see his son [Ibrahim], so brilliant and outstanding by every standard, languish in prison for months on false and preposterous accusations and though finally pardoned, not rehabilitated during his father's lifetime. The bitterness of this has remained with me to the present day, far surpassing any resentment over personal grievances I have felt as a result of later vicissitudes."[109]

The father was not able to protect his innocent son from a tyrant—a tyrant to whom both father and son had been loyal. As a practical consequence of the incident, Hasan and Ibrahim's promotions to higher ranks were held up until 1939 and were finally granted in a humiliating fashion that seemed to underscore the powerlessness of high-ranking officers:

> General Zarghami delivered to us the following Imperial message, "You are promoted to the rank of General and (my brother) Lieutenant Colonel, but you must always serve your country and not be influenced by foreigners." The allusion was transparent, and I found it insulting. I felt the blood rush to my face, and said to Zarghami: "My brother and I have served our Sovereign and Country loyally up to this day and without consulting him I can say that we are neither of us ready to accept these promotions, and we ask to be relieved of service in the Army!" General Zarghami allowed a half-smile of sympathy to appear for an instant on his bearded face and said calmly, "You realise that I could not possibly say that to His Majesty; accept the promotion, and time will dispel these ideas, as everybody knows that you are two faithful and patriotic officers."[110]

The personal status of Hasan as an elder brother did not count for much in this petty affair. His modest (and altogether legal) act of rebellion could not even be officially acknowledged by a general. The army, the source of Reza Shah's power, was no less immune from the emasculating effects of his rule—perhaps more so because of the military discipline to which all soldiers are subjected.

Even direct participants in the state's unveiling project remembered their role in terms of powerlessness. As scornful as he was of the demonstrators at Gowharshad, Amirteymour remembered his own efforts to avoid participating in the unveiling campaign in Mashhad—it is a memory that hinges on his lack of choice in the matter:

> A. [A man] came [from] the police and said, "You must invite the residents of Mashhad so that they will come and you will remove the veils." I was young, God help me. I said, "Sir, my wife [*'ayal*] is not here. My wife is in Tehran and this is not appropriate. My age will not permit me to do this to a person that is older than me." He said,

"It is impossible. This business has been ordered by Tehran and you must do these things." Oh, God. Well, in the end, that was the order from Tehran that I—I could not refuse a situation so desired by the shah. We invited four to five hundred of the residents of Mashhad and their wives. They came at night and removed their veils, without veils. We made a short speech [to the effect that] these are the requirements of the day and a man should be grateful and [so] it passed.

Q. To what extent did they welcome it? To what extent did they resent it?

A. Those that came that day, none of them resented it. Yes, the next morning it was put to me that "You do the inviting so that the clerics will come with a veil to [your] house."

Q. Without a veil.

A. Yes. I said, "I'm just not a cleric nor do I have a relationship with clerics. I cannot." They said, "Tehran has ordered this. You must do this job. This order from Tehran is an order." In the end, as ordered by Tehran, I invited a group of clerics. They came. Nearly sixty of these clerics came [that] night. But they were second-tier clerics. Initially, there were one or two [first-rank clerics?] who did not come.[111]

It is interesting that Amirteymour used his wife's absence from Mashhad as well as his own youth (he was forty-two at the time) as excuses to beg off organizing the event. At some level, he felt that regardless of his position, it was not his place to subject others to unveiling. In the end, he relented—just following orders. Every family had a least one female relative who simply refused to go out unveiled. In my own family, my grandfather, a brigadier general in the army, sent a car at night to convey secretly two conservative women relatives on various errands with their veils on. He managed to shield my grandmother from the first "unveiling parties" because she was recovering from the birth of my father—born on the eighteenth of Day (8 January); eventually, however, she removed her veil and never returned to it even after Reza Shah's abdication in 1941.[112] Resistance was risky, secretive, and, in the end, worked against the continuing presence of some women in "society." Amirteymour lamented the fate of Asadi, killed by Reza Shah, but also that of Iraj Matbu'i, killed by Khomeini, on the grounds of their essential innocence arising from a lack of power to influence the situation they were in. Matbu'i, as Amirteymour recalled for us earlier, had himself been threatened with death unless he attacked the protestors at Gowharshad.

With the violence of Gowharshad, the forced unveiling of women in the streets, and the coerced attendance at mixed gatherings, the Women's Awakening became much more than a symbol of ideological warfare between westernized modernists and religious traditionalists. It became a constant reminder of state power and proof of Reza Shah's villainy and tyranny—not just against women but against men. The stand taken at Gowharshad became the modern-day Karbala for Islamic revivalists, an event that underscored the tyranny of Reza Shah's brand of renewalism in its own day and ever after. Mohammad Shanehchi, a teenager living in Mashhad at the time of the massacre and having grown up to be a merchant and an advisor to Ayatollah Taleqani during the Islamic Revolution of 1978–79, recalled events this way:

> But regarding the events at Gowharshad, the mosque at Gowharshad, I said my father was an alert man [though] not on the basis of intense fanaticism. Of course, there was that kind of religion, it was not such that it could not exist. When Reza Khan wanted to remove the veil he would say, "Removing the veil in this way is not right. People must become aware and take off their veil in accordance with their conscience and preference. People's veils should not be taken by force. It is not right that people should be deprived of the veil. We must resist and not let this happen. If this is established, if dictatorship gets a foothold in Iran, it is not clear if all our efforts will come out all right [dorost az ab dar biayad]." On this occasion he was very involved with activities of the mosque—not to the extent that he would want to start a riot, but to the extent that he [would say] there should not be a dictatorship.[113]

Shanehchi's recollection is revealing in its confusion. Certainly, Reza Shah's "dictatorship" was clearly established well before the Women's Awakening. While all historians agree that Reza Khan's power was always somewhat precarious prior to his coronation and was challenged militarily as late as 1928, he was always able to outmaneuver and destroy threats to his power. The failed effort to create a republic in 1924 proved that Reza Shah was no demagogue. But his crushing of tribal autonomy in the decade following the coup d'état of 1921, his rigging of the legislature from the Fifth Parliament (1923–25) until the Twelfth Parliament (1941–43), his consolidation of state authority in all arenas during the 1920s—all pointed to a dictatorial bent before the banning of socialist ideology in

1931, before the arrests and executions of former advisors (starting with Teymourtache), and certainly well before Gowharshad in 1935. In 1926, observer Vincent Sheehan readily compared Reza Shah both to Napoleon and Mussolini (see chapter 1, note 2).

In the context of Iranian history, Gowharshad was the site of many "last stands" against tyranny before 1935. Amirteymour cast the event as a stand by the government against British infiltration of Iran by means of client "barbarians" from Afghanistan. British observers noted the anniversary of the Russian bombardment of the shrine in 1911. There was still another connection. On 4 April 1906, Asef al-Dowleh, the despotic governor of Khurasan whose taxes had compelled peasants to sell their daughters to Turcoman tribes and had been accused of later failing to prevent Turcoman raids that resulted in the kidnapping of women and children, quashed demonstrations against him at the shrine with military force.[114] In early summer 1935, as in the spring of 1906, the inability of Iranian men to protect their women from dishonor had been bloodily exposed.

In Shanehchi's recollection, unveiling appears to cause or, at least, to prove the existence of a dictatorship. His father has a "correct" read on all facets of the situation—religious but not fanatical, implicitly for unveiling but against state coercion, opposed to dictatorship but not at the cost of revolutionary chaos. The "aware" father would do nothing against Reza Shah's tyranny because, in the end, neither he nor anyone else could do anything. As a political man, Shanehchi's father is impotent. The veil is being taken away from "people" *(mardom)*, not only from women (whose honor is allegedly at stake) or explicitly from men (who are unable to protect "their" women from this dishonor). But as we have seen, in July of 1935 veiling was being discouraged, not banned. Men had been forced to change their personal appearance in the form of a hat. They protested this as well at Gowharshad, but all sources recall unveiling as the main issue, for this would change not just their personal appearance in public but their personal lives as well. On the issue of the veil, individual men were no longer the guardians of their households—the "great father" was.

On reading of the execution of Asadi (the official blamed for the events of Gowharshad), journalist and politician 'Ali Dashti, who was under house arrest at the time, recorded his reactions to Reza Shah's tyranny and unveiling in the journal that was to be published as *Prison Days*. It was one of the few entries from his incarceration from April 1935 to July 1936.[115] Asadi's execution and his own confinement were symptoms of the same problem—the paranoid tyranny of Reza Shah. He, more than

Shanehchi's father, was sympathetic to unveiling as a social reform but was also against the abrupt nature of Reza Shah's policies. He saw both the forceful enforcement of unveiling and the apparent lack of overt resistance to it as part of a pattern in which a "strong-willed leader 'leads [the people] to wherever his fancy lies'" and the people, rendered incapable of independent action and thought by this pattern, capitulate.[116] Reza Shah's court was simply another manifestation of a political system in which independent men were replaced by lackeys under the intolerant gaze of an authoritarian ruler.[117] The young men of renewal were no more free under the renewalist regime of Reza Shah than they were under the vilified despotism of Naser al-Din Shah—and the Women's Awakening seemed to prove it. Although, not surprisingly, the theme of powerlessness runs through *Prison Days,* the beginning of the Women's Awakening effectively concludes the work, for the next entry is Dashti's release in July of 1936. He did not, in later editions, add to his memoirs an account of his imprisonment under the prime ministership of Ahmad Qavam in 1946.

The loss of power on the part of Iranian men with respect to the shah predated both the Women's Awakening and the massacre at Gowharshad—and perhaps no class of men felt this loss of power more keenly than the Qajar aristocracy. Reza Khan and Sayyed Zia al-Din Tabataba'i's first act during their coup was to arrest prominent members of the Qajar aristocracy. It was not until after the coup of 1921, with the employment of Arthur C. Millspaugh from 1922 to 1927, that long-standing tax exemptions for Qajar aristocrats were phased out. The main consequence was to increase the power of the state with respect to the old aristocracy and the power of Reza Khan/Shah along with it as he maneuvered for control of the state.[118] But Reza Shah's domination of the ruling classes went well beyond removing their privileges under the law and included constant efforts to seize land and wealth for himself and the state.

As wealthy men, Qajar aristocrats were the primary targets of Reza Shah's extortion. As men with political experience, they could be useful to Reza Shah but were also suspected by him. Mohammad ʿAli Forughi (Zoka al-Molk), the president of the Parliament at the time of the short debate on the electoral law in 1911 and a longtime supporter of Reza Shah, lost his position as prime minister on 3 December 1935 as a direct consequence of the massacre at Gowharshad. He was related by marriage to Mohammad Valikhan Asadi, the man blamed (or, as Amirteymour would argue, framed) for the rise of disturbances that led to the massacre. He had intervened unsuccessfully on Asadi's behalf and was permitted to resign and retire from political life days before Asadi's execution.[119]

Another Qajar family that suffered some of the worst treatment Reza Shah had to mete out was the family of 'Abd al-Hosayn Mirza Farman-farma. His property was confiscated, and his eldest son, Prince Firuz Nosrat al-Dowleh, who in 1919 had been one of the architects of the failed Anglo-Persian Treaty, was killed in prison in 1937. The fear generated by Reza Shah's mere presence is well illustrated by this anecdote from Sattareh Farmanfarmaian's memoir on the occasion of a fire that engulfed her family home in Tehran in 1933:

> Suddenly some figures strode into the compound through the narrow east door from Kakh Avenue: a huge man in a brown general's uniform and a long blue cloak, flanked by two uniformed guards. Everyone froze with astonishment and shock. . . . We all bowed low, astounded and fearful . . . Everyone was very quiet. I could tell that my mother thought the end had come. But Reza Shah merely gazed at the flames with curiosity and interest. Then he turned to his old general and clapped him heavily on the shoulder. "Well, Shazdeh," he said affably, "old houses burn easily." I think he was trying to make my father feel better. Shazdeh bowed again and thanked the monarch for his magnanimous condescension and concern.[120]

Of course, Shazdeh was no longer a prince in 1933. Reza Shah's condescension could not have been more apt. Farmanfarma was no less able to protect his family from Reza Shah's predations than he was to prevent his home from being engulfed by flames—though not from lack of trying. Farmanfarma had supported Reza Khan in his bid to turn Iran into a republic in 1924, despite having been forced to hand over 30,000 *tuman*s to Reza Khan in 1923 (one of two confiscations Reza Khan ever admitted to).[121] Farmanfarma's later efforts to support Reza Khan materially and politically were rebuffed as the prime minister-who-would-be-king resented the fact that he had once served under Farmanfarma's command and that Farmanfarma was "too wealthy."[122]

For Iran's *'olama,* unveiling was one of a series of state encroachments on religious matters and the traditional jurisdiction of the religious bureaucracy. It followed enactment of a new conscription law in 1927 that did not exempt religious students, state regulation of *shari'ah* courts in 1928, introduction of the Pahlavi cap in 1928, regulation of religious schools, passage of the Marriage Law of 1931, aggressive enforcement of state control over pious endowments (a traditional source of income for the *'olama),* and introduction of the European hat in 1935. The Women's

Awakening of 1936 was followed by increased state regulation of *shari'ah* courts in 1939 so that *shari'ah* courts could not even hear cases without the approval of the Ministry of Justice. However, as Shahrough Akhavi's work illustrates, Reza Shah's anticlerical policies did not eradicate the *'olama*'s role in society (as had been effectively done in Atatürk's time in Turkey) or all of its infrastructure in Iran (to say nothing of that infrastructure in Iraq). Furthermore, as Faghfoory's work illustrates, the clergy were not moved very often to forcefully resist any of these changes.[123] It is significant that unveiling was one of the few times that they did. As the ranking *'olama* were all men, their resentment of the Women's Awakening was an important element of male resentment toward the policy.

The depths of male resentment toward Reza Shah only became apparent with his forced abdication and his exile in September 1941—an event that was greeted with a mix of glee and panic. It was as though Reza Shah had been able to intimidate the whole country (criminals and dissidents alike) with his mere presence, and suddenly the spell was broken. Arfa' recalled the day after the shah left:

> Immediately after the departure of Reza Shah, lawlessness, robbery and hold-ups started all over the country. My wife told me that the day after the departure of Reza Shah, as she was driving in the town, our driver turned down a one-way street and when she remonstrated, replied, "Oh, It does not matter, now Reza Shah has gone." Another story was told me at this time by an Englishman about a traveller who had been held up by a brigand. After having taken all his belongings, the robber noticed a paper in the pocket of his victim, and asked him what it was. "A telegram, announcing Reza Shah's return," said the traveller calmly. The brigand abandoning his booty fled at once without asking for any details.[124]

It was in the 1940s that Hosayn Makki's *Twenty Years of Iranian History*, a detailed indictment of the regime of Reza Shah, first appeared in serialized form in the pages of Majid Movaqqar's *Mehr-e Iran*. As harsh as this chronicle was to the memory of Reza Shah, it paled in comparison to Mohammad Mas'ud's fierce indictment of the regime and its collaborators in the prelude to his 1942 novel/autobiography *The Flowers That Grow in Hell*:

> Among the strange creatures of hell was a person who had the lips of a camel over his teeth and the brain of a jackass in his skull. He was appointed to fill the skulls of all the children of hell with the contents

of his little brain! Of course the job was extraordinarily difficult [and] its execution required complete authority. He was given authority to gather a number of his like-minded [friends] and working together they brought this momentous order to completion by all possible methods and means. They set out to raise the children. Mothers in the home, naked and without bread, were crying in the corners of rooms and they persuaded their children to play and dance in the parade grounds! "Dance to the whip!"[125]

It was the mothers who cried as the regime forced their children to comply with its propaganda and education policies. Husbands and fathers are absent from this passage; the male guardians are not even allowed the protest of tears. The culture of the "twenty years" had reduced them to obedience, as this lament from the Tudeh periodical *Mardom* affirms:

> In this country of ours everything is talked about. There is discussion of all pains, but lately the topic of culture has become trite. "Education and Nurture" is considered a base profession. The importance of a thieving accountant or a liar has become greater than one hundred ranking scholars and engineers. [This is because] in the last twenty years [the minions of Reza Shah's regime] endeavored with all their might to make a mockery of science and knowledge. They gave out bogus diplomas to many. They nurtured the thoughts of the young and the new generation of the country with the principles of flattery and obsequiousness. They made teachers and students dance as much as they wanted. They corrupted generations, and took an ax to the roots of the country but good [chenancheh bayad]![126]

Among the clergy, voices of resentment were not hard to find in 1941. They had been especially deceived by Reza Shah, who had learned to be wary of them in his failed bid to create a republic in 1924. No voice seems as important, in retrospect, as that of Ayatollah Ruhollah Khomeini in his *Kashf al-Asrar* (Revealing of Secrets). Even before he endorsed the idea of a clergy-led Islamic state, he saw the sartorial regulations of Reza Shah and the unveiling project as part of a grand deception in which all progress was really cover for European exploitation of Iran:

> The day everyone was forced to wear the Pahlavi cap, it was said, "We need to have a national symbol. Independence in matters of dress is proof and guarantee of the independence of a nation." Then a few years later, everyone was forced to put on European hats, and suddenly the justification changed: "We have dealings with foreign-

ers and must dress the same as they do in order to enjoy greatness in the world." If a country's greatness depended on its hat, it would be a thing very easily lost! While all this was going on, the foreigners, who wished to implement their plans and rob you of one hat while putting another on your head, watched you in amusement from afar and laughed at your infantile games. With a European hat on your head, you would parade around the streets enjoying the naked girls, taking pride in this "achievement," totally heedless of the fact that meanwhile, the historic patrimony of the country was being plundered from one end to the other, all its sources of wealth were carried off, and you yourselves were being reduced to a pitiful state by the TransIranian Railroad.[127]

Khomeini, echoing accusations found in Hosayn Makki's *Twenty Years of Iranian History* and elsewhere, saw Reza Shah's most tangible achievement as part of a British plot to establish a supply route to Russia in the event of war.[128] The railroad had been paid for by a regressive sugar tax that was surely most burdensome to the poorest Iranian households, as would have been the requirement that men and women wear Euro-American fashions to prove the regime's modernity.

It is clear that the Pahlavi regime—especially in the wake of Gowharshad—was desperate to blunt the rage against the Women's Awakening project because of unveiling (though, as we have just seen, it merely stifled the resentment). Given that the regime was aware of the hostility, one must consider the question of why the regime undertook this drastic policy. What benefits did the Women's Awakening promise to Iranian society? How did the propaganda of the Women's Awakening try to assure Iranians that the changes in their lives were for the best? What did those few Iranian women who arguably benefited from the Women's Awakening think had been achieved? To answer these questions, we must see the Women's Awakening as an attempt to address other aspects of the woman question besides unveiling—women's rights as wives and mothers, women's education, women's employment, and women's improved civic presence (including suffrage). It is to these arenas that we next turn our attention, starting with the first: marriage.

5

Renewal's Bride

In chapter 2, we read a letter from a "European-educated girl," printed in the pages of *Danesh* in 1911. She had written, "A woman must be the friend and intimate of a man. That means that she must be the ally and aid of her husband in all affairs." This, of course, served the interests of men, but there was also, we should recall, a benefit claimed for women. In allying herself with a like-minded husband, a modern Iranian woman could guarantee a long and happy marriage—free from the threat of polygyny and divorce, free from the anxieties of fading beauty. Serving him would "transform him into such a tender companion" for life. In the absence of political enfranchisement and legal reform, allying oneself with a "young man of renewal" through marriage could be seen as a political strategy as much as a measure of personal empowerment—a bargain with patriarchy, to borrow a phrase from Deniz Kandiyoti. Renewalist men, after all, had already signaled their intent to create agreeable life companions through education, thereby strengthening families and effecting the moral and material rebirth of Iran. In the present chapter we will visit men and women "courting" one another through press discussions of marriage and the Pahlavi state's appropriation of marriage reform in 1931 in response. As the Marriage Law of 1931 was the Pahlavi regime's first effort to engage the woman question, its importance faded with the coming of the Women's Awakening. Nonetheless, the issue of "companionate" marriage was revisited in propaganda,[1] in general, and in the marriage of Crown Prince Mohammad Reza Shah to Princess Fowziyeh of Egypt, in particular.

Marriage as a Metaphor for Alliance: Press Discussions

Marriage had long been an institution for cementing political relationships between two families. While Islamic scholars of all sects agree that marriage contracts are made between husband and wife, family politics traditionally have played a large part in the process. Renewalist thinkers and writers since Akhundzadeh had complained about "arranged marriages," but such marriages were as important in the reign of Reza Shah as they ever had been in Iranian history. As noted in the previous chapter, we have an account from Dowlatshahi family lore about Minister of War Reza Khan's efforts to marry a young woman named 'Esmat from the Dowlatshahi family in 1923.[2] Let us take a closer look at this marriage now, because it illustrates how indirect courtship could be and how much power senior men in elite families could have over their kin. At the same time it records the level of concern that could be expressed by the family patriarch for the young woman whose future he was unabashedly deciding. Reza Khan first sent an unnamed representative directly to 'Esmat's father, Mehrangiz Dowlatshahi's uncle. The father's reply was, "So he is Minister of War. I will not give my daughter to Reza Khan when it is not clear who his mother and father are." Some time later, 'Esmat's mother died due to complications from childbirth, and 'Esmat's father left her and her siblings in the care of his grandmother. Reza Khan then approached 'Esmat's uncle (and Mehrangiz's father), Mohammad 'Ali Dowlatshahi. As Mehrangiz remembered the story (and retold it in fits and starts), Mohammad 'Ali wrote to his brother:

"This is how it is. They have come again. What do you say?" At that time, somehow, and I'm not sure how. Due to [his experience?] abroad and in a manly way and so on, my father knew Reza Shah and they saw each other occasionally. Sometimes Reza Shah would consult with him. I mean my father had sympathy and respect for him. He wrote to my uncle, "They are really insisting. I approve of him in many respects. He is a worthy man. But, of course, he is older and he is married. What do you say about 'Esmat? You can't keep them [daughters] for long this way in a part of grandmother's house (and so on). Do whatever you think is best." Later they really persisted. One day Reza Shah invited my father to his office . . . My father said, "He [Reza Shah] took out a cigarette case and gave me a cigarette and was hospitable and we spoke a while. He started by saying, 'I am really eager to join with your family. I myself have no family and I want to—'" [interjecting]—Ah, before this time, between the last time he [Reza Shah] had asked for ['Esmat's] hand and this time, he had gone and married a granddaughter of Majd al-Dowleh, Ms. Malak Turan, the mother of Prince Gholamreza [Pahlavi]. But for whatever reason he had divorced her very quickly.

Some said Reza Shah believed in being bold. And before Gholamreza was born he divorced that woman—[*returning to her father's story*]—"'I [Reza Shah] want to join some families.'" My father raised many problems. He said, "You know, in our family divorce is very bad. And, basically, we also will not give a daughter to someone who has a wife." Of course, he did not say, "You are too old" and such things. [But] he did add that "She is a child and doesn't know how to do anything" and things like that. [Reza Shah] said, "There is no problem at all. I don't want any work from her. All of her living [needs] will be taken care of." Anyway, however it happened, he persisted. It was fate or whatever, I don't believe in fate, anyway a marriage engagement took shape, and the marriage contract ceremony took place in our house. At that time, fortunately, the situation was such that since Reza Shah wanted the business to take place secretly. Because on one side, her mother had died six months ago. One could not have a party with music and such. Reza Shah did not want before—

Q. A clamor to start.

A. A clamor to start over this matter. So, nothing. My uncle came from Kermanshah and my great aunt said he did not take off his black clothing [of mourning for his wife] . . . But anyway, the rest of the family took off their black clothes. In any case, there was a marriage ceremony. Naturally, the girl had not seen [Reza Shah] before and when she did first she took some exception. In the end, gradually, well, then, you know that she did not go to her husband's house right after the marriage ceremony. First there had to be an official wedding and they gradually became acquainted.[3]

It is ironic that the man who would outlaw child marriages in 1931 had sought a child bride himself in 1923. It was not a whim he indulged once he became king, suggesting that this marriage was, at least in part, an element in his dynamic and continual efforts to develop power for himself within a system he did not yet dominate. This fact, in turn, gave both Mehrangiz's father and 'Esmat's father power to negotiate with Reza Khan—a power they would no longer have in just two short years. The "union" that Reza Khan sought so eagerly in 1923 was with a prominent Qajar family, not with a particular woman. While 'Esmat's male guardians exhibited some concern over the age disparity, over polygyny, and over 'Esmat's "readiness" for marriage, it is clear that these concerns were negotiable. Reza Khan did not want 'Esmat as a partner or a helper. Indeed, he did not want "any work from her." 'Esmat's own doubts on the day of the marriage ceremony were not taken as a expression of her will, but of her immaturity, requiring only time and a wedding celebration to resolve. The indirect courtship and joyless wedding of Reza Khan and 'Esmat stood in contrast to the direct "courtship" of men and women that was taking place in the pages of the Iranian press. Since 1910, literate Iranian men and women had spoken to each other about marriage, about its significance, and about their expectations of it.

Indeed, marriage was the primary context in which *Danesh* addressed relations between women and men. The goal was to enlighten both sexes as to their roles. The first issue of *Danesh* contained an article entitled, "The Rules of Being a Married Woman."[4] An unnamed "wise" and "intelligent" woman advised wives to keep their promises to their husbands, refrain from asking for money, provide for their husbands' comfort, and not show disapproval of their husbands' actions so as not to compromise their role as confidantes. A complementary article, drawing on the same anonymous source, followed, entitled, "The Rules of Being a Married Man."[5] Men were urged to be forbearing and to communicate with their wives about what they had seen outside the home, to explain their decisions to their wives, and to leave the administration of the home to their wives. Men could also find articles on fatherhood, encouraging them to be loving and fair with their children.[6] There were also admonitions to unmarried men to refrain from swearing and acting rudely toward women.[7]

Taken together, these articles focused on smoothing the relationship between the sexes within the framework of male guardianship rather than challenging it. In addition to maintaining the link between modern Iranian womanhood and male guardianship, *Danesh* elaborated on the definition of modern Iranian womanhood. It accomplished this through comparisons with non-Iranian womanhood, which took a number a forms: (1) reports on the customs of foreign women in relation to such matters as marriage customs and child rearing, (2) biographies of famous and notable foreign women (see chapter 3), and (3) reports on the progress of women around the world (see chapters 3 and 6). We will focus here on the first category.

Danesh ran a series of articles detailing the marriage practices of foreign women—European, Ottoman, and Zulu. By addressing a culturally universal experience—marriage—and locating Iranian customs within a continuum of varying traditions, these articles created both a sense of connection to the world and a sense of what was distinctly Iranian. The reader would learn that in Russia[8] and France[9] marriages were arranged by the families of the bride and groom as in Iran. Interestingly, *Danesh* noted that in the case of France, young women were kept in a sort of seclusion, but their "seclusion" was spent in finishing schools where they learned all the necessary domestic sciences.[10] In England[11] and Germany[12] couples chose each other, and in the Ottoman Empire an official match-maker was used.[13] Though German women had the freedom to choose their mates, they were nonetheless expected to have mastered the "four arts" of child-rearing, clothes-making, cooking and housekeeping; they were also to know "the ways of their own religious law."[14]

As noted in chapter 2, Ottoman women were portrayed as resembling their European sisters in education, in the maturity of their relationships with their husbands, and in their gradual removal of the "face veil."[15] Perhaps most daring was Danesh's endorsement of the Ottoman "constitutional era," a rhetorical tactic often used by the more vituperative supporters of the Iranian Constitution during the civil war in Iran.[16] Also, despite the claim that the marital customs being discussed were distinctly Ottoman, wedding festivities in the Ottoman Empire were said to include changing into "ballroom clothes (dance clothes) in the style of Europeans."[17]

Such clear editorializing within this series of articles on marital customs was rare. For the most part, the customs of the foreign societies were presented without additional comment. However, the discussion of Zulu marital rituals was approached differently. While it is clear from the article that Zulu families arranged marriages for their sons and daughters and negotiated bride-prices, neither this nor any other Zulu marital custom was compared with European, Ottoman, or Iranian customs. The Zulu families were presented as a culture unto themselves. The article clarified that the Zulu were *mardoman-e seyah*, or "black people." The article closed with a rather disparaging remark: "In [the husband's] house, again in another custom, [the new bride] attempts to escape. This time the husband's family, to prevent this boldness [on the bride's part] guards her, for if they could not catch her and she escaped, it would be a great disgrace for her husband. The marriage would be voided, and this tomfoolery would have to be initiated all over again."[18] No such disparaging remark occurs in the discussion of European or Ottoman practices. While Ottoman customs had inclined toward those of progressive Europeans, and Iranian practices had an element in common with a couple of European countries, the Zulu were outside the pale of modernity and, in the final analysis, were somewhat silly. Iranian women could have someone to look down upon as well as someone to look up to.[19]

The ultranationalist "scientific" journal *Iranshahr* addressed the woman question from its second issue on 26 July 1922 onward. Marital relations, the social importance of educated women, and a host of familiar issues were discussed, and, starting in late 1923, a special section of *Iranshahr* entitled "The World of Women" was introduced. On 19 August 1924, issues 11 and 12 were printed together and were exclusively devoted to the woman question. The stage for the double issue had been set on 21 April 1924 when its editor, Hosayn Kazemzadeh, raised the issue of marriage between Iranians and non-Iranians, in particular, Europeans. This specific issue touched upon wider questions of family, morality, national identity, and the relations between sexes. According to Kazemzadeh, such marriages had direct consequences for Iran's independence and the prosperity of the Iranian "race" and were becoming more frequent because of the larger number of Iranians studying and traveling abroad.[20] He therefore posed six questions to his readers:

(1) In what ways are Iranian girls preferable to European girls for marriage?

(2) What benefits and positive aspects are there to marriage with European girls?

(3) In your opinion what qualities and characteristics should a woman have to be ready for marriage?

(4) What are the obstacles and drawbacks to marrying Iranian girls, and how can they be removed or reformed?

(5) Can European women live better in Iran or can Iranian women live better in Europe? What examples have you seen or heard about in this matter?

(6) Are there enough educated girls in Iran for the educated young men?[21]

The letters of four respondents to Kazemzadeh's questionnaire were printed—from two women, Sadiqeh Dowlatabadi and Badr al-Moluk Saba, and two men, Sayyed Mostafa Tabataba'i and ʿAbbas Zarkesh. The two women had been involved in the press for some time. Sadiqeh Dowlatabadi was the publisher of *Zaban-e Zanan,* and Badr al-Moluk Saba was the wife of the publisher of *Setareh-e Iran,* who had just been beaten up by the prime minister, Reza Khan—a fact to which she angrily referred in her letter.[22] The responses reveal conflicting feelings of self-hatred and national pride and of attraction and hostility toward Europe. And into this jumble was mixed competing notions of appropriate gender roles.

To the first question, Zarkesh and Tabataba'i and Dowlatabadi all responded that what was at stake was preserving the integrity of the Iranian race and Iranian culture.[23] Saba said that there was no advantage to marrying an Iranian woman because she was uneducated and did not know how to raise children properly.[24] But Saba, Tabataba'i, and Zarkesh all backed off some of the implications of their initial statements in responses to later questions. Although he asserted that marrying European women was an act of self-hatred and blind devotion to things European, Tabataba'i admitted that the lack of education and the wearing of the veil by Iranian women made marriages to them problematic for progressive Iranian men.[25] Also, he felt that European women could better adjust to Iranian life than the reverse.[26] Zarkesh felt that European women could run households and raise children better than Iranian women (despite the adverse effects of mixed marriages on Iranian culture) and that Europe possessed a better atmosphere for Iranian women.[27] Saba, in her response to question four, took the opportunity to criticize those who felt that Iranian women by their very nature were less capable than European ones and argued that Iranian men were ultimately responsible for the poor education that Iranian women received.[28] Although Saba ultimately opposed the idea of intermarriage between Europeans and Iranians, her reasons for doing so seemed to have more to do with contempt for Iranian culture than a desire to protect it. Poor treatment by men, the lack of freedom and fun, and the poor hygienic standards of Iran would drive European wives away: "I have spoken many times with two or three European and American women who have Iranian husbands about these issues. After expressing displeasure at the filthiness of our country, the rigid Iranian morality, and the differences in belief between themselves and their husbands, they believed that Iranian women were necessary for Iranian men."[29]

Sadiqeh Dowlatabadi put an even harsher edge to the problems inherent in marriages between Iranians and Europeans. Iranian men, she argued, were more interested in their pleasure than in the public interest.[30] Therefore, Iranian men would naturally succumb to charming European girls: "The European girl has been chest to chest with boys of various races since the age of twelve and has been pleasure-seeking since a young age. All the means of pleasure have been acquired for her. After dancing and partying every night till morning until the age of twenty-five or thirty, she then tires of pleasure seeking and thinks of taking a husband. It is natural that sleeping with her and putting your head upon her chest has more pleasure than with an innocent Iranian girl who has been barred from normal games since young childhood and then is married off to some unknown man at age fifteen or twenty."[31]

The European woman posed a dual threat to racial purity and cultural integrity because the children would naturally lose interest in their own culture under the influence of their foreign mother. Consistent with this position, she also argued that it was less problematic for an Iranian woman to marry a European man because the man would have to convert to Islam. Furthermore, their children would be more Iranian due to the civilizing influence of an Iranian mother.[32]

For Dowlatabadi, the strength of the Iranian woman was her superior sexual mores and her prime role as the determiner of Iranian ethnicity and culture of her children. In emphasizing this primary role for women in defining the modern Iranian moral order, Dowlatabadi was rather like Kermani in *The Hundred Sermons*. But the other respondents were also like Kermani in their use of Europe as a standard for excellence in maternal and wifely behavior. Whether as a superior temptress or as a superior domestic ally of the modern Iranian man, the modern European woman was in competition with the modern Iranian woman. The choice of arenas for this competition—the bridal chamber and the home—is telling. Implicitly left to men were the arenas of business, science, and politics.

Indeed, men's expectations could be quite high. In response to Kazemzadeh's question about what characteristics a woman should have to be ready for marriage, Tabataba'i wrote, "Loyalty, a sense of love, chastity, and a literary spirit, which is the mark of humanity, and also practical knowledge and housekeeping are the necessary conditions for any woman to be ready for marriage."[33]

Zarkesh was no less demanding: "In my opinion a woman should possess the qualities of good morals, Iranian patriotism, a knowledge of housekeeping, love for her husband, intrinsic innocence, knowledge of rights related to daily situations, free thinking, and things like that to be ready for marriage."[34]

The limitations placed by both men on the attentions and affections of their wives belie their claim to desire "free thinkers." Their wives were to be companions and domestic managers, and that was all. While clearly not responding specifically to these men, Dowlatabadi took aim at the hypocrisy of men in this matter. She told of an Iranian male friend who had married a European woman. Displeased with his wife's handling of a party, he complained to Dowlatabadi right in front of his wife: "'Damn the fathers of those that prefer European women to Iranian women, thinking that European women are knowledgeable, well-versed in philosophy, write articles well, and are involved in politics. [European women] don't understand family life. When my domestic situation is in order I can enjoy that other stuff, but when it isn't my soul is in torment.' Here I say to Iranian gentlemen: You who have come to Europe are of the first and upper second classes . . . [but] without doubt not one of the first-class women of Europe, who are adorned in all ways possible, will accept you in marriage, so that leaves the lower-second and third class . . . If you can have equality with your [European] wife, honor her, and give a little of the freedom that is naturally appropriate, why don't you try to make the society of women one with your own, and immerse a worthy Iranian woman in social education. . . . No? Oh, how tyrannical Iranian men are! There are two thousand girls with diplomas in Tehran who are without husbands, but our young men in Europe can't keep themselves from marrying maids, laundry maids, and coffeehouse waitresses."[35]

Along with the classist sentiments and resentment of European competition, this passage confirms the analogy drawn between marital relations and civic society. The "natural" equality, honor, and freedom that should exist for women in their relationships with their husbands set the standard for male-female relationships in society as whole. Remembering that Dowlatabadi was a public critic of the 1919 Anglo-Persian Treaty, one could extend the connection between married life and civic duty further: Marrying European women instead of Iranian ones was akin to selling out one's country rather than endeavoring to reform it and secure its independence.

In Iran, newspapers like *Setareh-e Iran* and *Shafaq-e Sorkh* were also addressing the woman question in the twenties. Somewhat less ideological than expatriate papers like *Kaveh* and *Iranshahr*, the domestic papers provided access to different points of view. For example, full transcripts of the mosque sermons of a cleric named Mohammad Mehdi Ayatollahzadeh Khalesi were regularly featured in *Setareh-e Iran* in 1923. Most of his sermons were exhortations for Iranian Muslims to struggle against the material and cultural encroachments of the West, but, in the midst of several sermons, Khalesi discussed the proper role for women in a modern Muslim Iranian society. He rejected the notion that women and men were "naturally" equal and reminded listeners that there were different religious commandments for men and for women.[36] In contrast to the young men of renewal, Khalesi saw Europe's treatment of women as a real threat: "If we were to advocate—like European civilization, which is nothing but the corruption of humankind, amorality, and the destroyer of humanity— that men and women are completely the same and that they must involve themselves in the special duties and occupations of one another, we would obtain nothing by the disruption of the social order of humanity. If we were to say that a woman, with the tenderheartedness, patience, and steadiness that is woman, should go to war, and if we were to say that a man with his crude and harsh nature should take up housekeeping, we have done nothing but wipe out humankind."[37]

Ultimately, Khalesi would link all social and political questions, including the woman question, to the single issue of protecting Iran's Islamic heritage from Western encroachment. He attacked "Mr. Renewal" for betraying his country and religion by taking a European wife.[38] But did the modern Iranian woman, as portrayed in the press, want the young man of the renewal movement as her husband and guardian?

'Alam-e Nesvan featured many articles on the subject of marriage and family relations.[39] Although 'Alam-e Nesvan attempted only to publish contributions by women, by 1925 men were regular contributors.[40] In 1930, half of its subscription representatives in Iran were men.[41] Like Iranshahr, it asked its readers to comment on marriage by asking men and women to describe their ideal spouses. In March 1930, ten women addressed the subject, including Afzal Vaziri, the daughter of Bibi Khanom Astarabadi. The common feature these women wanted in their husbands was "good morals" and even piety (diyanat),[42] but not once was Islam specifically mentioned. One woman emphasized this generic religiosity in this way: "He should not consider religion [mazhab] anything but morality and pure behavior, and should not consider worship anything other than serving people [khedmat be-khalq]."[43]

A woman named Malak al-Zaman made a point of rejecting the Islamic requirements of bride-price and dowry and added a curious test of her imaginary husband's piety: "He must demonstrate his piety by openly declaring before a government official that any time I disagree with his beliefs I can leave him right then and there, so as to prevent [his] corruption later."[44]

In effect, she proposed an alliance between herself and the state to ensure her husband's morality. Afzal Vaziri and Bala Khanom Sharif also called for state intervention in marriage laws and practices to prevent arranged marriages and other defective marriage practices. Although one woman specified that the ideal husband should be healthy so as not to sire sickly children who would burden the nation,[45] and two specified that he should be young, none insisted that the ideal husband be rich or handsome.[46] Actually, a woman identified only as M. M. wrote that a "pretty" (qashang) man would be nice, but that the odds of finding a good partner in "our environment" would be difficult enough in any case.[47] All these elements—youth, health, morality, alienation from traditional Islam, nationalism, and faith in state power—suggest that the composite "ideal man" selected by the editors of *'Alam-e Nesvan* would have much in common with the young men of the renewal movement.

The following month, this marital metaphor was extended further in a satirical short story by Delshad Khanom.[48] Her earlier satire of the clergy had been in the best tradition of renewal literature.[49] Her satire of the process of selecting an ideal husband begins with her narrator grousing about the superficial aspects of modernization—hats on illiterates, beautified cemeteries, and cinemas everywhere. She then finds herself on "Renewal Street." Here she sees women filing into a great building that she at first assumes is a doctor's office. Another woman tells her that the building is actually the Women's Literary Society and that she is welcome to attend. At first, the meeting is chaotic. The narrator refers to it as a *majles,* a word that, in modern parlance, could mean "gathering" or "parliament." It is clear that the ambiguity is deliberate when the president of the assembly calls it to order and declares that the assembly needs to respond to *'Alam-e Nesvan's* call for a description of the ideal husband. The president talks around the issue and then suggests that the participants write down their opinions so that they can be read aloud. In what can only be a clear lampooning of Iranian parliamentary practice, the assembly responds, exclaiming, "That is best; that is best *[ahsan ast]!*"

The list of opinions grows too long, so it is decided that they will be read aloud in a later session. After a very pleasant and luxurious recess, the floor is opened up to comments. In the course of this episode, the virtues of a love match over an arranged marriage are expressed. Also, a veiled woman attempts to pass herself off as being well educated, declaring herself too good for any husband. Questions from the other women reveal her to be a fraud and to be the "hick" she appears to be. At long last, the narrator presents her opinion to the assembly. She tells of how one of the wives of Naser al-Din Shah Qajar preferred to suffer the indignities of divorce rather than stay with a man who was not devoted to her, despite his lofty rank. The story ends with the narrator running home as fast as she can, fleeing her bizarre experience in the assembly.

The simultaneous respect for the institution of the Parliament and contempt for its practices was a definite feature of the renewal movement of the 1920s. In Delshad Khanom's satire, women can approximate political enfranchisement, but, ultimately, enfranchisement is not able to help them find what they really want: good husbands. Like a number of renewalist writers, Delshad Khanom shows contempt for superficial westernization and contempt for the wealth and power of the traditional Qajar establishment. Taken together with her earlier lampooning of the clergy, Delshad Khanom seems the perfect mate for the ideal man of the renewal movement.

There was only one problem with Delshad Khanom. She was a man—and a Christian one, at that. As Jane Doolittle recalled:

JD. One of the articles that was appreciated most was under the name of Delshad Khanom. Did you ever hear of Delshad Khanom?

Q. No.

JD. Delshad Khanom was Agha-ye Nakhostin, that is Nowzad, the uncle of Ahmad Khan. Did you know him?

Q. No.

JD. Well, he was a very interesting person and a very keen Christian. He used to write articles and sign them, Delshad Khanom and everybody thought it was a lady that was writing these articles. They were very well accepted at the time.[50]

Nowzad the man, Nowzad the Iranian Christian convert, represented himself as Delshad Khanom the (assumably) Muslim Iranian—fooling the reading public at the time and later researchers (including this one, until recently).[51] This is one of those moments of historical inquiry in which the truth is less important than the construction of the lie. Transgender authoring was nothing new in Iranian press culture—perhaps beginning with Mirza Malkam Khan in the pages of *Qanun* and continuing to this day, most recently in the pages of *Zanan* magazine in Iran.[52] In contrast to the ridicule inherent in Safavid-era transgender alter egos like Kolsum Naneh (see chapter 2), modern male transgender writers tended to use the shield of a female pseudonym to advocate for women's progress. In Delshad Khanom, we see more than that. We see an Iranian man's construction of modern Iranian womanhood—a woman who scorns the Qajars, shuns traditional dress, is not wed to superstition, has obtained a modern education, and can satirize the modern institution of parliament as well as any man. She is the ideal mate for the renewalist man—more sensible than the other women in the *majles*. It is a particularly fascinating construction of modern Iranian woman from a man who has reconstructed himself as a Christian—seemingly in order to be closer to his renewalist ideals.

'Alam-e Nesvan, like Iranshahr, asked men directly to imagine their ideal wives.[53] Three submissions were deemed worthy of publication. In his preamble, R. Namvar spoke of a loving partnership, but when he got down to specifics he was no less demanding than his counterparts who had written to Iranshahr some six years earlier: His ideal wife was to know her place, to act with circumspection, to be a good mother, to be of high moral character, to be kind to the poor, and to have an educated appreciation of music and literature.[54] Before marriage, she was to be unveiled—for how else would he be able to meet and evaluate her—and after marriage, she was "to have complete faith in me."[55] Another man wanted his wife to have sound morals, "enough" education to be the first teacher of their children, and a knowledge of housekeeping.[56] And the last respondent, Mehdi Movafeq, offered a couple lines of verse on how a wife's pure love and chastity would set her husband free from baseness.[57] Far from attacking these men for their limited perspective, 'Alam-e Nesvan tacitly endorsed these expectations by printing them and also by printing regular articles on morality, child-rearing, housekeeping, health, and beauty. So for all of its advocacy of women's education, women's work, and even women's political rights, 'Alam-e Nesvan, like Danesh and Shokufeh before it, nonetheless sought to advance women by finding them more agreeable male guardians—the "young men" of renewal.

The modern male guardian would support their education, permit them to work in certain professions, support their input on certain political and social matters, take only one wife from their ranks and treat her well. As many women noted, such men were rare indeed. But, according to the modern male guardians, so were ideal modern Iranian women. Actual Iranian women did not (and could not) live up the ideal, and even the ideal modern Iranian woman fared poorly in comparison with her ideal modern European and American sisters. But that was about to change. In addition to inventing the modern Iranian woman, the heirs of the nineteenth-century renewal movement created a Frankenstein they came to call Reza Shah. And he had plans for renewal's bride.

Courtship, Marriage, and State Propaganda

Before the Women's Awakening and before Gowharshad, the Pahlavi regime responded to women's calls for alliance through the institution of marriage. Parvin Paidar, and others, have criticized the Marriage Law of 1931 for being a mere codification of the shari'ah and for thus preserving gender inequities in traditional interpretations of Islamic law—a rubber-stamped piece of legislation that reflected the static patriarchal consensus. And certainly, the Marriage Law of 1931 did nothing to alter the many ways in which women were controlled by the men in their lives.[58] Husbands legally controlled their wives' right to work and travel, and the husbands chose their place of residence. Husbands could kill their wives if they caught them "in the act of adultery or in circumstances leading to adultery."[59]

But observers at the time could see that the Marriage Law of 1931 was proposed, debated, amended, and revised. It was debated both behind closed doors by members of a legislative committee of the Parliament and the Minister of Justice and in the open in the pages of the press. It was not debated on the open floor of the Parliament, however, and thus the debate among policymakers was off the record—somewhat reminiscent of the 1911 "debate" on women's suffrage that was quickly taken off the record at the nervous suggestion of Zoka al-Molk (see chapter 2). While there was little doubt that a marriage law would be passed, the regime decided to be flexible on certain specifics, permitted press debate on the law, and appears to have taken seriously objections raised in petitions by the clergy. In short, Reza Shah sought some level of consensus from among his men while clearly intending to respond to feminist demands for state regulation of marriage.

How did the law change between 16 July 1931, when it was first proposed, and 16 August, when it was finally passed? At the American Legation in Tehran, Charles C. Hart followed the progress of the law and addressed this very question in great detail in his dispatches to the State Department. The Pahlavi regime retreated on a number of points. First, it had initially provided stiffer penalties for failing to record marriages and would have taken clerics to task for failing to record marriages within a specified time. In the final version, only husbands were held accountable for failing to record marriages, and penalties were reduced from two years' to six months' imprisonment.[60] Nonetheless, the principle of state control over marriages was intact. Second, the original draft of the law had specified age limits (sixteen for young women and eighteen for young men) and would have held a wide variety of offenders responsible for violation (including, potentially, the parents). In the final draft, age limits were omitted, and specific references to "medical certificates" proving the "physical aptitude" of the bride or groom for marriage were also omitted. Again, only the bride or groom would be subject to prosecution for violating the law—although with an increased fine (from U.S.$10 to U.S.$100 in 1931 dollars).[61] Third, in the original draft of the law, the woman had been given the right to secure a divorce in specified cases: nonsupport, ill treatment, an attempt against her life, and the husband's conviction for a high crime or misdemeanor. In the final version, the husband's conviction of a high crime or misdemeanor was stricken from the list.[62] Also in the final version, marriages would no longer be voided for fraud on the part of either party, but either party could face prosecution for fraud. Included under this rubric was the man's failure to disclose the existence of another wife or intent to marry an additional wife.[63] The final version upheld the husband's right to choose the place of residence, with the woman only allowed to leave out of fear for her life or property. The most important compromise between the renewalist nationalism of the Pahlavi regime and Islamic law came in Article 17 of the final draft. The Ministry of Justice had proposed amending the original bill to specify that "The marriage of a Persian woman with a foreign national is subject to special authorization, and in each locality the Government will designate an authority for purposes of granting such permission. Any foreign national marrying a Persian wife without such authorization will be amenable to correctional imprisonment of from six months to three years."[64]

As Hart noted, this would be a direct assault on Islamic law, which traditionally holds that no Muslim woman may marry a non-Muslim man. The suggested provision would have replaced Islamic identity with Iranian identity as the relevant issue and did not categorically rule out marriage between a Muslim Iranian woman and a non-Muslim Iranian or foreign man. In the final version, the Iranian state retained the right to regulate marriage between Iranians and non-Iranians, but it also affirmed the Islamic prohibition against the marriage of Muslim women to non-Muslim men. The penalty for a non-Iranian man's failing to secure state permission for marriage to an Iranian woman was one to three years' imprisonment (a stiffer minimum than originally proposed).[65] In all versions, the state reserved the right of the Ministry of Justice to establish and enforce all regulations to ensure compliance with the law.

It is in this Article 17 of the Marriage Law that we see the clearest expression of modern (and, specifically, renewalist) male guardianship by the Pahlavi state. The state reserved the right to forbid a marriage between a non-Iranian Muslim man and an Iranian Muslim woman—national sovereignty transcended religious freedom and individual liberty. The state could, in theory, forbid a marriage contract between two consenting adults of different nationalities—even a marriage that their parents had approved and even if they were both of the same religion. By inserting state regulation into the process, the state provided women with an automatic (and powerful) third party to whom they could appeal but also to whom they must ultimately defer. Ultimately, this law ratified the idea that the male guardianship exercised by husbands and fathers was subject to the supervision of the state—an emasculating idea for men and not quite a liberating idea for women. Marriage was still a metaphor for unequal alliance, but the Marriage Law of 1931 did provide modern Iranian womanhood with the beginnings of the alliance it craved with the state. It also provided the Pahlavi state with a claim on the loyalties of modern Iranian womanhood.

Did the Pahlavi state act as a male guardian? In the short run, American diplomatic reports (drawing on Iranian press coverage) indicate that the regime moved quickly to find and prosecute violators of the Marriage Law of 1931. Regulations for the enforcement of the Marriage Law were established in September; two special courts (one for appeal) were established in October and November. The first case of violation of the Marriage Law was heard on 28 October. Hosayn the Waiter was convicted of violating the law by marrying Fatemeh, the twelve-year-old daughter of Ahmad the Baker and Ma'sumeh.[66] Hosayn received twenty-five months (reduced to twenty on appeal), Ahmad received two months (reduced to one on appeal), and Ma'sumeh received eight days (upheld on appeal). Hosayn was not convicted because of the victim's age per se, rather, he was convicted because medical reports (by government-appointed doctors) indicated that Fatemah had been brutalized on her wedding night—this, despite Hosayn agreeing in their marriage contract not to touch her for three years. In other words, he knew she was not "physically apt" for marriage. The parents were charged as accessories (using the preexisting penal code to bypass the fact that the Marriage Law did not provide for the culpability of parents or guardians). It is interesting to note that "spectators, principally women, jostled for admission" to the open proceedings of this first case, and that feelings "ran high" against Hosayn the Waiter as medical testimony was introduced against him. Women, it seems, wanted to witness the state's first effort to defend one of their own.

Using accessory charges, the Ministry of Justice was able to cast a wide net. The following four cases, recorded in Charles C. Hart's ongoing dispatches on the Marriage Law of 1931 to his State Department superiors illustrate the reasoning and methods of the court:

1. Inasmuch as Ramazan Mobarak, son of Hassan, 51 years old, having already another wife, married, on November 14, Seyed Masoumeh, daughter of Seyed Ali, who lacks physical aptitude for marriage:

And inasmuch as his defense is: firstly, that his wife is ill twice a month; secondly, that Seyed Masoumeh gave her consent to the marriage; and, thirdly, that a notice was published in the Official Gazette of the Ministry of Justice alleged to purport that the Law on Marriage and Divorce was to be put into effect only as of October 24, whereas the notice question dealt with Article 1 [recording of marriages] of the Law, not Article 3 [physical-aptitude requirement], under which the offense falls:

All these pleadings being ineffective, Ramazan Mobarak is, in conformity with Article 3 of the law in question, sentenced to correctional imprisonment of 22 months:

Further, Roqiyeh, daughter of Mashhadi Ali Akbar and mother of Seyed Masoumeh, who has confessed to having abetted the offense committed by Ramazan, is also amenable to punishment:

However, inasmuch as she gave countenance to the commission of the offense because of poverty, she is, in conformity with the said Article 3 and with due regard to Articles 28 (defining accomplices) and 45 (allowing the courts under extenuating circumstances, to mitigate punishment) of the Penal Code, sentenced to correctional imprisonment of eight days:

Also, Khanom Gol, daughter of Mashhadi Youssof, intermediary, who has confessed the truth of what is alleged by the prosecutor, is, also with due regard to the said articles of the aforementioned laws, sentenced to fifteen days correctional imprisonment. The judgement is appealable before the Court of Appeal.[67]

2. On December 9 Mirza Seyed Razi Khan Amid, Public Prosecutor attached to the Marriage Court in Pahlevi [sic], instituted a criminal suit indicting Azim Assadollahi, son of Hossain, 20 years old, for having married Seyedeh Kobra, daughter of Mir Hassan, 12 years old and lacking physical aptitude for marriage. He also charged Sheikh Mohammad Taqi Kabir, son of late Mashhadi Hossain Ali, 75 years old, with having abetted the offense by executing the marriage contract.

After examining the case and hearing the defense of the accused and the Sheikh's defending attorney, Rowhani:

Inasmuch as the accused have confessed to having committed the offense, and inasmuch as their ignorance of the law, which constitutes their only ground for defense, is not a plausible excuse:

Azim Assadollahi is, in conformity with Article 3 of the Law on Marriage and Divorce of August 15 1931, sentenced to 18 months correctional imprisonment;

And Agha Sheikh Mohammad Taqi Kabir is, with due regard to Articles 28 (defining accessories to an offense) and 29 (authorizing tribunals to reduce penalties in the light of special circumstances) of the Penal Code, sentenced to correctional imprisonment of one year. This judgement is appealable.

Pahlevi [Enzeli], December 9, 1931[68]

3. On November 2, 1931, Seiyed Mahmud Larijani, a mullah of Teheran having notarial authority to record marriage and divorce, together with his son, Seiyed Jelal-ad-Din Larijani, executed the marriage of a 23 year old resident of Teheran with a 14 year old girl lacking physical aptitude for marriage. On March 8, the court sentenced the husband, Seiyed Yahya, to one month of correctional imprisonment, Seiyed Mahmud Larijani (the mullah who executed the marriage) and his son to two months each, and the mothers of the couple, Galin Khanom and Roqeiyeh Khanom, to eight days of correctional imprisonment each.[69]

4. On March 6 the court sentenced Gholam Hossein, a 30 year old resident of Teheran who married a 13 year old girl to 16 months of correctional imprisonment. The mullah who pronounced the marriage formula, Aqa Seiyed Kazem Rozekhan (mourning preacher), was condemned to 45 days of correctional imprisonment. Seifollah, 65 years old, and his wife, Nushaferin, who gave their consent to the marriage of their minor daughter, were sentenced to two months and eight days of correctional imprisonment, respectively.[70]

These court records suggest that the regime had no trouble enforcing the Marriage Law of 1931 even without minimum age requirements and specific penalties for accomplices in the text of the law itself. Charles Hart clearly felt that the law was applied with a particular intent toward weakening the influence of the clergy, and the aforementioned cases certainly suggest this was true. But there is more; in going after the parents and matchmakers connected with illegal marriages, the regime was clearly trying to remove all cultural support for child marriages. Women did not escape the law, but seem to have been treated with greater leniency—mothers received token sentences, and the girls themselves were treated as victims rather than participants.

There was yet another theme to these courtroom performances, one that emphasized the connection between poverty and tradition. Whether due to differing customs of different social classes or due to different standards of enforcement by the state, the defendants and victims of these cases fit a profile that matched modernist constructions of all that was traditional in Iranian society. They were of humble backgrounds and possessed traditional religious (a renewalist might say superstitious) sensibilities. Poor and ignorant—is that not what some of the men pled in their own defense? In bringing the application of the Marriage Law to these particular defendants, the court educated and disciplined those seen as being most in need of reform. In staging public trials, as the regime did in its first case involving Hosayn the Waiter, the state could engage the emotions of the audience in favor of the law in a way that a dry reading of the legal code might not achieve. In displaying the court proceedings in the press, the regime educated and informed those Iranians and foreign diplomats who might read the press (and agree with the goals of the Marriage Law) that change was, in fact, taking place. The Pahlavi state was making good on its alliance—not that it had needed to wait long for support from some feminists. Even before the law was drafted in its final form, long-time women's activist 'Effat Kh^wajehnuri, whose husband had been jailed in 1923 for advocating the abandonment of the Islamic veil, endorsed the law in an open letter on the front page of *Ettela 'at*.[71] She praised the law as a solution to the disorderly and unregulated nature of marriage in Iran that she felt devalued women and prevented them from raising worthy sons for the nation. The terms of the alliance could not have been articulated more succinctly.

In 1937, in the midst of the greater reform of the Women's Awakening, the Marriage Law was amended without debate or even discussion.[72] The Parliament simply ratified the recommendation of the Ministry of Justice that a minimum age for marriage of sixteen for young women and eighteen for young men be reinserted into the law as had been the case with the original draft of the law in 1931 (of course, no mention was made of that). Unlike the Marriage Law of 1931 that served as propaganda fodder for well over a year, the changes to the law in 1937 received little public attention. *Ettela 'at* merely noted the ratification of the changes in its routine coverage of parliamentary activity on page four (page one being devoted to Reza Shah's tour of southern Iran).[73] Only a look at still unavail-

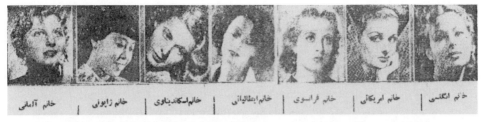

خانم آلمانی | خانم ژاپونی | خانم اسکاندیناوی | خانم ایطالیائی | خانم فرانسوی | خانم امریکائی | خانم انگلیسی

5.1a. From *Mehregan* 79 (28 December 1938), 12–13. Women from around the world choose their ideal husbands. *Right to left*: the English woman, the American woman, the French woman, the Italian woman, the Scandinavian woman, the Japanese woman, and the German woman.

able archival material might shed some light as to why the marriage reform was played down in 1937. It may have been to avoid provoking a public outcry from a population already aggravated by forced unveiling. It may have been because the regime was focusing on the more (in its own view) far-reaching Women's Awakening project. But while progressive reform of marriage laws seemed to be dead in 1937—leaving intact polygyny, temporary marriage, and strong male rights in the event of divorce—state interest in shaping attitudes about marriage and courtship through the public media was still keen.

One of the issues behind unveiling since the nineteenth century had been the social mixing of the sexes. Shirazi had seen nothing wrong with English boys and girls trying to impress each other, and Kermani had insisted that such social mixing was necessary for there to be true love matches. Akhundzadeh had his female characters demand to choose their mates, and on 29 December 1938, *Mehregan* gave its young women readers a chance to talk about their ideal man.[74] It presented foreign models and actresses as "typical" women from around the world answering questions about their ideal man (see illustration 5.1a). The answers were suspiciously stereotypical. The Swedish woman was coolly indifferent to how smart or rich her man was. The Japanese woman wanted a strong, intelligent man who cared about his own and his wife's honor. The English woman wanted her man brave, and the American wanted him to be rich and entrepreneurial. The Italian woman wanted him to dress in the latest fashions, while the German woman merely wanted him to be clean and to father a lot of children. The worst thing the German man could be was a coward in battle, and the worst thing an American man could be was poor. But what did the Iranian woman want in a man? *Mehregan* offered to print the pictures of the women with the "best" answers.

5.1b. From *Mehregan* 82 (9 February 1939), 12–13. Iranian women choose their ideal husbands. *Right to left:* Marziyeh Taheri, Mahin Damghanpur, Fari Khurshid, Mo'azzameh Nezhadpak, Badri Javadi, Shamsi Sa'id, Ajlaleh Giransar, Nuri Hassas, and Mahindokht Khaza'el. By permission of MEDOC, University of Chicago.

The nine women who won the contest were suspiciously unanimous (see illustration 5.1b).[75] Their ideal Iranian man had to be patriotic, smart, and serious rather than handsome and rich. The worst thing he could be was a traitor. Creating this ideal image of an Iranian man ostensibly through the eyes of the modern Iranian woman had several implications. On one level, it provided the image of an Iranian woman capable of choosing her ideal mate in the same way as her modern sisters around the world (and linked her to rather glamorous representations of her "sisters"). As we shall see, this message stood in contrast to the thoroughly arranged marriage of Crown Prince Mohammad Reza to Egyptian princess Fowziyeh that very spring. At the same time, the chosen favorable qualities were those that could be cultivated through moral, intellectual, and physical training rather than granted at birth. In a way, this contest was emblematic of the Women's Awakening as a whole. The Pahlavi state granted women "freedom," but it was a gift to be used in the service of the state and nation. In this case, an image of the sexual desires of the modern Iranian woman was used to reinforce an image of the modern Iranian man.

If discussions of marriage in the press illustrated the putative and actual power of the state to define and regulate that institution and served to highlight an alliance between feminists and the state, an individual marriage could represent both personal and national expressions of power (and powerlessness). Some men and women achieved the sense of partnership that renewalist ideology championed, while others lived with the ironic realization that whatever the act of marriage meant to them (or meant to the public), it was hard to slip loose from the obligations of male guardianship.

The Companionate Marriage in Practice: Some Examples

The producers and potential consumers of Women's Awakening propaganda about marriage and courtship were largely of the upper and middle classes. The lower classes served, as we have seen in state enforcement of the Marriage Law of 1931, as examples of what was wrong with tradition and ignorance in Iranian society. Indeed, for modern scholars (including this one), elite women have served as valuable counters to the popular images of veiled and downtrodden Muslim women. However, even the wealthiest of women could be vulnerable to the whims of the men in their lives. Two cases serve as powerful reminders of this fact. The first involves the second wife of the ill-fated court minister Teymourtache, and the second involves the first wife of Mohammad Reza Pahlavi, Fowziyeh.

In reporting on the progress of women in Iranian society, Charles C. Hart passed along news of discord in the Teymourtache household. The court minister had decided, during an illness of his second wife, to marry for a third time to a woman from Mashhad, the major city in his home province. Although Hart clearly chose the story to highlight the powerlessness of elite women in their personal affairs, his narrative has the jocular flow of a gossip column and the voyeuristic glee of a westerner peeking into an exotic and scandal-ridden Persian harem:

> Just after the news of the marriage got back to Tehran last December, wife No. 2, an Armenian society wife, with the Minister of Court, attended a dinner and soirée at the German Legation. Madame Teymourtache was very noticeably not herself that night. She spent most of the evening in front of the fireplace, glaring into the flames with the thought perhaps that the Minister of the Court would make excellent kindling material. She refused to dance and of course no one could offer to console her, although other guests divined the reason for her despair. As reported in my dispatch No. 411 of March 4, 1931, the marriage took place in Meshed while the Minister of the Court was accompanying the Shah on his tour of the country. It was then supposed that wife No. 3 would continue to reside in Meshed, but no! She showed up here soon afterwards and several persons who have seen her remark that she is so young and attractive as to justify the obvious fears of wife No. 2 that she may be crowded out of the Minister's favor.[76]

Teymourtache's marriage was, of course, a private affair. But eight years later, the marriage of Crown Prince Mohammad Reza Pahlavi to

Egyptian princess Fowziyeh was a spectacle to display both Iran's modernity and the legitimacy of its ruling house. Reza Shah himself had taken a Qajar wife to rise above his common origins, and the marriage of the crown prince into one of the more prestigious surviving families from the Ottoman era, the descendants of one of the first aggressive modernizers in the Middle East, must have seemed a real coup. But the marriage was problematic, both as public propaganda and as a private affair.

As public propaganda, the marriage posed logistic, symbolic, and legal obstacles. There were two wedding celebrations—one in Egypt and one in Iran. The Egyptian phase of the ceremony began on 15 March, and this was the date upon which the actual marriage contract was signed. Once the contract was made the royal couple was married in the eyes of traditional Islamic law. However, as American consul and special envoy to the Tehran ceremonies, C. Van. H. Engert, noted in his 27-page report, the Pahlavi regime did not definitively say they were married until after the Tehran celebrations were concluded on 25 April.[77] The official program published by the Iranian government did not even mention Fowziyeh by name until the royal couple was scheduled to begin its journey to Iran—two weeks after the marriage contract was signed.[78] The Tehran celebrations were timed to coincide with the thirteenth anniversary of Reza Shah's coronation—perhaps to underscore his intention of having a durable dynasty. This very point had posed a legal problem. The Iranian Constitution barred anyone from ascending the Iranian throne who was not the child of an Iranian-born mother. One of the details insisted upon by the Egyptian court during the marriage negotiations was that Fowziyeh's sons be eligible for the Iranian throne. In November 1938, Fowziyeh was granted Iranian nationality by imperial decree (speedily rubber-stamped by the Parliament) on the grounds that such a measure was in the compelling interest of the Iranian state as it had to do with dynastic succession. The journey from Alexandria to Iran was loaded with symbolic actions emphasizing Iran's rightful place among modern nations of the world:

> Upon leaving Egyptian and Sudanese waters the *Mohamed Ali El-Kabir* [an Egyptian royal yacht] was first escorted by Italian cruisers, then a French cruiser, and finally by the British cruiser *Norfolk* as far as the entrance to the Persian Gulf. There the Iranian gunboats [Italian made and with Italian-trained Iranian crews] *Palang* and *Babr* took over the escort and were later joined by a flight of Iranian military airplanes which accompanied the royal party to the new

port of Bandar Shahpur, the terminus of the Transiranian Railway, where they arrived on April 14th 10 A.M.[79]

Mohammad Reza Pahlavi's sister, Ashraf, remembered the betrothal of her brother to Fowziyeh this way: "This again was my father's own idea that his son would marry a woman from a royal house and because of the relations that he wanted to have with the Arabs and these sorts of issues. He really searched [for someone] and [to see if that person] would marry and, as a result, he [Reza Shah] picked Fowziyeh. Of course my brother and Fowziyeh had not seen one another. They were betrothed on the basis of a piece of paper and a picture, and the first time Fowziyeh saw my brother was the same time that he went to Egypt for the marriage. Of course, you know that they were both very young and very good looking. They were very pleased with one another from the beginning and liked each other."[80]

Granting Fowziyeh Iranian nationality appears to have been the fullest extent of Reza Shah's generosity toward Fowziyeh. It was rumored in Cairo that Reza Shah had stuck the Egyptian government with the costs of Fowziyeh's travel to Iran ($12,000—in 1939) and the bill for hosting the Iranian entourage in Cairo during that portion of the festivities.[81] Reza Shah also moved to separate Fowziyeh from her Egyptian entourage, sending it back to Alexandria.[82] The most interesting charge is that Reza Shah began demanding that Princess Fowziyeh's personal property be turned over to the crown prince. The last diplomatic report available stated that on 5 August, Hassanein Pasha, Fowziyeh's uncle, accompanied by a "Palace official and a [British?] Foreign Office official," was on his way to Tehran by plane to defend Fowziyeh's interests in negotiations with Reza Shah.[83] Ultimately, however, Fowziyeh was reported to have been driven from the Pahlavi house by the interference of her sister-in-law, Ashraf Pahlavi.[84]

Ashraf reports nothing but the warmest feelings among Fowziyeh, Reza Shah, and herself—indeed, Ashraf felt she got on better with Fowziyeh than with Mohammad Reza's second wife, Soraya. She does admit, though, that she spent all her time at her brother's house.[85] From 11:30 A.M. until after dark, Ashraf was at her brother's house with Fowziyeh. It is hard to imagine that, however warm her feelings toward Fowziyeh might have been, her constant presence would not have become tiresome for the hapless Egyptian princess.[86]

Until her decision to leave Mohammad Reza Shah in 1945, which apparently took everyone at the Pahlavi court by surprise, Fowziyeh was incorporated into Pahlavi propaganda as a very modern Iranian woman of the Pahlavi royal house. A regiment of the Iranian cavalry was named after her, and she, like the other princesses of the Pahlavi household, made public appearances in support of charities and appropriate societies. But rumors of her difficulties belied the public image and toward the end of the marriage in the 1940s became a matter of press speculation. For Fowziyeh, the emancipatory rhetoric of the Women's Awakening was no protection against the whims of her tyrannical father-in-law, and her marriage to the crown prince (and later king) seems to have accorded no advantages that she would not have enjoyed had she stayed with her family in Egypt— perhaps fewer. From 1945 to 1948, Queen Fowziyeh and Mohammad Reza Shah lived apart. The shah was advised (by then Prime Minister Ahmad Qavam and Court Minister 'Ala) to divorce Fowziyeh. King Farouk of Egypt had raised the matter of divorce, ostensibly on his sister's behalf. And Mohammad Reza Shah himself was inclined to divorce Fowziyeh as early as 1946.[87] But at that time, the personal matter of divorce had international implications. Everyone hesitated to act. The American ambassador reported:

Shah told me in strict confidence yesterday that he was contemplating divorcing the Queen but was hesitant to do so before finding out what British reaction might be in view of close British interest in Arab matters in general and Egyptian matters in particular. In response to my remark that I had heard there was already a divorce he said, smiling, "There is not a word of truth in the report—not yet." He asked if I would ascertain the British reaction. At a separate meeting, Qavam also broached the subject, saying that present situation was undignified and intolerable for Iran, that Fawzia enjoyed receiving social distinction as Queen of Iran but refused to come to Iran or assume any responsibilities of position and even refused to receive Iranian Ambassador in Cairo. He strongly favors divorce but also asked me if I could ascertain, very casually, what British reaction would be . . . Neither Qavam nor Shah knows other has discussed matter with me and both requested emphatically that I not tell the other. . . . [Both the Shah] and Qavam are especially anxious to avoid offending British sensibilities at the moment. Their attitude in this regard, while beneficial to our purposes at present, is a further indication that Iran's so-called independence remains a rather thin veneer, covering stout buttresses on the north and south. Iranians themselves would feel cost if either buttress gave and are doing their best to encourage us to build a third.[88]

Just as the marriage of Fowziyeh and Mohammad Reza had been orchestrated for national gain (or, at least, the gain of the royal houses of those nations), their divorce was coordinated with international interests and became just another angle for American and Iranian diplomats to exploit. In the end, there could have been no emptier a symbol for modern Iranian womanhood than Fowziyeh and no more incongruous a symbol of renewalist manhood than Mohammad Reza Shah Pahlavi. Like the Women's Awakening itself, their marriage had been designed for the needs of "the great"—and, now, absent—father, Reza Shah. Fowziyeh and Mohammad Reza were divorced in 1948, the stated reason being the inability of Fowziyeh to perform her duties as she was required to stay in Egypt for medical reasons.[89]

For other women, though, marriage to a man with the right mind-set could signal a change for the better, just as renewalist discussions of marriage had always suggested. Dreams of independence clashed with the expectations of male guardianship, and not always to the obvious advantage of the women involved except in that they felt empowered by their decisions to marry. Saffiyeh Firuz, the eventual founder of the Women's Party, married to escape the daily influence of her family upon her life.[90] Nayereh Ebtehaj-Samii, who remembers delivering a speech against the veil at her graduation from American Bethel (enjoying coverage in *Kushesh* and *Ettela'at*), received a marriage inquiry by a young man who was impressed with her speech. Her mother opposed the marriage because she wanted Nayereh to marry someone within the extended family back in her hometown of Rasht. Her father—described as quite progressive by Nayereh—also opposed the marriage but for a different reason: The young man's family had a reputation for taking multiple wives. For Nayereh, the decision to marry was very much about taking control of her own destiny: "I was not a receptive listener on this matter . . . especially because it was not because I was in love and not because I knew him. No, there was just a rebelliousness in my spirit that I wanted to show that I, also, have independence of thought. It was mostly in this vein that I decided [to marry the young man]."[91]

Nayereh remembered a good life with the young man until, indeed, he decided to take a second wife. Now, her mother opposed divorce on the basis of family honor. Her father, who must have inserted a condition into the marriage contract to the effect that Nayereh could divorce in the event that her husband took a second wife, supported Nayereh's decision to divorce. Her first marriage, then, would have satisfied neither traditional nor renewalist ideals. It was her antiveiling stance that seems to have attracted a "young man of renewal," but he was himself not true to renewalist thinking on the subject of monogamy. Her marriage was not for love—an implicit and often explicit expectation of renewalist discussions of marriage. It was, however, empowering because she felt that she was taking a decision by herself. Ultimately, the traditional well-negotiated Islamic marriage contract is what saved her from a polygynous marriage even though traditional sentiments on divorce and family honor were not with her. Nayereh Ebtehaj-Samii's first marriage is evidence indeed that human choices are not constrained by formal ideological rigor.

Nonetheless, the renewalist ideal of companionate marriage could affect the way a woman conceptualized her marriage. Parvin Moayyed-Sabeti regretted that marriage at seventeen kept her from pursuing her higher education until after her children were grown. Yet, she did not feel that her marriage (and motherhood) at such an age was driven by traditional family priorities:

Q. Was marriage important for [your] family or did you fall in love?

A. Yes, it must really seem that, at that time, it should be a family-run matter but it was not that way. I went to the American school. My husband went to Alborz College, and we played tennis and we were very modern. We fell in love and we married. It was not very customary in those days—I mean it was very rare to have such a marriage, and then I went to Mashhad and I studied there as well. I went to the university at night but not regularly. I went for a few months but then I became pregnant and I did not go. This studying was always something for me; it was a sorrow that "why didn't I continue this work?"[92]

A companionate marriage was modern. A secure, affectionate, and monogamous marriage had long been on the minds of women who embraced renewalism, for their own sake as well as that of the nation. Saffiyeh Firuz remembered happily that she was mistaken for her husband's mistress because she was seen horseback riding around town with him: "They [other men] could not believe that a woman could have something other than a sexual thing with a man. Friendship and the like was [considered] impossible. Of course, he was my husband."[93]

Firuz was living the marriage so coveted by Bibi Khanom Astarabadi in the nineteenth century and by the "European-educated girl" in the pages of *Danesh* in 1911. Simply to be included in her husband's interests and hobbies was symbolic of a more egalitarian relationship with men. Renewal's bride may not have expected much, but she did expect that some positive change would result from marrying a *modern* male guardian. That marriage and motherhood might limit a woman's options in life in a way that marriage and fatherhood did not limit her husband's options was not a detraction from companionate marriage. It was a goal women's rights activists had always cherished as a benefit of change, and it was the first goal that the Pahlavi regime endorsed in 1931 and continued to support throughout the Women's Awakening project. By 1936, however, marriage was only one part of a more complex program of state facilitation of women's entrance into society. The modern Iranian woman was to be celebrated as a student, a worker, and an active if not politically independent citizen. Celebrated as she was, the modern Iranian woman was not fully trusted in these roles. The tensions between male guardianship and modern Iranian womanhood were most obvious as the state toggled between encouraging and limiting women's entrance into society during the Women's Awakening. It is to an exploration of the tensions in women's education, employment, and civic presence that we now turn.

6

The Capable Woman

In the spring of 1997, I attended a memorial dinner for my aunt, Dr. Na'imeh Amin. There, one of her friends from medical school, "Dr. Maryam Tusi," shared pictures of herself and my aunt from their medical school days. In 1946, they were among the first women students admitted to the University of Tehran Medical School directly from Iranian high schools. I was fascinated by what I thought I saw in three of the pictures. One showed ten young women on the steps of the medical school, looking eager and confident (illustration 6.1). Another (illustration 6.2) showed men and women marching together in a street demonstration. The third (illustration 6.3) was of men and women on a country outing, huddled together to fit into the picture and seemingly unconcerned about traditional anxieties regarding mixed-gender socializing. These images of women's progress and activism could have been produced by the propaganda of the Pahlavi state during its Women's Awakening project. In fact, the picture of the demonstration went beyond Women's Awakening propaganda and was more resonant with a new demand for gender equality that appeared in the Iranian press in the wake of the Women's Awakening. Dr. Maryam Tusi's pictures and her recollections raised the possibility of answering a long-held question of mine: Did women who were in a position to benefit from the policies of the Women's Awakening take the messages of the Women's Awakening to heart?[1] Did they think of themselves as more than wives and mothers—as *capable* women: educated and professional?

The Changing Definitions of Women's Education

To answer Russian and British encroachment on its affairs and territory, the Qajar dynasty had sought to modernize education in Iran through various means, and its efforts centered on training men for a modernized military and bureaucracy. Although Europe was the ultimate source for

6.1. Ten women medical students at the University of Tehran in 1946.

6.2. Medical students protesting to increase the quota of students accepted into the University of Tehran Medical School, 1945.

6.3. University of Tehran medical students on an outing, ca. 1950.

new techniques and notions of what constituted modernity, the Qajar Empire took many of its cues from its neighbor and rival, the Ottoman Empire: Selim III's (d. 1807) *nizam-ı cedit* (new-order) military units were the inspiration for Qajar crown prince 'Abbas Mirza's *nezam-e jadid* military units; the first Qajar effort at a technical school, the Dar al-Fonun, was inspired by the Ottoman schools that the reformist minister Mirza Taqi Khan Amir Kabir (d. 1852) had observed; Iran's abortive attempts at administrative reform were called the *tanzimat-e hasaneh,* modeled on the more ambitious and successful Tanzimat reforms of the Ottoman Empire.

In one endeavor, however, the Qajar Empire was as quick to respond as either the Ottoman Empire or Khedival Egypt: sending student missions to Europe from 1811 onward. In the memoirs of one of these students, Mirza Saleh Shirazi (d. 1837), we see a clear appreciation for women's education in upper-middle-class English society—the purpose of such education being to make women better wives and mothers (see chapter 3).[2] Elite women had always had access to formal education (by tutors, if not in organized schools)—particularly religious education—in the Middle East. The key difference was Shirazi's appreciation for the notion of formally training women to better fulfill their "natural" roles. In the mid-nineteenth century, reform-minded critics of the Qajars, like their counterparts elsewhere in the Middle East, openly called for more education and better treatment for women in the name of national renewal. For men like Mirza Fath 'Ali Akhundzadeh and Mirza Aqa Khan Kermani, women's progress was integral to ridding Iran of superstition, despotism, and Western domination, thereby bringing about a moral and material rebirth of Iran.[3]

Although the Dar al-Fonun was neglected after its founding in 1851,[4] Qajar efforts to create a state-run modern educational system increased at the turn of the century. Despite the formation of a Council of National Schools in 1898, private citizens, foreigners, or missionaries ran most modern schools. It took the Constitutional Revolution to establish compulsory and universal elementary education (in the Supplementary Fundamental Laws of 1907), as well as the national bureaucratic infrastructure (through the Administrative Law of the Ministry of Education in 1910 and the Fundamental Law of Education in 1911), in order to realize such a dream.[5] The state even sought to gain regulatory control of private schools through licensing (1911) and by establishing curriculum guidelines for boys' and girls' education (1922).[6] But even the most progressive political party of the early constitutional period, the Social Democrat

Party, never envisioned complete equality in education for boys and girls, as is clear from this anonymously published explanation of the "women's education" plank (Article 5, Item 2) of its 1909 platform: "Surely intelligent people do not doubt that one big cause of the nation's misery and corruption of morals is the lack of education for women and ignorance of mothers. The meaning of women's education is instruction and education in housekeeping, health, marital etiquette, chastity, child raising, good morals, and liberation from superstition. Surely there is no one who will take issue with this."[7]

In the wake of the Constitutional Revolution, a number of schools for Muslim girls opened up, including some run by foreigners, such as the Ecolé Franco-Persan (opened by a French convert to Islam).[8] Girls' schools opened by Iranians adopted names that seemed designed to assure other Iranian Muslims of their good intentions and to counter the missionary presence in Iran: 'Effatiyeh (House of Chastity) in 1907 and Namus (Honor) in 1908. Newly formed women's organizations placed a premium on education as a ticket not only to social advancement but also to women's very inclusion in the imagined community of Iranians.[9] In 1913 *Shokufeh* counted sixty-three girls' schools in Tehran with a total of 2,474 students.[10]

With the exception of a women's teacher training college established in 1919 during the ill-fated prime ministership of Vosuq al-Dowleh, there was no avenue for women's postsecondary education in Iran until 1936. The college was created out of the Ecolé Franco-Persan secondary school, starting with ten students who initially seem to have received training as midwives rather than teachers.[11] Women who sought a postsecondary education were obliged to do so abroad. In 1933, there were nearly fifty women studying abroad (mostly in Europe) without any form of government assistance.[12] Fatemeh Sayyah, who in 1934 began her governmental career with Reza Shah's Ministry of Culture and later became the first woman professor (in Western literature) at the University of Tehran, earned her doctorate from the University of Moscow in 1920.[13] Sadiqeh Dowlatabadi, the editor and publisher of the magazine *Zaban-e Zanan* and, later, the president of the Women's Society under Reza Shah, interrupted her journalistic career to obtain a college degree in Switzerland.[14]

David Menashri has demonstrated that, from 1923 to 1941, the Pahlavi regime chose to put more resources into reform and expansion of secondary and postsecondary education than into other areas of education.[15] The old priorities of creating highly trained and loyal bureaucrats for a modernizing state apparatus that had motivated Qajar efforts at educational reform took precedence over extending basic education to all sections of society during the reign of Reza Shah as well. By any measure, though, education for men and women improved in Iran during the reign of Reza Shah. Between 1924 and 1944, the number of girls as a percentage of total students at all levels increased from 16.9 percent to 28 percent.[16] In 1910, only three girls completed sixth grade. The number of girls completing the sixth grade reached 5,667 in 1942. Although the numbers are lower in secondary education, there was a nearly tenfold increase in the number of boys completing twelfth grade between 1921 and 1938, while the number of girls completing the twelfth grade went from none in 1921 to 356 in 1936. Even though the number of boys receiving a state education was always greater than the number of girls, increases in the education of both boys and girls continued until the Allied occupation of 1941 when state action on a number of fronts was interrupted or curtailed. The effect on secondary education was delayed until 1943 for girls when the number of female twelfth-grade graduates dropped from 633 to 472 and until 1944 for boys when the number of male twelfth-grade graduates dropped from 2,703 to 1,575.[17]

The numerical differences between the sexes during the Pahlavi expansion of education do not tell the whole story. As far back as the 1922 attempts to standardize school curricula, notions of gender influenced the state's decision to simplify the program for girls and to include courses in drawing and sewing.[18] Maintaining different curriculum requirements persisted even to higher levels of education. By 1939, out of 170 hours of scheduled instruction in five years of secondary school, girls were to devote 2 to social etiquette, 4 to child rearing, 2 to nursing, 13 to sewing, 9 to handicrafts, 5 to drawing, 6 to housekeeping, and 8 to cooking.[19] In sum, nearly a third of their schooling was devoted to making them better wives, mothers, housekeepers, and hostesses.

As we shall see, especially in regard to women's education, the best elementary and secondary schools during the reign of Reza Shah were considered to be those run by missionaries and minorities. Not until 1940 did the regime bring all of these schools under the direct supervision of the Ministry of Education or close them. However, the Pahlavi regime was very active in standardizing curricula throughout Iran and bringing all schools under centralized national control. For example, there was no mistaking the reach of state authority for the principal of a girls' school in Sabzavar in 1936. She was dismissed by the Ministry of Education in Tehran for resisting unveiling but later was promptly reinstated when she acquiesced (see chapter 4).[20] Aside from nationalizing and centralizing education, most expansion in education during the regime of Reza Shah was in state-run schools, not missionary or private schools. Finally, although the regime centralized administration and standardized curricula throughout Iran before the Allied invasion of 1941, there were still loose ends. It was left to the revived Parliament of the 1940s to define the value of degrees from all the various institutions that had been brought under state control.[21]

The first of Dr. Tusi's pictures, depicting the ten women students on the steps of the medical school at the University of Tehran, suggests a womanly camaraderie, but this was only partially the case. Four of the women were Armenian, and Dr. Maryam Tusi, for one, felt much closer to the Muslim women.[22] They studied at each other's houses. My aunt, the daughter of a general killed in action against a Kurdish rebellion in 1941, was escorted to and from Dr. Tusi's home by a soldier assigned to my grandfather's household. The women stuck together in class to protect their reputations and to enjoy a sense of student fellowship that would not be forthcoming from their male colleagues until four years into the program (see chapter 7).

Although Dr. Tusi entered medicine with a patriotic commitment to serve Iranian women and although she felt close to her fellow Muslim women classmates while in medical school, she mused that she herself was not a typical Iranian but rather a "mixed European/Iranian." Her older brothers had brought her European books and magazines, which she preferred to the Iranian popular press. Feeling alienated from one's own culture could be more pronounced for others. For example, Mehrangiz Dowlatshahi, speaking five years after the founding of the Islamic Republic, admitted to a contempt for Islam as she saw it practiced:

> But my father was against clerics. Sure, he was Muslim but he was very opposed to much of the fakery and showiness and especially the superstitions that were connected with religion. I, too, [felt this way] as a result of his education, as a result of the books of Sadeq Hedayat . . . Of course, on the one hand, during the struggles that we had for the sake of women's issues we were obliged to take Islam's side and say, "No, we don't want anything outside of Islam. Everything we want is part of the same laws of Islam." Now let's just see about those clerics. I'll tell you about them in a minute; we went and saw many of them. For ourselves, we knew that it [Islam] was the cause of women's misfortune already.[23]

Both women retained their Muslim identity (or at least affirmed the Muslim identity of their families) but with some qualification. Dr. Tusi admitted an attraction to another culture, while Dowlatshahi believed that Islamic teaching was manifestly antifeminist, to the point where she chose to misrepresent her feminism rather than seek common ground with her faith. These impulses have been part of the processes of modernization and religious reform in the Middle East for over two centuries. For Akhundzadeh, an atheist and bureaucrat for the Russian Empire, as well as for Kermani, a Babi Iranian expatriate living in the Ottoman Empire, "superstition" meant Islam itself. But for most renewalist thinkers, the line between reforming Islam and forsaking it—modernizing Iranian culture and abandoning it—was problematic. It tended to be either deliberately (and deceitfully) blurred or sincerely rationalized away by those who wanted change.

In 1906, discussions of women's education in Iran's newborn Parliament had provided an important pretext for prominent cleric Shaykh Fazlollah Nuri's break with the renewalist constitutional order in which he used his now-famous "whorehouse school" imagery in the 1907 treatise, *For the Awakening and Removal From Error of Brothers in Religion*.[24] Although an initial supporter of the Constitution and Parliament, Nuri had come to see both as vehicles for Babi corruption of Iranian Islamic society and for Western imperialists' designs upon Iran. It is not an accident that education, the education of women in particular, served as evidence for Nuri's suspicions. In the late nineteenth century, schools for girls tended to be run by French, British, and American missionaries.[25]

Furthermore, as we have already seen, women who spoke out in the press for improvements in women's education often explicitly linked women's progress to renewalist notions of constitutionalism and nationalism. Indeed, "the main social activities of liberal men and women were channeled into the field of education,"[26] a sphere clearly endorsed by the Constitution itself. Therefore, for Shaykh Nuri, women's education was compromised by the influences of foreigners, heretics, and the otherwise misguided among Iran's Muslims. Of course, not all clerics opposed women's education or the Constitution.[27] Even some very conservative voices on the woman question in the Iranian press were not immediately swayed by Shaykh Nuri's rhetoric and condemned him for his break with the Parliament.[28]

In 1923, Ayatollahzadeh Mehdi Khalesi expressed more concern about Iranian Muslim women being educated by missionaries than about women's education per se. In one speech, he demanded that the state open more schools for them in order to counter the missionary threat: "The missionaries taught geography, and we said girls must know geography. As a result, girls have gone to American and other anti-Islamic schools in which they were told that they have the right to [political] representation and were baptized. Sirs! The way of reform is for *us* to build schools for women and tell girls, 'Enter *these* schools.'"[29]

The goal was not only to counter missionary activity but also to counter women's political empowerment. Khalesi's statement linked women's political empowerment and, by extension, the principle of gender equality to Christianity and Western culture. Sentiments such as Khalesi's appeared in the press well into 1924.[30] It did not help matters that American Presbyterian educators viewed Islam with suspicion[31] and that some American women missionaries—both Presbyterian and Baha'i—hoped to instill Iranian women with more progressive (and American) values about gender roles and everything else.[32] Let us recall, for example, that the Iranian women on the editorial board of the longest-running women's magazine, 'Alam-e Nesvan, were all graduates of the American Bethel Girls School in Tehran.

Education and the woman question, then, both helped define the battleground between competing religious and cultural expectations. The education of women became both a symbol of women's emancipation (from a vilified traditional order) and a symbol of men's protection of women (and, with them, a cherished traditional order or, in the case of many renewalist thinkers, a rediscovered "national" culture). In 1927, the Iranian government asserted its control over missionary schools, using its abolishment of extraterritorial legal privileges for foreigners in that same year as a general pretext. The main issue was the Christian content in the curriculum of missionary schools. Ironically, it was the modernizing and westernizing regime of Reza Shah Pahlavi that answered U.S. diplomatic concerns about religious liberty with assertions that in Islam "there is no separation of church and state."[33] By 1929, the Iranian government was threatening to conscript students of the American missionary schools if the schools did not adopt government-mandated curricula.[34] By 1940, all foreign schools except the German school were closed or nationalized. For American Presbyterian missionaries only a school for English-speaking students was allowed.[35]

It was not only a matter of controlling foreign schools at home but also of controlling Iranian students overseas. While the Qajars had been somewhat irregular about funding (and managing) student missions in the nineteenth century, in 1928 the Pahlavi government undertook to send 100 male students per year abroad to receive special training or advanced degrees. A student who stepped out of line while studying abroad could expect to receive a warning from the nearest Iranian legation and to have his funding threatened.[36] While men could find a number of options for secondary and postsecondary education in Iran (even before the formal establishment of the University of Tehran in 1935), women had fewer choices. But women's choices for modern education, even when located in Iran, seemed to take them away from being Iranian or being Muslim. At least, as we shall see, that is how some remembered it.

For secondary (and even elementary) education, Iranian families that desired a modern education for their daughters chose schools run by missionaries or members of Iran's religious minorities. Moloud Khanlari (b. 1920), a woman who was later to become active in the communist Tudeh Party in the 1940s and 1950s, came to Tehran in the 1930s from her hometown of Qazvin to complete her secondary education at the Zoroastrian School.[37] Ozma Adl-Naficy (b. 1920), the daughter of Iranian scholar and bureaucrat Sa'id Naficy, received both her primary and secondary education at the Joan d'Arc School for Girls run by French missionaries in the 1920s and early 1930s.[38] Mehrangiz Dowlatshahi came from an aristocratic, progressive family that started her in Iran's first kindergarten. It was a mixed-gender school, anticipating the Pahlavi regime's efforts to mix kindergartens in 1935. After kindergarten, Dowlatshahi's family seems to have debated whether to send her to a foreign-run school, and, largely because of the objections of Dowlatshahi's mother, they decided against it. Dowlatshahi's mother had been prevented from attending the Ecolé Franco-Persan due to the objection of Dowlatshahi's great-grandfather. "There goes my honor," Dowlatshahi reports her great-grandfather as saying. "You send these two daughters into the street every day? Don't!"[39] The fact that her mother didn't attend the Ecolé Franco-Persan wounded Dowlatshahi's sense of family pride because of the prestigious reputation of the school as being aristocratic and progressive: "Well, of course, not just then but later on also, many girls my mother's age attended it. Not much can be said, a number went, but my mother, unfortunately, did not go. Even though the Hedayat family was one of learning and distinction and members of it were the founders of the Science Ministry and the Education Ministry in Iran and gave their sons the best education, they came up short where their daughters were concerned."[40]

Dowlatshahi's own father persisted in exposing his daughter to a modern, European-style education. He hired a French governess who was eventually dismissed by Dowlatshahi's mother because household servants complained of her being ritually polluting *(najes)*. Ultimately, in 1925 at age six, Mehrangiz was permitted to attend the Zoroastrian School. It is interesting that she remembered the Zoroastrian School as the only Iranian school on a par with foreign schools, saying, "In actuality there were [only] three very good schools for girls at that time, one was Joan d'Arc, one was the American School, and one was the Zoroastrian."[41]

Even after missionary schools had been nationalized, the former status of a school as a missionary or foreign school could define its prestige. The American Bethel School for Girls became the Nurbakhsh Girls' High School. Dr. Tusi, one of the first nine women admitted to University of Tehran Medical School from the ranks of Iranian high school graduates, came to Tehran from Tabriz during World War II and attended Nurbakhsh. She reported feeling "apart" from the richer, Persian-speaking students who always seemed to have "high society" parties to talk about. She came from a self-described upper-middle-class family, and part of what lent prestige to Nurbakhsh in her eyes was the social status of the other students who attended it, in addition to its history as a former American school.

Sattareh Farman Farmaian, the daughter of a Qajar aristocrat whose fortunes were fading fast in the time of Reza Shah, was educated at home before being sent to a Baha'i school, Tarbiyat. When it was closed in 1933 by government order, many members of her large household compound rejoiced, considering the Baha'is to be heretics. She, of course, did not take this view in her memoirs, yet she admitted that Tarbiyat encouraged a different code of social conduct for girls than the secluded ideal championed by her mother: "[At Tarbiyat school] girls had not only been permitted to dance and sing, but even to pray aloud, just as men did. I had reveled in doing things that my mother, had I been so indiscreet as to tell her about them, would have considered immodest enough to rate a sound beating."[42]

Sent to the American Bethel School, instead, Farman Farmaian reports (contrary to Dr. Tusi's later experience) having had some middle-income classmates at the American School, "girls that I would never have met otherwise."[43] Another experience she might not have had without American Bethel was that of exposure to Christian evangelical zeal. Although she asserts that American missionaries were not trying to convert anybody, she recalls, "One of my strongest memories is of morning assemblies in the auditorium. There, after prayers, and after one of the Persian students had read a psalm from the Persian Bible the Presbyterians had translated, Miss Jane [Elizabeth] Doolittle, a bespectacled, authoritative lady of whom everyone stood in awe, would play the piano and we would sing a Christian hymn, also in Persian. Moslems were not required to participate in the prayers or hymn-singing, but I joined in lustily as soon as I picked up the words and soon knew all the hymns by heart."[44]

For other girls, the missionary character of the schools they attended could be problematic. Novelist Simin Daneshvar (b. 1921) attended a British consular school, Mehr-e A'in, in Shiraz before attending High College in Tehran in 1937. She recalled that the language of instruction was in English until the government started its attempts to bring all schools in line with a single, national curriculum.[45] The morality she was taught was based on Bible study. Even when she went to Tehran to attend the High College, she stayed at the American boarding school where "again everything was in English and [linked to] the Bible. Fortunately, we finished the Koran in the College of Literature."[46] In the novel *Savushun,* Daneshvar's alter ego, Zari, challenges her Christian teacher's attempts to devalue Islam and Iranian traditions.[47]

Even those inspired by Western tutelage embraced it with a mix of envy and admiration. Nowhere was this admiration clearer than in an article written in June 1926 by Jamileh Farrokh for *Shafaq-e Sorkh,* entitled "At the American College."[48] Farrokh was an irregular contributor to *Shafaq-e Sorkh* on women's issues. She took the occasion of a graduation ceremony at the Bethel School to lament that Iranian graduates of the school were not really applying their education productively. She, like the antimissionary cleric Khalesi,[49] believed that women's productivity was best confined to housekeeping and raising the children of tomorrow. She had been criticized for these views earlier by a woman reader named Haydeh Khanom. Farrokh used "At the American College" to respond to her: "This woman is also like the other educated women of Tehran who do not listen to straight talk, and who, upon hearing that women in America and Europe are equal in most of their rights to men, want to find equal rights with men without Iranian women obtaining the qualities that European women have."[50]

In other words, Iranian women were not yet good enough to have their rights. Unlike Khalesi, however, Farrokh believed that they would become good enough if they met the standards set by European and American women. However egalitarian Western gender roles may have appeared to some Iranians, American missionaries were not advocates of complete gender equality in theory or in practice. For example, Mehrangiz Dowlatshahi remembers being discouraged by Jane Elizabeth Doolittle herself from pursuing mathematics (for her, a practical step toward studying astronomy, which her father seems to have discouraged), in favor of literature.[51] Even in the freer world of missionary schools, some subjects were less suitable for young women than others.

What should we see in the picture of the ten women medical students on the steps of the University of Tehran? Were they a new generation of independent modern Iranian women, slaves of Western cultural imperialism, or simply decorative symbols of progress that never actually took place? Just as questions of identity were unavoidable for Iranians who embraced modern women's education, so too were tensions about the nature of that training. Was the purpose of education to make women better wives and mothers, or was it to make them something more as it made men more than just husbands and fathers?

The second picture, that of the street demonstration, caught my attention precisely because it seemed so far removed from the "home economics" curriculum of Pahlavi-era girls' education. In it, Dr. Tusi and my aunt seem to have much more on their minds than becoming educated companions for modern husbands. The young women in the protest march—Dr. Tusi and my aunt included—were students from Nurbakhsh High School in their twelfth and final year. They had been recruited for the protest by leftist, first-year medical students to join one of a series of protests that went on during the fall of 1945, demanding that more high school students be admitted to medical school.[52] The protests were successful. Quotas were increased from 150 to 200 students. Did this demonstration mean that Dr. Tusi was inspired by other women activists to go beyond the confines of "state feminism" and protest state policies they opposed? No.

Dr. Tusi avoided politics afterward, as did my aunt. She reported having no interest in politics or women's organizations, defining herself as "just a student." Dr. Tusi considered the leftists to be of a lower class than herself and rougher. By way of contrast, she emphasized how "polite" the march had been. It was no brazen act of rebellion. Her memory of what she did was distant from the more radical interpretations that I might have imposed on what she did. Her medical training and career were a source of great pride and sense of accomplishment; they were not associated in her mind with a more active social or political persona.

It was demanding enough to practice a profession without engaging in politics as well. And the doors to postsecondary education and prestigious professions had only been opened in Iran during the Women's

Awakening. The absence of a higher level of education for women translated into less rigorous secondary education for Iranian women. Even the most privileged women in Iran were aware that the education they could receive there—even at the best schools—was inferior to that made available to men. Sattareh Farmanfarmaian was fourteen when she realized that her education was not putting her on equal footing with her brothers. They were confident athletes, comfortable speaking in foreign languages, and they had visited foreign countries. She may have been attending the best school available to young women in Iran at the time, but her brothers' domestic education was better, and they could study abroad as well. She wrote: "Suddenly, it dawned on me: I was backward. I needed more education, and I wasn't going to get it staying at home. . . . [The] education Dadash and Aziz had received was brilliant. By comparison to them, I felt like an ignorant, untraveled yokel. Shazdeh [her father] wasn't even giving me a governess to teach me etiquette! I was certainly as smart as Aziz—I was the best of any of Shazdeh's children now in school. I should have the same advantages as he, my contemporary and equal. How was I going to get anywhere if I didn't have the best education?"[53]

Even though women had been calling for economic progress through education for a long time[54] (at least since the Constitutional Revolution of 1906 and earlier in the expatriate Iranian press), and male reformers had been calling for it since the mid-nineteenth century, not until 1934 did the government begin floating the idea of higher education for women in parliamentary debates[55] and in the press. From mid-August until the beginning of October 1934, *Ettela'at,* Iran's main daily, printed forty-one letters from readers on the question of higher education for Iranian women. Most (twenty-nine) were against the idea. Opinions were solicited from *Ettela'at*'s readers by an initial letter in which a man, Hosayn 'Ali, presented a debate between himself and his father, Hajj Aqa, over the fate of his sister—was she to be married off or allowed to pursue her dream of a higher education. Taking a hard line against his daughter's education, the family patriarch said:

A woman who has studied politics, who has flown an airplane, who has swum for fifty-four straight hours—what is a man going to do with this houri woman? Leave her to her sweet fancies! A woman must be like an angel in the sky or the beloved of artists and poets before she is worthy of a man's worship. If a woman has a broad chest, bulging muscles, and forelegs like Indian clubs in the *zur-*

khaneh,[56] then what good is she to a man? It is as I said: A woman should be educated enough to discern superstition [from fact], to manage household expenses and inventories, to know how to raise and educate a small child, and to make herself and her man, or rather I should say the family that he founded and created, happy and fortunate by means of her housekeeping and thrift. It is less likely that women who have a higher education will be that way. Therefore, I believe Parvin should marry.[57]

Of course, rather than ask Parvin what she wanted to do, Hosayn 'Ali turned to the readers of *Ettela 'at* for their opinions. Over the next month and half, out of forty-one respondents, twenty-nine essentially agreed with Hajj Aqa,[58] nine basically agreed with Hosayn 'Ali,[59] and three hedged or objected to the premise of his presentation of the problem.[60] This statistically meaningless classification of the responses (if they were indeed unsolicited and not part of any organized publicity campaign and completely forged) does not do justice to the full range of the discussion.

Sometimes, the reasoning invoked by respondents would work at cross-purposes to their stated positions. One woman supported Parvin's right to continue her education by arguing that too much education for women was not a problem, but that too much freedom for women was.[61] Freedom in this instance was interpreted as license to engage in immoral acts inspired in large part by the decadence of Europe, rather than as anything to do with the right to express an opinion or to vote. Sometimes, respondents with opposite positions could claim the same argument. For example, while one woman who supported higher education for women criticized men for not being able to accept women's "entering the arena of social life,"[62] another anonymous respondent argued against higher education for women precisely because men could not accept the idea of women being as educated and capable as they.[63]

Those correspondents who argued against higher education for women were often in full agreement with Hajj Aqa that a woman's place was in the home raising a family and serving her husband. But they also fully accepted the need for educated and well-trained modern mothers to raise a nation of productive patriots, just as had been advocated since the nineteenth century. This important element of modern Iranian womanhood was not in dispute, but now it seemed to mark the limit of what modern Iranian womanhood should be. One correspondent, 'Ala al-Din Farid 'Eraqi, put it bluntly and betrayed his unease with women's deviating from their "main" duty: "It is so clear that a single woman cannot be both a man and a woman and perform the duties of both simultaneously. [She cannot] participate along with men in all the routines of life including the army, war, or working in factories, mines, offices, and laboratories, and at the same time be separately responsible for the normal duties particular to herself such as pregnancy, nursing, raising children, organizing a household, and so on."[64]

Claiming to be inspired by the example of Mrs. Mussolini and encouraged by the policies of the new government of Germany and the intellectuals of France, 'Eraqi concluded that Iran needed to increase its population and to place "marriage above all other considerations."[65] Another correspondent, sympathetic to the desires of women for a higher education, nevertheless also concluded: "As I mentioned earlier, today these dreams are not practical. Today's generation of women must sacrifice themselves for future generations, and beat a trail toward prosperity and suffer so that they [later generations] might enjoy [it]."[66]

It seems that the old "mothers of the nation" argument for the educating of women had almost worked too well. Confronted with the image of powerful European women, the majority of respondents to Hosayn 'Ali's "conundrum" balked. Even those who supported Parvin's right to continue her education often did so without challenging the paramount duty of motherhood. One woman seemed to believe that "unlimited" education meant an education in the domestic sciences, rendering her conclusion that "there are no conceivable limits to education" rather ironic.[67] Another correspondent with a better appreciation of the implications of the term "higher education" challenged the assertion of an earlier correspondent that a woman would simply have no use for more advanced mathematics:

If you believe this then you are completely in error. Proofs and solving geometric cases serve only to strengthen the demonstrative power of the individual. However much extra education a mother may have, that much more will her intellectual horizons widen, and that much further away will she keep from superstitions. . . . It is well known that when the great Greek philosopher Plato was asked, "When should the education of a child begin," he responded, "Twenty years before its birth." Do you understand the meaning of this answer? The point is that first the mother must be completely educated before the child can inherit learning from its mother!![68]

This spirited defense of higher education for women was completely tied to the question of motherhood. The way in which the question exploring the compatibility of highly trained women with the institution of marriage was initially framed succeeded for the most part in preventing a full discussion of the other social implications of professional degrees for women. Discussion was restricted to the implications for the home, and even supporters of higher education for women stayed within this framework. The capable woman from the headlines of Europe ran headlong into the new rhetorical fortifications of male guardianship. Modern Iranian womanhood, at least in this discussion, was to be kept separate from the male spheres of work, government, and, most significantly, war.

Parvin's father's objections notwithstanding, the regime officially endorsed higher education for women one year later, in 1935. The government's new attitude was signaled through press coverage of a Women's Society meeting in November and was part of the general engagement of the woman question by the Pahlavi state in the wake of Gowharshad and before the move to forced unveiling of 7 January 1936 (see chapter 4). As we have seen, Hajer Tarbiyat, the president of the Women's Society, outlined a number of "appropriate careers"—old favorites like typing, bookkeeping, tailoring, handicrafts, and nursing (almost an exact match of the jobs ʿAlam-e Nesvan reported women doing in 1929) and new possibilities such as pharmacology, dentistry, and medicine. She also made clear that she was looking forward to Iranian women having a larger impact on social reforms in Iran, just like American women (see chapter 4).

Supporting women's entrance into society meant, in part, supporting their ability to work for wages. For at least a couple of decades before the Women's Awakening, Iranian women had been entering the workforce as teachers, nurses, journalists, and clerical workers. The only field for which we have employment data is teaching. During the first academic year following the Women's Awakening, 1936–37, there were 3,967 women teachers in Iran—very few of whom would have received much formal training by the state.[69] It was not enough, therefore, for the regime only to ride preexisting trends in women's employment and education. It celebrated the Iranian working woman as had never been done before, through the propaganda of the Women's Awakening.[70] But for there to be images of (as well as some actual) progress in women's employment, it was recognized that there had to be more vocational training and higher education for women.

In the 1936–37 academic year, 80 women entered the University of Tehran. They majored in archaeology (1), foreign languages (20), "special literature class" (37), Persian literature (5), mathematics (13), natural science (1), and philosophy and rhetoric (3). In addition, 75 women were enrolled in the government midwifery school.[71] The next year, the number of women students increased in all the aforementioned majors except mathematics and included additional majors (physics and chemistry, history, geography, and "special science class").[72] In the 1937–38 academic year, women gained entrance to programs in pharmacology (4 women) and dentistry (10 women).[73] In the 1940–41 academic year, 89 women were studying medicine at the University of Tehran,[74] though that number dropped to 42 in 1944 and to none in 1945.[75] No women graduates of the medical school are recorded in government statistics until the 1947–48 academic year, at which time there were five.[76]

In the 1934 debate about women's higher education in the pages of *Ettela'at,* opponents presented women's higher education as being incompatible with marriage. In a society where even educated women of the elite could marry in their teens, marriage could cut both ways. Badry Kamrooz-Atabai (b. 1927), for example, had to abandon formal schooling because "they gave me a husband in the beginning of [my] adolescence."[77] Moloud Khanlary did not go to college "because I married very young," but she was "granted" tutors and benefited from the private instruction of such luminaries of Iran's literary and political landscape as Malek al-Sho'ara Bahar (d. 1952) and 'Ali Akbar Dehkhoda (d. 1955).[78] Mehrangiz Dowlatshahi, on the other hand, was able to pursue the study of sociology and mass media in Germany precisely because her husband had been sent there to oversee the acquisition of German steel mill technology by the Iranian government in 1939.[79] Dr. Tusi's own parents preferred that she study medicine in Iran rather than abroad before she was married.

Although girls were tacitly prepared for marriage in school as part of their curriculum, it seems that schools were not imagined as places to facilitate and supervise courtship. The sexual maturity of students was denied even in government statistics. For example, although graduates of medical school would be in their early-to mid-twenties by the time they finished medical school (it was a six-year program, entered directly from high school), they were referred to as "boys" and "girls" in government statistics, as were all university students. The degree to which this convention in government statistics reflected a patriarchal attitude of the state, of institutions of learning, of society, or of all three is hard to evaluate. However, by considering students as boys and girls rather than as men and women, or even young men *(javan)* and young women *(dushizeh),* the potential social interaction between male and female students is rendered more innocent and less sexually charged.

The official image of men and women in school together evoked a sense of professional or intellectual collaboration rather than one of casual socializing. This is certainly true of yearbook images of extracurricular activities at the University of Tehran.[80] In the 1937–38 academic year, women held offices in the Literary, Forensics, and Yearbook clubs for the first time. The previous year, women had already entered the Foreign Relations, Sports, Library, Theater, and Music clubs, and women's membership in the executive committees of all these clubs (except the Library Club) increased in the 1937–38 academic year. No woman became president of a student organization during this time. In the Scientific Terminology Club, no women at all participated. The group dynamics of the men and women in these student organizations remains a matter of speculation for the time being, but we can infer that women were not expected to lead an organization in which men participated. Although Simin Daneshvar was the Second Secretary of the Foreign Relations Society in the 1937–38 academic year—the only woman officer of the club[81]—she makes no reference to the club in her recollections of her time at the University of Tehran. Formal student organizations seem not to have been emphasized in other branches of higher education or to have had much impact in the 1940s after the Women's Awakening project itself was left to wither on the vine. Informal socializing between the sexes was rare and problematic. In this exchange with Habib Ladjevardi, Mehrangiz Dowlatshahi clearly uses memories of such socializing to highlight the enlightened status of her family while still chafing against the memory of boundaries that did exist for her:

A. Yes, we were in Shemran when my father had a stroke. It was really a great sorrow for me. Under his tutelage I was really very free to learn to think and to live. Now, one cannot say "very free" about that time, but anyway . . .

Q. In relation to the times, then.

A. In relation to the times. *For example, just the [little] extent that we were able to socialize with our classmates, that by itself was a lot for the time* [emphasis added].[82]

Related to the question of marriage was the question of motherhood. Prior to the Women's Awakening, opponents of higher education for women had argued that a woman with too much education would not settle for the rigors and monotony of child rearing (after all, men did not) and would choose instead to devote her time to a rewarding career. Once the regime had committed itself to higher education for women, however, it was necessary in the propaganda of the Women's Awakening to place motherhood and careers in harmonious balance. During the first few months of the Women's Awakening in the winter of 1936, propaganda such as this passage from the pages of *Ettela 'at* portrayed a career outside the home as being *essential* to the success of modern Iranian motherhood: "What kind of mother could raise the [educated] woman and the [patriotic and well-raised] child that we have imagined? Is it a mother who sits at home and dons a veil, or a mother who enters the arena of life like a lioness, and who sings them lullabies of patriotism and sacrifice for the homeland while rocking their cradles on long nights?"[83]

If the image of a lullaby-singing lioness seemed implausible to critics of women's education, it could seem no less so to Iranian women who did pursue careers in the wake of the Women's Awakening. As an extern in pediatrics, Dr. Tusi would stay up all night researching conditions of patients she had seen during her hospital shift. While this extra effort certainly benefited her patients, her exertions were intended also to impress her supervisor during rounds the following morning. If her case presentation elicited an approving smile from her supervisor, she knew the work had been worth it. Was this truly "extra" work? No. She did it with the clear impression that it was expected of the best students. The pace of medical school and medical training was such that an aspiring "lioness" could not expect to be "rocking cradles" on long nights. She needed to work. Marriage to another University of Tehran Medical School graduate enabled Dr. Tusi to travel to America, receive additional training (as her husband did), and begin practicing in the United States. Eventually, she changed her specialty from obstetrics to pathology. She did this not to challenge professional limits for women in medicine but to have more time to raise her children.

Of course, state efforts to propagandize about ideal motherhood depended, in part, on the image of women who supported the Women's Awakening as members of the Women's Society. But those women who attended meetings, organized events, and provided lectures on a variety of domestic topics and public hygiene in support of the best intentions of the Women's Awakening could be stretched too thin, finding it hard to live up to anyone's standard of ideal motherhood. Pari Saberi's mother was an active member of the Women's Society in Kerman in the 1930s. One day, young Pari insulted a boy in the family. Furious, her mother chased her through the yard and grabbed her as she jumped into a shallow pool to escape, at which point the comical scene becomes a little monstrous: "She pulled me out and, like this, she pricked me with a pin on my lips three or four times, [saying] 'Don't talk bad.' This was good and bad because now I think it took away a measure of my courage in confronting people. But as a matter of discipline I think it was, well, correct that I should not, at least, swear [at people]—though maybe I should have. I don't know [laughs]."[84]

Aside from one instance of rather abusively correcting her daughter, Mrs. Saberi may have unintentionally sent a negative message about women and work. Or perhaps that message was already ingrained: "I mean, I don't know, they had set up a society at that time. Was it the Women's Society? I don't recall exactly. She [her mother] was working there and I, as a child, I always thought she should not leave the house. She should always be in the house and now, I think, I'm saying [to myself] 'Well, what can this mother do?' Because, I have also gone and done exactly the same thing with my own daughter. I mean, well, I had work; I went out, but when I return to my own past I say that, 'Well, at that moment I really needed my mother to be next to me.' How can this matter be resolved? I don't know."[85]

Traditional family roles asserted themselves in education policies, in the propaganda of the Women's Awakening, and in the lives of even the most professionally ambitious women. Behind the image of women marching in the streets for change were women's connections to family roles that undermined their actual independence from male guardianship. But how did male guardianship assert itself outside the immediate spheres of marriage and family? Did women remember better or worse treatment at the hands of instructors than did their male peers? What kind of relationships did women students have with their male peers?

In reference to these questions, the third picture was the most misleading of all. The country outing of men and women medical students captured in the third picture came only after four years of medical school. During those years, the men, at best, kept their distance from their female classmates and, at worst, verbally harassed them. At first Dr. Tusi would not elaborate on the nature of the abuse inflicted by male classmates. She would say only that they were "naughty," followed by a short, embarrassment-tinged laugh. Later she offered that sometimes a boy would be attracted to one of the women. If that woman did not show any interest, the boy might start saying "bad things" about her. But of course a woman could not show interest in the men (in public), or her reputation would be in shambles. It was an awkward double bind. A woman's reputation for modesty was crucial to her ability to work among men, and, at least in Dr. Tusi's case, it could also define her sense of identity (see chapter 7).

Dr. Tusi did not report any mistreatment from her professors at the University of Tehran. Rather, she felt the women students were treated more gently and respectfully, enjoying the address of *khanom* rather than the curt barking of their last name endured by the men in class or on rounds. At the same time, she was encouraged by everyone to be an "ob/gyn" because, as she herself agreed, "At that time no man would go to a woman doctor." In this broad, cultural sense, she felt that the practice of medicine in Iran was a "closed system."

Yet, when asked if she had any mentors in medical school, she initially responded, "I didn't want a mentor; didn't need guidance; I relied on books—that was enough." This forceful statement of independence and self-reliance was qualified later in the interview. She remembered, with fondness, the support and encouragement of her brothers, all of whom were highly educated professionals. One of her brothers threw a large party on the occasion of her gaining acceptance to medical school. Her experience stands in some contrast to Simin Daneshvar, who enjoyed an intimate and quasi-familial mentoring relationship with her dissertation supervisor, Fatemeh Sayyah. She described Sayyah's death in 1946 as one of the "[hard] slaps of fate" of her life although she made no mention of Sayyah's political activism with the Women's Party and any influence that may have had upon her.[86] Nonetheless, it seems that women who enjoyed some kind of mentoring or support from friends and family had the best chance of taking advantage of the opportunities the state had made available to them or in pursuing their own academic ambitions. Badry Kamrooz-Atabai, for example, benefited a great deal from the mentoring of historians, eventually earning a doctorate in history. She expressed her appreciation of them in familial terms: "I had a husband. I had children. I had a life. I could not sit in class. The great professors who are now no longer in the bonds of life—and I am very sorry about that fact—they gave me a great deal of help. *I mean, really I must say that each was a loving father to me.* My first professors were Professor Habib Allah Nurbakht and Professor Ibrahim Purdavud, because I really loved history. Then, whatever Iranian history I studied—before Islam, after Islam—I studied with those two professors. They guided me and they directed me so that I would not let go of my studies" [emphasis added].[87]

Mentoring could be a complex process, crossing gender and cultural lines. As the following passage shows, Mehrangiz Dowlatshahi's decision not to pursue mathematics was not a simple one. She, like Sattareh

Farmanfarmaian, bitterly resented the fact that boys received better training in the sciences and math. Responding to her talent and aptitude, her mentors encouraged her at first but ultimately steered her away from the sciences and the potential of earning the equivalent of a "male degree":

A. Miss Doolittle was very kind to me. She said, "Since you study so little chemistry in Iranian schools, I will advise you. Come study chemistry with the eleventh-grade class which I teach myself." It was really good, too, because in the girls' school they taught so little. The curriculum was just weaker at girls' schools of the time. For example, our math at the eleventh grade was like that of the boys in ninth grade. Our teacher at that time, Mirza Mohammad Naraqi, God bless him, would give me extra lessons. For example, one time he gave me a few problems and said, "Take these and let me see how far you get in solving them." The next morning I came and said I'd solved all four. He said, "Oh, you solved all four? I gave these to the boys' class and maybe only two people solved all four." He gave me extra lessons and would encourage me, saying, "Next year, come study some more and go take the test for twelfth-grade boys. [This way] you'll have a diploma that is worth something everywhere."

Q. You'll have a male diploma [diplom-e mardaneh].

A. A secondary school diploma, already. Because that diploma [from the Zoroastrian girls' school] was a secondary one but it just wasn't enough. Of course, they taught a little housekeeping and, I don't know, psychology and things like that but nothing suitable. . . . But, due to Naraqi's encouragement, my head was very much into mathematics . . . . At the American School, as a result of getting acquainted with English literature, my thoughts began to change [about a career as an astronomer]. Among them [i.e., the teachers], Miss Doolittle encouraged me not to always be thinking of mathematics.[88]

This may have been because Doolittle had low expectations of the Iranian girls she tried to educate. She felt that the 1,000 girls who had received diplomas "through the years" had not done much with them. It was as though she hung onto the notion that nothing had changed since 1891 when American Bethel began to offer twelfth-grade diplomas to girls. Education was a matter of personal achievement, not a step toward professional or political empowerment:

Q. And who was honoring it [the twelfth-grade American Bethel diploma]?

A. There wasn't anybody to honor it, at that time. The girls never applied for any work or anything; it was simply their pride and joy, that they had graduated. The diploma that we had in those days had a nice picture of the school, a nice little round one up at the top of it. They were very proud of those. To begin with, of course, they didn't have any alumnae association, because there weren't enough alumnae to have such. I think it was in 1915 that they first started an alumnae association, and there were only six graduates at that time that were members of it.[89]

Despite Doolittle's somber assessment, time did not stand still. Women entered the ranks of skilled professionals throughout the first half of the twentieth century. And, despite the propaganda of the Women's Awakening, "the professional woman" did not make her appearance only with policies of the Women's Awakening. The Pahlavi regime's contribution to the rise of the professional woman rested as much on celebrating and defining the image of the modern Iranian woman at work as in encouraging certain employment trends for women.

Celebrating the Professional Woman

As we have seen, education for women had long been advocated for the creation of better mothers and wives. However, within a few months of its first issue in 1910, *Danesh* began to advocate the next step for women's advancement in a modern Iranian society—feminine professions, specifically nursing and teaching. Although teaching was to become increasingly emphasized as a career path, nursing was the first profession to be advocated in a detailed fashion in the pages of *Danesh*. It initially discussed nursing in the context of family hygiene, not as a profession.[90] But on 1 March 1911, an article entitled "The Nurses of England" talked in no uncertain terms about nursing as a job and used the familiar tactic of discussing European development as a model for Iranian society and for Iranian women.[91] The article was reprinted in 1914 in the next major women's magazine, *Shokufeh*.[92] Interestingly, although the article discussed training requirements and fees, duties, hours, and vacation time, it did not discuss the average salary of nurses in England. Nonetheless, the description of duties made it quite clear that nursing was being discussed as a profession to be undertaken at a hospital or doctor's office but not as part of the domestic activities of a wife or mother.

Teaching was discussed in the context of the need for women's education and the establishment of women's schools and less as a profession with which a young lady might support herself. However, because many of the first schools for women and girls were staffed and managed by other women, and they—particularly the principals—were the visible advocates of women's education in the press, the idea of Iranian women as teachers was available quite early. But discussions about teaching focused less on professional considerations than on more abstract issues. For example, in 1913 an article in *Shokufeh* argued that any teacher must be the kind of person who can command respect in the classroom and must be religious so as to protect the morality of the students in his or her charge.[93]

In the spring of 1916, *Shokufeh* ran a series of fresh articles on nursing.[94] The series explicitly viewed nursing as an exclusively female profession[95] and declared nurses to be more important than doctors. While doctors only attended patients for a few minutes, nurses were responsible for their care twenty-four hours a day. Furthermore, doctors' orders were implemented by nurses.[96] Thus it was nurses who had to establish affectionate relationships with patients so as to secure their cooperation and help their recovery[97] and nurses who made the actual difference between life and death for a patient.[98] While it might seem that these observations point to an increased respect for women though nursing, many of the old suspicions about women's potential for moral weakness and creating mischief were applied to these female professionals as well.

For example, because of the nurse's sensitive position with respect to the patient, she had to be a woman of strong moral character; for *Shokufeh,* this meant she had to be a woman of faith.[99] If she were not a woman of faith, she might be tempted by bribes to poison a wealthy patient. The article asserted, "A nurse without religion would have no compunction [about this], like women who kill their husbands or children who kill their fathers for the same motive [i.e., greed]."[100] Furthermore, she would better be able to handle the physically intimate duties of washing and dressing patients if she were indoctrinated from the beginning that she was doing God's work.[101] In addition to her religiosity, the nurse had to be discreet because often a delirious patient would blurt out personal or family secrets. These secrets could "impinge upon the family honor, and revealing [them] could cause murder, treason, corruption, or discord, or could damage the reputation and morals of the patient."[102]

Thus, aside from her nurturing role that paralleled that of a mother, the nurse became a crucial element in the maintenance of the family honor of the patient. When the patient had taken leave of his senses, the nurse was to protect his secrets and therefore his well-being, as the Koran would have her protect her husband's honor and wealth during his absence.[103] In the example of nursing, then, we can clearly observe the tension between modern Iranian womanhood, which in this case valued women as indispensable to the practice of modern medicine, and male guardianship, which could not trust the nurse except by understanding her in terms of a familial metaphor and the moral controls associated with that metaphor.

Nonetheless, *Shokufeh* did become a forum for the advocacy of broader professional and economic opportunities. Earlier in the spring of 1916, the principal of the Towfiq School contributed an article defending the rights of women to engage in a variety of modest careers, vocational and professional.[104] He argued that although there were many women who were only able to handle housework and although that was certainly an honorable occupation, there were other women who squandered their potential by idling away their free time or refusing to work in order to guard their sexual innocence. He countered this concern by extolling the moral virtues of productivity: "It is held that women should not do work contrary to their innocence and chastity. But can you call a woman who tailors at home and is participating in her husband's livelihood unchaste?! Can you call a woman of today unveiled who like ancient women makes her way by spinning and weaving and in so doing lessens her husband's toil?! Is it impossible for women of the utmost innocence and chastity to work in teaching and educating young women? Of course it is possible! Anyone who thinks about this for a bit will affirm that work does not make a woman unchaste, but rather it increases her chastity and makes her modesty more complete."[105]

The entry of European women workers into state bureaucracies did not go unnoticed by *Shokufeh*. It reported that nearly 4 percent of France's four million government workers were women who were employed at the Ministry of Defense, on the railroads, at elementary and secondary schools, and in government factories.[106] However, rather than use these facts to inspire women to public service, the male author chose simply to make an unfavorable comparison between Iranian women and their

French sisters: "The aforementioned is not in any way expected of honorable Iranian ladies. It is merely hoped that they strive in their education and mastery of practical affairs so that at least they can administer their own homes."[107]

Notwithstanding the preference that women stay at home to tend to their families, the press in the twenties revealed a wider range of professional possibilities for women. Looking to Europe, for example, *Shafaq-e Sorkh* ran an article about the possibility of German policewomen in 1926.[108] The creation of a corps of policewomen was under consideration in the Reichstag, and the article speculated that the women would have to be uniformed although they would most certainly not be armed. Further, they would be responsible for monitoring the activities of women and girls and would turn lawbreakers over to "the constabulary." This tentative challenge to a male paramilitary preserve was portrayed as a radical step but was also a potential model for the modern Iranian woman.

Press discussions of the woman question in the 1920s created an expectation (dreaded and reviled by some) that the modern Iranian woman would be employed. Of course, most women had always worked to supplement the family income, but the notion of a woman as a highly trained professional was evolving in the public mind in the 1920s and was modeled on examples from Europe and America. As we have seen, the idea of a woman professional is what eventually drove the opening of higher education to women, but before there was much in the way of professional training for women in Iran, there were women professionals—doctors, nurses, teachers. Two themes followed this professional and civic expansion of modern Iranian womanhood into the 1930s: (1) a sense of inferiority with respect to the professional progress of European and American women and (2) a concern with distinguishing male from female professions. The messages about economic empowerment could be mixed. On the one hand, it was clearly portrayed as the key to women's success in America, Europe, Turkey, and Japan.[109] On the other hand, Iranian women were discouraged from crass displays of material wealth as though that were the only purpose to which they might apply their income.[110] Furthermore, while *'Alam-e Nesvan* championed the long-term potential of Iranian women, there was some degree of resignation about their abilities at the time. 'Effat Sami'ian's article on women's economic progress around the world admonished middle- and upper-class women not to think of work as "base and only for the third class." She suggested that they take up tailoring at home in their spare time and that there were decent employment prospects in nursing, medicine, and midwifery.[111]

Similarly, in talking about the industrious women of Europe, Rezazadeh Shafaq seemed to chastise Iranian women for their laziness as much as attempt to inspire them.[112]

In response to an essay contest in 1931 and 1932, women published articles in 'Alam-e Nesvan about their professional options. One option discussed was nursing, and here it was acknowledged that Iranian women were already entering this profession under the auspices of government programs and American missionary hospitals.[113] Another essay advocated that women could work as administrators in settings (night schools, hotel kitchens, laundries, housekeeping classes, hospitals, girls' schools, and charitable organizations) where "men did not participate."[114] A woman named Heshmat Hadashian noted that, although women had ruled kingdoms in the past and participated in a wide variety of professions, Iranian women were only recently "awakening" to their rights and duties.[115] Hadashian excluded Iranian women from political careers because they were not as educated and advanced as Europeans and also because such careers were inappropriate in the Iranian context: "We should not blindly follow them [Europeans] and, like a crow learning the ways of the partridge, give up our ancient customs. We must, then, not say that because, for example, English women can be members of Parliament or because they have put women in charge of ministries in Russia that women would be responsible for such affairs in Iran."[116]

Hadashian then enumerated appropriate professions for Iranian women. They could be doctors, dentists, nurses, teachers, principals of schools for girls and small children, and businesswomen. Their participation in offices was limited to "typing, translating, and such."[117] Women writers and journalists were to make other women aware of their rights and duties. At the top of her list of professions, even though she acknowledged that it was somewhat beside the point, Hadashian named housekeeping as the "most necessary and most honorable occupation."[118] Thus, the modern Iranian woman was imagined as segregated from or subordinated to men in every possible career path. Meanwhile, the modern American woman was flying airplanes.[119]

In the early 1930s, however, the idea of a woman professional working in a government office was not publicly embraced by the regime. Just before 'Alam-e Nesvan's essay contest regarding "suitable professions," two women decided to force the issue of women's employment in government offices in the spring of 1931. They submitted applications for clerical positions that had opened up at the Ministry of Economics.[120] Officials dithered for a while, searching for a specific reason to turn them down.

Finally, they did so by arguing that employing women was "not advisable at the present time."

Ironically, as American consul Charles C. Hart noted in his report on the incident, there already was a woman working for the Ministry of Economics. Her name was Zohreh Haidari, and her professional success had not come easily. Raised in Russia, the widow of a Russian killed during the Bolshevik Revolution, she fled to Iran.[121] After four months of wearing a veil (for the first time) and residing in her family's compound, she threw off her veil and obtained a job at the Ministry of Public Works as a typist— a feat she accomplished after tireless lobbying of the right people including then prime minister Mohammad 'Ali Foroughi. Not content with this success, she made a bid to join Hasan Taqizadeh as a member of the Iranian delegation to the Philadelphia Sesquicentennial Exposition. Although rebuffed by the cabinet, she left Iran on her own to catch up with the Iranian delegation in Paris en route for the United States. Members of the delegation then advocated her position to the government, and the government relented. She was still functioning as trade representative in 1931 when Hart made reference to her in his memorandum. The hypocrisy and conservatism that led to the denial of employment to these women seeking positions as simple typists was to crumble during the Women's Awakening. Women's Awakening propaganda was to embrace aggressively the "professional woman" while still seeking to remind her of her ultimate duties as a wife and mother. And yet, the case of Zohreh Haydari illustrated the fact that to occupy a professional position in the 1920s and 1930s was to act "foreign." As Sheehan observed:

> The difficulty with which she brought even the most intelligent of the Tehran leaders round to her plan displays more than anything else which came under my observation the Persian frame of mind with regard to women. Many Persians of the court and government seemed to me to be positively terrified by [Zohreh Haydari] . . . I saw her talking to Modarres . . . one day at a gathering of ministers; it seemed to me that old Modarres was in a perfect panic fright, afraid to even look at her face and afraid to answer what she said to him. To a man like Modarres there is something awe-inspiring, not to say demoniacal, in the idea that a Persian woman—a pure blood Persian woman—could have a mind of her own.[122]

Sheehan's misreading of Modarres's effort to follow Koranic injunctions to lower his gaze (he was a *mollah*, after all) when dealing with a woman (to say nothing of an unveiled woman) as a "perfect panic" should not distract us from an essential truth. Zohreh Haydari was likely perceived as foreign by her behavior as much as by the fact that she knew Russian better than Persian. In the end, her determined choice to leave Iran for the United States (albeit as a representative of her country) was a telling one.

It was not only women's magazines like 'Alam-e Nesvan that sought to assimilate images of women at work into Iranian culture. One magazine that anticipated the style of later Pahlavi propaganda was Sayf Azad's Iran-e Bastan (Ancient Iran), misleadingly titled since it was very much a magazine devoted to current affairs when it appeared in 1933. Azad was a Nazi, and his magazine looked for common ground between the Pahlavi regime and Nazi Germany. It was suppressed by the regime in 1935. Stuffed with pictures, Iran-e Bastan was in a position to show its readers what it meant by progress.

Despite its clear preference for women in their domestic role,[123] Iran-e Bastan depicted them as capable of much more and presented numerous examples of vigorous, active European women including a picture of a German woman parachutist[124] and a member of a Nazi motorbike club for women.[125] Pictorial advertisements for women's swimwear[126] complemented pictures of European women athletes and an article in support of female athleticism as part of a "fit" society.[127] This advocacy of athleticism was well anticipated by the Iranian expatriate and domestic press of the 1920s, but by summoning only European, and primarily German, examples of this athleticism Iran-e Bastan duplicated and propagated in Iran the fascist fascination with fitness that had evolved as part of modern European culture.[128]

Another way in which Iran-e Bastan emphasized the ability of women was to highlight prominent women in the Third Reich and elsewhere. These women were featured in a frequent but irregular section that, as in Iranshahr in the 1920s, was entitled "Women's World" (jahan-e zanan). For example, on 26 August 1933 the magazine printed the picture of a woman identified only as the person under whom all German women's groups had been subordinated.[129] A few months later, Henni Warringhoff, the head of the National German Women's Sports Organization, was pictured and featured along with writer Gabriella de Reuter. On the same page, a conference of the leaders of the girls' Hitler Youth groups was featured with a picture of uniformed girls participating in a gathering that gave the impression of a legislative meeting.[130]

These rather specific images of women functioning as administrators (however secondary) in the admired Third Reich were certainly an elaboration of the image of the professional woman that had been introduced by *Danesh* and *Shokufeh* just two decades before. And these professional images were placed against a backdrop of very public involvement by women in civic and political affairs. A French woman journalist was pictured making a speech in which she reportedly called for world disarmament.[131] Mrs. Goebbels is pictured helping her infamous husband, the Nazi minister of propaganda, by recording a radio spot.[132] A group of German city women was pictured helping with the harvest to help feed the poor, under the caption, "Worthy of the Attention of the Honorable Municipal Workers and Patriotic Statesmen of Iran."[133]

Assertive, industrious women could distinguish themselves in a variety of professions. One article featured a British police commander, a German clergywoman, American ambassador to Denmark Ruth Owen, and a host of other women making their marks in professions that were previously exclusively male.[134] Women were even shown as being capable of serving as soldiers in war—a marked elaboration upon the image of women supporting a war effort as had been portrayed in *Shokufeh*.[135] The "capable woman" in *Iran-e Bastan* was athletic, was educated, served in a variety of professions, was involved in the world outside her home, and was most definitely not from Iran. This was rather pointedly emphasized in a photo spread on technological advances showing European women enjoying a host of domestic and office conveniences from typewriters to electric irons. To bait Iranian national pride, the headline read, "Just a few other examples of things people today are using in their daily lives, and of which we Iranians are deprived."[136]

Women's Awakening propagandists worked very hard to make "the professional woman" an acceptable and even honorable aspect of modern Iranian womanhood. Like the earlier efforts of *Iran-e Bastan,* women's professional progress was linked to images of technical progress and prosperity—a prosperity from which Iran was "no longer" deprived. In 1939, Mohammad Hejazi's *Iran-e Emruz* (Today's Iran) appeared as the jewel in the crown of Pahlavi periodical press propaganda. The images of Iranian women in *Iran-e Emruz* were full of professional possibilities. Iranian women competed in athletic competitions (see illustration 6.4),[137] took college entry exams,[138] studied in laboratories (illustration 6.5),[139] flew airplanes (illustration 6.6),[140] worked in factories,[141] worked as nurses,[142] performed in the arts,[143] and received achievement awards for government service.[144] In many cases, women were pictured alongside men to emphasize the idea of the sexes working together shoulder to shoulder for the progress of the country.

a

b

c

6.4. Exercising for the nation-state: *a*, German Olympians pictured in *Iran-e Bastan,* 12 November 1934, 8; *b* and *c*, from *Iran-e Emruz* 1, no. 2/3 (April/June 1939): 23, and 2, no. 4 (June/July 1940): 7. They are similar in that they portray exhibitions of feminine fitness in the service of the nation. By permission of MEDOC, University of Chicago.

6.5. *Iran-e Emruz* 2, no. 11 (January/February 1941): 11. This photograph portrays women students working in a lab alongside men. Nevertheless, a man is pictured overseeing the process. By permission of MEDOC, University of Chicago.

Of all of these images, perhaps the most spectacular was that of women pilots. A 25-year-old clerk, Sadiqeh Dowlatshahi, was coming down the stairs from her office at the Treasury Ministry in Tehran when she heard a young newspaper boy announce, "By Order of His Majesty, Ever Powerful, Reza Shah the Great, a flight school has been opened and women, girls, and young men all may come and learn."[145] Born in 1914 to a Baha'i family, Dowlatshahi had attended the Tarbiyat School until the age of thirteen, when she accompanied her mother and brother to Beirut. Upon her return to Iran in 1932, she finished eleventh grade by attending night school, learned to type at a typewriter shop, and took a job with the National Bank of Iran (where her brother worked). Soon after starting there, she heard of an opening with the Anglo-Persian Oil Company in Abadan. She went there and worked as a typist in the translation department—one of the first Iranian women to work for the company. She returned to Tehran in 1936.

In 1938, she took a job with the Treasury Ministry after passing a typing exam—now open to male and female candidates. She was unusual in that she had always worked by choice and not from financial necessity, but, on that day in 1940, the newspaper boy seemed to be responding to

ابن یکی در انتظار نوبة خود بی تاب و الان است

6.6. *Iran-e Emruz* 2, no. 1 (March/April 1940): 36, 37. Iranian women pilots, who, as the Iranian women in the lab, are being helped and supervised by men. *Lower right:* The caption reads, "This one waits her turn eagerly." *Top left,* Sadiqeh Dowlatshahi sitting behind her instructor in a Tigermoth training plane (by permission of MEDOC, University of Chicago). *Lower left,* Sadiqeh Dowlatshahi, ca. 1940. In contrast to most public images of women pilots, this private portrait emphasizes a woman's personal achievement. By permission of Sadiqeh Dowlatshahi.

a long-cherished hope of hers: to fly. She recalled, "I would always think— I mean before this [boy] was shouting—'Would it be possible, could I fly?' I saw the planes that went up above. 'Is this possible? Such a thing is not possible. I, we, cannot fly.'—In one moment, I saw [the boy], took it [the newspaper], got a look at the address, and did not dither around."[146] She ran to the address given for the flight academy, the former house of Mr. 'Ala al-Dowleh on Sa'di Street, and encountered her first obstacle: soldiers who had not heard the news about the flight academy. She was unde-

6.7. The caption reads, "Brigadier General Nakhjavan, representative of the Ministry of War, presents the first young woman pilot with a silver vase." This woman appears to be Sadiqeh Dowlatshahi (although her profile is not completely visible). Dowlatshahi was married at the time, so it may have been more appropriate to call her *khanom* (lady) or *zan* (woman/wife) rather than *dushizeh* (virgin, young woman). It is interesting here that piloting is given a military and masculine air by the presence of Nakhjavan and, simultaneously, the military/masculine image is "softened" by the award of a silver vase, which has domestic and ornamental implications.

terred: "I took one look at this and went in. 'Well, where are you going, Miss?'"

Dowlatshahi recalled, "I said—I opened the newspaper and said, 'What's this?' He said, 'Well, man, I mean, you who are so little?' Really, I was very tiny . . . They said, 'Girl, child, you are just a child. Go and drink your milk!' I said, 'Stop talking nonsense [*mozakhraf nagu*]. I can go in.' I went [in]."[147]

The director's office was at the end of a hall, also flanked by soldiers. They teased her as well, but let her through. A servant showed her into the office, and at the desk was Dr. Mohammad Mosaddeq, the future prime minister of Iran. Turning on the charm, he tried to dissuade her as well:

He stood up and said, "Hello, Little Miss. How are you? Do you have a request?" I said, "Well, yes. Nobody comes here without something to say. Of course I have some business." I showed him the newspaper. He said, "Eh! You want to sign up, too!?" He was so well spoken and kind that I will never forget [it]. "Miss, you want to sign up?" I said, "Yes." He said, "Bravo. God's blessing. But you are a such a tiny little person now—I must tell you that flying airplanes requires big people." I said, "Man, no, look, tiny people [can] do it better." He said, "God's blessing. God's blessing." Then, he called for—no, then he said, "Let me tell you one thing, dear child. My daughter, these planes—all of them—are the most damaged and junky German planes"—they sent German and French [planes]— "You will go up, hit the ground, and die. What kind of business is this?" I said, "Doctor, sir?" I placed my hand on my chest, "Doctor, sir, a person—a human dies once, right?" He said, "No—twice is impossible, just once." I said, "Either I die on the ground, fall to the ground and die, or I have an automobile accident, or it is possible I'll die in bed if I get sick. Well, now I'll die in a plane. Does it make a difference?" He said, "BRAVO. I have no answer for you. Come here!" He called somebody in, "Come here and take a picture." I became the first student.[148]

Her eldest brother was not pleased to hear of his sister being the first person to register at the flight academy. But his objections were silenced by their mother who said, "It will be a source of pride for us."[149] There were no family objections to her course of action, and, now that she had registered, there were certainly no official objections. In fact, the government paid all of Dowlatshahi's flight academy expenses. Her office was notified as to which days she was to be excused from work to go for flight training. Depending on where she was, a car would pick her up from home or from work and take her to the airfield at Dowshan Tepe. Typically, they were scheduled for three half-hour flights per week. Sadiqeh Dowlatshahi took her first solo flight after only twelve flight hours, learning a variety of aerial stunts as part of her training—she was particularly fond of flying upside down. In the first weeks of training, Reza Shah was every bit the hands-on monarch as he came to watch the five women and six young men of the first class at the flight academy train. His presence had a profound effect on Dowlatshahi: "Whenever His Majesty was there, they would tell us to get started quickly and to start flying . . . This man was so . . . he wanted to see [our] progress—do you understand? He wanted to see the people, see the ideas of the young people [so much] that he would come to the airport. No one else would do something like this, and [all] to encourage us."[150]

Dowlatshahi described the whole enterprise as "tashviqi," for encouragement—she was never under the impression that she or any of her fellow students would *work* as pilots. Although the regime provided thorough and identical training to the men and women at the flight academy, it published pictures of the women flight students. Already a working woman with a modern education, Dowlatshahi could embody a bolder image of modern Iranian womanhood as a pilot. Of course, she could have done that by simply donning a flight suit and sitting in an airplane, as she is pictured doing in the pages of *Iran-e Emruz*. But it was clearly important that there be substance to the image. Like the American women in the pages of *'Alam-e Nesvan* in 1930, it was now Iranian women who mastered the very modern art of piloting aircraft. These images of women's progress no longer had to be imported from abroad to encourage Iranian women.

Despite these propaganda efforts, it remained true that the earliest generation of Iranian women professionals, just like the first women recipients of modern education, represented a foreign element in Iranian society. The first modern women professionals did not receive their training in Iran, and some, like Fatemeh Pakravan, had been away from Iran for much of their adolescence. What occasioned Pakravan's emigration from Iran was her father's separation from her mother, herself of Russian and Polish heritage. "My father convinced my mother to let my sister and me go to Paris with him where he had settled. He wanted to give—he believed very much in the French education and he loved France very, very much."[151]

Even though Pakravan's education in France began in 1929, seven years before the Women's Awakening, she seems to associate state-coerced unveiling with her education, her professional life, and even her independence from her own father:

[As] you know, in 1937 [1316] Reza Shah abolished the *chador* for women. He wanted them to really participate in life. He also more or less obliged them to wear a hat—starting with his own family: the queen and his daughters, and the wives of all the ministers, members of government, and high officials of his administration. Although my father wasn't a fanatical Muslim, he was very much against all that, but somehow there were things that he was attached to. So, he said, "You will study to be a midwife, because I'm sure that despite all the regulations, Iranian women will not agree to go to a male doctor to have their babies." So, I went to this school which I didn't like at all, and when I went back to Iran, I didn't know Persian very well. That's why many people think I'm French, because my natural language is French. I was quite a small child when I came [to France].[152]

Despite seeming to prepare Fatemeh for a career in midwifery in Iran, her father only grudgingly permitted her to return there and, even then, only on a trial basis. Her return was motivated by patriotism and idealism that were quickly dampened: "When I went back to Iran, I wanted very much to work. My idea was to work in a public hospital. Of course, I was full of ideals and I thought we have to serve—you know, things you have when you are very, very young. But there was no Ministry of Health at the time in Iran. There was a general directorate of hygiene, and I was offered a very, very minor job with a really ridiculous salary."[153]

In the end, it was not the Pahlavi state that gave Pakravan her first job, but the family of Mohammad Mosaddeq. A friend of her own family introduced her to Dr. Gholam-Hossein Mosaddeq (Mohammad's son), and she was hastily hired to replace a Swiss woman doctor as director of the private Najmiyeh Hospital in Tehran. Najmiyeh had been established as a charitable endowment by Mohammad Mosaddeq's mother. She replaced her Swiss predecessor not only as director but also as a "foreigner." As Fatemeh Pakravan explained, "Because the former director was always addressed as 'Mademoiselle,' I became 'Mademoiselle' in my turn. And everybody spoke French to me, because I didn't know enough Persian. And that's how the idea came about that I am either French or Armenian. Even people who know me very well, are sometimes surprised to find out that I am actually Iranian."[154]

Fatemeh worked at Najmiyeh Hospital until her marriage to then-Capt. Hasan Pakravan in February 1941. In her narrative, she is pulled away from work by "Eastern" culture acting through her "Western"-educated husband who could claim French and Austrian ancestors along with his Iranian ones. She recalled: "My husband suddenly became very, very Eastern and decided that his wife must not work, that he must provide for her. But, he couldn't provide for me, because he was a young captain and the army officers were very, very underpaid. So, we had to live with my mother-in-law [Emineh Pakravan], who was professor at the University of Tehran. She was also a writer in French."[155]

As her French-educated mother-in-law rescued Fatemeh and her husband from ignoble poverty, the "West"—this time in the form of the Allied invasion and occupation of Iran during World War II—rescued her from the life of a "kept woman" by creating such severe economic hardship as to require her to work. She continues: "And so I stopped working and had my first child, but we couldn't manage, because Tehran entered the war. Don't forget that the country was occupied by the Russians, the British with their colonial armies—that means Gurkhas, the Indians, the Sikhs, and what they call Anzacs—that's [a soldier from] New Zealand or Australia—and later by Americans. So life became very, very difficult in Tehran . . . There was a shortage of practically everything, and so naturally the price of everything shot up. . . . So I went back to work but this time at the hospital of the National Bank with Dr. [Abdolhossein] Raji."[156]

In these two passages we can see how in Fatemeh Pakravan's memory, the idea of a woman working is coded as "Western," even though her husband's idea that a man should support his wife financially would certainly have found sympathetic ears in many a European or American home. But, for someone with Fatemeh Pakravan's training and connections, economic necessity was also an opportunity. While she followed her husband to various diplomatic posts, marriage and motherhood alone did not keep her from working in prestigious management positions for hospitals, Iran Air, and the Office of Tourism. She was hired back to Najmiyeh Hospital by Mohammad Mosaddeq himself—a man with whom she was to become increasingly disillusioned. Of course, her husband's career as a royalist public servant (he was head of SAVAK from 1960 to 1965) no doubt colored her perceptions of Mosaddeq. But, in her narrative, it is her dealings with him as his employee that changed her opinion of the legendary Iranian statesman. In her memories of her second term as director of the maternity ward at Najmiyeh Hospital, memories referring to a period from 1943 to 1947, Mosaddeq changes from being a charming and supportive boss to being a stingy and irresponsible patriarch. Initially, he respected and supported her authority in the hospital, something she remembered insisting upon: "[I told him], 'You know, Dr. Mosaddeq, the first time I worked here, I was quite a young girl, I didn't know anything. I came straight from school to run a hospital. But since then, I have [developed] my own ideas of how to run a hospital—*I am the absolute master.*

Doctors, the surgeons, the nurses [and] absolutely the visitors must accept the rules that I am going to establish for this hospital.' He said, 'All right. Do that . . .' Mosaddeq, I must say, kept to his word" [emphasis added].[157]

Mosaddeq backed her against the fury of an unnamed general who was upset at not being allowed to visit his wife well after the visiting hours Pakravan had established. He allowed her to "get rid of the so-called practical nurses and trained nurses"[158]—women who would likely have received their training from the government or on the job during the interwar period. The quality of Mosaddeq's and Pakravan's professional relationship was not to last. He refused her requests to build showers for the hospital's pro bono patients and to increase the number of free patients the hospital would treat. She accused him of hiring two sisters as nurses with the secondary purpose of having them spy on her activities in the hospital. Yet, even in her critique of Mosaddeq's patriarchal and autocratic tendencies, Pakravan softens the blow by blaming his underlings—a final gesture of respect for male authority: "So, I realized that Mosaddeq, like many important people—[such as] the shah in his own way, and others that I don't want to name, especially if they are a little bit dictatorial or have great authority—are always in the hands of the so-called 'entourage.' . . . [All] big men have this weakness (which we don't realize) of giving part of their will and authority to people who don't deserve it. And these people are the ones who cause all the trouble."[159]

Pakravan's sense of empowerment through work contrasts with the recollections of Ozma Adl-Naficy. Encouraged in her study of French at the Joan d'Arc School in Tehran, she began showing a real talent for translation and spent a year in France starting in the summer of 1938. Her interest in the art of translation slackened with the realization that it was not terribly profitable work: "Later, as I became older, I discerned that my efforts were really misspent—meaning it did not have a material benefit, rather it was all [done at] a loss. It's that, for a while, I was so taken with the work that—a person can work and go to some trouble and have nothing material [to show for it]—it was a little strange."[160]

The theme of marginalization permeates Adl-Naficy's recollections. Although she was from a wealthy family (her father had paid for the publication of some of her early translation efforts), her family's wealth was tied up in agriculture in Azerbaijan. The Allied occupation of World War II disrupted her family's finances, especially toward the end of the war when the Soviet-sponsored Republic of Azerbaijan was defying the authority of the central government. In the fall of 1946, she decided to work for the Ministry of Labor and, like Fatemeh Pakravan, was not exactly encouraged by members of her family. As Adl-Naficy explained, "When I wanted to work for the Ministry of Labor, my uncle was Mr. E'temad al-Vozara', who was the father of Mr. Parviz Adl who later became Iran's ambassador to Canada. He was a very educated—I mean he studied in France and was very literate. Even such a man would come to our house to tell my mother that it was a shame for us to have a daughter in the family go and work. I mean, [the idea] of a woman working was ugly even for a person who was himself educated. For a woman, for example, to go and work for her living was very, very [much] a source of [embarrassment]."[161]

Adl-Naficy initially worked for the Public Announcements Bureau of the Ministry of Labor but was soon invited to work at the main office. She recalled her early days with the Ministry of Labor with fondness:

> When Mr. Mohammad Vali Farmanfarmaian became Minister [of Labor] he said, "That is not a very suitable environment for you. It's better if you come to the Ministry of Labor [main office]. At that time the Ministry of Labor was in [an old] imperial palace on Pasteur Street. I went [to work] there. Incidentally, the environment at the Ministry of Labor was a good one—a very, very good one. I don't think I've seen any place that I worked at or went to afterward with as good an environment in Iran. I mean, it was an environment in which everyone was very, very good to one another. It was a very rare thing that you would see people who would not speak ill of each other or strike at each other and [instead] work for each other during the days and even spend some of their free time together.[162]

It was there that she met her husband, Habib Naficy, then the deputy minister of labor. After their marriage in February of 1947, she reported that her husband preferred that she not work at the ministry but concentrate on housework instead. But before leaving the ministry, she was charged with organizing an Office for Women's Workers within the Ministry of Labor. Her recollections here provide a rare glimpse into the lives of Iran's earliest women office workers and the state of affairs inherited from the time of the Women's Awakening:

Q. Was there another woman besides you [at the Ministry]?

A. There were a lot of women who were members of the lower level of the Ministry of Labor. Later, when I became the head of the Office for Women Workers, these women worked with me.

Q. But they were not, so to speak, at the upper level.

A. No, not the upper level. I was not at the upper level. I entered that place as a Translator I. That [meant that], of course, I was given some letters and also foreign newspaper articles in which they had written something about Iran to translate. Sometimes they would give me Iranian newspapers that were interesting and told me to, for example, "underline this and make a note" and they would look at it later. At first my work was just translating. For a time, all I did was translate. But, at this same time that I was doing this work here [at the ministry], Her Highness Ashraf Pahlavi was at the Charitable Foundation and she would occasionally request information about the affairs of working women. Once, I remember, I brought all of these women to Her Highness for all these women to meet her and [she] would ask questions about working and so on.

Q. When was this?

A. At the time of Pishehvari (1946–47).[163]

Q. [Later in the interview] You still haven't spoken about your office.

A. Yes, I told you that there were these young girls in the office who were in Workers' Affairs. I said that these women workers were not typical and these girls also were mostly there to earn their living and none, perhaps I should include myself, were very knowledgeable of workers' affairs or the labor laws. [It was the case] that I studied the labor law and tried to make them understand how to operate.

Q. These were employees of the Ministry of Labor?

A. They were employees of the Ministry of Labor. They were the girls who had been moved to the Office for Women Workers and I was trying to acquaint them with women workers' rights so that later they would be prepared to go out to factories and, for example, make bosses responsible for observing their obligations towards women workers. They could [then] acquaint women workers themselves about their rights and what they should expect from these [bosses].

Q. So this work had not already begun. Now at least . . .

A. No, it had not started and then we were preparing these girls.

Later, well, they were people who did not have much education and, fundamentally, were not as clear on normal affairs of life as they ought to have been. I remember that I, myself, would speak to them and [another] person who would come at speak to them was Mr. Mohsen Kh^{w}ajehnuri—he spoke to them a lot. You first just have to give them a way of life so that they will know themselves what their rights are and how to manage their families and how they should act in the office so that afterward they can go help women workers. Like I said, I once took these girls to Her Highness Princess Ashraf to speak with them. She asked [questions] and showed interest.

Q. Were they part of the ESKI union or did they have any relationship to it? These women, I mean.

A. No, they were all members of the Labor Ministry.[164]

As we shall see later, men railed against their women coworkers in the 1940s. For the most part, women were shunted into low-level clerical positions with no expectation that they would rise up through the bureaucratic ranks. It is interesting that Ozma Adl-Naficy had such a broad vision of how to train her women workers at the Ministry of Labor. They were to be remade with guidance on all aspects of life, from office etiquette to domestic work. On an institutional level, the Ministry of Labor in the 1940s was following up on the promises of Women's Awakening propaganda to create a modern Iranian woman who could really balance the responsibilities of professional and domestic life—more "lionesses" to rock the cradles. In remembering herself as "not at the upper level" and as working so hard for such basic results in the Ministry of Labor, Adl-Naficy seems to minimize her pioneering efforts. This may be a reflection of the fact that she perceived herself to be displaced in the women's movement by "careerist" *(jah talab)* women like Mehrangiz Dowlatshahi and Mehrangiz Manuchehri.[165]

In assessing women who worked, we have come full circle back to the issue of education. And what of those women whose professional mission it was to educate? As we have seen, the Pahlavi state made an aggressive effort to expand, standardize, and monopolize education in Iran. As education became an increasingly state-controlled activity in the 1930s, the state would be the primary employer in one of the earliest professional areas to be opened up to women: education. On the eve of its downfall, the regime of Reza Shah was undertaking Iran's first census. The process was interrupted by World War II. We are fortunate that the Ministry of Cul-

Table 6.1 Elementary school teachers in Iran, 1937–1948 (1316–1327)

Academic year	Male		Female	
	Government	Private	Government	Private
1315–1316	2,880	1,381	1,441	1,035
1316–1317	2,974	1,494	1,843	1,149
1318–1319	No data	No data	No data	No data
1320–1321	No data	No data	No data	No data
1321–1322	No data	No data	No data	No data
1322–1323	4,617	1,143	3,612	774
1323–1324	4,889	1,025	3,804	734
1324–1325	6,071	915	4,339	651
1325–1326	6,855	894	4,858	649
1326–1327	7,946	933	5,180	722

Source: Ministry of Culture, *Salnameh va Amar, 1315–17*, vol. 2, 265, and *1322–27*, vol. 2, 29–31, 67–69

ture, which oversaw all education at this time, tracked its employees and students. It is the only data we have on women in the workforce before the 1950s (see tables 6.1 and 6.2).

The first thing the statistics confirm is that the Women's Awakening did not "create" a niche for women as teachers. In 1937 (1315/16), there were already 2,476 women elementary school teachers and 331 women secondary school teachers. Two-thirds of the women secondary school teachers were employed by private schools (consistent with the experiences and recollections of women regarding those times), but the state employed more than half of the women elementary school teachers. The number of state-employed teachers increased while the number of teachers working for private schools seems to have stabilized. This data is consistent both with the fact that the expansion of state education begun by the regime of Reza Shah was continued by the Parliament into the 1940s and with the Parliament's commitment to the more progressive aspects of Women's Awakening policies in education and hiring over the same period. Furthermore, there can be no doubt that the state facilitated the expansion of employment opportunities for women teachers. In 1936, women made up 31.4 percent of the teaching workforce, whereas in 1943, they made up 38.1 percent.

There is much that this data does not tell us. For example, we do not know what women teachers were paid (on average) in comparison to their male counterparts. The Iranian government recognized rank and seniority

Table 6.2 Secondary school teachers in Iran, 1937–1948 (1316–1327)

Academic year	Secondary and preparatory school teachers (government)		Secondary school teachers (private)	
	Male	Female	Male	Female
1315–1316	596	109	726	222
1316–1317	789	143	789	247
1318–1319	No data	No data	No data	No data
1320–1321	No data	No data	No data	No data
1321–1322	No data	No data	No data	No data
1322–1323	1,592	337	504	112
1323–1324	1,650	287	539	132
1324–1325	1,802	358	481	127
1325–1326	1,896	425	439	119
1326–1327	1,867	334	299	262

Source: Ministry of Culture, *Salnameh va Amar, 1315–17,* vol. 2, 265, and *1322–27,* vol. 2, 2–31, 76–89

in paying its Iranian employees. In any given year there would be more men with greater seniority. But we do not know if women were brought into the system with a different rank than their male colleagues. We also do not know if the women were promoted at the same pace or had comparable rates of dismissal or resignation as the men. However, we do know that, in 1938, the lowest-ranked elementary school teacher earned 340 rials per month—twenty rials a year more than the lowest-ranked office clerk.[166] The lowest-ranked secondary school teacher earned twice as much as his or her elementary school counterpart (680 rials per month), but that was slightly more than a judge who had been promoted once (620 rials per month). The highest-ranked and most senior secondary school teacher could expect a salary of 3,420 rials per month—more than any clerical administrator and more than all but the most senior doctors and judges on the government payroll. Similarly ranked elementary school teachers received slightly more than half the pay of their secondary school counterparts (1,660 rials per month).

Among the corps of government secondary school teachers, there was a fairly consistent ratio of six men for every woman from 1936 through 1948. However, in elementary education, the ratio of men to women improved from 2:1 in 1936 to 8:5 in 1948. So, even in the "growth field" of education, women occupied far fewer of the best-paying teaching positions than men both during and after the Women's Awakening. But allowing for this disparity, how did a teacher's pay compare to that of other occupations?

American diplomats did periodic assessments of wages in Iran. From a report in 1934, we are informed that skilled construction workers could earn as much as 16 rials per day, and typesetting superintendents could earn as much as 15 rials per day.[167] Assuming a six-day workweek, these wages would translate into approximately 384 rials per month and 360 rials per month, respectively. Long-haul truck drivers and bus drivers earned more per day but had to work considerably longer hours (up to sixteen hours per day for bus drivers). So, a first-year elementary school teacher could earn as much as a skilled worker in construction and a literate worker in publishing. The most skilled carpet weaver did not earn as much per day (12 rials) and an unskilled worker in construction earned considerably less (4.5 rials). By the standards of the urban workforce, then, teaching paid well.

But was teaching a prestigious job? Did the women who became K–12 educators in the 1930s and 1940s enhance the image of modern Iranian womanhood, day to day? This, of course, is hard to assess from employment data alone. Teachers could command the respect of their students. But for most teachers this would mean they would have authority over children. Perhaps the best indication that women were accepted (and perhaps valued) as teachers is that the backlash against women workers in the 1940s focused on office workers (see chapter 8), not teachers (or doctors and nurses, for that matter).

What of college- and university-level educators? In the 1936–37 academic year, there were three women serving as professors or lecturers at the university level (1.2 percent of the faculty) and four in the following academic year (1.5 percent of the faculty).[168] The number of women teaching at the university level seems to have fluctuated during World War II, but in the 1947–48 academic year there were eleven women teaching in Iran's universities and colleges (2.8 percent of the faculty).[169] By the standards of government employment, both lectureships and regular faculty positions were well paying and prestigious. In 1938, a first-year lecturer made 1000 rials per month (twice as much as a first-time judge), and a first-year professor made 1,100 rials per month.[170] The most senior lecturers and professors made 3,200 and 3,540 rials per month respectively. Furthermore, as we have already seen in the case of Fatemeh Sayyah, a woman professor could have an important impact on Iranian college students and serve as an important symbol of women's potential achievement. However, women were granted only a token presence at the highest levels of the Iranian educational system, and their token status had improved only minutely seven years after the end of the Women's Awakening (in contrast to women teaching at the K–12 level).

The effort to chaperone Iranian women into modernity through morally sound education and respectable employment was genuine, if not widespread. Few Iranian women could take advantage of the best opportunities the Women's Awakening provided, and even those who did so continued to experience contradictory expectations of what they should do with their opportunities. At first glance, the Women's Awakening would seem to have been a poor bargain. It increased state control over women's bodies, education, and public image rather than increasing professional acceptance by male colleagues, which was to have been the "reward" for women's obedience to forced unveiling. Indeed, the regime may have been more interested in the image of modern Iranian womanhood than its reality. But the images, however much they exaggerated the reality of women's progress, represented an important beginning. Women were celebrated for the work they did and the grades they earned. Some privileged Iranian women, rather than European or American women, could serve as inspiration for their countrywomen as to what was possible. In public discourse, the very meaning of male guardianship had been expanded from familial relationships (son, brother, father) to other socioeconomic relationships: teacher, mentor, supervisor, coworker, and classmate. This, of course, suggests an elastic boundary for women's emancipation. And, indeed, the images of "capable" Iranian women were placed alongside other images to create a complex set of guidelines for the new female citizen: She was to be progressive and active but not independent of male guardianship. The possibilities and limitations of this new civic presence for women in Women's Awakening propaganda are the subject of the following chapter.

7

The Limits of Emancipation

The Women's Awakening project was a precarious balancing act. Women's emancipation was not to be achieved at the expense of male guardianship. The regime's construction of the modern Iranian woman was a volatile synthesis of renewalist, missionary, leftist, and Islamic elements. Its volatility resulted not only from unveiling but also from the occasional implication—never realized—that gender equality was just around the corner. As we have already seen, the regime's enforcement of unveiling, reform of the marriage law, and encouragement of progressive trends in women's education and employment nevertheless maintained gender differences. Yet all of these efforts were linked to a vague concept of women's citizenship in Iran or, more precisely, the future of women's citizenship. To what end were women progressing? From what restrictions would they be finally liberated? The propaganda of the Women's Awakening exploited these ambiguities in the ultimate goals of the women's emancipation to imply simultaneously the coming of full and equal citizenship for women and the permanence of male guardianship. Even before the Women's Awakening, the regime moved to control the image of modern Iranian womanhood. And once the Women's Awakening was underway, it constantly flirted with the idea of full citizenship for women while offering reasons why women could not (because of their innate lack of potential) or should not (because of their moral laxity) achieve full citizenship.

Controlling the Image of the Modern Iranian Woman

The Women's Awakening represented the high-water mark of "state feminism" during the regime of Reza Shah. But it was not his regime's first attempt at co-opting the woman question. The Marriage Law of 1931 was the first attempt. It was followed by the regime's hosting of the Second Congress of Eastern Women in Tehran in 1932. The first conference had been held in Damascus in 1930, and it is clear that the regime wanted to show itself to be in step with the most progressive states in the region (most of the delegates were from the Middle East). The Second Congress of Eastern Women also confronted the regime with two potentially troubling images of women: as members of an international community and as a distinct constituency within Iranian society—one whose interests might not coincide with the regime's priorities. The awkward attempts both to embrace and contain the Second Congress of Eastern Women in 1932 represented the first effort of the regime and its supporters to draw meandering, semipermeable, and irregular boundaries around "acceptable" levels of feminism in Iranian society. It set a pattern that influenced the propaganda of the Women's Awakening—a pattern of adjusting the definition of male guardianship to embrace but, more importantly, at the same time to restrain the implications of modern Iranian womanhood.

The conference was announced in the pages of *Ettela'at* on 22 June 1932.[1] The Iranian government expressly asked for the cooperation of neighboring governments (including the British and French mandatory and colonial authorities in the region) in facilitating the travel of delegates to Tehran in the fall. For months, not much was said about the event. As we have seen, however, *Ettela'at* ran a special "letters to the editor" discussion about marriage for two months prior to the event. Ads ran for the book *Women in Society,* which was published by *Ettela'at*. In late October, shortly before the Congress was to begin, *Ettela'at* ran a front-page summary and translation of *La femme la société* (under the translated title of "Women in Contemporary Society") by Marguerite Faussecave.[2] Mas'udi, the editor and owner of *Ettela'at,* introduced Faussecave as a "learned woman of Egypt" whose writing was all the more impressive because she had risen from the "ranks of the working class."[3]

However, on the very eve of the Congress, Mas'udi ran an article on the front page, entitled, "The First Congress of Ugly Women."[4] It was presented as a lighthearted article about an actual conference of self-described "ugly women" in Philadelphia. The women reportedly were protesting the fact that pretty women seemed to have all the advantages in society while ugly women were ignored despite their superior virtues. The Congress of Ugly Women did not blame a patriarchal system so much as it blamed pretty women. Although men were to be educated regarding their errors in judgment, the fifth plank of the Ugly Women's platform stated, "[We should write] slogans of confrontation and war with beautiful women with whom we shall struggle to the end. Death to pretty women!"[5] Whether out of bad taste or malice, Mas'udi's inclusion of this inane "fluff" piece on the front page of Iran's major daily could only have served to undercut the Eastern Women's Congress. The following week, again on the front page, *Ettela'at* ran a copy of a speech by Gandhi to India's women, exhorting them to help raise good children and help India's struggle for independence by spinning their own yarn—a more favorable image of women to be sure, but also a more domestic image.[6]

Once the conference was under way *Ettela'at* did assign a special correspondent, 'A. H. Hashemi-Ha'eri. While his reporting was not to be Iranian journalism's finest hour, Hashemi-Ha'eri was refreshingly honest about his reaction to events (bordering on stream of consciousness) and his own limitations as a reporter. On one day of the Congress, for example, he witnessed an exchange between a religious-minded politician and the president of the Congress of Eastern Women, Nur Hamadah. He wrote, "Really, what would it hurt if I summarized his statements—I mean in so far as I remember them? I did not take notes there but I am hopeful that my memory will not betray me."[7]

Ettela'at's coverage presented the Second Congress of Eastern Women as a well-meaning, if disorganized, affair. It did not publish the minutes of the meeting; obviously, its summary of events sought to harmonize differences of opinion between Iranian government policy and issues raised by delegates to the conference.[8] In harmonizing differences, *Ettela'at* frequently emphasized that the Pahlavi regime, in all important respects, was at least as progressive as the platform of the Congress. The Congress's platform, adopted in Damascus in 1930, was reported in *Ettela'at* on 3 November as consisting of nineteen policy points: for equality in all matters (including, specifically, the right to work) as long as domestic responsibilities were not compromised, for support for the opening of kindergartens, for compulsory education, for vocational schools for girls and boys, for uniform education curricula (consistent with each country's needs), for the production of books for young children and the creation of scientific vocabulary in native languages, for the teaching of native languages in foreign-run schools, for the promotion of civilization *(madaniyat)* in Eastern countries, for setting minimum ages for marriage, for verifying the good health of couples who wish to get married, for lowering the bride-price and dowry[9] for marriage, for preventing polygyny by men (except in "necessary cases"), for giving women the right to divorce, for protecting women's inheritance rights, for participating in societies that combat the use of intoxicants and gambling, for fighting prostitution and slavery, and for fighting war while promoting freedom and peace.[10]

Hashemi-Ha'eri noted the appearance and demeanor of the three women he interviewed for the piece in *Ettela'at*. Haninah Khuri, the Egyptian delegate, "had a pleasant and cheerful face, was of medium height, fair, smiling, sweet spoken, and with charming gestures" and never lost a smile while speaking.[11] The Iraqi delegate, Fatimah Murad, was "wheat colored, thin, with black eyes and hair, and she possessed a special deliberateness and self-possession"—speaking less but always well and with a smile.[12] Nur Hamadah, the Syrian delegate and president of the Congress of Eastern Women, was smiling with a cheerful face.[13] Nur Hamadah sounded the right note, perhaps, by emphasizing that Tehran had been selected as the site of the Second Congress of Eastern Women because relative to other countries in the region, Iran enjoyed "complete independence and there was no foreign influence of any sort there."[14] She did not, however, emphasize Iran's progressive record on women's rights—that was left very much to Hashemi-Ha'eri's (and Mas'udi's) imagination.

The descriptions of the women's appearance, particularly the hair of one of the delegates, suggested a measure of "unveiling." Indeed, as noted in chapter 3, the very dark black-and-white pictures of Nur Hamadah and Haninah Khuri suggest that both women were at least "unveiled" in the Qasim Amin sense of that term (that is, no face veil).[15] That the pictures were declared "not ready" for publication the day of Hashemi-Ha'eri's report and were not published until the next issue (two days later on 5 November) raises the suspicion that there may have been some debate about printing the pictures or that it took some time to produce such very dark copies of the pictures so as to play down the level of unveiling involved (particularly in the case of Haninah Khuri, who as a Lebanese-born Christian may not have worn any sort of veil in 1932). Nonetheless, Hashemi-Ha'eri's warm and comfortable reception and interaction with the three foreign delegates, reported on 3 November, served as a model for proper and pleasant social mixing between the sexes in public—very much a renewalist ideal and, as we have seen, a key aspect of the Women's Awakening project. Hashemi-Ha'eri closed his article with the observation, "In truth, I can say that around the middle of the meeting, my interview took on more of a friendly aspect rather than that of an interview with a reporter who must be dry and diligent and tedious. I could not have been more satisfied with the discussion or the information from these learned women."[16]

The next installment of *Ettela'at*'s coverage contained an important subplot: the involvement of the Patriotic Women's League, at least from the perspective of one of its members, Mastureh Afshar. Hashemi-Ha'eri had gone to Afshar's house to speak again with the foreign delegates to the Second Congress of Eastern Women, only to find that they had left her house for another meeting. At this point, he decided to interview Mastureh Afshar on Iran's own women's society, the Patriotic Women's League. The information she offered him revealed an odd mix of pride and disdain for the league:

> Yes, we have a society, also. The Patriotic Women's League of Iran was founded ten years ago. On paper, it has 195 members. The founder of the league was Mohtaram Eskandari, who has since passed away. It has been ten years since she founded the league, and she invited me to join six months after she founded it. The truth is that I declined at first because I saw Iranian women and their sisters as idealists and as having not a particular goal. In the end, after meeting with them, I was convinced of her patriotism, and I proudly accepted membership in the league. For ten years, with only the efforts of a few patriotic women, has the league been maintained. It is true that there are 195 women with membership cards, but it is with the help and aid of a few women and with their efforts that the league has endured.[17]

In this statement, Afshar clearly positioned herself as one of the "few women" who had kept the Patriotic Women's League afloat. Furthermore, she established her independence from the league by assessing the group according to *her* standard of patriotism before joining. In so doing, she subordinated her loyalty to the league to a more direct loyalty to the nation. She went on to say that the Patriotic Women's League had three aims: setting a minimum age for marriage, preventing polygyny, and preserving the rights of women and children in the event of divorce. Hashemi-Ha'eri asked if these aims had not already been accomplished by the Marriage Law of 1931. Afshar responded affirmatively but suggested also that the Patriotic Women's League was working with the Ministry of Justice to improve the regulations in the administration of the law.[18] She pointed out that other countries represented at the conference had not yet found solutions to their problems with marital customs. This exchange established a theme that was to be repeated by Afshar and representatives of the Iranian government at the Tehran Congress: the Iranian government had already taken care of any meaningful changes that the congress's platform proposed. Furthermore, responsible activism, it was clearly suggested, consisted of working with the government.

Mastureh Afshar further ingratiated herself to the regime by taking issue with the congress's "peace" plank. She stressed that Eastern nations had to learn the arts of war eagerly—even as they wished for peace—

because recent historical experiences proved that they had to be strong to resist aggression, to "protect our homes and homeland." Approvingly, Hashemi-Ha'eri wrote that others (presumably in the household) were drawn to these words from the heart that spread through the room like waves. Afshar was speaking for Iran now—at least, the Iran that the Pahlavi regime wanted to portray. Afshar confirmed that the event was coming together rather haphazardly and that key elements of its program were not yet known. The "disorderliness" of the Congress was emphasized throughout *Ettela'at*'s coverage—as if to underscore that the actions of independent and international women were no substitute for loyalty to and cooperation with the nation-state.

The first organizational meeting of the Second Congress took place on 7 November. Hashemi-Ha'eri's reporting provides glimpses of tensions between men and women at the conference. Zahir al-Eslam Owrang, a parliamentary deputy, harangued a number of women who were waiting for the meeting to start, saying that there was no program for life that could be as comprehensive and useful as the laws of Islam. However, he conceded, there had been some in the past who had misused Islamic laws.[19] Hashemi-Ha'eri noted that some women "brightened" to these comments, but a woman asked why it was that not until now did men speak to women of rights (in Islam) and did not respect the rights of women. Hashemi-Ha'eri, seemingly not wanting to dwell on the awkwardness of the situation, summarized the women's comments: "The points that followed provided the substance of complaints that women have of us men—that in the past they were not treated well and the thrust of the speech is obvious."[20]

Hashemi-Ha'eri noted, once again, that a number of delegates were not present and that the program for the Second Congress had not yet been approved.[21] Owrang, serving as a translator (Arabic to Persian) for the conference and a de facto representative of the Pahlavi state, asked Nur Hamadah how long she would be staying in Iran and what the program of the Congress was to be. She responded—rather uncooperatively—that she would stay until the end of the Congress and that the scheduled end of the Congress had not yet been approved. Owrang addressed the full room of women, and some men, with his (and, we may assume, the Pahlavi regime's) definition of women's progress. Pointedly, it did not include unveiling. After declaring that women's previous attempts at activism had failed due to poor planning, radicalism, and lack of consideration for the necessities of life, Owrang offered this example: "Let's say, if our learned sisters who have gathered together, as their first step, begin thinking of the face veil and veiling. This would be like a woman who, at the beginning of winter and harsh cold, instead of gathering coal and other fuel to keep her body warm and to protect herself from the cruel cold of winter, begins thinking of what sort of *qolab-duzi* covering she ought to make to cover her *korsi* [heater] and day and night thinks about the beautification [of the *korsi*]. *She* is not thinking of the important fuel and material for generating warmth. Our sisters, also, must keep [the moral of this story] in mind and strive to attend to necessities as their first step."[22]

Owrang followed his speech with a poem emphasizing the themes of deliberate and learned and unified action. Nur Hamadah affirmed that, indeed, the veil was not the first priority for the women's congress. "The veil and face veil will not slow progress or impede its development [for women]."[23] This was less an endorsement of the veil than a recognition of the tone of the officials of the host country. Nur Hamadah added:

We have inserted broader principles in our platform because we wish to say to Western women that Eastern women do not [merely] have limited goals. We are also trying to bring ourselves to their level. Just as the women of Turkey have the highest degree [of progress] among [our] Eastern sisters, and after them the women of Egypt and the daughters of the land of the Pharaohs, and then Syria proper followed by Greater Syria. The women of Iraq have a new awakening, and most of the [progressive] women of the Hijaz are women from Syria and Greater Syria who have Hijazi husbands. And now that I have come to Iran and gathered with learned men and women, I am endlessly pleased that I am among them. I am also eminently satisfied that in Tehran, the imperial capital of Iran, with a great king such as the Pahlavi emperor, I see this awakening in [my] Iranian sisters. I can say that among the women of the countries I have listed, we can place them [the Iranians] in the middle—we should not exaggerate and say that they are in the highest level [of progress] nor be unfair and say they are in last place.[24]

Nur Hamadah, rather gently, disabused Owrang, and through him the Iranian government, of the notion that Iran's progress was exemplary in the Eastern world. She was tactful enough not to specify Iran's ranking (better than Syria, the Hijaz?) among Eastern women, but did stress the Euro-American standards to which Eastern women needed to aspire. *Ettela'at*'s coverage of the conference quickly became more limited and more critical. The next article, covering meetings on 9 November and not written by Hashemi-Ha'eri, simply listed the order of events and location

(Mastureh Afshar's house at 4:00 P.M. for the first meeting of the day) of the Eastern Women's Congress.[25] Only in the vaguest terms did it summarize the substance of what was discussed. The regime was sure to send two of its "official women"—the wife of Gen. ʿAbd al-Reza Khan Afkhami, vice president of the Red Lion and Sun Society, and the wife of ʿEffat al-Moluk Khʷajehnuri, treasurer of the Red Lion and Sun Society and director of the Women's Vocational School (and, as we saw in chapter 5, a public supporter of the Marriage Law of 1931). It was Mrs. Afkhami who welcomed the delegates on behalf of Princess Shams Pahlavi. Mastureh Afshar, reportedly, emphasized the role of Princess Shams in the progress of Iranian women (rather than the efforts of the Patriotic Women's League). In short, Ettelaʿat presented the Second Congress of Eastern Women as ratifying uncritically the progress of Iranian women under the auspices of the regime.

The Tehran Congress of 1932 was less a source of specific policy for the Women's Awakening of 1936 than a dress rehearsal for the kind of relationship the Pahlavi state wanted with the modern Iranian woman. In 1932, however, the regime could not claim ownership of the Congress. Furthermore, the Patriotic Women's League was one of a number of independent women's societies in Iran at the time. Although Mastureh Afshar was clearly an ally of the regime in spirit, she did not work for the regime in a formal sense and did not speak for all members of the Patriotic Women's League. To create the illusion of a unanimous and uncritical alliance between the state and Iran's feminists, Ettelaʿat minimized the substance of the congress's deliberations while trying to appropriate what progressive legitimacy it could.[26] The distorted reality of 1932 was to become the coerced reality of 1936.

Ettelaʿat's final word on the 1932 congress was a disparaging letter to the editor printed on page one in which the unnamed correspondent emphasized that there was nothing in the platform of the Congress of Eastern Women that the Pahlavi regime had not already brought into reality.[27] As if in direct response to Nur Hamadah's tepid appraisal of Iran's progress on women's rights, the letter mused about the benefits to non-Iranian delegates in interacting with the implicitly more progressive Iranian women. The Marriage Law of 1931 was again touted as proof of the regime's commitment to women's progress. It blamed the absence of women in certain professions in Iran on the fact that women did not have the requisite training or on the fact that entering such careers would compromise women's domestic duties (a condition of the platform of the Congress). This argument ignored the critical need for higher education for women that, as we have already seen, became an important part of Women's Awakening propaganda and policy later on.

Flirting with Full Citizenship for Women

One of the criticisms of the Women's Awakening has been the fact that women's suffrage was neglected. The denial of women's political rights during the Women's Awakening was in keeping with the short history of renewalism. The most progressive politicians of the early constitutional period had, in fact, acquiesced to the denial of women's basic political rights in 1907 and 1911, and it cannot be said that they ever put themselves at much risk in advocating change. Indeed, there was no immediate consensus on the extent of male political enfranchisement in the early years of the Constitution. The first Parliament was convoked in 1906, rather like the convening of the estates of the French Parliament before 1789, but along traditional Iranian conceptions of "classes" within society: princes, military commanders, clerics, landowners, craftsmen, merchants, and peasants—the same organization of people that might attend a *Now Ruz* (Iranian new year) audience at the king's palace. It was this initial group that ratified Iran's first Electoral Law of 1906. It took a civil war from 1908 to 1909 to convince Parliament to reduce property requirements from 1,000 to 250 *tumans* in 1909, roughly from US$1,150 to US$287 (in 1910 dollars).[28] Universal male suffrage was introduced in 1913 by removing the property requirement altogether, while women's suffrage, as we saw in chapter 2, was not raised again in Parliament after 1911.

Reza Shah, as eager as he was to link himself to the legacy of the early constitutional period, was certainly no advocate of democratic change—for anyone. To critique Reza Shah's attitude toward the women's movement, historian Eliz Sanasarian needed only to cite the words of his son, Mohammad Reza Shah: "Reza Shah never advocated a complete break with the past, for always he assumed that our girls could find their best fulfillment in marriage and in the nurture of superior children. But he was convinced that a girl could be a better wife and mother, as well as a better citizen, if she received an education and perhaps worked outside the home long enough to gain a sense of civic functions and responsibilities."[29]

This being said, it was the regime of Reza Shah that allowed for some discussion of women's suffrage. Even before the Women's Awakening, the regime allowed for the tantalizing possibility that women's suffrage was an eventual goal. On 21 December 1934, *Ettela 'at* noted Turkey's passage of a law forbidding the wearing of clerical garb or symbols of foreign nationality—on the front page.[30] On 22 December, the text of İsmet İnönü's speech on the occasion of the Turkish National Assembly's granting of women's suffrage was published as the lead article.[31] Turkish women were granted the right to vote and to be elected to the National Assembly. More than simply justifying this change, İnönü's speech made the alternative shameful:

> The effort we have undertaken today springs from the hopes of the Grand National Assembly of Turkey and the Turkish Nation, which had pursued [women's suffrage] for some time and had prescribed it as one of the requirements for the advancement of national reform. But the right to vote and the right to be elected must not be considered a gift or a favor to women. Rather, this right was the [religiously] lawful *[mashru]* right of our mothers that was taken from them in error. It has still not been forgotten that during the days of misfortune at a time when people of the country were devoting themselves to the path of independence, Turkish women struggled alongside men for the advancement of the people's cause by hauling munitions and preparing the means of defense while under enemy artillery fire. Those [women] who stayed in the interior were busy preparing supplies and mining raw materials from the earth for the sustenance of soldiers and others. So it is necessary that such valuable beings have the right to vote and [offer] their opinion on all national affairs. [Long applause][32]

The rhetoric of this speech drew on themes familiar to the discussion of the woman question in Iran. Improvement in the condition of women was linked both to progress and to restoring the fundamentals of a vague Islamic past. But, of course, this Turkish reform went beyond anything that had been seriously contemplated in the Iranian press. İnönü's speech made a very specific point: It was because women had proven themselves in war that they were to have their political rights restored. War was the ultimate test of the capable woman, and Turkish women had passed that test and earned full citizenship by fighting for their country. Turkish society—as seen through the eyes of *Ettela'at*—had accepted the full implications of the capable woman.

This report was as close as the regime of Reza Shah would come to endorsing the political enfranchisement of women. The regime's failure to endorse women as full citizens through suffrage was a glaring distinction between the regime's image of modern Iranian womanhood and Euro-

American images of modern womanhood. Writing in the first issue of *Iran-e Emruz,* Fatemeh Sayyah took on the question of women's suffrage as part of a general discussion of the European (and American) example in "Women in the West Fifty Years Ago."[33] Sayyah focused on struggles of Western women to obtain access to higher education, property rights, more equitable marriage rights, and political rights—making clear that Western women were starting from a thoroughly abysmal condition in all respects. Although she noted the advancements of Western women prior to the First World War, she ignored all history after 1917, thus avoiding specific mention of women eventually winning the right to vote in the United States and England. Toward the end of the essay, while summarizing issues raised during a women's conference in Washington, D.C., in 1888, she did mention that women in some American states (Wyoming and Kansas) had the vote. It was a right, however, that was not presented in the best possible light, linked as it was to domestic violence:

> Among the topics of discussion at the Women's Congress were family matters. It was in connection with this that the representative from the state of Kansas, in her report on the first participation of women in municipal elections in her state, stated that women's interference in these elections caused family adversity. She followed by telling the story of her own beating by her husband as an example. In the end, the incident was related to [her] interference in the election. At the same time, the woman was not all that vexed by the issue of being beaten. She had mentioned this case so that they [the other delegates] would know that she did not think that [even the risk of being beaten] should keep women from participating in elections. This is because, after some inspection of the matter, it was the case that the woman's husband was [simply] in the habit of beating his wife [whatever the provocation]. An English representative emphasized that in the northern provinces of England, wife beating was an accepted tradition and was rampant among husbands of some classes.[34]

From here, Sayyah segued into glowing praise for Reza Shah for having bestowed rights upon Iranian women for which Western women had been forced to toil for fifty years to obtain. Of course, Sayyah must have known full well that in mentioning Western women's achievements such as suffrage (and the right to serve as judges) at all, she was undercutting the praise she heaped upon her king. Given her later critique of the premise that women's suffrage would adversely affect family life and child rearing in Iran (see chapter 8), it is reasonable to assume that Sayyah was sending a deliberately mixed message about women's political enfranchisement. Women's suffrage might lead to violent reprisals, but they were reprisals worth enduring. The alleged risk posed to the family by women's suffrage implied at the beginning of the paragraph is all but disavowed by the end.

Sayyah seemed amused by the morality expressed at the Women's Congress of 1888. She quoted the president of the Congress, Miss Willard, as saying, "Smoking is not appropriate nor beneficial to women. The waltz is a dance that offends morality, and women must severely restrain themselves from it."[35] To this, Sayyah responded, "It is not clear what the lady would have had to say if she had seen today's fox-trot and tango!"[36] Sayyah's gentle dismissal of such moral concerns may have been pointed since the regime's propaganda machine did not fail to underscore the moral laxity of Iranian women—particularly those who saw themselves as modern (see the section after next). At the same time, as if recalling İnönü's speech from 1934 about women's right to vote based on military service, the regime cultivated a martial image of modern Iranian womanhood—really, girlhood—through scouting.

Although there were never as many Girl Scouts as Boy Scouts, they were on the front lines of Women's Awakening propaganda—appearing at parades, posing for front-page press photographs, and being deployed to celebrate no less an occasion than the wedding of Crown Prince Mohammad Reza and Fowziyeh (as was the case for their Egyptian counterparts, see chapter 6). Marching and saluting but unarmed, the Iranian Girl Scouts offered a martial image of modern Iranian womanhood that stopped short of being threatening. Anniversaries of the Seventeenth of Day were celebrated with uniformed and beretted Girl Scouts marching in formation at flag-raising ceremonies in local schools.[37]

The activities of the Girl Scouts did not meet with the approval of some parents, however. Safiyyeh Firuz's family balked at the notion of her joining the Girl Scouts—apparently on the grounds of unsupervised contact with male scout troop leaders. She recalled someone saying, "What do you mean we should hand our girls over to this guy [mardikeh] to go, I don't know, go camping?"[38] Sattareh Farmanfarmaian recalled scouting as a positive part of her experience at American Bethel while mindful of how the activities were harnessed for the Pahlavi regime's propaganda efforts. Scouting was an extension of the wholesome physical exercise for girls encouraged by missionary educators and adopted by the regime during the Women's Awakening. And for Farmanfarmaian, the regimented activity of organized sports like basketball and the paramilitary drilling of scouting were part of "an encouraging and liberal atmosphere."[39] Though she was aware, even then, that an American named Thomas Gibson had persuaded the regime that scouting produced a loyal citizenry and that the flag-waving, pro-shah patriotism that went along with scouting was more than a little contrived (especially given her own family's history with the regime), she reports marching enthusiastically, wearing a "hot green Girl Scout uniform with shiny brass badges."[40]

Perhaps the most martial of images was that of women pilots. As illustrated in chapter 6, even though the flight academy was established for the benefit of civilians, it was surrounded by soldiers—some of whom took it upon themselves to interfere with Sadiqeh Dowlatshahi as she made her way to register. All of her instructors were military officers, training her in daring and life-threatening stunts.[41] The trainees (cadets?) were rounded up from their homes and civilian jobs and transported with military precision to Dowshan Tepe Airfield, which was also guarded by soldiers. The flight school was as close to military training as women could get. Sadiqeh Dowlatshahi was not motivated by this dimension of the experience, but she was aware of the military potential of flight training, at least in retrospect. She recalled that one of her fellow trainees, an artist, stood out because he was so much older than the others. She learned later that he was a Communist who eventually used his flight skills to escape to the Soviet Union. This later escape, with its vague implications of treason and espionage, seemed to explain (to her) why this odd man wanted to fly in the first place. Through his story and not her own, the association of flying with soldiering drifts fleetingly into view. Yet, for all of this encouragement and flirtation with images of women as warrior-citizens, the propaganda of the Women's Awakening was careful to imagine limits for women as well as possibilities.

Limiting the Potential of Modern Iranian Womanhood

Through its emphasis on secondary education and higher education, the Pahlavi regime seems to have realized that Iranian women could actually become not only well-educated wives and mothers but also well-paid professionals with a more visible social and economic presence. The state allowed a certain amount of speculation about the potential of women in this regard. Fatemeh Sayyah wrote a series of articles on women's creative history and potential for *Iran-e Emruz* in 1939 and 1940. Having largely accepted women's creative inferiority to men as a matter of historical record and current fact, Sayyah turned to Auguste Comte and John

Stuart Mill to consider "nature versus nurture" explanations for this inferiority. Dissatisfied with the stark choice between the two explanatory paradigms, she suggested that both played a part in the current state of affairs. Pregnancy and nursing weakened women's minds, but society had also closed off many opportunities for women to develop their creative and intellectual talents.[42] She concluded on an optimistic note: "[Without] changing the important womanly duty of motherhood, civilization has gradually reduced the extraordinary burdens of family life and has freed [women] from some chores of motherhood. In this way it has both increased the possibilities for women and allowed more of women's physical strength to be applied to social and intellectual matters. . . . [It] is possible that one day as a result of long-term changes the intellectual power of women that has lost its distinctiveness [tamayyoz va khosusiyat] will approximate the intellect of men."[43]

The recognition that the "chores of motherhood" were potentially incompatible with a woman's full development as a creative individual was, perhaps, as radical a feminist statement as was possible during the Women's Awakening. Male privilege and male guardianship are implicitly criticized because, clearly, the "chores of fatherhood" presented no such obstacles to an individual man's development. Yet, in Sayyah's scheme, even if some lost, primordial intellectual capacity could be reclaimed by women, there would still be boundaries to its potential. The standard of intellectual maturity was set by men's abilities. Women could aspire to approximate the male standard, but not to set a new or higher standard. This vision of women's potential reflects the difficult chore of balancing justifications for male guardianship with visions of women's emancipation through educated self-improvement. Women's intellectual and creative potential needed to be contained even when it was being encouraged, or the rational grounds for male guardianship would be undermined.

In the late spring of 1941, an article entitled "The Natural Differences between Men and Women" appeared in Iran-e Emruz.[44] The author, Mahmud Sanna'i, drew on the latest American scientific research into the process and reported conclusions that today seem rather familiar: (1) The intelligence of men and women is roughly equal, and (2) on average men are physically larger and stronger than women. However, in the area of "affect" Sanna'i could report, "Thorndike, the American scientist, believes that in men the instincts for belligerence and quarrelsomeness are strong, while in women the instinct for motherhood is strong. The strengths and weaknesses of many male and female inclinations can be seen as stemming from these [basic instincts]."[45]

جشن
دانشسرای
دختران

پیشاهنگان دختران دانشسرای

مقدمائی تهران ظهر روز فرخنده؛ جمعهٔ بیست و چهارم
اسفند جمعی از بانوان و دبیران آموزشگاهها و چند تن
از ممتحنین و اولیای دبیرستان را برای صرف نهـار و
مشاهدهٔ اولین آزمـایش خوراك پزی بزی دوشیز گان
پیشاهنگ در دانشـرای دختران دعوت نموده بودند
زیرا طبق برنامهٔ درجـهٔ دوم تعلیمات پیشاهنگی عموم
دختران پیشاهنگ باید فن خوراك پزی را بخـوبی
آموخته باشند ، بعد از صرف نهـار یك پرده نمایش

7.1. *Iran-e Emruz* 2, no. 2 (April/May 1940): 31. The crafting of "educated house-wives" is celebrated at a graduation ceremony at the Academy for Girls. By permission of MEDOC, University of Chicago.

Although Sanna'i cites another American researcher, Watson, to cast doubt on the notion that motherhood is an instinct rather than a learned behavior, he nevertheless concluded, "It can be said that either from the perspective of the individual or society, the most important duty of a women is to form and manage a family."[46] No matter what "scientific" criteria were applied, no matter what field of endeavor was examined, and no matter what a woman *could* do, motherhood with its related responsibilities was the career to which a woman should devote herself.

Women who did more could be noted and praised, but the modern Iranian woman was ultimately to be judged by what kind of mother she was. Just because she could fly airplanes did not mean that flying was her first and best destiny. Indeed, the academy for girls prepared them for a life of entertaining and household management (see illustration 7.1).[47]

In the end, *Iran-e Emruz* assured women that the best contribution they could make to the regime's propaganda efforts was to help instill the ideals of patriotism and industriousness in their children.[48] The only article in

Iran-e Emruz that highlighted professional women in a supervisory capacity was a feature on the history of Iranian kindergartens in which the principal and all the teachers were women.[49] In a collection of moralizing essays for high school students, Mohammad Hejazi—the publisher of *Iran-e Emruz*—devoted only one essay to the question of women and work, but the article was very telling.[50] It was called "Honor," and it criticized a family for choosing to starve rather than have the daughters of the family work outside the home following the death of their father. When Hejazi asked one of the brothers why his sisters were not working, the brother responded, "We have our honor. [This] is easier than putting the women to work."[51] As was usually the case in Hejazi's artless prose, he turned to lecturing the brother: "I said, 'You are making a mistake. Dishonor comes from idleness. If you want people to be without honor, keep them from working and provide their bread for free. They will give up ambition and honor and become despicable and disreputable. They will be good for nothing but dependence and hopelessness.'"[52]

The message of this little essay is mixed. It advocates gainful employment for women. However, it does so only after establishing that the primary male guardian, the father, was "out of the picture" and that the remaining male guardians could not provide for the family on their own. Ironically, the story also suggests that women at home do not perform meaningful work—they are "idle."

Thus, in the way the Iranian press framed her, the modern Iranian woman was at once made capable of many things and yet restricted to one societal role. Even in that role, she could be devalued. And although the modern Iranian woman was being pictured alongside, or instead of, her European and American sisters, doing great things, she was not entirely free from "the European example" because her capabilities and limitations were being evaluated against European history and culture (by Sayyah) on one hand, and measured within the paradigms of American scientific research (by Sanna'i) on the other. "The European example" had more than one implication, however. If the women of Europe and America could represent the best in modern womanhood, they could also represent the worst.

Women's Awakening propaganda was not content simply to remind women of their limits and their "appropriate" roles. Male guardianship also depended on the notion that unsupervised women were immoral women who posed a real danger to society. The moral laxity that was identified with European and American women in the nineteenth century was now associated with modern Iranian womanhood—especially with those women who might seek to be independent from or equal to men. Shadowing the capable modern Iranian woman who worked alongside her modern male guardian was a dangerous modern Iranian woman threatening to rebel against him.

The Dangerous Woman

In addition to the limitations constructed around her, the capable woman was stalked by another frame in the Iranian press, that of the dangerous woman. Male guardianship could not trust women to exert upon themselves the moral control that male guardianship demanded of them. This mistrust manifested itself in a demonized image of women as the source of evil and discord. Nothing seemed to smack of immoral rebellion more than the idea of political rights for women—in any measure. Progressive constitutionalists portrayed European suffragettes as brave but shrill, while Iranian women were either lazy or deceitful thieves undermining public safety (see chapter 2). Debates on miscegenation in the 1920s suggested that more educated and liberated European women were also more prone to sexual impropriety than their Iranian sisters (see chapter 5). But when Iranian women entered dance halls to tango in Mohammad Mas'ud's *Night Amusements,* they brought with them a chaotic sexual energy. Even when Iranian women pursued an education from European mentors, they might be warned that they were still too lazy in pursuing their potential to merit equality (see chapter 5). In short, the moral laxity of European and American women was combined with the ignorance and sloth of the "traditional" Iranian women to produce a potent and dangerous foil to the "capable" modern Iranian women. The "dangerous woman" remained part of public discourse in the 1930s as well as part of Women's Awakening propaganda.

During the discussion of Hosayn 'Ali's "marriage versus higher education for women" conundrum in 1934 (see chapter 6), a number of respondents did not simply characterize women as ill suited for anything but domestic chores; they took things one step further. Hosayn Barjasteh, who had opposed the idea of women obtaining a higher education, offered this misogynous nugget: "I dare say that 80, 90 percent or more of today's girls are basically unacquainted with their natural duties. . . . They are considered the enemies of civilization and progress. . . . If someone were to tell [these girls] that women have been created to go to the cinema, goof around, and dance in the wind, they would idolize him."[53]

Another respondent who opposed higher education for women, Sayyed

Nurollah Sotudeh, was more explicit in asserting that Iranian women were being corrupted by modern amusements. He argued that too much education would make women uninterested in marriage by exposing them to corrupting forms of entertainment, writing "Novels destroy the morals of individuals, especially women, and have negative effects on society. Why? Because the insubstantial yet sweet sentences attract the reader and instill inappropriate desires in her, and it is the same in the matter of cinemas. A girl sees an actor who, even if he is behaving strangely, is at the same time handsome. Of course, she is human, and no matter how hard she tries, she cannot control herself. Then she wants a husband like the actor who plays these exciting roles."[54]

The day after news of Turkish women obtaining the right to vote and to be elected was splashed on the front pages of *Ettela'at*, an article appeared in the "Social Questions" column. It opened by saying that moths destroy fabric by eating it and that there are "morality moths" that destroy the fabric of society. Women who engage in gambling, drinking, smoking, dressing, and acting provocatively were the moths who destroyed society's moral fabric. The article exhorted readers, "These women have been introduced as educated, modern, and intellectual(!) . . . Women argue how is it that men can do these things, and they cannot. They argue that men and women must be equal . . . But when the tie that holds their lives together comes undone, they will understand how expensive these amusements turned out to be. . . . Ladies, be careful that the 'gambling moth' does not rend your morals to pieces, because this 'madness moth' is unusually apt to wreck homes, [to cause] black days, misfortune, and disaster, and to eat the moral roots of society. For you are the trainers of [society's next] generation!"[55]

This passage is very lethal indeed. It equates women who seek equality with men—"modern women"—with women of bad character and equates the notion of equality of the sexes with gambling, smoking, drinking, and loose behavior. The combined impression of these passages is that women are frivolous, especially corruptible, and irresistibly corrupting once they themselves have been tainted. In short, women are dangerous—the potential "enemies of civilization and progress."

Although it seems to have been accepted regime doctrine that the entrance of women into society through unveiling would raise the moral standards of society, it was also true that there was still a great deal of anxiety about the moral consequences of male and female strangers socializing together. There was as much of Rezaqoli Mirza's immature awkwardness about such socializing as there was an ideological commitment to the natural goodness of such interaction. As the Ministry of Education memorandum of November 1935 suggested would happen (see chapter 4), there was an effort by the regime to publicize the rules of social protocol to ensure the same level of moral sanctity that the physical veil had guaranteed. For example, in January and February 1936, *Ettela'at* ran excerpts from Amir Hekmat's *The Protocols of Social Intercourse and Etiquette.*[56]

It was a work devoted to the premise that the true veil that protects innocence and chastity is the training of the spirit and morals of the individual. It is doubtful how useful most of the series was to the average Iranian since it seemed to assume a rather high standard of living (with rules for attending the theater or throwing a banquet). Nonetheless, it occasionally did address the specific question of how the sexes should interact. Men were to greet only women whom they knew or who had taken notice of them.[57] The act of a handshake could get downright complicated: "An older woman must first extend her hand to younger men and women, and young ladies. Married men may extend their hand to young ladies, but a single man has no right. If a single man extends his hand to a young lady, she should not refrain from giving her hand, but she must treat [the matter] with the utmost coolness so as to make it [almost] reproachful."[58]

In addition to these excruciating rituals devoted simply to saying hello, there were specific rules for the behavior of women in public. Women were not to leave their homes without their hats, were to make sure to remove their coats and gloves if they were going to stay for any period of time at anyone's house, and were to ask for things in a gentle voice at the store.[59] In many ways, it might have seemed that these European-inspired rules of etiquette were no less restrictive than the veil was supposed to be!

Oddly enough, the goal of protecting society from the dangerous woman was subverted by an aspect of the "capable woman": women's athleticism. Although the subject of women's education had been considered for more than a century before the Women's Awakening, the subject of women's physical education did not receive much attention until after World War I. Partisans of the Renewal Party seem to have raised the issue first.[60] Although women's magazines like *Danesh* and *Shokufeh* had written about women's health and hygiene since 1910, they did not talk about women's athletics or physical education. However, shortly before the Women's Awakening, some women's magazines did publish articles and other features regarding women and sports.[61] One magazine that had a great deal of impact on the form of Pahlavi regime propaganda was *Iran-*

e Bastan, published by Iranian Nazi sympathizer Sayf Azad (see chapter 6). *Iran-e Bastan* regularly published articles on women's athletics.[62] Physical education for Iranian women had been pioneered by the American missionary schools in the first quarter of the twentieth century.[63] Thus, in Women's Awakening propaganda, the modern Iranian woman was supposed to be physically fit, and the pages of *Mehregan, Iran-e Emruz,* and even *Ettela'at* glorified the image of women performing healthy exercise.[64]

But since the days of *Danesh,* matters of health had been closely associated with matters of beauty, and it was no different during the Women's Awakening. In *Mehregan,* beauty tips for Iranian women[65] appeared along with news of European beauty contests,[66] leaving no doubt as to what the standards for modern Iranian womanhood were to be. The glamorous beauty of Hollywood and the European film industry also penetrated the Iranian periodical press at this time with features on film dance numbers with exotically dressed women[67] and on stars like Ginger Rogers.[68] Physical health and glamorous beauty were conflated in articles showing scantily clad and provocatively posed starlets under the headline, "Do You Want to Be Beautiful and Ravishing?" (see illustration 7.2)[69] The content of the article was about the favorite exercises of the starlets, and also pictured were rather unglamorous German women performing some sort of team gymnastics.

There were also celebrity workout features and glamorous health/ beauty features.[70] The glamorous beauty that was dangled before the modern Iranian woman conflicted with other articles that appeared in *Mehregan* admonishing her to dress simply: "Everyone knows and it is clearer than the sun in the sky that ladies mostly wear chic clothes and make themselves up for the approval and praise of other women, not men. . . . One of the most famous movie stars who at first acted in the theater wrote this about plain clothing and its importance, 'I owe my fame most to a way of dressing, and my happiness from the beginning started with wearing plain clothes.' Nobody can prove false the benefits of dressing simply, or protest the attractiveness of natural adornment."[71]

So, glamorous beauty actually lay in simplicity and not in the fashions featured in *Mehregan.* The unnamed "most famous movie star" had said so. Furthermore, women were not supposed to dress up to please other women (that would be vain!), but were supposed to be attractive to men. This pearl of wisdom clashed somewhat with an article in *Ettela'at* that protested that women were not just pretty faces or placed on earth "for the

7.2. *Mehregan* 73 (16 September 1937): 12–13. The conflation of health and beauty. The article asks, "Do you want to be beautiful and ravishing?" The top center picture is of women engaging in wholesome athletics, but the pictures to the left and right are of Hollywood starlets (Martha Ray, *top left,* and Sonya Henne, *bottom right)* in provocative poses, skimpy outfits, and high heels. The ostensible purpose was to show how even beautiful actresses kept themselves in shape. By permission of MEDOC, University of Chicago.

pleasure of men"[72] —this, from a publication that had given over all of page eight to glamorize stylish movie stars in its "special page for theater, cinema, radio, and concerts" for most of 1938!

Of course, glamorous beauty was potentially corrupting. Starlets' moral problems also graced the pages of *Mehregan.* An American starlet confessed to her lifelong struggle with selfishness and a bad temper, and a French actress fell from grace for an unspecified crime and was imprisoned.[73] Just two days before the third anniversary of the Seventeenth of Day, *Kushesh* ran a story about the inherent evil of glamorous beauty—on the front page.[74] "Chic" and possessing a "good figure," Anna Schneider captured the heart of a Polish count. She manipulated him into a marriage proposal, then jilted him and made off with some very expensive presents.

She ran off to Germany where the gambling operation she oversaw in her home caught up with her and landed her in jail. In case the point of this "front-page news" was lost on anybody, the editors of *Kushesh* prefaced it thus: "Beauty is God-given capital for women, which, if they choose to misuse it, will lead to a bad end. The protagonist of this story is an example of the sort of woman who imprisons others with [her] beauty and in the end is duly punished for her acts."[75]

In the late nineteenth century, some Iranian travelers to Europe had feared that the sexual permissiveness there would corrupt Iranian men who went there to study. In the pages of *Iranshahr* in 1924, Sadiqeh Dowlatabadi speculated that the charms of European women had seduced away European-educated Iranian men from sexually inexperienced Iranian girls. Before the Women's Awakening, some had blamed the corruption of Iranian girls on the influence of modern European and American culture, and after the Awakening these very corrupting elements were simultaneously sold and condemned by the Pahlavi-controlled press.

The images of modern European and American success that were claimed for modern Iranian womanhood were placed alongside images of modern European and American vice. The images mixed along the frontier of male guardianship, a frontier marked by women's suffrage or any hint of women's moral independence from men. The result from this balance was the ultimate expression of modern Iranian womanhood that could exist within the boundaries of male guardianship. Although this particular balance was to prove too precarious to maintain itself in the wake of the collapse of Reza Shah's regime in 1941, it remained influential on the course of the woman question in the press in the years immediately following that collapse, as we shall see.

At some level, women themselves were concerned about "dangerous" women, because such women undercut either their personal efforts or the progress of women generally. In chapter 4, we met Parvin Moayyad-Sabeti, who proudly recalled how the women in her Mashhad Nurbakhshiyan Society "never" wore the veil—even in the 1940s as the enforcement of unveiling slackened. But she was not sure that her unveiled colleagues fully appreciated the importance of unveiling. She recalled:

Q. But how did they go in the streets?

A. In the streets they went without the *chador* and, indeed, wore very good clothes. They minded their clothes and, unfortunately, all they took from "the equality of rights"—or perhaps they understood this from their Western sisters—is that they must be chic and make themselves up better. They never sensed how they were coming up short. They were not aware *[agah]*.[76]

But the disdain that Moayyed-Sabeti expressed for "chic" women—those who were only going through the motions of modernity and missing the point—became a common charge in the wake of the Women's Awakening in the 1940s. Men used it to criticize activist women, and women would use it against one another. Messages about women's achievement continued to be mixed. The conflation of health and beauty underscored an ornamental function for women and colored their achievements with the vibrant hues of scandal and glamour (see illustration 7.3).[77] For ex-

7.3. *'Alam-e Zanan,* August/September 1944, back cover. The endurance of Western glamour. Every issue of *'Alam-e Zanan* featured at least one full-page photo like this one, along with tips on fashion and beauty (conflated with health) taken from American and European magazines. It is a legacy of the Women's Awakening that has endured even past the Islamic Revolution of 1979.

ample, looking back on the 1940s and 1950s, Sadiqeh Dowlatshahi, Iran's first woman pilot, could remember women's magazines covering her regular flights for the encouragement of other women. But she also remembered the editor of a women's magazine organizing groups of young women to enter beauty contests abroad—like the contests *Mehregan* had reported in the late 1930s.

Despite the Euro-American standards of beauty that were emerging in the Iranian press, it remained important for the ideal modern Iranian woman to be moral and purposeful in her actions. To do otherwise was to risk not being taken seriously. Dr. Tusi scornfully recalled a classmate named "Firuzeh." Firuzeh was "not smart" and only succeeded "because of [her] looks." She was engaged to a fellow student but broke it off in favor of a new suitor, an Iranian man who had completed his medical training in France. She went on to a successful career in Europe which, Dr. Tusi insisted, was the result of riding her husband's coattails. I was fascinated by Tusi's assertion that Firuzeh was "not a Muslim; she had boyfriends." Earlier, she had listed Firuzeh as one of the Muslim women by virtue of not being Armenian. For a moment, when she equated being a Muslim with being modest, Dr. Tusi's sense of identity was keen and uncompromising. What is clear also is that concern regarding a women's modesty and her physical attractiveness was part of how male students evaluated their female colleagues. The men stayed clear of the women except, of course, when they did not. And if they said anything about the women, somehow the thrust of their comments made it back to the women. It was men who set the rules (albeit contradictory ones) and the pace at which woman could gain true, collegial acceptance.

This sense of acceptance was very important. Despite the obvious similarities in their histories, Dr. Tusi's memories of her medical training cast Firuzeh as her opposite. Whereas she, Dr. Tusi, was hardworking, modest, Muslim, and yet cosmopolitan, Firuzeh was a flirt, an opportunist, and a willing outcast from her own culture. What seems to reinforce this contrast in Dr. Tusi's mind is the hard-won acceptance she eventually obtained from her male colleagues and that Firuzeh never obtained and never truly merited.

And acceptance only came, Dr. Tusi recalled, after the male students were convinced that the women students were "good girls, decent" as well as "hardworking." They were only convinced of this after the women had finished their coursework in their fourth year of medical school. Even so, a social outing captured in a group picture (see chapter 6) was not a comfortable mix of men and women colleagues. In recalling the outing, Dr.

Tusi seemed a bit anxious to frame it as "proper," quickly stressing that the excursions were day trips, "no overnight." Also in the picture was my father, eight years junior to my aunt. He was not "tagging along" with her for more mature and sophisticated company. He was my aunt's chaperone, her guardian.

Dr. Tusi's recollections have a number of themes in common with the propaganda of the Women's Awakening. Alongside the moral, hardworking, and capable modern Iranian women (herself), there is an immoral and dangerous woman (Firuzeh), symbolizing the excesses of westernization with her sexual freedom and flamboyance, who shadows Dr. Tusi. Upon Firuzeh, Dr. Tusi—and perhaps her fellow students—could project her own concerns about being a "mixed European/Iranian." Even in her recollections of protesting medical-school quotas in 1945, she distances herself from the Marxists who organized the protest and takes the edge off the fact that she was challenging state authority (an obvious extension of male guardianship) by emphasizing the politeness of her participation. Thus, her social interactions stay within the boundary prescribed by Women's Awakening propaganda in the 1930s, and, in her memory, her brief experience with social activism more resembles an extracurricular activity at school than an experiment in political protest. She was capable, but not rebellious against male guardianship. She (eventually) integrated herself into a male-dominated profession but never came close to compromising her reputation. She became the perfect example of modern Iranian womanhood as it was imagined in the propaganda of the Women's Awakening, intentionally or not.

It would likely be a mistake to assume that the Pahlavi state orchestrated a double bind for Iranian women with regard to morality and beauty. In making possible images of unveiled Iranian women, the regime also made possible the increased use of diverse and contradictory images from Euro-American culture to sell products and periodicals. The conflation of health and beauty that became so obvious in the press during the Women's Awakening was in conflict with the moral qualities the regime wanted to instill in modern Iranian womanhood through education and propaganda. At the same time, it provided regime propagandists (as it would social critics of all political persuasions in the 1940s) with a ready source of negative examples to caution Iranian women against open defiance of male guardianship. The dangerous woman was less a creation of the Women's Awakening than a new synthesis of long-standing concerns over westernization, modernization, and the woman question. It was a synthesis that was made more salient and pressing because Iranian society was being forced by the state to consider new possibilities and images of modern Iranian womanhood.

All of these elements—state control over women's images, the suggestion that women might become full citizens, and the suggestion that women were not worthy of full citizenship—set the stage for the aftermath of the Women's Awakening. The call for gender equality that emerged in the 1940s both built upon the successes of the Women's Awakening and struggled against the new form of male guardianship that accompanied those successes. The effort of some "modern Iranian women" to break with male guardianship in the 1940s, though it did not result in its immediate goal of women's suffrage or its broader vision of gender equality, established a new frontier in gender relations. It is to the creation of that new frontier that we now turn.

8

Breaking with Male Guardianship

It was only in the wake of the Women's Awakening that women made clear demands for gender equality in the pages of the Iranian press—and not just in women's magazines. The image of the modern Iranian woman was never more available than after the Women's Awakening. In its most optimistic expressions in the 1940s, the image held the promise of work, education, more equitable social relationships with men, and new respect for the "science" of motherhood (see illustration 8.1).[1] At the same time, male hostility toward working women (particularly those in offices) and in the civic arena was never more acute. For the first time in Iranian history, a campaign for women's suffrage was undertaken. But its quiet failure was more telling than if there had been political fireworks over the issue. Iranian feminism was in the difficult position of declaring its independence from male control while at the same time trying to retain (and expand) its place in the main arena of male dominance—the state—even as a junior partner. Complicating matters further was the weakness of the state during the Allied occupation of World War II. The throne was no longer a reliable or indispensable partner in furthering women's progress, but Iranian feminists could ally (and subordinate) themselves to a number of political organizations. There was some reason to hope for change through parliamentary action; during the 1940s the Parliament finally approved funding for Iranian women to pursue higher education overseas.[2] The political left emerged as the principal ally in the women's suffrage campaign, but Islamic revivalists were also recruiting women to their cause. This dynamic political landscape shifted along a new cultural fault line: For the first time in Iranian history, there emerged equal-rights arguments to counter complementary-rights arguments against women's progress. And both sides of the new frontier took the Women's Awakening of 1936–41 as their point of departure.

آبان ماه ۱۳۲۳
بها ۸ ریال

عالم زنان

شماره (۵)

8.1. 'Alam-e Zanan (Women's World), October/November 1944, front cover. Iranian women might portray themselves as industrious, adventurous, athletic, romantic, and maternal in the periodical press after the Women's Awakening.

Male Backlash and the Call for Equal Rights

The backdrop for the male backlash against women in the office place was the economic crisis caused by the Allied occupation of World War II. The brunt of the effects of the occupation was felt hardest in 1943, when Iran's gross national product was estimated to have fallen 15 percent (since 1941) before it began to work its way back to preinvasion levels over the next two years.[3] In the wake of Reza Shah's regime, the state was the single largest employer of skilled clerical labor, with an estimated total bureaucratic workforce of 90,000[4]—this in an economy that was considered to have few modern industrial features outside of the oil industry and thus few suitable outlets for the growing number of people with secondary- and college-level education. In the unstable economic environment of the war years, a reliable government job with a steady (if rarely extravagant) paycheck and opportunities for advancement (and, for the unscrupulous or desperate, illegal financial gain) would be highly prized. But, as noted earlier, the government not only employed women as office workers. It employed women as teachers and medical professionals as well. That these women professionals did not come under attack in the press in the 1940s (indeed, they continued to be praised) suggests that there was something especially troubling about women in the office. Was the backlash due to the increasing number of women employed as office workers during the Women's Awakening? This coupled with the widespread disruption of state activities during the Allied occupation might have made fewer entry-level bureaucratic positions available for men. Or was the backlash due to an increasing number of men looking for such work during the war years? More studies on Iranian labor history need to be done before any definitive answer to these questions can be attempted.[5] However, as a matter of cultural history, it is completely clear that women in the office place created anxiety regarding public morality, women's fundamental competence as workers, the security of men's privileges in modern Iranian society, and, among some feminists, the esteem women felt they had won over the years as educated housewives and mothers.

On 29 December 1941, not quite four months after the collapse of Reza Shah's regime, a correspondent for *Kushesh* (an old 1920s renewalist paper that, like *Ettela'at,* had continued publishing through Reza Shah Pahlavi's reign) addressed the issue of women working in offices.[6] Identifying himself only as "M," he raised the specter of nine million women typists who would take over offices and become burdens to men rather than partners. "M" reminded "our modernized ladies," who had benefited from modern education in Iran and Europe, that their place was in the home. He "proved" this point by pointing out that the original of the Persian word for girl (*dushizeh*)was "the one who provides milk."[7] In a follow-up article, "M" pointed out that he was raising the question of women at work "after [the return] of freedom of the press."[8] This is a clear indication that the Women's Awakening had gone too far even for some long-standing allies of Reza Shah. "M" summarized the arguments of men and women in the office and then appointed himself as discussant. Not surprisingly, he gave men both the first and last word:

Summary of the Opinions of Men . . .

(1) Women are taking the places of men. As a result, some family men are being kept out of office work.
(2) Young ladies who work in offices are not willing to start families. Office salaries—especially after recent raises—have made [young women] so selfish that they will no longer take on family life.
(3) The presence of women in offices causes the moral corruption of both men and women.
(4) Women cannot work like men. Married women in the late months of pregnancy have to take leaves and burden men with their workload.
(5) Nobody expects women to have an education. [Women] just need basic literacy in Persian and ten hours' practice on a typing machine to be employed. In contrast, [employers] expect a great deal of education and diplomas from men before employing them.

The Answers of Women . . .

(1) Women are not taking the place of men. With the exception of one or two offices, the number of women relative to men is low.
(2) If the young women who work in offices have not started families, it is because they have not found young men worthy of marriage.
(3) The presence of women in offices does not cause the corruption of morals as long as the men do not already have corrupted morals.
(4) It should not be considered abnormal that married women take off one or two months [near the end of a pregnancy] because men also take time off when feeling ill.

(5) In contrast to men's perceptions, most of the women who work in the office possess an education and a diploma.

(6) Everything else aside, men and women are equal in rights and there is no reason that men should reserve office jobs for themselves.[9]

After faulting women for the "emotional" nature of their response, "M" put himself in the role of mediator. While accepting that men's and women's rights were equal, he stressed that they were not identical. The occasional Joan of Arc notwithstanding, he argued, it was men who fought and died in wars, which was, of course, "the greatest of life's duties." By excluding women from military service, he excluded them from full citizenship as well as full rights to economic participation. Furthermore, he objected that pregnancy was not comparable to illness because an illness could not be avoided. Nonetheless, he agreed that women were competent at their jobs, were well enough educated, and were, in fact, not overrunning government offices at the moment.

But "M" wanted to keep the number of women in the office low. Those women did not make good wives because "thoughts of office life would remain in their brains for all eternity," and he encouraged men to seek mates among other sorts of women.[10] He agreed that men and women working together was problematic and noted that some office managers had actually segregated their male and female workers. His great concern was that if current trends continued there would be "nine million lady typists" taking male jobs and not starting families. Among his solutions were training women to be mothers and wives foremost and diversifying women's professional education in fields like dentistry, pharmacology, and medicine so that those who did go to work would not all be sent into offices. Not only should women be encouraged to form families, but married women should by law be "returned from offices to their homes."[11]

Support for male guardianship did not come only from men. In 1942, the head of Reza Shah's Women's Society, Sadiqeh Dowlatabadi, responding to "this moment which is the most dangerous in the lives of Iranian women,"[12] revived her periodical *Zaban-e Zanan*. But *Zaban-e Zanan* was filled with articles stressing the virtues of motherhood and tips on "domestic science." An American article on the subject of women and work, translated and published in *Zaban-e Zanan*, declared that a woman's "first important job" was taking care of a husband, and her second was giving birth to and raising children.[13] It took a dim view of young unmarried women who "learned how to type with a full measure of errors" and then went from office to office looking for work, "not afraid of the thousand ways of corrupting her morals that could result from interacting with ill-mannered men who are everywhere."[14] Although the author of the article agreed that working for a wage was an honorable thing and that a woman could contribute to her household by working for money, the author felt she should not do so if her husband disapproved. Women with young children should stay at home, and those with school-age children were given a number of guidelines to follow: "First, their husbands should be informed about the conditions of the offices where they work, and should know with whom they interact. Also, male co-workers should know a lady's husband and show him respect. Second, the work should not be too tiring. Attention to this point is important because, after returning home from the office, the woman is responsible for providing for the comfort of herself and her husband. She should find the opportunity to clean up after the mistakes of the help and look in on the kitchen. She should feed the children dinner earlier. If she becomes tired and worn out at this time with all this work, the outlook is black."[15]

Women's presence in the office served as a new point of departure for the woman question and, despite the attitudes expressed in *Zaban-e Zanan,* provoked demands for gender equality rather than simply enhanced rights for women. These new demands surfaced in the most unlikely places in the periodical press. In the spring of 1942, the editor of *Eqdam* (Endeavor), ʿAbbas Khalili (d. 1972),[16] invited women to address issues of social reform in the paper with the challenge, "Where Are the Lionesses?" The first response came from Fakhri Estifa, who titled her response, "Where Are the Lions?"[17] She criticized the men of her day for being self-serving and not seeing to the needs of the country. Despite the criticism, she implicitly left the running of the country to men. Another woman, Tuba Mofidi, was the first to respond in a column that came to be entitled "Woman and Life." She took no issue with the substance of Estifa's article but instead thought it appropriate to address the larger question of women in society. She declared, "Women can only perform delicate tasks, and therefore women should not enter into frays and dangerous affairs, especially involvement in politics and war. In my opinion any woman who claims competence in such matters is deficient in her womanly nature. Woman was created for a normal life, housekeeping, raising children, and fine crafts such as painting, flower arranging, music, and occasionally poetry and prose writing."[18]

Other women also weighed in with similar opinions.[19] In her letter, Iran Nezhi added, "Dear Young Ladies! Cherished Sisters! By God, you are the protectors of the Iranian nation. God has granted an exalted and unique position. The greatest name, that of 'mother,' he gave to you. . . . You must know that if you perform your motherly duties, your own loving mother, Iran, will be pleased with you. If you do not, she will curse you forever. You must reform yourselves."[20]

'Abbas Khalili wrote a front-page editorial that encouraged women to focus on their primary duties as wives and mothers.[21] In a sympathetic response, Parvin Modabber began her editorial by defending Iranian women's patriotism and willingness to be self-sacrificing good mothers, but she conceded that women had an image problem. In an interesting twist, she laid women's moral downfall at the palace threshold of Reza Shah Pahlavi: "You cried twenty years of your life away over the condition of women. You saw with your own eyes how instead of learning sacrifice, patriotism, chastity, strength, and circumspection, the pure-hearted women of Iran learned dance, fashion, excessive makeup, idle talk [herzeh-dara'i], and a thousand other wicked behaviors."[22]

The power of men's pent-up grievances was nowhere so apparent in the Iranian press as in Mohammad Mas'ud's Mard-e Emruz (Today's Man). The essential misogyny that had so animated his literary works in the 1930s translated well into his revived career as the publisher of one of the most controversial and sensational independent weeklies in the 1940s. One cartoon depicted an attractive woman in an office, dressed in slacks, with a somewhat disdainful look on her face as she said to the men, "I won't elaborate. Just like when I was with the [foreign] advisors, the 5000–rial salary, afternoon tennis, night outings, dinner, dancing, and choice of hose and clothes are up to you."[23]

The "foreign advisor" to whom the cartoon alluded was likely Arthur Chester Millspaugh, head of the second American Financial Mission to Iran from 1942 to 1945. Mas'ud was one of a chorus of journalists who dogged Millspaugh relentlessly during his tenure as the chief financial officer of the Iranian government. In Mard-e Emruz, Millspaugh's fiscal administration was likened to the tyranny of Reza Shah and the decadence of American playboys.[24] By linking the female office worker to foreign advisors, Mas'ud transformed the modern Iranian woman into a willing and immoral collaborator with Euro-American economic imperialism. Continuing in this vein, Mard-e Emruz criticized a wealthy woman named Fakhr al-Dowleh for serving as a representative of the Ford Corporation in Iran, noting, "At a time when good, hardworking men lay pipe for 1 shahi, Ms. Fakhr al-Dowleh pulls at least 10,000,000 rials out of thin air."[25] In the pages of Mard-e Emruz, working women could only profit at the expense of men. She was, just like her "traditional" foil, an economic parasite rather than the productive partner imagined in the press in the 1920s (see chapter 3).

The modern Iranian woman had been further satirized in *Mard-e Emruz* for her shallow consumerism and devotion to Western fashion.[26] Sympathy for women tended to manifest itself only when they seemed vulnerable. For example, a series on prostitution in 1945 emphasized that women had fallen on hard times because men were unable or unwilling to provide for their families.[27] Women who seemed independent of men were derided, and those who seemed to be failing without the help of men were pitied, but the core of the message was the same: Women could not and should not do without the guidance and protection of men. On the other hand, *Mard-e Emruz* also published an article that argued that the government should regulate houses of prostitution to ensure public health (as was and is the case in the Republic of Turkey) and accept both prostitution and temporary marriage as sexual outlets.[28]

This combination of misogyny and sympathy took a lighthearted turn in the pages of the satirical weekly *Baba Shamal*. One mock announcement to women read:

(1) Your tears are your decisive argument [in any quarrel]. Use this decisive argument often.
(2) In love, money is more attractive than anything else.
(3) Be like a slow clock in measuring your age after twenty.
(4) If you don't like philosophy and science, say, "We women are the philosophy of life and the original cause for the appearance of science."
(5) Believe that most of your faults come from men, and most of men's virtues come from you.
(6) If someone talks about the ugliness of a friend of yours, immediately agree because it is in your interest.[29]

That all women might be considered vain and shallow was reinforced on the cover of the issue of 12 May 1943 that portrayed a group of women, veiled and unveiled, trying to seduce Baba Shamal, the fictional character and namesake of the magazine.[30] Taken alone, these examples of misogyny would wholly misrepresent the opinions expressed in *Baba Shamal* on the woman question. *Baba Shamal*, as part of a consortium of left-leaning periodicals, wrote in favor of women's right to work. Furthermore, it was one of the first periodicals to signal the political left's support of women's suffrage. And discussions of women's political enfranchisement grew out of debates over women's right to work.

Some of *Eqdam*'s correspondents in 1942 attacked male guardianship while defending the rights of women to participate politically and economically. Citing examples of women political leaders in world history, Tahereh Yazdanfarr took issue with the fact that Fakhri Estifa had left the world of politics to men: "We [women] forget that the intelligence, insight, and aptitude of women is often greater than that of men, or at least is no less. I am very surprised to hear Lady Fakhri Estifa say that women should not interfere in political matters."[31]

Of course, Fakhri Estifa had not actually said that in her letter, but she provoked a reaction nonetheless. This repudiation of male guardianship took the form of a positive assertion of female ability to rule. Another correspondent, Farangis Mazandarani, attacked the results of male guardianship directly.[32] She declared that it was men, not women, who wasted the nation's money on foreign fashion and on entertaining themselves with debauched nights on the town. If Iran was in a mess, it was because men were running things:

> The gentlemen have the initiative. The programs of girls schools are established by their hands. The country's laws, office organizations, and such are all in the hands of the gentlemen. Instead of our gentlemen striving to improve themselves, the organization of the schools, and the rest of it, they go after the powder and cosmetics or women's actions, behavior, or working in offices. It is really shameful how, at such a time and during this regrettable situation for our country with all these deficiencies in the country's affairs, every day the columns of newspapers fill up with criticisms of women. It is so embarrassing to have a country whose men think of nothing but women. I remember last August, when this unfortunate situation for our country occurred [i.e., the Allied occupation], one of the government offices distributed a circular about women's stockings. During those same two or three days they spoke about coloring fingernails and proper toiletry on the radio. Two or three days afterward I went to see an American friend who had noticed the same thing, and I wished a bomb would drop on my head so I would not have to live in this shameful society.[33]

Mazandarani clearly rejected male scapegoating of women for the country's problems, but she also called into question men's good faith as guardians. Her remarks also display the continued problem of the European example. On the one hand, she condemned Iranian men for following European fashions, and on the other hand, she never felt more ashamed than before the judgment of her American friend. Another woman, Puran Hajilu, complained of the same double standard when it was applied to women and challenged male supremacy: "We ladies do not know which tune of yours to dance to![34] One moment you wrap us in a shroud, and place a face veil upon our face, and the next moment you give us freedom. You take us to parties, to cinemas, and onto the streets in makeup and respectable clothes so that you can teach us social protocol and principles of civility, and admit us to offices and to governmental and nongovernmental work, and then you yourselves block our way . . . Why should you be in offices and not us? Who made you better than us? . . . Aren't we brothers and sisters?"[35]

A respondent known only as "M. H. F." was not amused by Hajilu's complaint, her "selfishness," or her familial metaphor: "It must be said that they brought you out of the tyranny of the veil. Did they tell you to wear a blouse that shows all your parts underneath? Did they tell you to wear stockings that show your legs, or not to wear stockings at all? . . . Hundreds of women have been seen fighting with their husbands and divorcing them, relying on their salaries after entering the office. These actions lead to a decrease in population and the strength of the country."[36]

As with "M" in *Kushesh*, "M. H. F." was given the last word in this particular exchange of opinion in the pages of *Eqdam*. These exchanges recall the nineteenth-century treatise of Bibi Khanom Astarabadi, but there is an important difference: Astarabadi never questioned the principle of male guardianship, just its practice. As we have seen, however, men and women who were comfortable with the link between male guardianship and modern Iranian womanhood could now expect to be challenged in the press by those who rejected this link. The fact that a conservative paper like *Eqdam* would publish such sentiments (even if only to refute them) marked a significant change in discussions of the woman question in the Iranian press. As has been noted by Afsaneh Najmabadi and others, women used similar critiques of men in the press during the early constitutional period in an effort to shame them into proper conduct politically and socially. Certainly, that meaning is more than implied here. However, when women wrote to *Sur-e Esrafil* and *Iran-e Now* during the First and Second Parliaments (1906–11), they were supported by the male editorial staff of those papers. In the 1940s, women could publish letters in papers even when the editors disagreed with the tone or content of their letters. Furthermore, some women who spoke out against male guardianship in the 1940s were not simply rejecting the terms of male guardianship but, rather, the very idea of male guardianship.

By late 1943, the question of women's political enfranchisement had become a regular feature of the woman question in the press. *Baba Shamal* advocated women's rights while parodying the "women's column" format in the rest of the press. It printed letters from fictional women called Khaleh Kukumeh (Auntie Old Cuckoo), Naneh Shushul, president of the Granny Party (ra'is-e hezb-e naneh-ha), Rudeh Deraz (Long Winded), and Khanom-e Kuchulu (Little Lady). Given a folksy voice by the editors at *Baba Shamal*, Khaleh Kukumeh had this to say on the question of political enfranchisement: "I swear on yer life, if us women had the right to vote, and they counted us as human bein's, I would-a voted a few thousand times fer ya and other decent people too. . . . I mean, fer God's sake, where in the world is it a custom that some-a us women who are as smart as any man, and who got as much learnin' and sense as men got, can't vote, but then, uneducated men who can't tell up from down, and who don't even understan' jes' what electin' a representative is all about, have all kindsa rights?"[37]

On 16 February 1944, *Baba Shamal* ran a poem entitled "Women and the Right to Vote":

Dear Baba, every night this crazy heart
Talks with this distracted head
About why an ordinary man has a vote,
But a women of a hundred talents does not.
Men and women are not different in nature.
Their differences come through science, virtue, morals, and dispo-
   sition.
An ignorant man is like an animal,
As an empty brain is worth less than a pumpkin.
A learned woman is better than a man without substance
(For even a learned enemy is better than an ignorant friend).
Even with its thorns, there is value in the flower.
With its hundred fragrances and colors why is the flower scorned?
Why does she have no vote?
The right belongs to the one who gives life.[38]

The Tudeh Party, through its unofficial organ, *Mardom* (The People), called forthrightly for women's political enfranchisement on 6 February

1944.[39] The article blamed the political exclusion of women, workers, farmers, and craftsmen on the "reactionary economic structure" of Iranian society and announced the formation of the Women's Committee (Tashkilat-e Zanan). The Women's Committee was at the forefront of the women's suffrage campaign (as well as the case for equal pay for equal work) in its periodical, *Our Awakening (Bidari-ye Ma)*—but soon found itself on the wrong side of Iranian politics by following the Tudeh line in endorsing a Soviet oil concession as part of the resolution to the Azerbaijan crisis of 1946. Nonetheless, Iran's political left retook the initiative on the woman question by championing women's suffrage, challenging other political forces in the country to react.[40] Prime Minister Qavam's 1946 creation of the Democrat Party, an affiliated women's organization, and an alternative labor union (ESKI), was designed to counter the influence of the Tudeh Party generally and the Soviet-sponsored Azeri Democrat Party specifically.

Maryam Firuz, a half-sister of Sattareh Farmanfarmaian and sister-in-law to Saffiyeh Firuz, was a member of the Women's Committee that was affiliated with the Tudeh Party. Interviewed in 1994 in the Islamic Republic, she was questioned about her sentiments toward the Tudeh. Was she a feminist first or a communist first? Did she feel the Tudeh Party was sincere in its commitment to women's rights? The obvious skepticism of her interviewer provoked a spirited defense of her two ideological commitments as well as a desire to distinguish them from one another:

Q. [After confronting Firuz with a document stating that the Women's Committee was a tool of the Tudeh with no autonomy of action or ideology] Please give your opinion on whether or not it is reasonable for an organization to draw the masses to one political ideology with deception, without the possibility of choice or recognition. Please explain.

MF. I have explained all my reasons at the time for choosing to join the Women's Committee. The Tudeh Party was the only organization that considered a woman to be a human being and recognized her rights. Yes, with all of its mistakes, with all of its leftism, it was the only organization that accepted women; and we grew gradually. Those that did not support this [leftist] line split off and left. I have said many times that I was opposed to women joining the Women's Committee and then being recruited [to the Tudeh Pary] by [means of Tudeh] party propaganda. Any woman who joined the committee was a member of that committee, and if she was inclined to and wanted to join the party, I did not oppose it even though joining the party had responsibilities and was difficult. But these were two completely separate issues. I was against recruitment for the party from within the Women's Committee and [they] had to recruit from outside the party.

Q. This Women's Committee that you mention, was it a party-affiliated organization? Did those who were in contact with it know officially that they were seeds of [class] struggle sown by the hands of the [Tudeh] party?

MF. Yes, it was affiliated and completely independent. The goal of the Women's Committee was securing and defending women's rights. People joined the commission from any group and any party. Those who were members of the [Tudeh] party could, upon receiving instructions, engage in political activity, but the Women's Committee was about protecting women's rights and securing mothers' rights, and this work did not depend on what was said regarding party struggles.[41]

Even in the face of a skeptical interrogator, Maryam Firuz defended the Tudeh's commitment to women's rights. Nonetheless, a sense of futility and regret for a cause lost permeates her defense:

Q. What has the Tudeh Party done for women in fifty years? Except for slogans, did it pursue women's rights seriously, or [simply] use [the issue] in the service of the party?

MF. The party could not do anything or pass a law, but it kept the rights of women in its platform. The party calls for resistance, but it cannot carry out this goal by itself, and I did not have this expectation of the party. It was enough that in the party's regular activities my say was equal to a man's. I should say the contempt for women is in all men and I was fighting because of this.

Q. Even among party men?

MF. It is obvious. I did not have any other expectation of them. They are of the same environment, but should one not struggle?

Q. Do you recall any party programs for the growth of women and promotion of Iranian womanhood? Fundamentally, did it have serious programs and passion for the cultural and social situation of women?

MF. I do not recall what programs it had. The party was a small group in a large society. We believed that women had to become aware and struggle for their own rights and at the same time we also [would] struggle. This was the course of our struggle and also one of our duties.[42]

Even the question of women's political enfranchisement could be contained—symbolically and intellectually—within the bounds of male guardianship. By the very nature of the male-dominated political system, women's suffrage would be something granted to women by men (even if this came as the result of political pressure generated by women activists). When Dr. Feraydun Keshavarz of the Tudeh Party attempted to introduce a women's suffrage amendment to the Electoral Law on 12 August 1944, he introduced it in this way: "Considering that Iranian women have enjoyed the blessings of freedom these past few years, and that they have proven themselves worthy by performing any duty that has been assigned them, and that they rightly deserve equality of rights and social privilege with men, we, the undersigned, request the passage of the single item below."[43]

The "blessings of freedom" could only be a reference to the bygone era of the Women's Awakening. At a minimum, the statement ties into the fiction of the Women's Awakening that emancipation was something that could be achieved without political empowerment. Women proved themselves worthy of equal rights and social privilege by performing "assigned duties." Male tutelage was complete, and so now women could be declared equal. This approach to women's suffrage was consistent with the way the Women's Awakening was utilized by the Left. For example, articles in *Our Awakening* support unveiling while criticizing Reza Shah's ham-fisted approach to the matter in the 1930s.[44] In any case, Keshavarz was shouted down, and the amendment was passed on to a committee from which it failed to emerge. On 5 September 1944, the Fourteenth Parliament referred the matter of election law reform to a committee (which seems to have excluded members of the Tudeh Party) that finally met on 9 March 1945.[45] The first part of the committee's report was published on 19 March 1945 in the *Official Gazette of the Imperial Country of Iran*.[46]

The commission rejected literacy as a precondition for the right to vote. It did so because "Most of the members of the commission recognized the right to vote as an individual right, believed that elections had to be general, and that this right could not be taken from the majority [of the country]."[47] This was the only debate the commission reported on the matter of voting rights. The rest of the proposed reforms were procedural and designed to make for better election monitoring and to reduce election fraud. According to Article 11, Item 6, and Article 13, Item 7 of the committee's revised Electoral Law, women were still barred from voting and from being elected.[48] When the report was finally discussed at the insistence of Dr. Mohammad Mosaddeq on 11 March 1946, the only matter raised was in connection with the right of an indigent person to be elected.[49] No vote was taken on the law.

As part of his negotiations with the Pishehvari government of the Soviet-sponsored Azerbaijan Republic in the summer of 1946, Iranian prime minister Ahmad Qavam had promised to introduce a bill granting women the right to vote.[50] But, as with all of the promises to the separatist government in Azerbaijan (and to the Soviets regarding an oil concession in the north), it was apparently forgotten after Soviet troops withdrew. When Qavam introduced his government's programs to the Fifteenth Parliament on 13 September 1947, he made no mention of politically enfranchising women and was not called to task on that score by anyone present.[51]

Such indifference to the question of women's political enfranchisement did not go unnoticed by women in the Iranian press. While *Zaban-e Zanan* was obviously still committed to the connection between male guardianship and modern Iranian womanhood, there were signs of strain. In December 1944, Sadiqeh Dowlatabadi wrote:

> We cannot be separate from men for even one minute. In every case and in every situation our lives are connected. But from today onward, when we take our first step along the path of the duty of motherhood until twenty years from now when our young men become the true children of the homeland, we will ignore men along our way and will not have the smallest expectation of them because they were not raised by mothers like us. But twenty years from now when the fruits of the strong trees that are our lives ripen, and our young daughters and sons clasp each other's arms and turn to their goal . . . , [the independence of Iran] will be secured by their sacrifice. In their young shadow our old world will be free and independent.[52]

Dowlatabadi's frustration with the state of the country had led her to question male guardianship ever so slightly. Her generation of men was to be abandoned in favor of the next generation, whose character could be cultivated by modern, moral, and patriotic mothers. It was only a slight variation on a familiar theme, but suggestive in that any group of men was to be ignored. Motherhood was more than a duty; it was a source of power. Iran as a whole would surely benefit, but the era of "freedom and independence" ushered in by the next generation would surely reward women in particular—perhaps with greater political and social rights. In March 1945, shortly after the report of the Parliamentary Committee on Reform of the Electoral Law, Dowlatabadi lamented:

> After forty years of constitutional rule, we woman are in the same category as children and the insane in the first section of the Constitution. We have gone to school for forty years and sent our children to school for forty years and we still do not know the ins and outs of high school and are deprived of obtaining the education and knowledge it provides, to say nothing of college. For ten years the women of Iran have benefited from the gift of freedom and still do not know the protocols of social intercourse or even how to wear clothes, and a thousand other faults—why are we this way? Because all of our efforts are hollow and have no basis or foundation. Because we are extreme in all our efforts. Those who unite together do so against other united groups [instead of working with them].[53]

Thus, it was not just men that she blamed. She felt that, even after the Women's Awakening to which she had dedicated herself, women were simply not sufficiently aware of their rights.[54] All the same, by June 1945 a new contempt for the male politicians was all too evident. An angry editorial, which both expressed disdain for the Parliament and argued for women's enfranchisement, asked how men could expect freedom from the Constitution that considered half of those who wanted freedom to be as good as insane.[55] In reference to the articles of the Constitution banning women from voting or being elected, the editorial concluded sarcastically, "We also assure you that if you remove this unfortunate effect, the tree of freedom will bear good fruit. This is based on the condition that our intelligent men—in contrast to the past—will cease to buy and sell votes."[56]

This tone was striking in that it called into question male guardianship, not just of women but of the entire nation. Men had so debased the constitutional order that even the enfranchisement of women could not easily set things right. Again, this overt hostility to male guardianship emerged only gradually in the pages of *Zaban-e Zanan* and was directed at the Parliament rather than the throne (Dowlatabadi remained loyal to the throne as she tried to keep Reza Shah's Women's Society going with *Zaban-e Zanan* as its press organ).

Even a relatively progressive male voice on "the woman question" like

Ahmad Kasravi still sought to ensure clear limits on women's progress—limits that would preserve male guardianship in the face of change. Staunchly anti-Islamic, he endorsed Reza Shah's policy of unveiling as a "great and valuable event on the whole" despite his qualms about the state-sponsored violence and resulting devotion to European fashion.[57] He endorsed basic education for both sexes but expected women to receive special instruction in the domestic sciences. He endorsed higher education for women only in medical specialties, concluding, "[There] is no need for women engineers and lawyers."[58] On the matter of women in the office, he sniffed: "One of the caprices that has turned up among Iranian women is that they have taken to going to the offices and doing men's work. They also learned this from the Europeans. There is a group of men that like to drag women into offices and shops. They see it as in their interest."[59]

Women's most important job was as wife and mother, and except for medical professions, teaching, and handicrafts, Kasravi did not support women in the office unless they were indigent or there was a war on.[60] On the issues of war and governance, Kasravi walked a fine line:

I know somebody will say, "Women are members of Parliament and involved in politics in England and nothing unpraiseworthy has happened." I say, "All people are not the same. The English are more level headed than others. Even in England the number of [female] representatives is but a few. . . ." All this aside, being members of Parliament and ministers in cabinets does not add to the value of women. The housekeeping and raising of children that is of their nature[61] is not less than those things. . . . I say again, "Women should be aware of the situation of the country and the masses, should be aware of events, should join associations, should read newspapers, and should participate in the selection of representatives . . . But being a representative, a minister, a judge, and those sorts of things are inappropriate to their natures. Now that wars are so frightful . . . , [women and men] should learn and teach their children how to protect the land, and to train and exercise. Perhaps some women could take up first aid and such things. This is all to the good. But soldiering and making war is not a job for women and girls . . . If a woman or girl shows a talent for fighting or piloting every so often, that cannot be taken as a reason [to think all women capable of soldiering]."[62]

Women could vote but should not rule. Women could train for defense but should not make a career of soldiering. The association of piloting with soldiering and fighting casts an interesting light upon Women's Awakening images of women pilots. Flight school graduate Sadiqeh Dowlatshahi may not have been fully aware of the connections between flying, military service, and full citizenship (see chapter 7), but Kasravi clearly had taken notice. Women could be educated but should not enter most professions. As ever, the most valuable contribution of the modern Iranian woman was as a wife and mother.

In the spring of 1946, *Atesh* (the Fire) opened up a forum in its first issue for readers to debate the question of women's political enfranchisement. Within the confines of the section devoted to the world of "women, the arts, and literature," *Atesh* included a section entitled "If a Woman Became a Representative of the Nation."[63] Noting that women had been agitating for action on political enfranchisement during the Fourteenth Parliament to no avail, the editors of *Atesh* said they expected it to be an important issue in the Fifteenth Parliament and asked its readers, "Given the conditions of life and situation of today, would women's participation in parliamentary elections as voters and candidates be an improvement for the country and to the benefit of society, or not? If you think it would be in the country's interest, what conditions should be stipulated?"[64]

This call for a public debate was raised amid pictures of Rita Hayworth and a leggy Japanese showgirl named Chiyuko putting on a revealing outfit in preparation for entertaining U.S. troops (see illustration 8.2).[65] Despite this frivolous backdrop, the debate became a regular feature in *Atesh* for eight months. The first pro-enfranchisement correspondent, Dr. Maryam Mir Hadi, argued—like the fictional Khaleh Kukumeh in *Baba Shamal*—that it was a disgrace that a woman with a doctorate should be denied the vote while an uneducated man enjoyed it.[66] She further argued that as a member of the United Nations, Iran was obliged to respect the rights of women and warned that women would fight for their rights because "they believe that rights are taken, not given."[67]

Dr. Hadi's opponent argued that politics was a filthy business that women should have no part of and that just because Western societies included women politically did not mean that Iran should blindly follow. Besides, "M. B." argued, "What do you think the fate of the man would be whose wife was a parliamentary representative? Can one say to such a woman, 'Iron my shirt and pants.' 'Why is tonight's dinner so salty?' Does such a woman even have a chance to see to the grievances of a husband and child?"[68]

Mir Hadi and M. B. were talking right past each other. He left no room for the possibility that a woman could be more than a wife and mother,

8.2. *Atesh*, 17 April 1946, 4. "If a Woman Represented the Nation . . ." This ongoing discussion of women's political enfranchisement in *Atesh* in 1946–47 was contained in a section titled "The World of Women, the Arts, and Literature." Placing the letters to the editor on the subject of women's political enfranchisement opposite a picture of Rita Hayworth put the entire discussion in a frivolous context that belied its earnest content.

and she provided no assurances that political enfranchisement for women would benefit the Iranian family in any way. Later, another woman also opposed women's political enfranchisement because of its inherent (in her view) incompatibility with domestic duties.[69] There was no answer, however, to the fact that male guardianship was challenged on a national level by Mir Hadi's appeal to a supranational authority, the United Nations.[70] Feminist historiography also entered the press when a woman named Afsar Sadqadar characterized the history of civilization under male rule as an "era of fear and brutality" from which humankind was only just now emerging and the effects of which accounted for male opposition to female political enfranchisement.[71]

The argument for women's political enfranchisement did not have to rest solely on attacking male guardianship, and it did not. Women now elaborated on the images of the Women's Awakening by publishing interviews with such people as Professor Fatemeh Sayyah of the University of

Tehran and Dr. Iran A'lam of the Tehran Obstetrical Clinic.[72] These images of Iranian women in public life could be favorably compared to images of prominent European women, such as the first woman member of the British Parliament, Lady Astor.[73] In contrast to the early years of the constitutional period, advocates of women's suffrage could draw upon images of European and American women wielding political power soberly rather than images of rioting suffragettes (see chapter 2). Despite the opposition to women's suffrage, there was an emerging respectability and prevalence of women in politics—perhaps as ratification and extension of the civic space that women acquired during the Women's Awakening. For example, the Patriots Party, which briefly flirted with the idea of supporting women's political enfranchisement in its official press organ *Mihan Parastan,* covered a visit to Iran by British member of Parliament Irene Ward.[74] The most telling symbol of women's political independence from men was the Women's Party (Hezb-e Zanan)—not the Iranian Women's Party or the Tudeh Women's Party—just the Women's Party, formed in 1944 by Saffiyeh Firuz and Fatemeh Sayyah.[75] Also, women of the royal family could make more public political gestures. For example, when Iranian troops reoccupied Zanjan in late 1946, it was Ashraf Pahlavi, not her brother and king Mohammad Reza Shah, who was pictured delivering a speech at the Zanjan train station (see illustration 8.3).[76]

Indeed, contrary to the expectations of Ms. Sadqadar, a couple of men did respond in favor of women's political enfranchisement in the pages of *Atesh.* However, even in their support, they were unable to dispense with the frame of male guardianship. A man named Ahmad listed seven reasons in support of women's suffrage: (1) it was the way of modern civilized countries; (2) women comprised half the population of the country and should not be excluded; (3) illiteracy afflicted both men and women, so it should not be used against either sex; (4) women would not abandon the domestic sphere if politically enfranchised; (5) women would exert a civilizing influence on parliamentary proceedings; (6) no society or social movement had ever succeeded without women; and (7) women had indeed performed well in other areas such as office work despite the criticism of some men.[77] The first, second, and sixth arguments had been part of the woman question in the Iranian press since 1890 in the pages of Mirza Malkam Khan's *Qanun* (see chapter 2). Ahmad's third argument seems to be an effort to diffuse the most strident proenfranchisement rhetoric, while his fourth responds to the very crux of anti-enfranchisement rhetoric. It was as if to assure readers that male guardianship would

برای اینکه از مصائب

در امان بمانیم باید گذشته را درس آینده قرار دهیم .

والاحضرت شاهدخت در ایستگاه   و چنین بیان فرمودند
زنجان حضار را مطرف مخاطب قرار داد.

بقیه در صفحه ۹

8.3. *Atesh,* 24 December, 1946, 4. Princess Ashraf reclaims Zanjan. Princess
Ashraf (Mohammad Reza Shah's sister) is pictured in the statesmanlike act of
addressing the residents of Zanjan at the railroad station after the city was liberated by Iranian troops from Soviet occupation. During the Women's Awakening
she, her sisters, and her mother had undertaken public appearances at charities,
public health organizations, and Women's Society events, but this image elevated
Ashraf to a symbol of Iran's national sovereignty. Her brother was never comfortable with her political assertiveness, and her later reputation for corruption and
drug smuggling did not serve the Pahlavi dynasty well. Nonetheless, this image of
an actual woman (as opposed to a feminine, symbolic "Mother Iran" in political
cartoons) serving as a triumphant symbol of restored national sovereignty was impossible before (and even during) the Women's Awakening project and stands in
great contrast to nineteenth-century images of Iranian women (see illustration 2.1).

persist even if women obtained the vote, that is, that illiterate men would not be disenfranchised and that women would not abandon their "natural" role. The sixth argument—that women could extend the safety and civility of the domestic sphere into the rest of society if they could mix freely with men—had started in the Iranian context with Kermani and had been a central assumption of Reza Shah's Women's Awakening (see chapters 2 and 4).[78]

Another male respondent, Habibollah Shamluli *[sic]*, also supported the political enfranchisement of women in principle but had serious misgivings about the readiness of Iranian women (and of Iranian society) for such a responsibility. He concluded, "To women who desire with heartfelt sincerity to see themselves in Parliament, I shout, 'As long as there are veiled women, and as long as ignorance and superstition predominates among the people, your wish will not be fulfilled.'"[79]

Nonetheless, he included his conditions for women's political enfranchisement: (1) Only ten women could be elected to Parliament, (2) only educated and married women could vote, (3) only women between the ages of twenty-five and forty-five could vote, (4) those women elected must be married and have good reputations, (5) those women elected must be between the ages of thirty and forty-five, (6) the Women's Party could only have two representatives, and (7) women who participated in elections had to be Iranian and known to be residents of the districts in which they ran and voted.[80] In other words, this man could only envision the women's political enfranchisement under conditions that would ensure male control of the political machinery. Taken together with Kasravi's notion that women could vote but not be elected, this text suggests that male guardianship could adapt itself to any proposed or actual change in the social structure.

Even staunch women advocates of women's political enfranchisement, such as Women's Party's secretary and former member of the Women's Society, Fatemeh Sayyah, continued to negotiate within the boundaries of male guardianship to some extent. Sayyah was completely dismissive of men who argued that women were too unstable to be trusted with real political power, writing, "One does not train a cannon on sparrows."[81] However, she did seriously engage concerns that women were not yet educated enough to vote and hold office and that political responsibilities might keep women from their duties as mothers. She argued that countries in which women had greater political rights were increasing in population and that political rights in Iran would allow women to secure better rights in the family that would make them better mothers. Furthermore, if un-educated men could vote, then why not women? She wrote, "If [men] really want women to perform their duties, they must give them the rights to make the performance of these [motherly] duties possible."[82]

Sayyah did not trust male guardians with her future, but she nonethe-less was willing to accept motherhood as the most important national duty. Furthermore, she suggested that if women were to be elected they should serve as a moral force in the Parliament and devote themselves to "social issues, public welfare, education, and the protection of mothers, the infirm, children, and others."[83] She expected women to be a highly scrutinized minority in the Parliament who would have to serve as ex-amples for men by being particularly committed to these sorts of causes and by demonstrating superior moral character. Even in the publicly ex-pressed visions of those who craved it, women's emancipation still had limits. Although the desire to break with male guardianship could now be expressed almost anywhere in the periodical press, those expressions could themselves renew the connection. As ever, the parameters of male guardianship itself continued to change as the parameters of modern Ira-nian womanhood changed.

The unfulfilled promise of the Qavam government to introduce women's suffrage as part of its program in 1947 was an obvious political failure of the various women's groups that had lobbied for it since 1944. The very idea of gender equality was often compromised even as it was expressed. The fact that women activists had to work with male politi-cians to advance their cause had a dampening effect on the tone they could take. Just as Zandokht Shirazi had been forced by the Pahlavi regime to change the name of her short-lived women's organization in 1931 from Enqelab-e Zanan (Women's Revolution) to Nahzat-e Zanan (Women's Movement or Awakening), the founder of the Women's Party, Saffiyeh Firuz, felt compelled to change the name of her organization. Her recollec-tions suggest that pressure to change the name of the Women's Party was more informal (and even well intentioned) than was the case with Shirazi. An unspecified "they" told her that the word *hezb* (party) implied that her organization had a policy platform and that she wanted to be prime min-ister, and that to be effective she should change the name to the Women's Council (Shura-ye Zanan)—which she did.[84]

Mehrangiz Dowlatshahi's first women's organization, formed in 1946 upon her return to Iran from Germany, was affiliated with Ahmad Qavam's Democrat Party—although she had insisted that it not be completely subsumed into the Democrat Party (just as Maryam Firuz said was the case with the Tudeh-affiliated Women's Committee). Nonetheless, when Qavam's political fortunes changed in 1947, the Democrat Party and its women's organization fell apart.[85] While the organization existed, however, Dowlatshahi claimed that it was able to undertake charity work in cooperation with the government. Interestingly, Saffiyeh Firuz reported that one of her great frustrations with the Women's Party was the difficulty she had actually carrying out charitable work in partnership with the government because of "red tape"—particularly on the matter of prison reform, which was an original part of the Women's Party platform.[86] The Women's Party was clearly not as useful to the Democrat Party as its own women's organization. Likewise, after 1946 and after about three audiences, Saffiyeh Firuz could not secure any further appointments with the shah to lobby the court for change.[87] Cooperation with the state, a state controlled by male politicians, was both a goal and an obstacle for women's organizations. The realities of the political system that equal-rights feminists were struggling to change from within worked against their commitment to gender equality. The failure of the women's suffrage campaign of 1944–46 was only a symptom of the larger problem: Women were unable or unwilling to embrace the implications of the gender-equality vision that found articulation in the Iranian press.

The other side of the coin, as Eliz Sanasarian has argued, was the lack of organizational unity among women's groups in the 1940s. There were generational splits and ideological divides based on wider affiliations of women's organizations to other parties or to the court and personality conflicts. Saffiyeh Firuz—seemingly embittered by the experience of trying to form a single independent women's organization in the Women's Party—mused first that all social endeavors were difficult because "nobody stays to work with another person." She noted that the first meeting of the Women's Party in 1944 had 350 participants, and only a year later many women had split off to join or to form as many as thirty-five other societies.[88] For her, "The Iranian has no social consciousness."[89] Of her contemporaries in the wider women's movement, she had little good to say: "They were very self-satisfied with their own information—very self-satisfied, very. And it was very difficult to work with them. It was not possible to reach them with straight talk [such as] 'In the end you have one opinion and I have another opinion. We must try to meet in the middle.' It wasn't possible. They all thought that they were more intelligent because they had a little education—[and] most of them didn't have much education [either]."[90]

The politics of the women's movement in the 1940s mirrored the larger political scene in Iran—partisan and a tad chaotic. But just as the wider body politic was able to find a high degree of consensus on certain issues (national sovereignty, for example), the women's movement also had common concerns. The impetus for feminist action was not merely the general backlash against the Women's Awakening in the 1940s but religiously inspired backlash. It was in response to the threat of religious fanaticism that modern Iranian women hoped to mobilize some expressions of support from their modern male guardians. Saffiyeh Firuz, for example, remembered the threat of "reveiling" as her prime reason for becoming an activist and recalled the only published attacks against her as coming from clerics.[91] And while it was true that clerical opposition to the unveiling was very apparent in the 1940s, opposition to the veil should not obscure a much more complicated response to the Women's Awakening by Iranian Islamic revivalists. Even as Islamic revivalists were attacking the image of modern Iranian womanhood that emerged from the Women's Awakening, they were positioning themselves as new male guardians as well.

The Lingering Rhetoric of Dependence

On 27 August 1943, nearly two years after the fall of Reza Shah, a group of women wrote a letter of protest to Prime Minister Qavam that they sent to a number of newspapers, prominent government officials, and the Parliament. The letter protested an act of violence against unveiled women:

Those government statesmen, those national leaders, and freedom lovers of this country—or at least those who for many years joined with the Organization of Public Enlightenment (OPE) and the Women's Society, and those who showed the day-brightening progress of Iranian women to the world with pride, and those who introduced by means of newspapers and magazines gatherings of groups of girls, women, Girl Scouts, and pictures of their leaders, Shams, and Ashraf Pahlavi,[92] to our progressive neighbors and the civilized world as being the masses of this country's women, and those who drew the eyes of our Turkish, Egyptian, and Caucasian sisters to us—should have been there on 2 Shahrivar (24 August) at 10:00 A.M., they could have been present on Shahpur Street in front of Police Station #4 to see with their own eyes a mollah-like person who, wearing a big turban and long-bearded artistic [artistik] face, spun around, went up and down, called pedestrians faithless calves, and introduced himself as the propagator and agent of the ideas of

Ayatollah Qommi. [They should have seen] how he set upon a handful of unveiled women with his cane, how he dishonored them and
the masses of Iranian women (who are famous throughout the Islamic world for their modesty, chastity, and innocence) in front of
pedestrians and foreigners and guests of this country with his asper-
sions, curses, and immodest language, and how he attacked them for
the crime of being unveiled. Her Majesty, the beloved queen of Iran,
will be saddened by these dark days and misfortunes of her Iranian
sisters, and must be ashamed before her great and noble family. Oh
King, the successor of Cyrus and Anushiravan! Oh Prime Minister,
the successor of Bozorjmehr! Oh guardians of the state! Oh leaders
of the nation! Oh freedom lovers of the country! Now that the
rabble-rousers, game players, and deceivers of the public have run
out of political rhymes in this country, they want to play with the
honor and chastity of you and this ancient nation. They want to
make our chastity a trump card in their game in the name of "the
veil." They want to dishonor us. Will you, our men, sit quietly? Will
you not show the bravery and zeal in the defense of honor which is
proper to the men of Iran?[93]

The letter opens with a reference to the former display of Iranian
women's progress; the assault threatened an image of civility and modernity that was part of the Women's Awakening propaganda. But the heart
of this appeal for justice was a call for the protection of male guardians.
The assault upon the honor, or *namus,* of these women on Shahpur Street
became an assault upon the queen and upon every Iranian woman. The
king, the prime minister, and all Iranian men were called to their "ancient"
duty—their duty as the guardians and protectors of women. If not for
nation, if not for progress, then the men had to act to defend the honor
that was embodied in *their* women.

The women sent copies of their letter to *Ettela 'at, Eqdam, Mardan-e
Kar* (Men of Action/Work), *Nahzat-e Melli* (National Uprising), *Iran-e
Ma* (Our Iran), *Baba Shamal, Kushesh, Khorshid-e Iran* (The Iranian Sun),
Mehr-e Iran (The Light of Iran), and *Tehran-e Mosavvar* (Tehran Illustrated). Although we do not know the responses of all of these papers to
the incident,[94] the responses we do have are intriguing. *Ettela 'at* ignored it.
Kushesh urged the religious establishment to prevent such violent extremism on the part of "uneducated clerical pretenders [*'eddeh'i mollanama-ye
bisavad].*"[95] *Mardan-e Kar* encouraged women to ignore "the handful of
honorless, country-sellers who want to reopen their stores by placing veils

on your head and who want to gamble with your honor once again," and laid the blame for the incident upon the head of Prime Minister Qavam for allowing a situation of social chaos and upon the heads of "charlatan" clerics who cheapened religion.[96] It demanded the defense of Iranian women's honor so that the nation would not lose face in the eyes of the foreigners who were now in Iran and called upon women to take heart in the accomplishments of English, French, American, German, and Turkish women—an oddly nonpartisan statement considering the presence of Allied censors.[97]

Iran-e Ma, which identified itself as the organ of the leftist Paykar Party, actually anticipated the event by a couple of days. In reaction to a Tehran preacher's sermon that advocated assaulting journalists who spoke out against the veil, *Iran-e Ma* responded with a front-page editorial. The sarcastic headline read, "Alas, that the Allies were not here so that you could cut us to pieces: Do you call this *chador* and violence 'the Islamic veil'?"[98] In response to the incident itself, *Iran-e Ma* urged criminal punishment for the perpetrators. *Iran-e Ma* framed its response completely in terms of male guardianship, writing, "If you are men, why do you attack women? . . . We will defend our Iranian mothers and sisters and their honor, until our last breath."[99]

Mehr-e Iran also condemned the violence as a national disgrace and urged clerics, in particular Ayatollah Qommi, to prevent such extremism.[100] A couple of days later, Majid Movaqqar himself published an editorial praising the efforts of Allied female military personnel and noting the apparent pride of those stationed in Iran.[101] There was an implicitly negative comparison between the state of affairs in Allied countries and the "fires of domestic discord" regarding the issue of veiling in Iran. Two days after that, however, another article appeared that placed some of the blame for the intensity of the veiling debate upon Iranian women themselves. Unlike some Iranian women, it was argued, European and American women worked side by side with their men, and they did not fuss with their makeup, seduce young men, or tell lies.[102] They were not dangerous women. There was also some venom for veiled women who embarrassed the nation by their backward and misguided religiosity. Women were to blame for the affront to national honor by perverting both modernity and tradition. Explicitly or implicitly, all the periodicals that responded to the open letter of the women did so in terms framed by male guardianship. Those who carried out the assault are excluded rhetorically from the nation, from true religion, and even from manhood. Women, as the repositories of national and male honor, could not be trusted with their own defense (even though it was they who insisted on justice in this instance) or even with their own sense of moral propriety because of the risk of inciting attack. Feminizing national vulnerability and nationalizing feminine vulnerability were not limited to this particular incident. Such notions could find extremely graphic representation in the press.[103]

On 22 March 1946, Dr. ʿAbd al-Karim Faqihi Shirazi's *Parcham-e Eslam* (The Banner of Islam) introduced itself to the shared tradition of the Iranian press. *Parcham-e Eslam* was concerned with actively integrating Islamic teachings into modern life. In the course of its year-long run, it aggressively weighed in with the Islamic perspective on social questions, world events, and national politics. It advocated a new concern for the affairs of the poor, and although it was suspicious of bribe-taking officials and the absence of religious guidance in governmental affairs, *Parcham-e Eslam* also endorsed the idea of a strong state with a wide range of responsibilities and powers as had the renewalists of the twenties.[104] Another element it shared in common with the renewal movement and the regime of Reza Shah was a vital stake in the woman question.

On one level, its concern was highly reactive. For example, starting with its eighth issue and continuing until its last, space on page three was devoted to a series on the history of the 1935 massacre at Gowharshad (see chapter 4).[105] It was a constant reminder of the sacrifices and bloodshed that had accompanied Reza Shah's dress codes and, by extension, his Women's Awakening. Like a serialized *taʿziyeh* performance, this grim reckoning formed the backdrop for *Parcham-e Eslam*'s frequent articles on Islam and women. Just as national renewal was impossible without women, so too was Islamic revival. It was argued that Islam needed and cherished women and that it had been a progressive force in the history of their sex:

> [Islam] considered men and women equal before God. Honor and virtue were joined in a man or woman who virtuously and piously strove to perform his [or her] religious duties. In accordance with Islamic laws, men and women set up and administer the court of life in the palace of creation, helping each other. The effect of women upon society is greater than that of men, and they are more beneficial to its orderly formation than men because their womanly nature and motherly love can endure any hardship, difficulty, sleeplessness, or exhaustion. [Women] would risk their lives to save their newborn from death, open themselves up, and deliver fit and healthy children. So that the Arabs would see the value and worth of their girls, the

Prophet (PBUH) would say, "Girls are a sign of God's mercy, and you must never offend Him." He also ordered, "When you caress your children, first inquire and see after the girls. When you are preparing food and clothing, put girls before boys." In a loud voice he ordered, "What I esteem in this world—love and affection—is from the world of women." With the utmost justice and fairness, he declared a program of rights and duties for married men and women and entrusted its ordering and execution to mortals.[106]

Parcham-e Eslam reclaimed for Islamic revival "the cult of domesticity" that had been so much a part of modern Iranian womanhood and that had been so valued by the renewal movement and Reza Shah's Women's Awakening. Portraying Islam as historically progressive on the woman question had been a part of the Women's Awakening propaganda, as well. In contrast, however, there was no interest in the capable woman who could do more than work at home.

The dangerous woman, on the other hand, lurked everywhere in the pages of *Parcham-e Eslam*. She shamelessly flirted with strangers in the street right in front of Dr. Shirazi on a Friday (the Muslim Sabbath).[107] She danced and made love on the corrupting screens of the cinema.[108] In a complaint similar to those leveled by the propagandists of the Women's Awakening, *Parcham-e Eslam* condemned the fashion worship of the dangerous woman that destroyed families, elicited the "shameful" attentions of men, corrupted morals, and siphoned off the country's wealth to the clothes makers of England and America.[109] Echoes of *Shokufeh*'s "economic nationalism" from the 1910s and the renewal movement's laments about a corrupt society in the 1920s were harnessed for a different ideological task but to a similar end. Just as the Women's Awakening could rescue women from ignorance and the poor morals that resulted from superstitious tradition, Islamic revival could save women from the moral peril that resulted from mindlessly aping the ways of Western modernity. Unlike Mas'ud's *Mard-e Emruz,* which saw the following of Western fashions as merely silly, Shirazi's *Parcham-e Eslam* saw it as a cause for action: "To oppose this great source of corruption, let us work together today and struggle against the shameless fashion worshippers and thoughtless imitators who are seen in public with half-naked bodies. With all possible means let us admonish those who simplemindedly and thoughtlessly shorten their sleeves and nakedly display their bodies to imitate the ways of chastity instead."[110]

As had been the case in the propaganda of the Women's Awakening, women were central to both the preservation and corruption of society's morals. Despite the "honored" position of women in Islam, *Parcham-e Eslam* unequivocally asserted that "a woman's mental power and natural ability is less [than a man's]. Her heroism, bravery, and especially her ability to rule are extremely weak, and her muscles are unable to withstand outside rigors and difficulties."[111] Accordingly, God through Islam had "exempted women from all sorts of suffering and toil with the exception of managing the home, nursing, and raising children."[112] In a series of articles rather misleadingly titled "Koranic Teachings about Women in Islamic Society," a "learned" man by the name of Mr. Monshi-bashi (who oddly declared that he would be writing under the pen name of F. Shakibi) set out to attack the notion that women had any but a domestic function. He did so, not by recounting Koranic teachings, but by citing Western intellectuals on the topic. Western thinkers like Montesquieu and Comte were summoned to advocate that women would be miserable and lost with too much power or freedom.[113]

Just as advocates of women's progress could draw upon sympathetic European voices, so now could Islamic revivalists draw upon European misogyny to buttress their point of view. The West itself was clearly not unanimous on the woman question, and there were Westerners who in fact agreed with the substance of Islamic revivalist opinion on the subject. This also removed the need to employ explicitly misogynous *hadith* or Koranic verses to emphasize the restrictions placed upon women. Women were not "forbidden" from entering the rough-and-tumble world outside the home; they were "exempted" from doing so. Even on the specific issue of unveiling, one contributor to *Parcham-e Eslam* chose to set aside all the specific scriptural reasons for veiling and to focus instead on emphasizing the alleged practical result of removing the veil: moral decay, and not just by the standards of religion. "A sense of religiosity, patriotism, friendship, and mercy towards one's own—all of these are given up."[114] In tone, the article was a perfect response to Tarbiyat's pseudorational articles about the harm caused by wearing the veil in the pages of *Ettela'at* during the opening months of the Women's Awakening (see chapter 4).

As for the question of women working outside the home, *Parcham-e Eslam*'s rather uncompromising adoption of the renewal movement's "cult of domesticity" would seem to put it at odds with the way in which the meaning of modern Iranian womanhood expanded to embrace the reality of the professional woman. This is not surprising given that even the propaganda of the Women's Awakening itself had not confronted all of the implications of women's "entrance into society."

The modern Iranian woman was important to a variety of irreconcilable causes in the press. Communist, royalist, Islamic revivalist, and renewalist men might talk past each other on many issues, but they were in agreement on the notion of the educated housewife—the cutting-edge idea of late nineteenth-century Iranian feminism and certainly an assumption of Women's Awakening propaganda and policies. Furthermore, the male backlash against women at work was so focused on the office that it in effect endorsed the idea of women as teachers and medical professionals. As we saw in chapter 6, women's horizons continued to expand in employment and education in the 1940s. And clearly, veiled or unveiled, women's enhanced presence in the civic arena was acknowledged by the fact that political activists of all stripes addressed their rhetoric to women as well as men.

But this rough consensus on certain aspects of the woman question in the 1940s did not keep religious extremists from silencing Kasravi with a bullet in 1946 or renegade Tudeh operatives from dispatching Mohammad Mas'ud in 1948. No male "political utopias," to borrow a phrase from Afsaneh Najmabadi, emerged to completely claim modern Iranian womanhood. And some women advanced utopias of their own. If anything, the woman question became more charged with the emergence of gender equality in the public discourse of Iranian feminists. The very idea of male guardianship, and not merely its terms, was finally being publicly challenged. This was (and is) a new cultural frontier for Iranian society. While gender equality is not a dominant cultural value in Iran (or anywhere else), no lingering feminist rhetoric of dependence and no subsequent redefinition of male guardianship has yet removed it from Iranian public discourse.

9

The Legacy of the Women's Awakening

In the fall of 1992, Iran's most celebrated postmodern Islamic intellectual, 'Abd al-Karim Soroush (the pen name for Hosayn Dabbagh), conducted a series of lectures in Tehran on the topic of women in contemporary Shi'a society. A former darling of the Islamic Republic, used to great effect against remnants of leftist opposition to the regime in the 1980s, he became in the 1990s an intellectual spokesman for the forces of political reform identified with President Khatami. Just as the woman question became a battleground for renewalists and the Qajar elite at the turn of the twentieth century, it is one of the many fronts in the current contest between reformists and hard-liners at the turn of the twenty-first. His lectures took issue with the more misogynous passages of the *Nahj al-Balaghah*, a document said to be written by the first Shi'a Imam, 'Ali, and therefore as vital a scripture for the Shi'a as the canonical collections of reports on the life of the Prophet Muhammad. The misogyny in the text, Soroush noted, flew in the face of contemporary notions of gender roles in Iranian society:

> The very fact that it's now accepted that a woman's presence in society doesn't violate her womanhood and Muslimhood is due to the immense changes that have occurred in the realms of thought and practice; these have also found their way into our religious consciousness and our society. Women's presence in society is now as natural and logical as their absence once was. This tells us the extent to which, in our understanding and practice of religion, we act unconsciously and involuntarily; this isn't to be taken negatively but in the sense that we're guided by elements that aren't in our control. They do their work, shape our lives, our mind, our language.[1]

The "immense changes" that Soroush argued were relentlessly and silently compelling Iranian society to question the validity of religious expressions of male guardianship in the 1990s originated in the complex propaganda and policies of the Women's Awakening project. The Women's Awakening dominated Iran's cultural landscape from 1936 to 1941, forcing into being a single vision of the modern Iranian woman as unveiled, educated, and employed, yet comfortably dependent on the stewardship and goodwill of her many modern male guardians.

Yet, this single vision was a tapestry of many visions. Iranian feminists had worked hard to expand the potential of modern Iranian womanhood beyond "scientific housewifery" to "respectable employment" in the pages of the Iranian press. Women's organizations such as the Patriotic Women's League had provided a model for women's civic participation alongside images of European and American suffragettes. American missionaries and many of the "young men of renewal" had championed the removal of the veil. In response, Islamic critics of renewalism struggled to ensure that the modern Iranian woman was held to some level of moral accountability in Islamic terms. The Pahlavi regime's synthesis of these impulses—so often viewed as a break from both progressive and conservative trends—was, in fact, a catalyst for an enduring change in Iranian culture: the emergence of a public call for gender equality.

This study leads us to five general conclusions.

First, the Women's Awakening of 1936–41 represented the culmination of decades of debate regarding the woman question. It clearly linked women's progress with state legitimacy. Despite its coercive policies and domination of the woman question with propaganda and censorship, it is clear that the regime's image of the modern Iranian woman was a creative synthesis of many viewpoints. Its chief innovation in the context of the Iranian culture was to use Iranian women (rather than images of foreign women) to express images of modernity, progress, and potential—all without ceding women's symbolic independence from male guardianship. However, the terms of male guardianship clearly changed in public discourse in the wake of the Women's Awakening. Male guardians were no longer simply the fathers, brothers, and husbands or other male relatives of a woman. They were also office mates, classmates, supervisors, teachers, and colleagues.

Second, the groundwork for the Women's Awakening was laid between the enactment of the Marriage Law of 1931 and the holding of the Second Congress of Eastern Women in Tehran in 1932. It was in crafting the Marriage Law of 1931 that Reza Shah attempted to forge an alliance with Iranian feminists and to "steal the thunder" of the political left and rivals within the renewalist movement. The regime's effort to contain and control the Congress of 1932 foreshadowed its dismantling of nongovernmental women's organizations such as the Patriotic Women's League in favor of the government-run Women's Society. These changes were not wholly unilateral: Marriage reform was a long-standing issue with Iranian feminists, and it is clear that some members of these nongovernmental women's organizations wanted access to the power of the state and all that that implied. In the final analysis, it was the Marriage Law of 1931 that signaled state engagement with the woman question because it was on the basis of this reform that the regime claimed to represent the interests of Iranian women rather than the Patriotic Women's League at the congress of 1932.

Third, the forced unveiling that accompanied the Women's Awakening was something of a paradox. On the one hand, it came to define the image of the modern Iranian woman in the 1930s and the ruthlessness of the regime's modernizing policies. On the other hand, it was beside the point—the regime's propaganda emphasized unveiling in relation to more substantial progress in marriage and courtship, education, and employment and an expanded civic presence for women. Women who felt they benefited from the Women's Awakening were very aware of the stressful aspects of unveiling upon other women (especially older women). Another fact of unveiling was that it represented an extension of state power over men as much as it did over women. During the Women's Awakening, the state assumed guardianship over individual women in requiring them to unveil—an extension of the powers of guardianship it had formally assumed under the Marriage Law of 1931. Even men who were sympathetic to the goal of unveiling expressed a sense of powerlessness and resentment since they could do nothing to protect "their" women from the law.

Fourth, it was only in the wake of the Women's Awakening that gender equality became an enduring part of public discourse in Iranian culture. By taking the complementary-rights perspective to its most extreme expression, the policies and propaganda of the Women's Awakening held the irreconcilable demands of women's emancipation and male guardianship in a precarious balance. The regime itself flirted with "masculinizing" images of women, suggesting the eventual realization of full citizenship for Iranian women. The public backlash against women office workers notwithstanding, the overwhelming response to the Women's Awakening in the 1940s across the political spectrum was to appropriate some aspect of its message or to push beyond it (as was the case in the political left's support of women's suffrage or the Islamic revivalists' discovery of "the cult of domesticity"). Against the backlash, some women expressed clear equal-rights retorts in the pages of the press—offering feminist interpretations of history, threatening to go to an international arena to seek justice from the male-dominated nation, and resisting the long-standing trend in the woman question to link women's rights to their domestic responsibilities.

Fifth, the emergence of a new and enduring frontier between equal rights and complementary rights in Iranian public discourse is less visible in the memories of individual women. Some women internalized the battle between the "dangerous woman" (subversive, rebellious, seductive, and thus immoral) and the "capable woman" (productive, educated, supportive of men's personal and civic ideals, and thus moral) that defined the public record of "woman question" debates. It colored their perceptions of what they and other women achieved. Even when new opportunities arose for women in education and employment, for example, there were less-visible social pressures working against women as they moved to exploit those opportunities. Furthermore, a commitment to equal rights in one sphere of life did not translate to such a commitment in all spheres of life. It was the effort (and limitations) of the few women who supported or took advantage of the opportunities of the Women's Awakening project of 1936–41 and, subsequently, sought to build upon its achievements that defined the effective boundaries of male guardianship.

How do these conclusions change our perspective on the Women's Awakening specifically and Iranian history generally? After all, the judgment of most historians has been that the Women's Awakening was a failure. For Haideh Moghissi, following Eliz Sanasarian, the state's "coercion and co-optation" of the women's movement in Iran "circumscribed and discredited the women's movement."[2] Guity Nashat reminds us that Reza Shah's policies helped only a small group of women, alienated most others, and precipitated a backlash in the 1940s.[3] Furthermore, there is still the question of Reza Shah's brand of patriarchy being merely another expression of a "patriarchal consensus" offered by Parvin Paidar (see chapter 1).

Responding to the last issue first, I have shown conclusively that the "patriarchal consensus" was not at all static. I do not mean this only in the sense of a dynamic process of "bargaining with patriarchy" in a given moment (though a number of oral histories do illustrate this). There is also a historical process through which the very meaning of male guardianship changes—extending itself to new social situations (for example, the workplace), new implications (for example, state control over women's education and marriage to non-Iranians), and new political arrangements (for example, the press "negotiations" over women's suffrage during the

1944–46 campaign for women's suffrage). Certainly, these changes in meaning are observable in the more elite aspects of Iranian cultural production such as parliamentary debates, schools, and the periodical press. This, of course, brings us to the second issue: How did the effects of the Women's Awakening (indeed, the whole "woman question" debates) extend into Iranian society and when?

Clearly, we are looking at the beginning of a process through which women were gaining new (or reframing old) roles in Iranian society. That the process began first among a small group of people who in many ways did not represent the majority of Iranians should not distract us from the fact that the process began. Furthermore, whatever our judgments about the pace of change, there is no doubt that the process expanded throughout the period under study and that the Women's Awakening was an integral part of that process. The Marriage Law of 1931 provided meager legal gains for Iranian women, but that was not its main purpose. The law's chief significance lay in establishing a basis for state engagement of the woman question. The active recruitment of women into government bureaucracy (as teachers, nurses, and, most significantly perhaps, as office workers) during the 1930s—and celebration of these facts in propaganda ad nauseum—unquestionably set precedents (in public discourse as well as in fact) that withstood the male backlash in the 1940s.

The backlash in the 1940s was telling because it was an argument about existing social conditions (primarily, women in the office). In the mid-nineteenth century, the woman question was a largely male vision of reform. It was only at the turn of the century that discussion of the woman question began to coincide with the changing social conditions in Iran. The public discourse did not have a life of its own, unconnected to social realities or emerging constituencies, but it required very little "reality" to inspire it. Slowly changing patterns in women's education and employment began with an elite of urban and educated Iranians. Indeed, there is no evidence that any sort of progressive attitude toward women, let alone gender equality, influenced rural life even at the end of the twentieth century.[4] Nonetheless, the culture toward which rural Iranians would gravitate as they migrate to the cities, the culture in which children are educated, the culture that produces news and entertainment on a mass scale—that urban literate culture—was permanently changed by the Women's Awakening. And this brings us back to the first issue: Did the Women's Awakening help or hurt the women's movement; did it provoke or forestall the call for gender equality?

The moderate changes in gender roles that were discussed—even obsessed over—by the propaganda of the Women's Awakening created a cultural point of departure for literate, urban Iranian society. Some Iranian feminists (independent ones and those allied with the political left) pushed for more improvements in the 1940s based on a gender-equality argument. Others tried to continue the modernist complementary-rights agenda of the Women's Awakening in alliance with the court or other political groups. Perhaps the most significant development was the beginning of a sophisticated engagement with the woman question by Islamic revivalism.

The Pahlavi effort to engage the woman question was enduring and successful in one respect: The legitimacy of the modern state was tied to the principle of women's progress. The state did no more to co-opt and coerce the women's movement in the 1930s than did the various intellectual and political causes that preceded and succeeded the Women's Awakening. However, through its enforcement of laws, its control over and expansion of education, and its domination of communication and the economy in general, the Pahlavi State created a more Foucauldian discourse on gender for Iranian society. The Women's Awakening of 1936–41 was not mere propaganda. With its sheer power over Iranian society, the Pahlavi state could dispense real benefits to those who accepted its synthesis of modern Iranian womanhood as well as real punishment for those who did not. The "co-optation and circumscription" of the women's movement, thus, had its collaborators.

The foundations of the 1930s Pahlavi synthesis are still visible in twenty-first century Iran. Contrary to the expectations of some archconservatives in Iranian culture, and despite many setbacks for women in the Islamic Republic, the official stance of the government toward women in Iran was more of a return to 1936 than to 1836 (much less to the seventh century). Women's athleticism, first championed by the Pahlavi regime during the Women's Awakening, has been accommodated—even celebrated—by the Islamic Republic despite the complications associated with veiling and seclusion. Women's civic participation was considered crucial to the success of the revolution. The need for women professionals in medicine and the legal system is still recognized—and even celebrated—despite early impulses to force working Iranian women back to a domestic setting.

Salam Iran, a web site sponsored by the Embassy of the Islamic Republic of Iran in Ottawa, has an interesting mix of propaganda and substance to illustrate modern Islamic womanhood.[5] Supported by statistics and commentary from two National Reports on Women (1995 and 1997), originally published by the Women's Bureau of the Presidential Office of the Islamic Republic, the site is organized around themes with obvious roots in the Women's Awakening of 1936 and the woman question in general: Women and Art, Women and Sports, Women and Education, Women and the Family.[6] The Islamic Republic echoes the Women's Awakening formulation of women's work, civic presence, and family responsibilities as complementary and indissoluble: "Women enjoy a rich Islamic culture from which they draw their strength. They rely on the power of religion to bring vitality, justice and equality to the family, and to revive their cultural identity. Islamic rules account for strong family ties, deep positive changes in gender relations, and raising the status of women. The family, in the wide sense of the word, is a shelter for its own members, and Iranian women have successfully combined family obligations with career responsibilities and participating in public life."[7]

Even the additional themes of "Women and Revolution" and "Women and the Constitution"—direct responses to the more recent legacy of the White Revolution—have their roots in the first major legal alliance between the state and women: the Marriage Law of 1931 (see chapter 5). Perhaps the most interesting theme is "Women and Mythical Deities." It makes a case for respect for women based on pre-Islamic Iranian mythology—a curious ghost of the secular nationalism of the Pahlavi period. Indeed, in making a case for the political rights of women in the Islamic Republic, the web site offers a fabulously ahistorical construction: "Islam granted women suffrage some 1400 years ago, when Prophet Muhammad (PBUH) established the first Islamic government in Medina. Though certain reactionary secular powers gradually restrained women's rights, Islamic ideology and principles remained as a source of inspiration for Muslims in general and Muslim women in particular, until the day came to revive their religious and cultural heritage."[8]

The "reactionary secular powers" can only be a reference to the long line of caliphal and imperial dynasties that ruled Iran through the end of the Pahlavi dynasty. The facile substitution of "reactionary secularism" for the renewalist construction of "superstitious religion" is especially ironic since the first state-sponsored arguments for Islam as a progressive force for change were made by the regime of Reza Shah Pahlavi in support of its Women's Awakening policies (see chapters 4 and 7).

Iranian society, like all others, has yet to decide if it will reject, embrace, or qualify the principle of gender equality. At present, it does all of those things. There is no promise of steady progress toward an egalitarian consensus about gender, just as there is no history of such progress. Nor is there a history of a static "patriarchal consensus," blunting the forces of change without compromise. What we can point to, as a matter of historical record, is that the principle of gender equality first found meaningful expression in Iranian culture in the 1940s under the pressure of contemporary politics that, in turn, were a reaction to a drastic state feminist program in the 1930s, which itself was a synthesis of ideas from decades of "woman question" debates that began in the mid-nineteenth century.

Notes

Chapter 1. The "Women's Awakening" Reconsidered

1. *Koran* 24:31 (The Light) tells Muslim women to avoid temptation, to preserve their chastity, to draw a veil over their bosoms, and not to display their adornments (except to close family). *Koran* 33:59 (The Confederate Tribes) tells the wives and daughters of the prophet Muhammad and the wives of believers to draw their veils close so that they may not be recognized and troubled. Drawing on the body of accepted *hadith,* or reports on the sayings and actions of the Prophet (for Twelver Shi'ite Muslims, this would include the sayings and actions of the twelve imams), Islamic scholars seem to agree that Muslim women should cover their entire bodies except for their faces and hands. The practice of veiling has varied regionally and historically. For more on the development of the meaning of the veil in Islamic law, see Barbara Freyer Stowasser, *Women in the Qur'an, Traditions, and Interpretation,* 90–94, 115–18, 127–32. See also *The Encyclopaedia of Islam: The New Edition,* ed. H. A. R. Gibb, J. H. Kramers, E. Levi-Provençal, and J. Schacht, s.v. "Hidjab" by J. Chelhod; and *Encyclopaedia Iranica,* ed. Ehsan Yarsharter, s.v. "Cador" by Bijan Gheiby, James R. Russel, and Hamid Algar.

2. Ervand Abrahamian, *Iran: Between Two Revolutions,* 118–65. American journalist and writer Vincent Sheehan portrays Reza Shah in the dawn of his reign as a minor, Iranian version of a European "great man of history": "[He is] a Napoleon or a Mussolini of a different stripe, to be sure; he has neither the military genius of one nor the intellectual audacity of the other. But the essential quality of them both he possesses: a fundamental independence of spirit, a fearless arrogance of purpose, which has at last raised him to the throne of the vicegerent of God." (Vincent Sheehan, *The New Persia,* 32)

From Amin Banani, we have this description:

Reza Khan was tall, broad-shouldered, and possessed a natural air of authority. He was strong-willed and impatient, quick-tempered and uncouth; but he had to perfection the politician's talent for opportunism. Most of the qualities that alienated him from the refined, Europeanized, and often effeminate sections of society were the same that won him the support of the hero-worshipping lower classes. Although in the early, uncertain days of his career he showed that he knew how to play upon the religious emotions of the people, he was basically apathetic to religion and antagonistic toward the clergy. . . . He possessed a keen mind, an excellent memory, and an unusual ability to absorb information and briefings even if of a highly technical nature. He seldom made public speeches, but when occasion demanded he was always brief and to the point. . . . His personal morals were above reproach. His conduct as a public figure, however, showed some serious faults, for as he grew in power, his desire to accumulate a fortune developed into a voracious greed, and he became very suspicious and ill-tempered. (Amin Banani, *The Modernization of Iran*, 39–40)

3. For a thoughtful exploration of this issue, see Cyrus Amir-Mokri, "Redefining Iran's Constitutional Revolution."

4. For a consideration of just how varied and dynamic the religious response was to the perils of Reza Shah's regime, see Mohammad Faghfoory, "The Impact of Modernization on the Ulama in Iran, 1925–1941."

5. Afsaneh Najmabadi, "Hazards of Modernity and Morality," in *The Modern Middle East*, ed. Albert Hourani, Philip S. Khoury, and Mary C. Wilson, 663–87; and Najmabadi, "Zanha-yi Millat: Women or Wives of the Nation?" See also Parvin Paidar, *Women and the Political Process in Twentieth-Century Iran.*

6. Afsaneh Najmabadi, *The Story of the Daughters of Quchan: Gender and National Memory in Iranian History*; and Janet Afary, *The Iranian Constitutional Revolution, 1906–11: Grassroots Democracy, Social Democracy, and the Origins of Feminism.*

7. Mohamad Tavakoli-Targhi, "Imagining Western Women: Occidentalism and Euro-eroticism." For other considerations of interactions between "East" and "West" involving issues of gender, see Carter Vaughn Findley, "An Ottoman Occidentalist in Europe: Ahemed Midhat Meets Madame Gülnar"; and Billie Melman, *Women's Orients: English Women and the Middle East, 1718–1918.*

8. Shahla Haeri, *Law of Desire: Temporary Marriage in Shi'i Iran.*

9. Eliz Sanasarian, *The Women's Rights Movement in Iran: Mutiny, Appeasement, and Repression from 1900 to Khomeini*; Pari Shaykh al-Eslami, *Zanan-e Ruznameh-Negar va Andishmand-e Iran*; Tal'at Bassari, *Zandokht: Pishahang-e Nahzat-e Azadi-ye Banovan-e Iran*; and Badr al-Moluk Bamdad, *From Darkness into Light: Women's Emancipation in Iran*, 100.

10. Mohammad Mas'ud, *Golha'i keh dar Jahanam Miruyad*, 29.

11. Mohammad Khatami, "On the Virtues of the West."

12. Paidar, 112–17; and Sanasarian, 53–75.

13. See, for example, Fatemeh Ostad Malek, *Hejab va Kashf-e Hejab dar Iran.* The Islamic Republic's efforts to document the abuses of the Women's Awakening resulted in two published document collections: *Khoshunat va Farhang: Asnad-e Mahramaneh-e Kashf-e Hejab (1313–1322)* and *Vaqe'eh-e Kashf-e Hejab: Asnad-e Montasher Nashodeh.* Hereafter, the two collections will be referred to as KVF and VKH, respectively.

14. Ashna, KVF, dah-yazdah [pages x–xi].

15. See, for example, Geraldine Brooks, *Nine Parts of Desire: The Hidden World of Islamic Women.*

16. This is certainly the tenor of Iranian historical treatments of the reign of Reza Shah that were published during the period following his forced abdication in 1941. See Hosayn Makki, *Tarikh-e Bist Saleh-e Iran,* vol. 1. Makki's canonization of the accusation that Reza Shah was merely a British lackey is still the focus of continuing scholarly discussion. See Michael P. Zirinsky, "Imperial Power and Dictatorship: Britain and the Rise of Reza Shah, 1921–1926." For a typical criticism of the regime's modernizing efforts see Amin Banani, *The Modernization of Iran.*

17. Many of the most fawning treatments of Reza Shah, by Iranian and Western scholars, were produced in the time of his son, Mohammad Reza Shah. He took a keen interest in restoring his father's image. In the fifties, he had his father's remains returned to Iran from South Africa (where his father had been exiled by the Allies and where he had died in 1944) and had the Parliament bestow upon his father the title of *kabir* (the great). See Sa'id Nafisi, *Tarikh-e Mo'aser-e Iran: Az Kudeta-ye Sevvom-e Esfand Mah ta Bist va Chaharom-e Shahrivar, 1320 (Tarikh-e Shahriyar Shahanshah Reza Pahlavi)* for examples of such posthumous celebrations of Reza Shah's reign. For a more blunt, yet favorable, treatment, see Donald N. Wilber, *Riza Shah Pahlavi: The Resurrection and Reconstruction of Iran, 1978–1944.* Favorable biographies were produced in English and Arabic in Reza Shah's own time, presumably to serve as international propaganda for the regime. See, for example, Ahmad Mahmud al-Sadati, *Rida Shah Bahlawi: Nahdat Iran al-Hadith;* and Mohammed Essad-bey, Paul Maerker Branden, and Elsa Branden, *Reza Shah.*

18. *Iran under the Pahlavis,* ed. George Lenczowski.

19. *Reza Shah: Khaterat-e Solayman Behbudi, Shams Pahlavi, 'Ali Izadi,* ed. Gholamhosayn Mirza Saleh; Mostafa Eslamiyeh, *Reza Khan Maksim;* and Khosrow Mo'tazed, *Fowziyeh: Hekayat-e Talkhkami, Qesseh-e Jodayi.* Also recently published is a eighteen-volume compilation of memoir material pertaining to the reigns of both Mohammad Reza Shah and Reza Shah, rather in the tradition of Hosayn Makki's historiographical style of presenting selected sources with a bare minimum of overt commentary. See Dr. Mostafa Alamuti, *Iran Dar 'Asr-e Pahlavi.*

20. Cyrus Ghani, *Iran and the Rise of Reza Shah: From Qajar Collapse to Pahlavi Power,* 376–94.

21. The full treatise is reproduced in Mirza Fath 'Ali Akhundzadeh, *Maktubat-e Mirza Fath 'Ali Akhundzadeh.* See also *Encyclopaedia Iranica,* s.v. "Akundzada" by Hamid Algar; Sho'leh Abadi, "Mirza Fath 'Ali Akhundzadeh va Mas'aleh-e Zanan"; and Juan R. I. Cole, *Modernity and the Millennium: The Genesis of the Baha'i Faith in the Nineteenth Century Middle East.*

22. Some even doubt if Qorrat al-'Ayn actually removed her veil. See Abbas Amanat, *Resurrection and Renewal: The Making of the Babi Movement in Iran, 1844–1850.* Nonetheless, the story that she did remove her veil has become a

permanent part of Iranian historical memory and has been appropriated by both feminist and nationalist myth makers. For example, see Mo'in al-Din Mehrabi, *Qorrat al-'Ayn: Sha'ereh-e Azadikh^wah va Melli-ye Iran,* 91–97. Certainly, it must be noted, Babism (in its eventual expression in Baha'ism) gave rise to a group of Iranians who would be receptive to feminist impulses and contribute to discussions of the woman question.

23. An ongoing discussion in gender studies involves the merits of examining historical and social processes in terms of discourse versus interpreting them in terms of women's reported experiences. To get a fuller sense of the issues involved, see Joan Wallach Scott, *Gender and the Politics of History;* and Dorothy Smith, *The Everyday World as Problematic: A Feminist Sociology.* Balaghi and Göçek note Joan Scott and Kathleen Jones's objections to positioning the experiences of women as "real" (and thus true) versus other systems of meaning, but nonetheless Göçek and Balaghi are attracted to Smith's attempt to get at experience in *Reconstructing Gender in the Middle East,* ed. Fatma Müge Göçek and Ashiva Balaghi. Offering a useful synthesis of these two approaches, Penny Summerfield's (University of Lancaster) paper, "'You Were Just One of the Boys': Women's Constructions of the Disruption of Gender Divisions at Work in World War II Britain," presented on Saturday, 8 June, at the 1996 Berkshire Conference on the History of Women in Chapel Hill, North Carolina, influenced me to attempt a closer integration of reported experiences in reference to the gendered discourses that manifested themselves in the institutional and urban popular culture in Iran in the first half of the twentieth century.

24. Mohammad Sadr-Hashemi, *Tarikh-e Jarayed va Majallat-e Iran;* L. P. Elwell-Sutton, "The Iranian Press, 1941–1947"; Go'el Kohen, *Tarikh-e Sansur Dar Matbu'at-e Iran; Asnad-e Matbu'at (1286–1320 h.s.),* ed. Kaveh Bayat and Mas'ud Kuhestani Nezhad and *Asnad-e Matbu'at-e Iran 1320–1332,* vol. 1; and Camron Michael Amin, "'The Attentions of the Great Father': Riza Shah, 'the Woman Question,' and the Iranian Press, 1910–1946," 40–64. See also Nassereddin Parvin, "The Sources of Historiography of the Iranian Press"; E. G. Browne, *The Press and Poetry of Modern Persia;* and Husayn Abu Torabiyan, *Matbu'at-i Irani.*

25. I found it useful to conceptualize the press as a window on Iranian society's "cultural scheme" that both shapes and is shaped by the flow of history. For more on this, see Marshall Sahlins, *Islands of History,* 151–52. Space prevents a more thorough literature review here, but for more on the rise of the press as an institution in the Middle East and the press as a reflection of framing of ideas and societal conventions, see Erving Goffman, *Frame Analysis;* Gaye Tuchman, *Making News: A Study in the Construction of Reality;* Michael Schudson, *Discovering the News: A Social History of American Newspapers;* Todd Gitlin, *The Whole World is Watching: Mass Media in the Making and Unmaking of the New Left;* Elizabeth L. Eisenstein, *The Printing Revolution in Early Modern Europe;* George Roper, "Faris al-Shidyaq and the Transition from Scribal to Print Culture," in *The Book*

in the Islamic World, ed. George N. Atiyeh; Allen Douglas and Fedwa Malti-Douglas, *Arab Comic Strips: Politics of an Emerging Mass Culture;* and Ami Ayalon, *The Press in the Arab Middle East.*

26. The Pahlavi state had a fairly sophisticated view of propaganda, viewing press propaganda as just one element in a coordinated effort to influence public opinion through the media, education, and art. The regime's Sazman-e Amuzesh va Parvaresh Afkar-e 'Omumi (Organization for the Teaching and Nurturing of Public Thought, or, in slightly more idiomatic English, Organization of Public Enlightenment), established in 1938, was the formal realization of a coordinated propaganda scheme envisioned by intellectual supporters of the regime as far back as 1922. See, for example, "Jang ba Fesad," *Iranshahr* 1, no. 5 (25 October 1922): 91–104.

27. Sidney Bolkosky, "Of Parchment and Ink: Varieties of Survivor Religious Responses to the Holocaust"; and "Interviewing Victims Who Survived: Listening for the Silences That Strike."

28. Bolkosky, "Interviewing Victims," 33.

29. As a case in point, see Rosemary Sayigh, "Engendered Exile: Palestinian Camp Women Tell Their Lives"; and Ellen Fleischmann, "Crossing Boundaries of History: Exploring Oral History in Researching Palestinian Women in the Mandate Period."

30. Habib Ladjevardi, *Reference Guide to the Iranian Oral History Collection,* 8–9.

31. Samuel Schrager, "What is Social in Oral History?"

32. Haeri, 15. See an example of an occasionally awkward interview with the case of "Mulla Amin Aqa," 167–75.

33. Habib Ladjevardi, speaking at the University of Chicago Conference on Middle Eastern History and Theory in the spring of 1997, recalled with amusement the case of a general disavowing a transcript of his tape-recorded interview. When Ladjevardi's staff checked the recording against the transcript, they found no error. Ladjevardi drew laughs from the audience in recalling the general's protest: "I don't know what idiot said these things, but it certainly wasn't me."

34. Margot Badran, *Feminists, Islam, and Nation: Gender and the Making of Modern Egypt,* 19–21.

35. For a critique of static definitions of patriarchy that reduce it to formal expressions of culture (e.g., Islamic law), see Deniz Kandiyoti, "Islam and Patriarchy: A Comparative Perspective," in *Women in Middle Eastern History,* ed. Nikki Keddie and Beth Baron, 23–42.

Chapter 2. Tradition and Renewal

1. For a fascinating account of the strained relationship between the Safavids and their *qezelbash* followers, see Kathryn Babayan, "The Safavid Synthesis: From Qezelbash Islam to Imamite Shi'ism."

2. There is little doubt that official Qajar ideology perceived its military cam-

paigns into Georgia in this way. The Qajar historian Mohammad Saravi reported in his late-eighteenth-century chronicle, *Ahsan al-Tavarikh* (The Best of Histories), that Agha Mohammad Khan Qajar sent a missive to the Georgians in 1795 warning that they should return to their place within the empire "because according to ancient principles and agreements Georgia belonged to Iranian kings, has been so from the reign of Shah Esma'il Safavi until our royal state." See Mohammad Fathollah Ibn Mohammad Taqi Saravi, *Tarikh-e Mohammadi, "Ahsan Al-Tavarikh,"* ed. Gholamreza Tabataba'i Majd, 272.

3. For example, the Qajars expanded on late-Safavid-era efforts to popularize Shi'ism by supporting the production of *ta'ziyeh* plays, commemorating the martyrdom of the Imam Hosayn (and countless other topics that were linked to the original themes of the plays). See Peter Chelkowski, "Majlis-i Shahanshah-i Iran Nasir al-Din Shah," in *Qajar Iran*, ed. E. Bosworth and C. Hillenbrand, 213–42.

4. See Shaul Bakhash, *Iran, Monarchy, Bureaucracy, and Reform under the Qajars, 1858–1896.*

5. On pre-Islamic conceptions of womanhood in this area, see Mehrangiz Kar and Shahla Lahiji, *Shenakht-e Hoviyat-e Zan-e Irani dar Gostareh-e Pish-e Tarikh va Tarikh.* In this volume, which is apparently seen as part of a bigger project, the authors draw upon archaeological research regarding cultures in Mesopotamia and the Iranian Plateau from the Neolithic Age to the time of the Sassanians.

6. Adele K. Ferdows and Amir H. Ferdows, "Women in Shi'i Fiqh: Images through the Hadith," in *Women and Revolution in Iran,* ed. Guity Nashat, 55–68.

7. *'Aqa'ed al-Nesa va Mir'at al-Bolha: Du Resaleh-e Enteqadi dar Farhang-e Tudeh,* ed. Mahmud Ketra'i, 1.

8. Kathryn Babayan, "'The 'Aqa'id Al-Nisa'': A Glimpse at Safavid Women in Local Isfahani Culture," in *Women and the Medieval Islamic World,* ed. Gavin R. G. Hambly, 358.

9. Maria Szuppe, "The 'Jewels of Wonder': Learned Ladies and Princess Politicians in the Provinces of Early Safavid Iran," in *Women and the Medieval Islamic World,* 323–47.

10. Leslie Peirce, *The Imperial Harem: Women and Sovereignty in the Ottoman Empire.*

11. Eskandar Beyg Monshi, *History of Shah 'Abbas the Great,* 1:337.

12. Ibid., 1:370. It was not only at the highest levels of Safavid politics that we find examples of active women. We also have information of a dynasty based in Gilan around Fumen and Rasht that rebelled against the Safavid monarch Esma'il I (reg. 1501–24). Hosam al-Din Dabbaj Fumeni's clan had ruled the area since the time of the Mongols. When Shah Esma'il I established the Safavid dynasty, he eventually subdued Hosam al-Din and made him his governor. After Hosam al-Din's death, his daughter, Amireh Dabbaj, ruled Gilan and made an unsuccessful bid for independence from Shah Esma'il I. Ghiyas al-Din Khʷandamir, *Habib al-Siyar,* ed. Jalal al-Din Homa'i, 4:483–85 and 4:563. For more on women in the

Safavid period, see Maria Szuppe, "La participation des femmes de la famille royale à l'exercice du pouvoir en Iran safavide au XVIe siècle."

13. Twelver Shiʿism had been split between two mutually antagonistic schools, called *osuli* and *akhbari*. After decades of sometimes violent rivalry, the *osuli* school came to dominate the scene in the eighteenth century. Scholars of this school defined Twelver Shiʿite orthodoxy in the nineteenth century.

14. See chapter 1 n. 25.

15. Sepehr, translated in Amanat, *Resurrection and Renewal*, 321.

16. Boshra Delrish, *Zan dar Dowreh-e Qajar*, 186–224.

17. See Abbas Amanat, "The Downfall of Mirza Taqi Khan Amir Kabir."

18. *Qanun* 2 (22 March 1890): 4.

19. Delrish, 65–66.

20. Ibid., 58.

21. *Vaqayeʿ-e Ettefaqiyeh* 485, 7 March 1861, 5.

22. Its "author," Mohammad Hasan Khan Eʿtemad al-Saltaneh, has a mixed legacy as a censor and as a public educator in his capacity as the director of the press office—a Qajar counterpart to the Ottoman Empire's Ahmet Midhat Pasha, perhaps. In contrast to Ahmet Midhat Pasha, Eʿtemad al-Saltaneh is alleged to have supervised the writing of his books rather than authoring them personally. See E. G. Browne, *The Press and Poetry of Modern Persia*, 154–66.

23. *Sharaf* 51 (June 1887): 1–4.

24. *Sharafat* 28 (September 1898): 1–2.

25. *Sharafat* 32 (January 1899): 3.

26. The letter is cited in the introduction to *Ruznameh-e Khaterat-e Eʿtemad Al-Saltaneh, Vazir-e Entebaʿat dar Avakher Dowreh-e Naseri, 1292–1313 Hejri-Qamari,* 9.

27. See, for example, the writings of Malek al-Shoʿara Bahar, "Bazgasht-e Adabi," *Armaghan*, 1311 [1932/33], and 1312 [1933/34], reprinted in *Bahar va Adab-e Farsi*, 1:43–66. For more on the *bazgasht* movement, see *Encyclopaedia Iranica*, s.v. "Bazgast-e Adabi" by William L. Hanaway Jr. For an excellent re-evaluation, explication, and appreciation of the *sabk-e hendi* (Indian-style) poetry produced in the Safavid and Mughal courts, see Paul E. Losensky, "'Welcoming Fighani': Imitation, Influence, and Literary Change in the Persian *Ghazal*, 1480–1680."

28. Paidar, 46–49. See also Feraydun Adamiyat and Homa Nateq, *Afkar-e Ejtemaʿi, Seyasi va Eqtesadi dar Asar Montasher Nashodeh-e Dowran-e Qajar.*

29. The full treatise is reproduced in Mirza Fath ʿAli Akhundzadeh, *Maktubat-e Mirza Fath ʿAli Akhundzadeh.* See also *Encyclopaedia Iranica*, s.v. "Akundzada" by Hamid Algar. For Akhundzadeh in a comparative perspective, see Juan R. I. Cole, "Marking Boundaries, Marking Time: The Iranian Past and the Construction of the Self by Qajar Thinkers."

30. Akhundzadeh, *Maktubat*, 54–55.

31. Ibid., 119–32.

32. Ibid., 126.

33. Ibid., 136–38.

34. Sho'leh Abadi, "Mirza Fath 'Ali Akhundzadeh va Mas'aleh-e Zanan," 31.

35. Ibid., 33–34.

36. Ibid., 31.

37. Akhundzadeh, *Maktubat,* 54.

38. Afsaneh Najmabadi, "A Different Voice: Taj os-Saltaneh," in *Women's Autobiographies in Contemporary Iran,* ed. Afsaneh Najmabadi, 19–20. Najmabadi also provides a brief summary of Kermani's discussion of the woman question in *The Hundred Sermons.*

39. Feraydun Adamiyat, *Andishah-ha-ye Mirza Aqa Khan Kermani,* 56–59.

40. Feraydun Adamiyat, "Seh Maktub-e Mirza Fath'Ali" and "Seh Maktub va Sad Khetabeh-e Mirza Aqa Khan." Adamiyat's comparison of Kermani and Akhundzadeh is interesting if perplexing. He produces topic indexes for both treatises to demonstrate that, while Kermani closely simulated the opening of Akhundzadeh's work, he soon diverged to explore different things. He also found Kermani more knowledgeable and more elegant in his use of Persian. His argument that Kermani's work should not be referred to as "The Three Letters" because it consists of only one letter is beside the point; Akhundzadeh's work was not actually a collection of three letters, either. Also, his topic index of Akhundzadeh's *The Three Letters* is suspicious. For example, it completely subsumed Akhundzadeh's discussion of the woman question under the heading "Learning and Religion." His distancing of Kermani from Akhundzadeh goes a step further in his book on Kermani when Adamiyat summarizes his earlier articles in *Yaghma.* Adamiyat writes, "The 'Three Letters' of Mirza Aqa Khan is something other than 'Three Letters' of Mirza Fath 'Ali. . . . 'The Hundred Sermons' has no relationship to Mirza Fath 'Ali and is an original work of Mirza Aqa Khan." (Adamiyat, *Andishah-ha-ye Mirza Aqa Khan,* 56–57) Adamiyat also fails to see that the general concerns of both men—the desire for political liberalization, the admiration for Europe, the hostility toward Islam and other manifestations of "traditional culture," the discomfort with the condition of women, and hope for the national rebirth of Iran—speak to a profound influence of Akhundzadeh upon Kermani.

41. They are reproduced in "Arshiv: Bakhshha'i az *Sad Khetabeh*-e Mirza Aqa Khan Kermani" and summarized in English in Najmabadi, "A Different Voice," 19–20.

42. Kermani, "Arshiv," 101. The phrase "zendeh beh gur" literally means "entombed alive," but I think my freer translation better captures the spirit of the term in this context.

43. Ibid., 104.

44. Ibid., 101.

45. Ibid.

46. Ibid., 102–3.

47. Ibid., 102.

48. Ibid., 103–4.

49. Ibid., 101–2.

50. *Koran* 4:3.

51. Kermani, "Arshiv," 106. For more on the institution of temporary marriage, see Shahla Haeri, *Law of Desire.*

52. Kermani, "Arshiv," 107.

53. Ibid.

54. Ibid., 109.

55. Ibid., 108–9.

56. Ibid., 109.

57. Ibid., 110.

58. Ibid., 111.

59. Ibid., 112.

60. Ibid., 110.

61. Kermani and Ruhi cited in Afsaneh Najmabadi, "Crafting an Educated Housewife in Iran," in *Remaking Women: Feminism, Modernity, and the Middle East,* ed. Lila Abu-Lughod, 94–95.

62. Juan R. I. Cole, *Modernity and the Millennium,* 163–97.

63. Ibid., 174. For more on Tahtawi, Kemal, and al-Afghani, see Albert Hourani, *Arabic Thought in the Liberal Age, 1798–1939;* Nikki R. Keddie, *An Islamic Response to Imperialism: Political and Religious Writings of Sayyid Jamal ad-Din "al-Afghani";* and Bernard Lewis, *The Emergence of Modern Turkey.*

64. Nikkie R. Keddie, "Religion and Irreligion in Early Iranian Nationalism," in *Iran Religion, Politics, and Society: Collected Essays,* 13–52.

65. *Mirza Aqa Khan Kermani, Namehha-ye Tab'id,* ed. and intro. Homa Nateq and Mohammad Firuz, 38.

66. Ibid., 64. The letter in question is undated, but its references to *Qanun* suggest it was written in late 1890 or early 1891.

67. Rowshanak Mansur, "Chehreh-e Zan dar Jarayed-e Mashrutiyat," 14, 15.

68. *Qanun* 7 (August 1890?): 3.

69. *Qanun* 10 (October or November 1890?): 3–4.

70. Ibid.

71. *Qanun* 15 (n.d.): 4.

72. Ibid.

73. Ibid.

74. *Qanun* 19 (n.d.): 3.

75. Ibid.

76. For more on the vagaries of Malkam Khan's ideas of political reform, see Amir-Mokri, 86–89; and Hamid Algar, *Mirza Malkum Khan: A Study in the History of Iranian Modernism.*

77. *Qanun* 21 (n.d.): 3.

78. Kermani, "Arshiv," 111.

79. For an exhaustive discussion on the history of these texts, see Najmabadi, introduction to Bibi Khanom Astarabadi, *Ma'ayeb al-Rejal*, 1–26.

80. Ibid., 49, with a partial translation on page 12 of the English introduction.

81. Ibid., 84.

82. Ibid., 87–88.

83. Ibid., 88–94.

84. Ibid., 58.

85. Ibid.

86. Ibid., 60.

87. Najmabadi in Astarabadi, *Ma'ayeb al-Rejal*, 25.

88. Beth Baron, *The Women's Awakening in Egypt: Culture, Society, and the Press*, 5. See also Beth Baron, "Mothers, Morality, and Nationalism in Pre-1919 Egypt," in *The Origins of Arab Nationalism*, ed. Rashid Khalidi, Lisa Anderson, Muhammad Muslih, and Reeva S. Simon, 271–88.

89. Najmabadi, "Crafting," 101.

90. Mansur, 15, 16. Unfortunately, Mansur has not provided specific citations for this five-part series, and I could not confirm them with the issues of *Sorayya* that were available.

91. For a partial translation of the text of the debate, see Paidar, 60–63.

92. *Mozakarat* (Parliamentary Proceeding), 2: 1528–35.

93. Ibid., 1531. It is possible that this modest affair has been raised to the status of legend. In his collection of biographies of famous people in modern Iranian history, Mehdi Bamdad reports that "they say" Vakil al-Ra'aya was tossed out of the Parliament by prominent cleric Sayyed 'Abd Allah Behbahani for raising a suggestion that women should vote. Bamdad, who does not seem to have consulted parliamentary proceedings on the matter, claims to have found a report in British Foreign Office correspondence that an unnamed deputy was tossed out of the Parliament by Sayyed Mohammad Behbahani (the son of 'Abd Allah) for raising an unspecified issue. Bamdad assumes that the name of the cleric in the British report is an error and considers this to be corroboration of the popular account of Vakil al-Ra'aya's defense of women's rights. See Mehdi Bamdad, *Sharh-e Hal-e Rijal-e Iran* 3:325–26 [Hereafter *BAMDAD*]. Mangol Bayat-Philip refers to two *Times of London* articles in regard to this incident. The first account, dated 22 August 1911, portrayed the deputy from Hamadan in a bolder light than the official record, but nothing like the Bamdad account. The unnamed cleric condemned Vakil al-Ra'aya's speech and claimed that women had neither souls nor rights. The president reportedly motioned to move on and to strike the discussion from the record. The second *Times of London* account, dated 28 August, which is viewed with obvious suspicion by Bayat-Philip, was printed as a "correction" to the earlier account and is closer to the official record cited here, except that it reported that the cleric responding to Vakil al-Ra'aya was "Sheikh Assadollah," instead of Sayyed Hasan Modarres. Mangol Bayat-Philip, "Women and Revolution in Iran, 1905–1911," in *Women in the Muslim World*, 3d ed., ed. Lois Beck

and Nikki Keddie, 301. Vakil al-Ra'aya and Sayyed Hasan Taqizadeh had both argued in favor of women's right of association in the First Parliament. See Najmabadi, "Zanha-yi Millat," 52–56; and Paidar, op. cit.

94. *Mozakarat*, 2:1531.

95. The presidency of the Parliament had changed hands several times in 1910. Before it came back to Mo'tamen al-Molk on 7 February 1911, it had gone to Zoka al-Molk and Esma'il Momtaz al-Dowleh, see *Mozakarat*, 2: 4. Mo'tamen al-Molk had received some education in Paris and had served as the director of the Foreign Ministry school. He was the son of Nasrollah Khan Moshir al-Dowleh and the younger brother of Hasan Moshir al-Dowleh Pirniya, who had played a role in writing the initial drafts of the constitution and who had held several ministerial spots in his career. See *BAMDAD:* 1:388–89.

96. Sayyed Abu al-Hasan Esfahani resigned without attending Parliament on 18 December 1909, and Haj Mirza Sayyed 'Ali Saberi resigned on 2 September 1910 without ever attending. His replacement, Haj Shaykh Mohammad Baqer Hamadani, resigned on 10 September 1910. Shaykh Mehdi Mazandarani was selected to replace Hamadani, but he refused and officially resigned on 16 January 1911. *Mozakarat*, 2: 5. For more on Modarres, see Hosayn Makki, *Modarres Qahraman-e Azadi;* and *Modarres*.

97. *Koran* 4:34, of course. See chapter 1, note 1.

98. *Mozakarat*, 2: 1531.

99. *Iran-e Now* 104, 9 August 1911, 3.

100. *Danesh* 1, 15 September 1910, 1.

101. See Sanasarian; Najmabadi, "Zanha-yi Millat"; and Paidar, op cit.

102. *Shokufeh* 1, no. 4 (18 February 1913): 1.

103. Reference to *Koran* 95:4 (*al-Tin*, The Fig), "*Laqad khalaqna al-insana fi ahsani taqwimin*" (Certainly We created humans in a most noble image).

104. Ibid.

105. See the letter dated 18 Mizan 1331 (3 October 1913) in *Asnad-e Matbu'at*, 2:86. Unfortunately, that issue of *Shokufeh* was not available to me.

106. Ibid., 87.

107. For more on this school, see chapter 6 n. 11.

108. *Danesh* 27, 27 May 1911, 2–3.

109. Ibid. Here I have employed a freer translation of *sharh va bayan* (literally, "explanation and narration").

110. Ibid.

111. Ibid. In the text: *Wa fina rabbena 'adhab al-nar*. However, the "*wa fina*" is almost certainly a typesetter's error for *faqina*, or "save us," making the final line of the couplet a likely reference to *Koran* 3:191: "*Rabbana ma khalaqta hadha batilan sobhanak faqena 'adhab al-nar,*" or "Lord, You have not created this in vain. Glory be to You! Save us from the torment of Fire."

112. It is an intriguing Koranic reference. The *surah* to which it refers, *Al-'Imran,* in addition to exhorting believers to be steadfast in their faith and con-

demning infidels, has two other themes. First, the *Koran* claims as Muslims biblical figures, such as Adam, Noah, and Abraham, and New Testament figures such as Mary and Jesus. Second, it uses a discussion of these figures to distinguish Islam from Christianity and Judaism and, of course, to exalt Islam over both. The author of the letter calls on Islam by referring to a passage in the *Koran* that endorses the adaptation, absorption, and complete co-option of ostensibly pre-Islamic or, more importantly perhaps, non-Islamic religious mythology.

Further, the line to which the allusion is made, *Koran* 3:191, occurs in one of the concluding passages of *Al-'Imran,* just before the next *surah, The Women* (Al-Nisa). The Koranic (*Koran* 3:190–93) context of the line is thus:

> In the creation of the heavens and the earth, and in the alternation of night and day, there are signs for men of sense; those that remember God when standing, sitting, and lying down, and reflect on the creation of the heavens and the earth, saying: "Lord, You have not created this in vain. Glory be to You! Save us from the torment of the Fire. Lord, those whom You will cast into the Fire You will put to eternal shame: none will help the evil-doers. Lord, we have heard someone calling to the true faith, saying: 'Believe in your Lord,' and we believed. Lord, forgive us our sins and remove from us our evil deeds and make us die with the righteous. Lord, grant us what You promised through Your apostles, and do not hold us up to shame on the Day of Resurrection. You never break Your promise." Their Lord answers them, saying "I will deny no man or woman among you the reward of their labors. You are the offspring of one another."

What is a prayer to the Lord in *Al-'Imran* could be a suggestion to the men, encouraged by the author of the letter in *Danesh,* to support women's education and to select wives on the basis of their inner merits and that their actions and promises have divine sanction. There is even a suggestion that God has promised equal attention to the conduct of men and women, and God's word that the fate of men and women are necessarily linked. Whether or not this intertextuality between the *Koran* and the *Danesh* letter was specifically intended to this extent or at all is a matter of speculation, but it exists regardless.

Chapter 3. Imagining the Modern Iranian Woman

1. I have discussed the history of the Iranian press in greater detail elsewhere. See Camron Michael Amin, "Selling and Saving 'Mother Iran': Gender and the Iranian Press in the 1940's." See also chapter 1, n. 24.

2. Abrahamian, 118–65.

3. For a consideration of Shirazi's encounter with European progress, see Feraydun Adamiyat, "Ashna'i-ye Iran ba Tamaddon-e Gharbi va Pishruvan Taraqqi-ye Jadid," in Mohammad Mirza Saleh Shirazi, *Majmu'eh-e Safarnamehha-ye Mirza Saleh Shirazi,* ed. Gholamhosayn Mirza Saleh, 1–12.

4. See Mohammad Esma'il Razvani, "Mirza Saleh Shirazi va Ruznameh Negari," in Shirazi, 13–33.

5. Shirazi, 169–70.

6. Since the sixteenth century, Iranian travelers to Europe had noted European women, and their impressions helped them define their culture in opposition to that of Europe. See Tavakoli-Targhi, "Imagining Western Women."

7. Shirazi, 184.

8. Ibid., 185.

9. Ibid.

10. Ibid.

11. Ibid., 191.

12. Ibid.

13. Ibid., 291–92.

14. Ibid., 293.

15. Ibid., 311.

16. Ibid.

17. Ibid., 316. Shirazi's favorable impression of the education of English women was anticipated by an eighteenth-century Iranian traveler to England, E'tesam al-Din, who was in England from 1766 to 1769. See Tavakoli-Targhi, "Imagining Western Women," 79.

18. Shirazi, 317.

19. The term *foyuj* or *feyuj* means "messenger(s), page(s), or attendant(s)." My speculation is that *ahl-e feyuj* ("those [who have to do with] attendants") is a euphemism for sex with boys or young men. It could also be read here as sexual activity distinct from pederasty—perhaps indicating prostitution, generally speaking.

20. Shirazi, 316.

21. Rezaqoli's account of events are a little vague. See J. B. Fraser, *Narrative of the Residence of the Persian Princes in London in 1835 and 1836*, 1:6–48, and *BAMDAD*, 4:367–78.

22. Rezaqoli Mirza, *Safarnameh-e Rezaqoli Mirza Naveh-e Fath 'Ali Shah*, ed. Asghar Farmanfarma'i Qajar, 345.

23. Fraser, 1:82–85.

24. Rezaqoli Mirza, 361–62.

25. Ibid., 394–95.

26. Tavakoli-Targhi, "Imagining Western Women," 76.

27. Ibid., 78–79.

28. *Sur-e Esrafil*, 27 February 1908, 4–5.

29. 'Ali Akbar Dehkhoda, "Charand va Parand," *Sur-e Esrafil*, 23 April 1908, 7–8.

30. "Zan-e Azadi Talab," *Iran-e Now*, 25 August 1909, 4.

31. "Zanan-e Haqq Talab," *Iran-e Now*, 27 August 1909, 4.

32. *Danesh* 11, 29 December 1910, 2.

33. "Sharh-e Hal-e Malekeh-e Holand," *Danesh* 16, 25 January 1911, 6–7.

34. "Sharh-e Hal-e Malekeh-e Alman," *Danesh* 19, 23 February 1911, 2.

35. "Madar-e Jorj, Padeshah-e Englis," *Danesh* 22, 3 March 1911, 8.

36. "Malekeh-e Rowmayn," *Danesh* nos. 29 and 30, 8 and 25 July 1911, 6 and 5.

37. "Malakeh-e Japon," *Danesh* 27, 26 June 1911, 5–8.

38. *Danesh* 29, 8.

39. *Danesh* 27, 6.

40. *Danesh* 16, 6–7.

41. "Mo'avenat-e Zanan-e Vokala-ye Parlemant-e Englis Be-showharan-e Khud," *Danesh* 23, 29 March 1911, 7.

42. "Mohabbat-e Madaranah-e Zanan-e Englis be-mosaferan-e Keshtiha," *Danesh* 26, 7.

43. Ibid., 8.

44. "Taraqqi-ye Zanan-e 'Osmani," *Danesh* 24, 14 March 1911, 4.

45. "Tafsil-e 'Arusiha-ye Mamalek-e Kharejeh," *Danesh* 13, 12 January 1911, 5. This passage appears as part of a larger discussion of foreign marriages to which we shall return later.

46. "Ghayrat va 'Asabiyat-e Khanomha-ye 'Osmani," *Shokufeh* 4, no. 4 (24 January 1916): 1–2.

47. "Falsafeh-e Hejab," *Shokufeh* 2, no. 23 (21 February 1914): 4.

48. "Falsafeh-e Hejab," *Shokufeh,* 2, no. 24 (3 March 1914): 3.

49. Just as arguments for unveiling bear the mark of the Egyptian Qasim Amin (and probably entertain the same limits as he for unveiling), opponents of unveiling seem to have used arguments similar to those of Tal'at Harb, who countered Qasim Amin's work.

50. *Shokufeh* 2, no. 24 (3 March 1914): 3.

51. Fakhr Afaq, "Moqayeseh-e Halat-e Zanan-e Urupa'i ba Zanan-e Irani," *Shokufeh* 2, no. 24 (3 March 1914) 3.

52. Ibid., 4.

53. "Avval Madraseh-e Dokhtaran dar Iran," *Danesh* 8, 2 December 1910, 5.

54. "'Avatef-e Khanomha-ye Irani," *Setareh-e Iran* 9, no. 42 (21 October 1923): 3. The article listed the donors by name and announced that their giving was a "sign of their awakening."

55. *Setareh-e Iran* 9, no. 60 (15 November 1923): 4.

56. "Dar al-Mo'allamat," *Setareh-e Iran* 9, no. 27 (23 September 1923): 3. For more on the origins and debatable purpose of this school see chapter 5 n. 11.

57. The process began with publication of the translation of a written plea for help by Iraqi women, see "Eblaghiyeh-e Majma' va Kongereh-e Nesvan," *Setareh-e Iran* 9, no. 34 (7 October 1923): 1–2. This was followed by the announcement of a conference and subsequent reports on that conference. See *Setarah-e Iran* 9, no. 44 (25 October 1923): 2; "Konferans-e Jam'iyat-e Ershad al-Nesvan, *Setareh-e Iran* 9, no. 52 (6 November 1923): 5; and "Bayanat-e Jam'iyat-e Ershad al-Nesvan," *Setareh-e Iran* 9, no. 53 (11 November 1923): 3–4.

58. *Setareh-e Iran* 9, no. 40 (18 October 1923): 4.

59. *Shafaq-e Sorkh* 466, 3 March 1926, 4.

60. The other women's periodicals of this period include *Zaban-e Zanan* (Women's Voice), edited by Sadiqeh Dowlatabadi in 1918; *Nameh-e Banovan* (The Ladies' Paper), edited by Shahnaz Azad in 1920; and *Jahan-e Zanan* (Women's World) edited by Fakhr Afaq Parsa in 1921. Later, supposedly with the secret aid of Reza Khan, a group called the Society of Iranian Women and Patriots started a magazine entitled *Majalleh-e Jam'iyat-e Nesvan va Vatankhʷah-e Iran* (Magazine of the Society of Iranian Women and Patriots) in 1923, and it had a two-year run. See Shaykh al-Eslami, 72–152. For a list of magazines targeted at women or operated by women between 1919 and 1974, see Shaykh al-Eslami, 181–90. See also Eliz Sanasarian, "Characteristics of the Women's Movement in Iran," in *Women and Family in Iran*, ed. A. Fathi, 86–106; and Sadr-Hashemi.

61. The owner of the publishing license was Navaveh Safavi. In 1929, the only member of the board of directors listed was Mrs. Boyce, the principal of the American Girls' School. In 1932, two Iranian women, Taybeh Khanom Mir Damadi and Ashraf Khanom Nabavi, and two Americans, Mrs. Boyce and Miss Doolittle, were listed as directors. See *'Alam-e Nesvan* 9, no. 5 (September 1929) and 12, no. 5 (September, 1935): 201 and 193 respectively.

62. Ibid., inside cover. In 1929, the non-Iranian representatives were Mrs. Ziegler in Molayer, Miss Eden in Yazd, and Mr. Miller in Mashhad. In 1932, the non-Iranian representatives were Mrs. Ziegler in Molayer, Miss Eden in Yazd, and Mrs. Elder in Kermanshah.

63. Cited in Shaykh al-Eslami, 123–25. Shaykh al-Eslami was unable to provide an exact date for the first issue of *'Alam-e Nesvan*, but the sixth (and it was a bimonthly magazine) was dated Tir 1300 (June/July 1921). That would place the first issue's appearance in the summer of 1920.

64. Ibid., 145.

65. *The Reminiscences of Jane Doolittle*, 1983, pages 9–11, in the Oral History of Iran Collection of the Foundation for Iranian Studies.

66. Shaykh al-Eslami, 100.

67. Ibid., 89.

68. Sadr-Hashemi, 3:125–31.

69. Sayyed Hasan Taqizadeh, "Dibacheh-e Sal-e Dovvom-e *Kaveh* (Dowreh-e Jadid)," *Kaveh* 2, no. 1 (11 January 1921): 1.

70. Ibid.

71. For examples, see "Melliyat va Ruh-e Melli-ye Iran," *Iranshahr* 2, no. 4 (17 December 1923): 193–206; and "Az Ketab Aqa-ye Soltan Assadollah Khan Arbabi: Favayed-e Varzesh-e Badani va Espor," *Setareh-e Iran* 12, nos. 116–18 (12–16 January 1927): 4, 4, and 3; and Azad Hamadani, "Manzum: Varzesh," *'Alam-e Nesvan* 10, no. 1 (January 1930): 16.

72. Ibid., 2.

73. Ibid., 2–3.

74. "Arshiv va Asnad: Ruznameh-e *Kaveh*," *Nimeh-e Digar* 7 (summer 1988): 134.

75. Zhazi Khanom Jamalzadeh, "Asas-e Enqelab-e Ejtema'i—Tarbiyat-e Zanan," *Kaveh* 1, no. 6, n.s. 41 (18 June 1920): 1–2. Reprinted in *Nimeh-e Digar* 7, 134–38.

76. Ibid., 134–35.

77. Ibid., 136.

78. Ibid., 137.

79. "Falj-e Sheqqi, Pasti-ye Halat-e Ejtema'i-ye Zanan," *Kaveh* 1, no. 12, n.s. 47 (18 December 1920): 1–2. Reprinted in *Nimeh-e Digar* 7, 138–40.

80. Ibid., 138–39.

81. Ibid., 139.

82. Ibid., 140.

83. "Zan-e Geda'i, Makkareh va 'Ayyar," *Iran-e Now* 10, 5 September 1909, 2.

84. Jamalzadeh, *Once Upon a Time,* 97.

85. Iraj Mirza, "Arefnameh," in Brian Spooner, *Suppressed Persian: An Anthology of Forbidden Literature,* 88–90. I will quibble with Spooner's translation of these last couplets. While *sar* and *sineh* are most meaningfully translated as "hair" (rather than head) and "breast" (rather than chest), *'esmat* is best translated as "chastity" or "innocence" and *naz* is best translated as "coquetry." Admittedly, these translations would totally ruin the rhyme in English, but they put the contradictions of the couplet in sharper relief.

86. Qasim Amin, *The Liberation of Women,* 35–61.

87. Afsaneh Najmabadi first drew scholarly attention to the "inner veil" idea in Iraj Mirza's poetry in "Veiled Discourse—Unveiled Bodies," 510–11.

88. Yahya Aryanpur, *Az Saba ta Nima,* 2:280–81.

89. Ibid., 2:280.

90. See Ebrahim Golestan, "Esmat's Journey," and Moniru Ravanpiur, "The Long Night," in *Stories From Iran: A Chicago Anthology,* ed. Heshmat Moayyad, 145–52 and 531–42; and *Sadeq Hedayat: An Anthology,* ed. Ehsan Yarshater.

91. Mohammad Mas'ud, *Tafrihat-e Shab,* 3–7.

92. Ibid., second page (unnumbered).

93. Ibid., d-h. Sayyed Kazem Khan Sar Keshik Zadeh, also known as Ettehad, was the founder and publisher of a daily newspaper, *Ettehad,* which began publishing in 1921, and a weekly satirical magazine, *Omid,* which began publishing in 1929. By 1932 both had been shut down by the authorities. See Sadr-Hashemi, 1:46, 1:277–81.

94. Ibid., z.

95. Sadr-Hashemi, 4:255–59.

96. For example, see "Namayandeh-e Majma'e Bayn al-Mellali-ye Nesvan," *Nahid,* 20 April 1928, 1; and M. Shaydush, "'Aqebat-e Sigheh-ravi," *Nahid,* 30 April 1928, 8. The first was a front-page story of a certain "Madam Shuflakher" who was a representative to the International Women's Congress in Iran. The second was the versification of a "true story" of a woman who, after being di-

vorced by her husband, became the temporary wife of a cleric. The first wife of the cleric found out, and the second wife was driven to the margins of society, ending up as a poor, disease-ridden prostitute.

97. Farrokhi's personal political journey was nearly classic for active members of the Iranian intelligentsia in the early twentieth century. He supported the Social Democrats during the Constitutional Revolution; he joined the anti-Entente Committee of National Defense in Kermanshah during World War I. Unlike many others with this history, however, his troubles with Reza Khan/Shah were immediate as he was arrested during the coup of 1921. His publication of *Tufan* set him on a collision course with the regime, and after his imprisonment, one term as a parliamentary deputy, exile, and reimprisonment, he was finally murdered in his cell in 1939. For an excellent biography and introduction to the literary and political significance of Farrokhi, see Ali Gheissari, "The Poetry and Politics of Farrokhi Yazdi."

98. Mirza Mohammad Farrokhi, "Tazakkor beh Majles-e Chaharom," *Tufan* 2, no. 6 (12 September 1922): 1.

99. *Tufan* 2, no. 40 (21 February 1923): 1.

100. *Tufan* 2, no. 102 (14 August 1923): 1.

101. *Khalq* 31, 18 December 1925, 4; and *Nahid,* 11 May 1928, 4 and 5.

102. *Khalq* 29, 11 December 1925, 4; and *Khalq* 33, 25 December 1925, 4. These cartoons are similar to those of an earlier leftist periodical published in Azeri, entitled *Molla Nasr al-Din* (ca. 1908). For examples, see Hasan Javadi, *Satire in Persian Literature,* 220–23.

103. Haideh Moghissi, *Populism and Feminism in Iran: Women's Struggle in a Male-Defined Revolutionary Movement,* 34.

104. Ibid., 35. For more on the editor of this paper, Ms. Rowshanak Now'dust, see Sadr-Hashemi, 2:92–93.

105. Tal'at Sh., "Khatar-e Bozorg dar Pish," *Tufan,* 2, no. 23 (23 October 1922): 2–3.

106. Ibid., 2.

107. Ibid.

Chapter 4. Unveiling and Its Discontents

1. "Jashn-e Ruz-e Tarikhi-ye Hefdahom-e Day," *Ettela'at* 2715, 7 January 1939, 1.

2. "Beh yadbud-e 20 shahrivar," *Kh^w andaniha* 8, no. 6 (Mehr 1323), cited in Mahmud Hakimi, *Dastanha'i Az 'Asr-e Reza Shah,* 334–36. The poem seems to have been first published in *Iran-e Ma,* a leftist newspaper. It is not clear why *Kh^w andaniha* chose to reprint it in the fall in 1944—perhaps in reaction to Reza Shah's death in exile that year. The word *pardeh* has been translated as veil or curtain, depending on the context—I think this ambiguity was deliberate on the anonymous author's part. It is the Persian equivalent of the Arabic *hijab.*

3. Sepehr Zabih, *The Communist Movement in Iran,* 21, 36; and Cosroe

Chaqueri, *The Soviet Socialist Republic of Iran, 1920–21: Birth of the Trauma,* 229–30, 253, 419–21.

4. Houchang E. Chehabi, "Staging the Emperor's New Clothes: Dress Codes and Nation-Building under Reza Shah," 212. Chehabi does not name the publication in which Kh^wajehnuri's article appeared.

5. Mohammad H. Faghfoory, "The Impact of Modernization on the Ulama in Iran, 1925–1941," 292. The action may have been for her own protection, as she was quickly assaulted by "veiled Moslem sisters" after venturing outside. This courageous act by Mohtaram Eskandari, the wife of Rokn al-Saltaneh, had some analogous precedents elsewhere in the Middle East after World War I, for example, in Egypt in 1922. In the Iranian context, she stands in contrast to Qorrat al-ʿAyn in the mid-nineteenth century, whose act may have had overtones of Islamic mysticism as much as those of feminism.

6. Afsaneh Najmabadi, "Feminism, Nationalism, Secularism and the Contemporary Quest for Civil Society in Iran," 32.

7. VKH, documents 1–22. See also Chehabi, 209–33; and Faghfoory, 290–94.

8. Guity Nahsat, "Women in Pre-Revolutionary Iran: A Historical Overview," in *Women and Revolution in Iran,* ed. Guity Nashat, 25.

9. U.S. State Department File 891.405/11, Charles C. Hart to the Secretary of State, 17 April 1931, 3.

10. Mehrangiz Dowlatshahi, in an interview recorded by Shahrokh Meskoob in Paris on 18 May 1984 for the Iranian Oral History Project, tape 5, page 22 of transcript.

11. Ghani, 383–88. Iran Teymourtache was inspired to avenge her father. She doggedly pursued the prosecution of the prison doctor who poisoned him, and she published her father's letters (to the embarrassment of the Pahlavi regime) in the 1940s. Her opposition to the regime forced her into exile in the late 1940s. Reportedly, she gleefully listened to the demise of the Pahlavis in 1979 on her radio in Paris. See Behnud, *In Seh Zan.*

12. Mehrangiz Dowlatshahi, tape 1, 5–8.

13. Lois Beck, *The Qashqaʾi of Iran,* 138.

14. See examples of press coverage of the trip in *Ettelaʿat,* 2, 9, 12, and 17 June and 10 and 30 July 1934.

15. Hassan Arfa [Hasan Arfaʿ], *Under Five Shahs,* 249. Loraine was instrumental in helping Reza Khan increase his power and remove the Qajar dynasty during the 1920s.

16. Ibid., 250.

17. Ibid., 248.

18. Ibid., 252.

19. *Ettelaʿat,* 17 and 23 July 1934, both on page 3.

20. John Perry, "Language Reform in Turkey and Iran."

21. Makki, 6:252.

22. VKH, 23.

23. Badr al-Moluk Bamdad, cited in VKH, 23.

24. U.S. State Department File 891.405/15, Chargé d'Affairs ad interim J. Rives Childes to Secretary of State, "Westernization of Iran: Greater Freedom for Women," 29 May 1935, 2–3.

25. U.S. State Department File 891.4051/19, William H. Hornibrook to the Secretary of State, "Westernization of Iran: Shah's Attitude Towards the *Chadar [sic]*," 18 June 1935.

26. U.S. State Department File 891.4051/20, William H. Hornibrook to the Secretary of State, "Westernization of Iran: Movement Towards Unveiling of Women; Discarding of Titles; Simplification of Funeral Ceremonies and Other Reforms," 27 June 1935, 1–2.

27. U.S. State Department File 891.4051/22, William H. Hornibrook to the Secretary of State, "The Unveiling of Women and Its Possible Effect on the Present Dynasty," 2 July 1935, 4.

28. U.S. State Department File 891.4051/23, William H. Hornibrook to the Secretary of State, "Proposed Removal of the Chador," 9 July 1935, 2.

29. U.S. State Department File 891.4051/21, William H. Hornibrook to the Secretary of State, "Riots in Meshed," 18 July 1935.

30. "Be-yad-e Hamaseh-e Khunin-e Gowhar Shad," *Sorush* 2, no. 90 (6 March 1981), cited in Makki, 6:254–56.

31. *Ettela'at Dar Yek Rob'-e Qarn,* cited in Makki, 6:274–76.

32. Mohammad Ebrahim Amirteymour, in an interview recorded by Habib Ladjevardi in La Jolla, California, 3 February 1985 for the Iranian Oral History Project, tape 9, page 13 of transcript.

33. Ibid., 13–15.

34. Arfa, *Under Five Shahs,* 255–56. In pointing the finger at Bahlul, Arfa implicitly exonerated "Assadi . . . who was hanged . . . for having instigated the Mashad people to revolt in protest at the adoption of the European hat." Arfa also noted that when the unveiling order was lifted with Reza Shah's departure in 1941, even the "lower classes" adopted a form of the veil that did not include a face covering.

35. FO 14906/26(I), "Disturbances in Meshed," Lt. Col. C. K. Daly to Mr. Knatchbull-Hugessen, 15 July 1935, document 270 in *BDOFA IIB.27/Persia viii.*

36. Ibid.

37. Ibid.

38. FO E4876/308/34, "Intelligence Summary No. 15 for Period Ending 27 July 1935," Major G. D. Pybus, 27 July 1935, document 273 in *BDOFA IIB.27/Persia viii.*

39. U.S. State Department File 891.4051/33, William H. Hornibrook to the Secretary of State, "Removal of the Chador," 19 August 1935.

40. U.S. State Department File 891.4051/34, William H. Hornibrook to the Secretary of State, "Shah Proposes to Ban Chador From Iran," 30 October 1935, 1–2.

41. KVH, document 3.

42. Ibid.

43. Ibid.

44. "Dar Kanun-e Banovan—Vaza'ef-e Akhlaqi-ye Zanan," *Ettela'at* 2617, 19 October 1935, 1, 8.

45. Esfandyari, *Ettela'at* 2617, 8.

46. Ibid.

47. "Dar Kanun-e Banovan," *Ettela'at* 2628–32, 2–8 November 1935, 1 (2628 only), 2.

48. "Dar Kanun-e Banovan," *Ettela'at* 2628, 1.

49. Ibid.

50. "Dar Kanun-e Banovan," *Ettela'at* 2630, 2.

51. Ibid.

52. "Dar Kanun-e Banovan," *Ettela'at* 2631, 2. She neglected to mention that the conference in Istanbul was the International Women's *Suffrage* Conference.

53. "Dar Kanun-e Banovan," *Ettela'at* 2632, 2. A picture of Pari Khanom in full uniform appeared on page one of the previous issue.

54. "Masa'el-e Ejtema'i: Saliqeh dar Sadagi Ast," "Vazifeh-e Nokhostin-e Ma dar Nazar-e Qanun-e Tabi'at," and "Tavaffoq-e 'Elm va 'Erfan," *Ettela'at* 2680, 6 January 1936, 2.

55. "Masa'el-e Ejtema'i: Vazifeh-e Bozorg," *Ettela'at* 2681, 7 January 1936, 2.

56. Mahmud Jam, "Khaterat," *Majalleh-e Rowshanfekr* (3 January 1962), cited in Makki, 6:259–68.

57. *The Reminiscences of Jane Doolittle,* pages 15–18, in the Oral History of Iran Collection of the Foundation for Iranian Studies. Doolittle confused the year of the event—remembering it as 1937—but it was a significant day in her mind. As she remembered it, "The day of freedom of women was really a very exciting time."

58. "Ruz-e Hefdahom-e Day Mah," "Entezar-e Shahanshah-e Iran az Zanan-e Keshvar," and "Banovan-e Iran, Ru be-jelow," *Ettela'at* 2683–85, 10–12 January 1936, 1, 8 (2685 only). Portions of the speech could also turn in up in "Letters to the Editor." See Vahid Mazandarani, "Yek Ruz-e Tarikhi," *Ettela'at* 2686, 13 January 1936, 3.

59. "Du Notq-e Mohemm-e Molukaneh," *Ettela'at* 2682, 8 January 1936, 1.

60. Unquestionably, the regime was (publicly) committed to the idea that women could work in low-ranking but necessary office/clerical positions. For example, see "Banovan Dar Zendagani-ye 'Amali—Amukhtan-e Fann-e Telegraf," *Ettela'at* 2704, 3 February 1936, 1. The brief discussed women's learning to use the telegraph and the typewriter. Women were pictured in telegraph class and exercising.

61. "Tashrif Farma'i-ye 'Olyahazrat Malekeh va Valahazratayn Shahdokht beh Dar al-Aytam-e Shahpur," *Ettela'at* 2685, 1; and "Tashrif Farma'i-ye 'Olyahazrat

Malekeh va Valahazratayn Shahdokht beh Parvarshgah-e Nowzadehgan va Zayeshgah-e Baladi," *Ettela 'at* 2692, 20 January 1936, 1, 8.

62. *Ettela 'at* 2685, 1.

63. "Pazira'i-ye Dishab dar 'Emarat-e Majles-e Shura-ye Melli," *Ettela 'at* 2685, 1, 8.

64. "Nashriyat: Tafsir-e Qor'an," *Ettela 'at* 2682, 3.

65. "Khetabeh-e Ma'aven-e Tavliyat-e Astaneh dar Jashn-e Nahzat-e Banovan-e Qom," *Ettela 'at* 2694, 22 January 1936, 3; and "Majles-e Jashn-e Banovan-e Qom," *Ettela 'at* 2705, 4 February 1936, 1.

66. "'Olama va Ruhaniyan," *Ettela 'at* 2707, 7 February 1936, 1; and "Qazvin—Sherekat-e Aqayan-e 'Olama Dar Nahzat-e Banovan," *Ettela 'at* 2711, 1.

67. Zanjani, "Zan dar Eslam va Sharaye'-e Qadim," *Ettela 'at* 2721–23, 24–26 February 1936, 2. Unfortunately, part 1 was not available. Zanjani may have specifically addressed the issue of unveiling here, but he did not in the remaining parts.

68. Zanjani, "Zan dar Eslam va Sharaye'-e Qadim," parts 5 and 6, *Ettela 'at* 2724–25, 28–29 February 1936, 2.

69. Zanjani, "Zan dar Eslam va Sharaye'-e Qadim," parts 7–9, *Ettela 'at* 2726–28, March 1–3 1936, 2.

70. H. Tarbiyat, "Zararha-ye Jesmi va Ruhi-ye Hejab," *Ettela 'at* 2706, 5 February 1936, 1.

71. "Chador az Janbeh-e Qaza'i," *Ettela 'at* 2707, 1.

72. "Takanha-ye Ejtema'i Pas az be-Dur Andakhtan-e Chador," *Ettela 'at* 2708, 7 February 1936, 1.

73. "Beh Afkar va Tasmim-e Jame'eh Bayad Ehteram Gozard," *Ettela 'at* 2705, 4 February 1936, 1.

74. Shayesteh Sadeq, "Maqam-e Zan dar Iran va Torkiyeh," *Ettela 'at* 2709–11, 9–11 February 1936, 1 and 8 (2711 only).

75. "Nofuz-e Adabi-ye Zan," *Ettela 'at* 2715, 16 February 1936, 1.

76. See, for example, *Ettela 'at* 2681, 8.

77. For example, see "Khanom-e Dorrat al-Sadat Tabataba'i," *Ettela 'at* 2686, 1; "Konferans-e Banovan Dar Esfahan," *Ettela 'at* 2688, 18 January 1936, 1; "Dar Jashn-e Banovan-e Fars," *Ettela 'at* 2693, 21 January 1936, 1; and "Dar Khorramabad—'Esmat Khanom Vahdati," *Ettela 'at* 2694, 1.

78. Bahar's "Zan," in "Dar Kolub-e Iran," *Ettela 'at* 2693, 1. See also "Setayesh Dar Nahzat-e Banovan," *Ettela 'at* 2690, 2; "Dar Jalaseh-'e Kanun-e Banovan," *Ettela 'at* 2692, 1; "Hadiyeh beh Banovan-e Hassas," *Ettela 'at* 2696, 2; "Jashn-e Baladiyeh," *Ettela 'at* 2697, 1; and "Dar Kolub-e Iran," *Ettela 'at* 2726, 2.

79. "Tashrif Farma'i-ye Valahazratayn Shahdokht—Khetabeh-e Aqa-ye Vosuq," *Ettela 'at* 2691, 19 January 1936, 1, 4.

80. Ibid., 4.

81. "Khetabeh-e Aqa-ye Vosuq [part 2]," *Ettela'at* 2692, 2. This theme of "equality of importance" as one of God's creatures was also trumpeted in an anonymous essay, "Adam va Hava'," *Ettela'at* 2691, 2.

82. "Khetabeh-e Aqa-ye Vosuq—3," *Ettela'at* 2693, 2.

83. "Khetabeh-e Aqa-ye Vosuq—3–6 [*sic;* actually 4–6]," *Ettela'at* 2694–97, 22–26 January 1936, 2.

84. *Mehregan* 2, no. 1 (20 March 1936): 8.

85. "Java'ez-e *Mehregan* be-Shagerdan-e Avval va Dovvom-e Emtehanat-e Naha'i-ye Sal-e Jari-e Markaz va Velayat," *Mehregan* 51 (16 July 1937): 11.

86. For example, see the picture of an American woman stumping for U.S. presidential candidate Alf Landon in *Mehregan* 2, no. 7 (21 June 1936), and a short feature on women royalist soldiers in the Spanish Civil War in "Eqdamat-e Zanan-e Vatan-parast dar Espani," *Mehregan* (22 September 1936): 11.

87. "Bigonah," *Mehregan* 2, no. 10 (6 August 1936): 19. See responses by Abu'l-Qasem Sadra'i, Gholam Reza Bozorgar, Hamid Salehi, Amineh Shaykh al-Eslami, and 'A. Homayunfar in *Mehregan* 2, nos. 11, 12, 13, 14, and 22 (22 August, 6 and 22 September, 7 October 1936, and 4 February 1937): 20, 19, 20, 21, and 21 respectively.

88. VKH, document 30.

89. VKH, documents 109–12.

90. VKH, documents 61, 62, 69, and 70.

91. VKH, document 210 (dated 5 June 1943).

92. *Reminiscences of Parvin Mo'ayyed-Sabeti,* 1988, pages 3–4, in the Oral History of Iran Collection of the Foundation for Iranian Studies.

93. See, for examples, *Reminiscences of Nayereh Ebtehaj-Samii,* 1984, pages 5–6, in the Oral History of Iran Collection of the Foundation for Iranian Studies; and *Reminiscences of Safiyyeh Firuz,* 1984, 705–17 on the tape counter, in the Oral History of Iran Collection of the Foundation for Iranian Studies; and *Reminiscences of Jane Doolittle,* 1983, page 26, in the Oral History of Iran Collection of the Foundation for Iranian Studies.

94. VKH, documents 129–32; and KVF, document 31.

95. VKH, document 83.

96. KVF, document 279.

97. KVF, documents 59, 60. The sense of trauma that a family could feel in response to these state-enforced social occasions is captured in Jalal Al-e Ahmad, "The Joyous Celebration," in *Modern Persian Short Stories,* ed. Minoo Southgate, 19–33.

98. FO E 1155/405/34, Mr. Butler to Mr. Eden, 20 February 1936, document 50 in *BDOFA IIB.28/Persia viii.*

99. The wife of a Parliamentary deputy from Mashhad, Parvin Mo'ayyed-Sabeti remembers hearing of similar episodes. She did not claim to have witnessed such a thing—raising the question in my mind as to whether this was something of

an "urban myth" during the early days of the Women's Awakening. *Reminiscences of Parvin Mo'ayyed-Sabeti*, 1988, pages 4–5, in the Oral History of Iran Collection of the Foundation for Iranian Studies.

100. FO 15370/43(i), Consul Urquhart to Mr. Butler, 20 February 1936, document 56 in *BDOFA IIB.28/Persia viii*.

101. FO 15665/24 [T 14283/69/379], Mr. Seymour to Viscount Halifax, 31 October 1938, document 220 in *BDOFA IIB.28/Persia viii*.

102. KVF, documents 135–37.

103. KVF, document 117.

104. KVF, document 118.

105. U.S. State Department File 891.24/88, William Hornibrook to the Secretary of State, "Major Arfaʿ Imprisonment," 26 July 1935. Hasan Arfaʿ remembers the accusations differently. According to his memoir, Ibrahim was charged with delaying the purchase of airplanes during Iran's confrontation with the British over the APOC from 1932 to 1934 in order to put the Iranian army at a disadvantage—far more treasonous (and outlandish) charges. Arfaʿ, 262.

106. U.S. State Department Record 891.24/108, William Hornibrook to the Secretary of State, "Efforts to Obtain the Release of Major Arfaʿ," 9 December 1935. Arfaʿ, 262–63.

107. U.S. State Department Record 891.24/103, William Hornibrook to the Secretary of State, "United Aircraft Exports Corporation Representations to the Iranian Government," 23 October 1935.

108. U.S. State Department Record 891.24/125, William Hornibrook to the Secretary of State, "Ex-Major Ibrahim Arfaʿ," 17 July 1936. Hasan Arfaʿ concurs with the terms of his brother's release but attributes it to an appeal he prepared on his brother's behalf that was brought to the attention of Reza Shah by General Zarghami. Arfaʿ, 263.

109. Arfaʿ, 263–64.

110. Arfaʿ, 270.

111. Mohammad Ebrahim Amirteymour, in an interview recorded by Habib Ladjevardi in La Jolla, California, on 3 February 1985 for the Iranian Oral History Project, tape 9, page 13 of transcript.

112. Conversation with my father, Mohammad Amin, on 26 November 1999 (the day after Thanksgiving, in Chicago!).

113. Mohammad Shanehchi, in an interview recorded by Habib Ladjevardi on 4 March 1983 in Paris for the Iranian Oral History Project, tape 1, page 2 of transcript.

114. Najmabadi, *The Story of the Daughters of Quchan*, 24.

115. J. E. Knörzner, *Ali Dashti's Prison Days: Life Under Reza Shah*, 176–83. *Prison Days* was a work in progress as Dashti was imprisoned a number of times under Reza Shah and once during the prime ministership of Ahmad Qavam in 1946, under Mohammad Reza Shah. The first edition was published in 1922, the

third in 1948, and the version analyzed by Knörzner was the fifth edition, published in 1960, Knörzner, 59–60.

116. Ibid., 180–81.

117. Ibid.

118. Ghani, 274–76.

119. For a convenient biography of Foroughi and his relationship to Reza Shah, see Ghani, 292–93. See chapter 2 of this book for his role in the brief parliamentary discussion of women's suffrage in 1911.

120. Sattareh Farman Farmaian, *Daughter of Persia*, 85.

121. Ghani, 283 and 310.

122. Ibid., 357, 373 n. 17.

123. Shahrough Akhavi, *Religion and Politics in Contemporary Iran: Clergy State Relations in the Pahlavi Period*, 23–60. Faghfoory, op. cit.

124. Arfaʿ, *Under Five Shahs*, 305.

125. Mohammad Masʿud, *Golhaʾi keh dar Jahanam Miruyad*, 39.

126. "Farhang va Zayeʿat-e Maʿnavi," *Mardom*, 23 April 1943, 1.

127. Cited from *Islam and Revolution: Writings and Declarations of Imam Khomeini*, trans. and ann. Hamid Algar, 172.

128. As an antidote to this paranoid assessment, see Patrick Clawson, "Knitting Iran Together: The Land Transport Revolution, 1920–1940."

Chapter 5. Renewal's Bride

1. Beth Baron has explored the notion of the companionate marriage in the context of Egyptian feminist struggles for legal reform in "The Making and Breaking of Marital Bonds in Modern Egypt," in *Women in Middle Eastern History*, 275–91.

2. See chap. 4 n.10.

3. Ibid.

4. "Rasm-e Showhar-dari," *Danesh* 1, 5, 6.

5. "Rasm-e Zan-dari," *Danesh* 6–8, all on page 8.

6. "Pedar-e Khub," *Danesh* 18, 16 February 1911, 7, 8.

7. "Be-mardan va Javanan," *Danesh* 2, 2.

8. "ʿArusiha-ye Mamalek-e Kharejiyeh: Rusha, Englisha," *Danesh* 14, 18 January 1911, 5.

9. "Tafsil-e ʿArusiha-ye Mamalek-e Kharejeh," *Danesh* 13, 12 January 1911, 6.

10. Ibid., 6–7.

11. *Danesh* 14, 5.

12. *Danesh* 13, 4.

13. "Ezdevaj-e Ahl-e Eslambul," *Danesh* 26, 12 May 1911, 3.

14. *Danesh* 13, 5.

15. See chapter 3 n. 44.

16. For example, see any issue of *Ruh al-Qodos*, 1909–11.

17. *Danesh* 26, 4.

18. "Tariq-e Nekah-e Zulu (Mardoman-e Seyah)," *Danesh* 30, 24 July 1911, 8.

19. A nationalism defined against the barbarity of others was evident elsewhere in the pages of *Shokufeh* and in relation to other topics. True to post-Kermani renewalist sentiment, "pure" Iranian virtues and "correct" Islamic virtues were portrayed as foil to the barbarity of Zoroastrians, Chaldeans, Mongols, and Arabs whose superstitions were propagated through Iranian society by "Jewish charlatans." See R. H. M., "Ma'aref Zanha-ye Irani: Yeki az Sar-cheshmehha-ye Badbakhtiha," *Shokufeh* 1, no. 9 (10 May 1913): 1; R. H. M., "Ma'aref-e Zanha," *Shokufeh* 1, no. 10 (31 May 1913): 2; and "Dokhtar-e Khub Kodam Ast?" *Shokufeh* 1, no. 11 (17 June 1913): 3.

20. Hosayn Kazemzadeh, "Ezdevaj ba Dokhtaran-e Irani va ya Farangi," *Iranshahr* 2, no. 8 (21 April 1924): 494.

21. Ibid., 494–95.

22. Badr al-Moluk Saba, "'Aqideh-e Khanom-e Badr al-Moluk Saba," *Iranshahr* 11–12 (19 August 1924): 668. She had addressed the same issue one year earlier in *Setareh-e Iran*, see Badr al-Moluk Saba, "Ekhtelat-e Nezhad," *Setareh-e Iran* 9, no. 13 (13 August 1923): 2, and the subsequent endorsement of her views in 'Ali Sadeqi, "Dar Atraf-e Ekhtelat-e Nezhad," *Setareh-e Iran* 9, no. 14 (15 August 1923): 2–3.

23. 'Abbas Zarkesh, "Maseleh-e Ezdevaj ba Irani ya Farangi," Sayyed Mostafa Tabataba'i, "Qesmat-e Falsafi," and Sadiqeh Dowlatabadi, "'Aqideh-e Khanom-e Sadiqeh Dowlatabadi," *Iranshahr* 2, nos. 11–12, 676, 629, 707.

24. Saba, 668.

25. Tabataba'i, 629.

26. Ibid., 630.

27. Zarkesh, 676.

28. Saba, 668–69.

29. Ibid., 669–70.

30. Dowlatabadi, 702.

31. Ibid., 703.

32. Ibid., 707.

33. Tabataba'i, 630.

34. Zarkesh, 676.

35. Dowlatabadi, 704–5.

36. "Notq-e Hazrat-e Ayatollahzadeh Khalesi," *Setareh-e Iran* 9, no. 23 (17 September 1923): 2.

37. Ibid.

38. "Notq-e Hazrat-e Ayatollahzadeh Khalesi," *Setareh-e Iran* 9, no. 26 (21 September 1923): 2.

39. For examples, see "Raftar dar Khʷanavadeh," trans. Fetaneh Khanom Dayhim, *'Alam-e Nesvan* 9, no. 3 (May 1929): 142–49; R. Namvar, "Ezdevaj Dar Iran," *'Alam-e Nesvan* 9, no. 5 (September 1929): 240–49; Habibeh Mojallel,

"Dar Atraf-e Ezdevaj Dar Iran," '*Alam-e Nesvan* 9, no. 6 (November 1929): 270–71; 'Abbas Aryanpur Kashani, "Zan-e Shahri ya Dehqani," '*Alam-e Nesvan* 10, no. 1 (January 1930): 6–10; Tayibeh Shimi, "Javab-e Zan-e Dehqani," '*Alam-e Nesvan* 10, no. 3 (May 1930): 117–20; 'Effat Khanom Sami'iyan, "Rahnama-ye Khanavadeh," '*Alam-e Nesvan* 11, no. 3 (May 1931): 134–42; Mr. Niri, "Su-e Ezdevaj," '*Alam-e Nesvan* 11, no. 5 (September 1931): 216; Amir Arsalan Khal'at-Bari, "Qanun-e Jadid-e Ezdevaj," and Musa Rahmat-pur "Sa'adat ya Khowshi Dar Khanavadeh," '*Alam-e Nesvan* 12, no. 3 (May 1932): 97–103, 136; and 'Abbas Aryanpur Kashani, "Entekhab-e Showhar," '*Alam-e Nesvan* 12, no. 6 (November 1932): 283–87.

40. See '*Alam-e Nesvan* 5, no. 2 (March 1925).

41. '*Alam-e Nesvan* 10, no. 2 (March 1930): inside cover.

42. S. A., Afzal Vaziri, and Malak al-Zaman Ebrahimiyan, "Showhar-e Khiyali-ye Man," '*Alam-e Nesvan* 10, no. 2 (March 1930): 75–77, 79, 80.

43. Ibid., 76.

44. Malak al-Zaman Ebrahimiyan, '*Alam-e Nesvan* 10, no. 2, 79.

45. R. Aryanpur Kashani, "Showhar-e Khiyali-e Man," '*Alam-e Nesvan* 10, no. 2, 80.

46. M. M., and Bala Khanom Sharif, '*Alam-e Nesvan* 10, no. 2, 78, 80.

47. Ibid., 78.

48. Delshad Khanom, "Showhar-e Khiyali-ye Man," '*Alam-e Nesvan* 10, no. 3 (May 1930): 108–11.

49. Delshad Khanom, "Geda-ha ra Migirand," '*Alam-e Nesvan* 9, no. 4 (July 1929): 153–58. Without mentioning the author, Sanasarian has also taken note of this short story. See Sanasarian, 34.

50. *The Reminiscences of Jane Doolittle*, 1983, pages 9–11, in the Oral History of Iran Collection of the Foundation for Iranian Studies.

51. See note 50 of the present chapter.

52. Ziba Mir-Hosseini, op. cit.

53. "Hamsar-e Khiyali-e Shoma!" '*Alam-e Nesvan* 10. no. 2, 57. The call was directed to "all youths and men who have an interest in the progress of women."

54. R. Namvar, "Cheguneh Zani Mikh^{w}aham?" '*Alam-e Nesvan* 10, no. 3, 144. In an earlier exchange on marriage, Namvar was taken to task for his high expectations by Habibeh Mojallel. She insisted that until men recognized women as social and political partners *(sharik)*, there could be no meaningful discussions of ideal marriages. See Habibeh Mojallel, "Dar Atraf-e Ezdevaj Dar Iran," '*Alam-e Nesvan* 9, no. 6 (November 1929), 271.

55. Ibid., 144–45.

56. 'A. A., "Hamsar-e Khiyali-ye Man," '*Alam-e Nesvan* 10, no. 3 , 145–46.

57. Mehdi Movafeq, "Qet'eh," '*Alam-e Nesvan* 10, no. 3, 146.

58. Sanasarian, 60–61, and Paidar, 109–11.

59. Ibid. Killing a sister or mother under the same circumstances cost only three

months in prison. The irony here is that legalized violence against women was codified in the Penal Law of 1940, which owed more to Italian penal law than Islamic law. "Honor killing" has received similar legal ratification in other modernizing Middle Eastern countries that adapted European legal codes as part of their programs of legal modernization. For example, see Lama Abu-Odeh, "Crimes of Honor and the Construction of Gender in Arab Societies," in *Feminism and Islam,* ed. Mai Yamani, 141–95. It has no legal justification in Islamic law.

60. U.S. State Department File 891.4054/8, Charles C. Hart to the Secretary of State, 19 August 1931, 1.

61. Ibid., 5.

62. Ibid., 6.

63. Ibid.

64. U.S. State Department File 891.4054/7, Charles C. Hart to the Secretary of State, 11 August 1931, 7 and 8.

65. U.S. State Department File 891.4054/8, page 5 of the translation of the Marriage and Divorce Law.

66. U.S. State Department File 891.4054/10–11, Hart to the Secretary of State, 6 and 28 November 1931.

67. U.S. State Department File 891.4054/12, Hart to the Secretary of State, 19 December 1931, 2, 3

68. Ibid., an attached translation of "Second Marital Sentence Rendered by Pahlevi Court: Sheikh Condemned to One Year's Imprisonment," *Iran,* 25 December 1931.

69. U.S. State Department File 891.4054/16, Hart to the Secretary of State, "Two Further Sentences in the Application of the Law on Marriage and Divorce in Persia," 8 March 1932, 1.

70. Ibid., 2.

71. 'Effat Khʷajehnuri, "Tashakkor az Qanun-e Ezdevaj," *Ettela'at* 1379, 2 August, 1931, 1.

72. Mozakarat 10:94, 29 Farvardin 1316, 964–1023. Of much greater interest that day was proposed Ministry of Justice regulations for the insurance industry.

73. "Eslah-e Qanun-e Ezdevaj," *Ettela'at* 2108, 17 April 1938, 4.

74. "Yak Mosabeqeh-e Delkash," *Mehregan* 79 (28 December 1938): 12–13.

75. "Pasokhha-ye Mosabeqeh-e Delkash-e Makhsus-e Banovan," *Mehregan* 82 (9 February 1939): 12–13.

76. U.S. State Department File 891.405/11, 2.

77. U.S. State Department file 891.0011/113, Engert to the Secretary of State, "Festivities for the Wedding of the Crown Prince and Princess Fawzieh," 13 May 1939, 3. Mohammad Hejazi's *Iran-e Emruz,* the new official publication of the Organization of Public Enlightenment, was able to capitalize on the royal wedding for optimistic and patriotic material. The gymnastics exhibitions featured Iranian

girls—further displaying modern Iranian womanhood's disciplined and wholesome athleticism. We will examine this aspect of Women's Awakening propaganda further in chapter 7. See *Iran-e Emruz* 1, nos. 2/3 (April/June 1939).

78. "Barnameh-e 'Arusi-e Valahazrat-e Homayun Valiahd ba Valahazrat Shahzadeh Khanom Fowziyeh," included in U.S. State Department File 891.0011/numbers. Picture portraits of Reza Shah, King Farouk, Crown Prince Mohammad Reza, and Princess Fowziyeh were included with the program. The first mention of any ceremonial action by Fowziyeh is on the day after the marriage contract was signed, 16 March. On that day, the princess was presented with flowers at a flower festival in Abedine Palace in Cairo. She vanishes again until the journey to Iran begins. It is not known whether the royal couple shared quarters on the yacht.

79. U.S. State Department file 891.0011/113, 3.

80. *Reminiscences of Ashraf Pahlavi*, 15 June 1982, page 13, in the Oral History of Iran Collection of the Foundation for Iranian Studies. This was also Engert's impression.

81. U.S. Department of State File 891.0011/110. Bert Fish to the Secretary of State, "Marriage Celebrations in Teheran for the Crown Prince of Iran and Princess Fawzieh," 30 May 1939.

82. Ibid.

83. U.S. State Department Records 891.0011/112 and 115–16, Bert Fish to the Secretary of State, 10–11 July and 5 August 1939. In 891.0011/112, Bert Fish related that the shah had demanded Fowziyeh's "inheritance and property" for the crown prince in an obvious violation of Islamic legal traditions on this matter. It is unlikely that the Egyptian royal family would have made a gift of such property (especially as a portion of it was in the form of landholdings in Egypt) during the negotiations over the marriage contract.

84. Khosrow Mo'tazed, *Fowziyeh: Hekayat-e Talkhkami, Qesseh-e Joda'i.*

85. Ashraf, 14, 17.

86. Fowziyeh's story was taken up in the Arab press and circulated in Iran. This journalistic, and undocumented account, casts Fowziyeh's brother, King Farouk of Egypt, as the real villain who interfered with Fowziyeh's and Mohammad Reza's attempts to reconcile once Fowziyeh returned to Egypt in 1945. See *Fowziyah, Malekeh-i Ghamghin: Tarjomeh az Majalleh-e al-Maw'id (Chap-e Bayrut).*

87. U.S. State Department File 891.001 REZA SHAH *[sic]*/8–2645, Allen to the Secretary of State, 24 August 1946. It is amazing that the new king, Mohammad Reza Shah, did not yet have a new file.

88. U.S. State Department File 901.001 REZA SHAH *[sic]*/8–2646, Allen to the Secretary of State, 26 August 1946.

89. The official communiqué is reproduced in *Fowziyeh, Malakeh-e Ghamgin,* 323. Even amid the political news from Iran, the divorce made it into the pages of the American press. See "Shah Divorces Empress Fawzia," *New York Times,* 20 November 1948, sec. 1, p. 6. Incidentally, the *New York Times* devoted more

coverage to the wedding of Fowziyeh and Mohammad Reza than to any other news from Iran in 1939.

90. *Reminiscences of Saffiyeh Firuz,* 1984, 687–705 on the tape counter, in the Oral History of Iran Collection of the Foundation for Iranian Studies.

91. *Reminiscences of Nayereh Ebtehaj-Samii,* 1984, page 3, in the Oral History of Iran Collection of the Foundation for Iranian Studies.

92. *Reminiscences of Parvin Mo'ayyed-Sabeti,* 1988, page 1, in the Oral History of Iran Collection of the Foundation for Iranian Studies.

93. Firuz, 947–56 on the tape counter. Firuz believed that she brought horseback riding around town into fashion for Tehran women in 1927, 88–111 on the tape counter.

Chapter 6. The Capable Woman

1. Dr. Maryam Tusi (her name has been changed to protect her privacy) in a phone interview with the author, 28 May 1998.

2. See chapter 3.

3. See chapter 2.

4. The legacy of this institution, which laid the foundation for what was to become the University of Tehran, is complex. The translation bureau and printing press associated with the Dar al-Fonun were of critical importance to the process of adapting European modernity to Iranian needs and to the rise of the periodical press in Iran. However, as early as 1859 the administrators of the Dar al-Fonun were hard pressed to find funds for the school's operating expenses. See Maryam Dorreh Ekhtiar, "The Dar al-Funun: Educational Reform and Cultural Development in Qajar Iran," 133–35.

5. David Menashri, *Education and the Making of Modern Iran,* 77–78.

6. Rudi Matthee, "Transforming Dangerous Nomads into Useful Artisans, Technicians, Agriculturalists: Education in the Reza Shah Period," 315–16.

7. Mansureh Ettehadiyeh, *Maramnamehha va Nezamnamehha-ye Ahzab-e Seyasi-e Iran dar Dowreh-e Dovvom-e Majles-e Shura-ye Melli,* 46.

8. Paidar, 67–70.

9. Najmabadi, "Zanha-yi Millat: Women or Wives of the Nation?"

10. Janet Afary has translated and reproduced the information from *Shokufeh.* See Afary, *The Iranian Constitutional Revolution, 1906–11,* 182–83 (see table 7.1).

11. Gholam'ali Sarmad, *E'zam-e Mohassal beh Kharej az Keshvar dar Dowreh-e Qajar,* 109. This college has been described as a teachers training college, based on the reading of its name as dar al-mo'allemat. However, Sarmad's information on the intent of the "place of women's training," or *dar al-mo'allamat,* raises a question as to whether it was a teachers college at all, at least in its initial incarnation. Women were being "trained" (hence the term *mo'allam,* in Arabic *mu'allam),* but they were not themselves in the business of training

others as teachers *(mo'allem,* in Arabic *mu'allim).* This would be consistent with
the use of the term in other contexts; for example, Ottoman Sultan Mahmud II's
new military unit was called "the Victorious Trained Soldiers of Muhammad"
(muallem asakir-i mansure-i Muhammadiye—in Turkish an "e" is used to represent the Arabic "a"). See Stanford J. Shaw and Ezel Kural Shaw, *History of the
Ottoman Empire and Modern Turkey,* 2:22–23.

12. Menashri, 130.

13. Fatemeh Sayyah, *Naqd va Sayyahat: Majmu'eh-e Maqalat va Taqrirat
Doktor Fatemeh Sayyah,* ed. Mohammad Golbon.

14. For more on the life of this remarkable woman, see *Sadiqeh Dowlatabadi:
Nameh-ha va Neveshteh-ha va Yad-ha,* 3 vols., compiled and introduced by
Mahdukht San'ti and Afsaneh Najmabadi.

15. Menashri, 118.

16. Ibid., 110.

17. All of the statistics in this paragraph that are not attributed to another
source are drawn from Ministry of Culture, *Salnameh va Amar-e Vezarat-e
Farhang-e Dowlat-e Shahanshahi-ye Iran, 1322/23–1326/27,* 140–41.

18. Matthee, 315.

19. *Salnameh va Amar, 1322/23–1326/27,* 333, 351.

20. VKH, documents 61, 62, 69, 70.

21. *Salnameh va Amar, 1322/23–1326/27,* part 2, 507–47.

22. It is interesting to note that Dr. Tusi recalls nine students, the picture shows
ten women, and official records indicate that there were seven.

23. Mehrangiz Dowlatshahi, in an interview recorded by Shahrokh Meskoob
in Paris on 8 May 1984 for the Iranian Oral History Project, tape 1, page 3 of

24. Fazlollah Nuri, "Matbu' dar Astaneh-e Moqaddaseh-e Hazrat-e 'Abd al-
Azi (Salam Allah 'Alayhi wa 'Ala Aba'ih al-Karam) Bara-ye Entebah va Raf'-e
Eshtebah az Baradaran-e Dini," in *Rasayel, E'lamiyehha, Maktubat, va
Ruznameh-e Shaykh-e Shahid Fazlollah Nuri,* vol. 1, ed. Mohammad Torkaman,
262.

25. Delrish, 126–28. She notes that the Qajar monarch Naser al-Din Shah (d.
1896) used to provide annual financial assistance to both the Presbyterian girls'
school and the French school run by the Sisters of St. Vincent de Paul.

26. Paidar, 69.

27. Delrish, 135–39.

28. "Yahudan-e Ommat-e Mohammad Sal'am," *Da'vat al-Eslam* 22, 25 August 1907, 1. The article compared Shaykh Nuri to the "hypocrites" and to Jews
who opposed the Prophet while he struggled to establish the Medinan Muslim
community.

29. "Notq-e Hazrat-e Ayatollahzadeh Khalesi," *Setareh-e Iran* 9, no. 27 (7
October 1923): 1.

30. Matthee, 327.

31. Michael P. Zirinsky, "Render unto Caesar the Things Which Are Caesar's: American Presbyterian Educators and Reza Shah."

32. Michael P. Zirinsky, "A Panacea for the Ills of the Country," 124–25; and Michael P. Zirinsky, "Presbyterian Missionaries and American Relations with Pahlavi Iran," 78, 85.

33. Michael P. Zirinsky, "Render Unto Caesar," 347.

34. Ibid., 349.

35. Ibid., 356.

36. For example, novelist and journalist Mohammad Mas'ud was sent to Belgium at government expense to study journalism in 1935. However, when he wrote an article for a Belgian newspaper on the subject of communism, he was warned by Minister of Education 'Ali Akbar Hekmat via the Iranian embassy not to write such articles in the future. See Nasr Allah Shifteh, *Zendegi-nameh va Mobarrazat-e Seyasi-e Mohammad Mas'ud, Modir-e Ruznameh-e Mard-e Emruz*, 373–74.

37. Moloud Khanlary, interviewed by Ziya Sedghi in Paris on 7 March 1984 for the Iranian Oral History Project, tape 1, page 1 of transcript.

38. Ozma Adl-Naficy, interviewed by Habib Ladjevardi in Cambridge, Massachusetts, on 10 February 1984 for the Iranian Oral History Project, tape 1, page 2 of transcript.

39. Dowlatshahi, tape 1, page 14 of transcript.

40. Ibid.

41. Ibid., page 15 of transcript.

42. Sattareh Farman Farmaian, *Daughter of Persia*, 50–51.

43. Ibid., 59.

44. Ibid.

45. Simin Daneshvar in an interview with Naser Hariri published in *Honar va Adabiyat: Goft va Shonud ba Parviz Natel Khanlari va Simin Daneshvar*, 8.

46. Ibid., 15.

47. Simin Daneshvar, *Savushun: A Novel About Modern Iran*, trans. M. R. Ghanoonparvar, 200–203.

48. Jamileh Farrokh, "Dar Kolej-e Amrika'i," *Shafaq-e Sorkh* 528, 14 June 1926, 3.

49. "Notq-e Hazrat-e Ayatollahzadeh Khalesi," *Setareh-e Iran* 9, no. 23 (17 September 1923): 2.

50. Farrokh, 2.

51. Dowlatshahi, tape 1, page 23 of transcript, and tape 2, page 8 of transcript.

52. Dr. "Said Rafiq," husband of Dr. Tusi, in a phone interview with the author, 28 May 1998. Again, his name has been changed to protect his privacy.

53. Farman Farmaian, 88.

54. See the next section in this chapter.

55. Menashri, 109.

56. A traditional gymnasium and typical male preserve.

57. Hosayn 'Ali, "Mo'amma-ye Ezdevaj va Tahsilat-e 'Aliyeh," *Ettela 'at* 2263, 15 August 1934, 2.

58. Hosayn Barjasteh, "Tahsilat-e 'Aliyeh-Ghowgha-ye Ezdevaj," *Ettela 'at* 2267–71, 20–25 August 1934; 'Ala al-Din Farid 'Araqi, "Mo'amma-ye Ezdevaj ya Tahsilat-e 'Aliyeh," *Ettela 'at* 2274, 28 August 1934; M. Rasekh, "Mo'amma-ye Ezdevaj ya Tahsilat-e 'Aliyeh," *Ettela 'at* 2275, 29 August 1934; M. N., "Dar Atraf-e Tahsilat-e 'Aliyeh-e Dokhtaran," *Ettela 'at* 2276–77, 31 August and 1 September 1934; Zaynat Movahhed and B. Bahrami, "Mo'amma-ye Ezdevaj va Tahsilat-e 'Aliyeh," *Ettela 'at* 2279, 3 September 1934; Mahmud Dehdashti and Mas'ud Zara'i, "Mo'amma-ye Ezdevaj va Tahsilat-e 'Aliyeh," *Ettela 'at* 2282, 7 September 1934; Z. 'Azizi and Ahmad Kayvan Kashani, "Mo'amma-ye Ezdevaj va Tahsilat-e 'Aliyeh-e Dokhtaran," *Ettela 'at* 2284, 9 September 1934; Esma'il Katuziyan, "Mo'amma-ye Ezdevaj / Tahsilat-e 'Aliyeh-e Dokhtaran," *Ettela 'at* 2285, 10 September 1934; 'Ali Azari, "Mo'amma-ye Ezdevaj / Tahsilat-e 'Aliyeh," *Ettela 'at* 2288, 14 September 1934; Shapur Mihan, "Mo'amma-ye Ezdevaj / Tahsilat-e 'Aliyeh," *Ettela 'at* 2289, 15 September 1934; Turandokht Saqqafi, "Ezdevaj va Tahsilat-e 'Aliyeh-e Dokhtaran," *Ettela 'at* 2290, 16 September 1934; 'Abd Allah Amjadi, "Mo'amma-ye Ezdevaj / Tahsilat-e 'Aliyeh-e Dokhtaran," *Ettela 'at* 2292, 18 September 1934; 'A. Nowruzi, "Ghowgha-ye Ezdevaj / Tahsilat-e 'Aliyeh," *Ettela 'at* 2293, 19 September 1934; Dr. Shafe', "Mo'amma-ye Ezdevaj va Tahsilat-e 'Aliyeh," *Ettela 'at* 2294, 21 September 1934; Sayyed Nurollah Sotudeh, "Mo'amma-ye Ezdevaj / Tahsilat-e 'Aliyeh," *Ettela 'at* 2295, 22 September 1934; Dr. Sharifi, "Dar Atraf-e Tahsilat-e 'Aliyeh-e Dokhtaran," *Ettela 'at* 2300–1, 28 and 29 September 1934; H. 'Alavi, "Mo'amma-ye Ezdevaj va Tahsilat-e 'Aliyeh-e Dokhtaran," *Ettela 'at* 2302, 30 September 1934; Ne'matollah Amir Khalili and 'Ali Asghar Jaberi, "Dar Atraf-e Tahsilat-e 'Aliyeh-e Dokhtaran va Mo'amma-ye Ezdevaj," *Ettela 'at* 2303, 1 October 1934; 'A. Taqavvi, "Ezdevaj va Tahsilat-e 'Aliyeh," *Ettela 'at* 2304, 2 October 1934; and Behjat Rahimi Larijani, "Mo'amma-ye Ezdevaj / Tahsilat-e 'Aliyeh-e Dokhtaran," *Ettela 'at* 2305, 4 October 1934, all on page 2.

59. 'A. B., "Mo'amma-ye Ezdevaj va Tahsilat-e 'Aliyeh," *Ettela 'at* 2272–73, 26 and 27 August 1934; Shokufeh Nowrasteh, "Mowzu'-e Tahsilat-e 'Aliyeh-e Dokhtaran: Janjal-e Mardaneh/Ghowgha-ye Haqq Be-Janeb," *Ettela 'at* 2280, 4 September 1934; Fakhri Hojjati, "Mo'amma-ye Ezdevaj va Tahsilat-e 'Aliyeh-e Nesvan," *Ettela 'at* 2283, 8 September 1934; Mostafa Shah 'Ala'i, *Ettela 'at* 2285; Hormoz Qarib, "Mo'amma-ye Ezdevaj / Tahsilat-e 'Aliyeh-e Dokhtaran," *Ettela 'at* 2286, 11 September 1934; Ruha Arfa', "Mo'amma-ye Ezdevaj/ Tahsilat-e 'Aliyeh," *Ettela 'at* 2287, 12 September 1934; H. M., "Ezdevaj va Tahsilat-e 'Aliyeh," *Ettela 'at* 2291, 17 September 1934; 'Ali Qotbi, *Ettela 'at* 2292; and Jalal Ajlal, *Ettela 'at* 2304, all on page 2.

60. M. Mir Safavi and Khoshkish, "Mo'amma-ye Ezdevaj va Tahsilat-e 'Aliyeh," *Ettela 'at* 2278, 2 September 1934; A. M. Danesh, "Mowzu'-e Ezdevaj va Tahsilat-e 'Aliyeh," *Ettela 'at* 2281, 5 September 1934; Mahmud Mostashari,

"Moʿamma-ye Ezdevaj: Amal-e Zananeh," *Ettelaʿat* 2296–99, 23–26 September 1934, all on page 2.

61. Fakhri Hojjati *Ettelaʿat* 2283, 2.

62. Shokufeh Nowrasteh used the expression "vared-e maʿrakeh-e hayat-e ejtemaʿi" in *Ettelaʿat* 2280, 2.

63. M. N., *Ettelaʿat* 2277, 2.

64. ʿAla al-Din Farid ʿEraqi, *Ettelaʿat* 2274, 2.

65. Ibid.

66. M. Rasekh, *Ettelaʿat* 2275, 2.

67. Turandokht Saqafi, *Ettelaʿat* 2290, 2.

68. H. M., *Ettelaʿat* 2291, 2.

69. Ministry of Culture, *Salnameh va Amar 1315/16 and 1316/17*, part 2, 272–73.

70. In addition to the aforementioned example of women pilots, see *Ettelaʿat* 4062, 31 December 1939, 1; "Shirkhʷargah-e Tajrish," *Iran-e Emruz* 3. no. 4 (June/July 1941): 23–25; "Komisiyun-e Namayesh-Honarestan-e Honarpishagi," *Iran-e Emruz* 1, no. 1 (March/April 1939): 51–52; "Edareh-e Musiqi-ye Keshvar," *Iran-e Emruz* 2, no. 9 (November/December 1940): 2–8; and *Iran-e Emruz* 3, no. 5 (July/August 1941): 12–14; *Iran-e Emruz* 3, no. 2 (April/May 1941): 22; "Banovan Dar Zendagani-ye ʿAmali—Amukhtan-e Fann-e Telegraf," *Ettelaʿat* 2704, 3 February 1936, 1. See next section of the present chapter.

71. Ministry of Culture, *Salnameh va Amar 1315/16 and 1316/17*, part 2, 2 and 4.

72. Ibid., 3 and 5.

73. Ibid.

74. Ministry of Culture, *Salnameh va Amar, 1319–22*, part 2, 2.

75. Ministry of Culture, *Salnameh va Amar, 1322–27*, part 2, 1.

76. Ibid, 3.

77. Badry Kamrooz-Atabai, in an interview recorded by Habib Ladjevardi in Cambridge, Massachusetts, on 11 April 1984 for the Iranian Oral History Project, tape 1, page 1 of transcript.

78. Moloud Khanlary, tape 1, page 1 of transcript.

79. Merhangiz Dowlatshahi, tape 2, pages 8–14 of transcript.

80. *Salnameh-e Daneshsara-ye ʿAli 1315/16 va 1316/17*, 171–202.

81. Ibid., 182. There had been no women members the previous academic year (1936–37).

82. Dowlatshahi, tape 1, page 22 of transcript.

83. "Tarbiyat Pas az Vorud-e Zan beh Ejtemaʿ," *Ettelaʿat* 2710, 1.

84. *The Reminiscences of Pari Saberi*, 1985, pages 4–5, in the Oral History of Iran Collection of the Foundation for Iranian Studies.

85. Ibid., 5.

86. Daneshvar interview in *Honar va Adabiyat*, 16.

87. Kamrooz-Atabai, 2.

88. Dowlatshahi, tape 1, page 23 of transcript.

89. Doolittle, 15.

90. "Parastari," *Danesh* 11, 29 December 1910, 6, and "Taklif-e Parastari," *Danesh* 17, 9 February 1911, 2.

91. "Parastaran-e Englis," *Danesh* 20, 1 March 1911, 3.

92. "Parastaran-e Englis," *Shokufeh* 2, no. 17 (27 August 1914): 4.

93. "Dar Sharayet-e Mo'allem va Mo'allemi va A'za-ye Ruhani," *Shokufeh* 2, no. 19 (20 December 1913): 2, 4.

94. Only three installments of the series are available. "Parastar-e Khub Pish-nahad-e Sehhat Ast," *Shokufeh* 4, nos. 8, 9, 10 (16 and 23 April, 13 May 1916): 1–2 in the first two issues, 2–3 in the following issue.

95. *Shokufeh* 4, no. 8, 1.

96. *Shokufeh* 4, no. 9, 1.

97. *Shokufeh* 4, no. 8, 1, 2.

98. *Shokufeh* 4, nos. 8 and 9, 1.

99. *Shokufeh* 4, no. 9, 1–2.

100. Ibid., 2.

101. Ibid.

102. *Shokufeh* 4, no. 10, 3.

103. In reference to this rather murky passage in Koran 4:34—"*fa'l-salihatu qanitatun hafizatun li'l-ghaybi bi-ma hafiza allah*" (Good women are obedient. They guard their unseen parts because God has guarded them)—Al Tabari cites a *hadith* that clarifies the passage to mean that a woman would protect her husband's property (including herself) in his absence. According to his *Tafsir* (explication), "The Prophet said, 'The best woman is one that pleases you when you look at her, obeys you when you command her, and keeps for you herself and your property when you leave her.' The Prophet then recited *Koran* 4:34." See *Hadith* 9328 in Muhammad Ibn Jarir al-Tabari, *Tafsir al-Tabari, Jami' al-Bayan 'an Ta'wil Ay al-Qur'an*, vol. 8, ed. Mahmud Muhammad Shakir, 295.

104. Ahmad, "Kar," *Shokufeh* 4, no. 4, 4.

105. Ibid.

106. Ziya al-Din Nadim-bashi, "Nesvan va Khedmat-e 'Omumi," *Shokufeh* 1, no. 21 (13 January 1914), 1.

107. Ibid., 2.

108. "Polis-e Zananeh dar Alman," *Shafaq-e Sorkh* 501, 7 May 1926, 4.

109. 'Effat Sami'iyan, "Hojum-e Zanan dar 'Alam-e Eqtesad," and "Taraqqi-e Zanan-e Torkiyeh," *'Alam-e Nesvan* 9, no. 5 (September 1929): 201–7, 231.

110. Sami'iyan, 206; and "Pul," *'Alam-e Nesvan* 5, no. 2 (March 1925): 1–2.

111. Sami'iyan, 206–7.

112. Dr. Rezazadeh Shafaq, "Zan va Kar," *'Alam-e Nesvan* 12, no. 6 (November 1932): 241–44.

113. "Mashaghel-e Nesvan: Zan Irani Cheh Mitavanad Bokonad? U Mitavanad Parastar Shavad," trans. [from English?] by Ms. Afshar Sadeqi, *'Alam-e Nesvan* 11, no. 5 (September 1931): 214–16.

114. "Mashaghel-e Nesvan: Zan Irani Cheh Mitavanad Bokonad? U Mita-vanad Modireh-e Moqtasedi Shavad," trans. [from English?] by Ms. Afshar Sadeqi, 'Alam-e Nesvan 12, no. 3 (May 1932): 110–12.

115. Heshmat Hadasheyan, "Zan-e Irani Cheh Mitavanad Bokonad?" 'Alam-e Nesvan 12, no. 5 (September 1932): 198–201.

116. Ibid., 200.

117. Ibid., 201.

118. Ibid.

119. "Zanan-e Havapayma," 'Alam-e Nesvan 10, no. 2 (March 1930): 56.

120. U.S. State Department File 891.02/13, Charles C. Hart to the Secretary of State, 4 May 1931. Hart followed the story in Shafaq-e Sorkh, which seemed to suggest in its coverage that women be "educated" not to aspire to professional positions. Hart did not read this as satirical, but given that Shafaq-e Sorkh had been a fairly consistent supporter of women's progress in the 1920s, this seems likely to me.

121. The information on Zohreh Haidari comes from Vincent Sheehan, The New Persia, 258–62. Sheehan calls her Sara Khanum. It was Charles C. Hart who asserted in his aforementioned memorandum that Sara Khanum was, in fact, Zohreh Haydari.

122. Ibid., 261–62.

123. Mahmud Azar Yaghma'i, "Dushizagan Be-kh^wanand . . . ," Iran-e Bastan 1, no. 14 (4 May 1933): 5; 'A. Amirani, "Ta'lim va Tarbiyat-e Banovan," Iran-e Bastan 1, no. 18 (1 June 1933): 2; Mozaffar Karimlu, "Haqiqat-e Zan," Iran-e Bastan 1:21 (29 June 1933): 8; and Mohammad 'Ali Qahramanzadeh Qahramani, "Mohabbat va Mehr-e Madari," Iran-e Bastan 2, no. 3 (2 February 1934): 8.

124. Iran-e Bastan 1, no. 2 (28 February 1933): 11.

125. Iran-e Bastan 1, no. 32 (16 September 1933): 4.

126. Iran-e Bastan 1, no. 25 (29 July 1933): 9.

127. For example, see "Namuneh'i az Varzeshha-ye Kohneh va Now keh Emruzeh dar Donya Ravaj Darad," Iran-e Bastan 2, no. 21 (23 June 1934): 6; and "Chera Khanomha Bayad Varzesh Konand?" Iran-e Bastan 2, no. 43 (10 January 1935): 8, 10.

128. See George L. Mosse, Nationalism and Sexuality: Middle-Class Morality and Sexual Norms in Modern Europe.

129. "Lider-e Zanha-ye Alman," Iran-e Bastan 1, no. 30 (26 August 1933): 10.

130. Iran-e Bastan 2, no. 14 (5 May 1934): 8.

131. Iran-e Bastan 1, no. 20, 7.

132. Iran-e Bastan 1. no. 18, 2.

133. Iran-e Bastan 1, no. 36 (21 October 1933): 6.

134. "Taraqqi va Pishraft-e Bozorg-e Banovan dar Donya-ye Motamadden," Iran-e Bastan 3, no. 4 (9 July 1935): 14.

135. See the picture of Japanese women training to shoot down enemy planes with rifles in Iran-e Bastan 1, no. 10 (15 April 1933): 3 and the picture of a bare-

breasted Ethiopian woman standing at attention with a rifle while training to fight Italian invaders, *Iran-e Bastan* 3, no. 2 (16 June 1935): 2.

136. *Iran-e Bastan* 2, no. 40 (29 November 1934): 9.

137. *Iran-e Emruz* 1, no. 2/3 (April/June 1939): 22–23; *Iran-e Emruz* 1, no. 7/8 September/November 1939): 12; *Iran-e Emruz* 2, no. 4 (June/July 1940): 6–8 and back cover; *Iran-e Emruz* 2, no. 8 (October/November 1940): 5; and *Iran-e Emruz* 3, no. 2 (April/May 1941): 18.

138. *Iran-e Emruz* 2, no. 5 (July/August 1940): 2–7.

139. *Iran-e Emruz* 2, no. 11(January/February 1941): 11.

140. "Havapayma'i," *Iran-e Emruz* 2, no. 1 (March/April 1940): 36–37. The name of one of the pilots was Ina Owshid; see "Dar Forudgah-e Dowshan Tepeh: Parvaz-e Nokhostin Banu-ye Khalaban," *Ettela'at* 4131, 4 March 1940, 1. Another highly educated woman named Tayereh Dimyad entered the flight school earlier that year and got her picture in the paper for it; see "Yak Dushizeh-e Daneshmand Davtalab-e Fann-e Khalabani," *Ettela'at* 4062, 31 December 1939, 1.

141. *Iran-e Emruz* 2, no. 10 (December 1940/January 1941): 19; and *Iran-e Emruz* 3, no. 9 (October/November 1941).

142. "Shirkhʷargah-e Tajrish," *Iran-e Emruz* 3, no. 4 (June/July 1941): 23–25.

143. "Komisiyun-e Namayesh-Honarestan-e Honarpishagi," *Iran-e Emruz* 1, no. 1 (March/April 1939): 51–52; "Edareh-e Musiqi-ye Keshvar," *Iran-e Emruz* 2, no. 9 (November/December 1940): 2–8; and *Iran-e Emruz* 3, no. 5 (July/August 1941): 12–14.

144. *Iran-e Emruz* 3, no. 2 (April/May 1941): 22.

145. Interview with Sadiqeh Dowlatshahi, 5 February 2000, tape 1, side A, 200–7 on the tape counter.

146. Ibid., 220–35 on tape counter.

147. Ibid., 249–55 on tape counter.

148. Ibid., 271–95 on tape counter.

149. Ibid., 430 on the tape counter.

150. Ibid., 343–49 on tape counter.

151. Fatemeh Pakravan, *Memoirs of Fatemeh Pakravan: Wife of General Hassan Pakravan: Army Officer, Chief of State Intelligence and Security Organization, Cabinet Minister, and Diplomat,* ed. Habib Ladjevardi, 50.

152. Ibid., 50–51.

153. Ibid., 52.

154. Ibid.

155. Ibid., 53.

156. Ibid., 53–54.

157. Ibid., 70–71.

158. Ibid.

159. Ibid., 78.

160. Ozma Adl-Naficy, in an interview recorded by Habib Ladjevardi in Cambridge, Massachusetts, on 10 February 1984 for the Iranian Oral History Project, tape 1, page 6 of transcript.

161. Ibid., 13.

162. Ibid.

163. Ibid., 14–15

164. Ibid., 18.

165. Adl-Naficy, tape 2, page 2.

166. Ministry of Culture, *1315–17*, 2:289.

167. U.S. State Department File 891.5041/2, Vice Consul Raymond Hare to the Secretary of State, "Current Wages in Persia," 5 June 1934. It would have been preferable to compare wage data from the same year, but it is worth noting that after a large crash in value in 1930–31, the rial's value remained more or less stable until the onset of World War II.

168. Ministry of Culture, *1315–17*, 2:4–5.

169. Ministry of Culture, *1322–27*, 2:3.

170. Ministry of Culture, *1315–27*, 2:289.

Chapter 7. The Limits of Emancipation

1. "Tashkil-e Kongereh-e Zanan-e Sharq dar Tehran," *Ettela 'at* 1636, 21 June 1932, 1.

2. *Ettela 'at* 1734–35 and 1738–39, 18–19 and 23–24 October 1932, 1.

3. *Ettela 'at* 1734, 1. Faussecave is not mentioned by either Badran or Baron in their histories of the Egyptian women's movement.

4. 'Abbas Mas'udi, "Avvalin Kongereh-e Zanan-e Zesht-ruy," *Ettela 'at* 1740, 5 October 1932, 1.

5. Ibid.

6. "Be-Zanan-e Hind," *Ettela 'at* 1745, 21 October 1932, 1.

7. 'A. H. Hashemi Ha'eri, "Dat Jalaseh-e Dishab-e Banovan," *Ettela 'at* 1751, 7 November 1932, 1.

8. Afsaneh Najmabadi had limited access to actual minutes of the Second Eastern Women's Congress in Tehran as they were published in the newspaper *Iran* (the relevant issues of which are not available in the United States). She reports that there was obvious tension between Mr. Owrang, a parliamentary deputy sent as a representative of the government and who was ostensibly there to serve as a translator for Arabic-speaking delegates, and some Iranian delegates, particularly on the issue of veiling and the question of whether or not men should be allowed to speak at all at the women's conference. Also, Mastureh Afshar, who figures so prominently in *Ettela 'at*'s coverage of both the conference and Patriotic Women's League, seems to have broken ranks with her fellow society members and taken a much more progovernment line. Much of my interpretation of *Ettela 'at*'s coverage of the conference owes a great deal to information shared with me by Afsaneh Najmabadi in e-mail correspondence and via telephone 15–25 August 1999.

9. The term used is "jahizeh," which Dehkhoda gives as a synonym for "jehaz"—the household items and clothes that would accompany a bride to the home of her new husband.

10. ʿA. H. Hashemi Haʾeri, "Sharh-e Mosahebeh ba Raʾiseh-e Kongereh-e Zanan-e Sharq," *Ettelaʿat* 1747, 2 November 1932, 1.

11. Ibid.

12. Ibid.

13. Ibid.

14. Ibid.

15. *Ettelaʿat* 1748, 4 November 1932, 1.

16. *Ettelaʿat* 1747, 1

17. ʿA. H. Hashemi-Haʾeri, "Jamiʿat-e Nesvan-e Vatankhʷah-e Iran," *Ettelaʿat* 1750, 6 November 1932, 1.

18. Namely, requiring a blood test—a suggestion that Hashemi-Haʾeri claimed had been made by *Ettelaʿat* when the law was first being discussed in the Parliament.

19. *Ettelaʿat* 1751, 1.

20. Ibid.

21. Ibid.

22. Ibid.

23. Ibid.

24. Ibid.

25. "Konferans-e Zanan-e Sharq," *Ettelaʿat* 1752, 8 November 1932, 1.

26. The capital's hosting of delegates did not abate. The Grand Hotel advertised an elaborate variety show for "honored women of the Eastern Women's Conference" on Sunday, 6 Azar, at 7:30 P.M. that would be an "embodiment" of women's progress in Iran, expressed in song, dance, and sketch comedy. *Ettelaʿat* 1757, 15 November 1932, 4.

27. ʿA. B., "Az Maqalat-e Varedeh: Maram-e Kongreh-e Zanan-e Sharq," *Ettelaʿat* 1755, 12 November 1932, 1.

28. Abrahamian, 100–101. In "real" US dollars (1982–84), that would be roughly from $11,500 to $2,870.

29. Mohammad Reza Pahlavi, *Mission for My Country*, 231, cited in Sanasarian, *The Women's Rights Movement in Iran*, 86–89. Of course, the fuller context for this quote was Mohammad Reza Shah's attempts to justify his own denial of the vote for women at that point in history. The haunting of Mohammad Reza Shah by the legacy of his father and his resentment of strong women like his sister Ashraf provide an interesting foundation for interpreting the motivation of White Revolution policies toward women. See Marvin Zonis, *Majestic Failure* and, for a direct encounter with Mohammad Reza Shah's misogyny, see his comments in Oriana Fallaci, *Interview With History*, trans. John Shapely, 269–72.

30. "Qanun-e Lebas-e Ruhani va Esteʿmal-e Neshanha-ye Khareji," *Ettelaʿat* 2371, 21 December 1934, 1.

31. "Dar Atraf-e Qanun-e Haqq-e Entekhab-e Zanha-ye Torkiyeh," *Ettelaʿat* 2372, 22 December 1934, 1.

32. Ibid.

33. Fatemeh Sayyah, "Zan dar maghreb-zamin panjah sal pish az emruz," *Iran-e Emruz* 1, no. 1 in *Naqd va Sayyahat,* 64–72.

34. Ibid., 71–72.

35. Ibid., 70.

36. Ibid., 71.

37. See, as examples, "Pishahangan hengam-e dafileh dar yeki as jashn-ha," and "Marasem-e barafrashtan-e parcham," *Ettela'at* 3015, 7 January 1937, 1; "Dar Dabirestanha-ye Dushizegan," *Ettela'at* 3016, 8 January 1937, 1; and "Pishangan-e dabirestan-e Nurbakhsh dar jashn-e 17–e Day," *Ettela'at* 3018, 11 January 1937, 2.

38. Safiyyeh Firuz, 746–51 on the tape counter.

39. Sattareh Farmanfamian, 60.

40. Ibid.

41. Sadiqeh Dowlatshahi, tape 1, side A, 353–70 on the tape counter.

42. Fatemeh Sayyah, "Mas'aleh-e Nobugh dar Nazd-e Zanha," *Iran-e Emruz* 2, no. 8 (October/November 1940): 32.

43. Ibid.

44. Mahmud Sanna'i, "Ekhtelaf-e Fetri-ye Zan va Mard," *Iran-e Emruz* 3, no. 3 (May/June 1941): 33–35.

45. Ibid., 35.

46. Ibid.

47. "Jashn-e Daneshsara-ye Dokhtaran," *Iran-e Emruz* 2, no. 2 (April/May 1940): 31.

48. Hosayn Farhudi, "Vazayef-e Banovan dar Parvaresh-e Afkar," *Iran-e Emruz* 2, no. 2, 25–27.

49. See Mohammad 'Ali Daneshvar, "Kudakestan," and "Tarikhcheh-e Pay-dayesh-e Avvalin Kudakestan-e Irani, 'Barsabeh' va Barnameh-e An," *Iran-e Emruz* 2, no. 11(January/February 1941): 19–25.

50. Hejazi, *Andisheh,* 129–31.

51. Ibid., 130.

52. Ibid. The original subject of the passage is in the singular, but to preserve its inherent gender ambiguity in English, it has been rendered in the plural.

53. Barjasteh, *Ettela'at* 2217, 2.

54. Sotudeh, *Ettela'at* 2295, 2.

55. "Sus-e Akhlaq!?" *Ettela'at* 2273, 23 December 1934, 2.

56. Amir Hekmat, "Adab-e Mo'asherat va Adab," *Ettela'at* 2698–705, 2. The effort was not restricted to *Ettela'at,* of course. See "Az Jarayed-e Emruz," *Ettela'at* 2685, 2689, and 2691, 4.

57. Hekmat, *Ettela'at* 2700, 2.

58. Hekmat, *Ettela'at* 2701, 2.

59. Hekmat, *Ettela'at* 2702, 2.

60. See Sayyed Hasan Taqizadeh, "Dibacheh-e Sal-e Dovvom-e *Kaveh,*" *Kaveh* 2, no. 1 (11 December 1921): 1; Hosayn Kazemzadeh, "Melliyat va Ruh-e Melli-

ye Iran," *Iranshahr* 2, no. 2 (12 December 1923) 193–206; and "Az Ketab-e Aqa-ye Soltan Asadollah Khan Arbabi: Favayed Varzesh-e Badani va Espor," *Setareh-e Iran* 12, nos. 116–17 (12–16 January 1927): 2.

61. See, for example, Azad Hamadani, "Manzum: Varzesh," ʿ*Alam-e Nesvan* 10, no. 1 (January/February 1932): 16.

62. For example, see "Chera Khanom-ha Bayad Varzesh Konand?" *Iran-e Bastan* 2, no. 43 (8 January 1935): 8 and 10.

63. See Michael P. Zirinsky, "A Panacea for the Ills of the Country: American Presbyterian Education in Inter-War Iran."

64. *Iran-e Emruz* 1, no. 2/3 (April/June 1939): 22–23; *Iran-e Emruz* 1, no.: 7/8 (September/November 1939): 12; *Iran-e Emruz* 2, no. 4 (June/July 1940): 6–8 and back cover; *Iran-e Emruz* 2, no. 8 (October/November 1940): 5; and *Iran-e Emruz* 3, no. 2 (April/May 1941): 18. Of course, it was not only the female form that was being celebrated. For example, see "Mosabeqeh-e Varzidehtarin Andam va ʿOzolat," *Mehregan* 23 (1 March 1937): 11.

65. "Cheguneh Khud-ra Arayesh Mideham?" *Mehregan* 75 (21 October 1938): 12–13; and "Banovan: Baraye Zibaʾi," *Mehregan* 112 (30 May 1940): 17.

66. "Malekeh-e Vejahat-e Donya," *Mehregan* 19 (21 December 1936): 9; and "Mis Fenland: Malekeh-e Vejahat-e Orupa-ye 1938," *Mehregan* 75, 5.

67. "Dar Ghar-e Dozdan-e Daryaʾi," *Mehregan* 134 (24 April 1941): 17.

68. Rolan Miklivi, "Zhinjer Rowjers: Setareh-e Amrikaʾi—Tarikhcheh-e Zendagani va ʿAvamel-e Pishraft-e Vay dar Jahan-e Sinema," *Ettelaʿat* 3688, 11 December 1938, 8.

69. "Mayl Darid Ziba va Delroba Bashid," *Mehregan* 73 (16 September 1937): 12–13.

70. "Dasturha-ye Sudmand—Zibaʾi: Afatha-ye Chehreh, ʿEllat va Rah-e Modavi-ye An," *Mehregan* 80 (12 January 1939): 15; and "Varzesh-e Banovan: Yek Robʿ-e Saʿat ba Mishelin Persel," *Mehregan* 113 (13 June 1940): 6.

71. "Lebas-e Banovan Bayad Sadeh Bashad: Banovan Namidanand ba Cheh Lebashaʾi Zibatar va Delrobatar Khʷahand Shod," *Mehregan* 20 (5 January 1937): 1.

72. "Zan," *Ettelaʿat* 3676, 29 November 1938, 5.

73. Meryl O'Brown, "Ari, Akhlaq-e Man Khub Nist," *Mehregan* 47 (21 May 1937): 19–21. The note on the French actress accompanies an inset picture on page 20.

74. "Suʿe Estefadeh az Vejahat Baraye Zan Badbakhti Ast," *Kushesh* 3888, 4 January 1939, 1.

75. Ibid.

76. *The Reminiscences of Parvin Moʾayyed-Sabeti*, 1988, pages 3–4, in the Oral History of Iran Collection of the Foundation for Iranian Studies.

77. ʿ*Alam-e Zanan*, August/September 1944, back cover.

Chapter 8. Breaking with Male Guardianship

1. *'Alam-e Zanan,* October/November 1944, front cover.

2. Amin, "Propaganda and Remembrance: Gender, Education and the 'Women's Awakening' of 1936," 384. Twenty-eight women were supported this way in 1328 (1949/50).

3. K. S. Maclachlan, "Econcomic Development, 1921–1979," in *The Cambridge History of Iran,* 7:618.

4. Abrahamian, 136–37.

5. There are a number of studies and document collections that focus on the history of labor movements in Iran and their political activities in Iranian history. See Willem M. Floor and Abu al-Qasim Sirri, *Sana'ti Shudan-e Iran va shuresh-e Shaykh Ahmad Madani, 1900–1925;* and Willem M. Floor, *Ettehadiyah-ha-yi Kargari va Qanun-e Kar dar Iran, 1900–1941.* The intrepid Marxist historian Cosroe Chaqueri is the editor of a number of collections including Cosroe Chaqueri and D. Bozorg, *Asnad-e Tarikhi: Junbesh-e Kargari, Susiyal Dimukrasi, va Kumunisti-i Iran;* and Cosroe Chaqueri, *Conditions of the Working Class in Iran: A Documentary History.* But these works have not yet been utilized to produce a comprehensive history of workers and their working conditions through the course of various economic changes in Iran. Such a study would be especially difficult before World War II as the first complete census of Iran was undertaken only in 1956.

6. M., "Dushandeh-e Shir: Anha'i Keh Sarbar Jame'eh Kh^w ahand Shod?" *Kushesh,* 29 September 1941, 2.

7. Ibid.

8. M., "Khanomha va Khadamat-e Edari," *Kushesh,* 16 November 1941, 1, 2.

9. Ibid., 1.

10. Ibid.

11. Ibid., 2.

12. Sadiqeh Dowlatabadi, "Tarikh-e Tolu'-e *Zaban-e Zanan* va Ta'til-e Bist Saleh-e An," *Zaban-e Zanan* 1, no. 23 (December 1942): 2–4.

13. "Zan va Kar," *Zaban-e Zanan* 24, no. 5 (September 1944): 4. The article was taken from a magazine entitled *Rider Gent* (Rayder Jent).

14. Ibid., 5.

15. Ibid., 6.

16. Sadr-Hashemi noted that 'Abbas Khalili had always been a firebrand journalist, even from *Eqdam*'s inception in 1921, as well as a translator and writer of fiction, Sadr-Hashemi, 1:226–29. For more details on him, see *Chehreh-ye Matbu'at-e Mu'asir,* 17–18.

17. Fakhri Estifa, "Shir-Mard Ku?" *Eqdam,* 24 April 1942, 3.

18. Tuba Mofidi, "Zan va Zendagani," *Eqdam,* 26 April 1942, 2.

19. See Kowkab Behzadi, "Zan va Zendagani," *Eqdam,* 4 May 1942, 2; Iran Nezhi, "Zan va Zendagani," *Eqdam,* 7 May 1942, 2; and Fakhr Al-Moluk Shahgoli, "Zan va Zendagani," *Eqdam,* 23 May 1942, 3.

20. Nezhi, 2.

21. ʿAbbas Khalili, "Be-Shoma Banovan-e Iran," *Eqdam,* 11 May 1942, 1.

22. Parvin Modabber, "Shir-Zan Mikhʷahim," *Eqdam,* 13 May 1942, 3.

23. *Mard-e Emruz,* 10 June 1944, 6.

24. *Mard-e Emruz,* 7 April 1944, 1; and *Mard-e Emruz,* 22 April 1944, 6.

25. "Khanom-e Fakhr al-Dowleh, Namayandeh-ye Kompani-ye Ford," *Mard-e Emruz,* 17 August 1944, 2.

26. Untitled, *Mard-e Emruz,* 28 October 1942, 7; "Seh Rokn-e Zendegi-ye Khanomha: Varzesh, Tabbakhi, Mod," *Mard-e Emruz,* 20 July 1942, 9; "Modha-ye Mozhek," *Mard-e Emruz,* 26 August 1942, 6; and "Jens-e Khub Kharidan Kar-e Asani Nist," *Mard-e Emruz,* 2 September 1942, 9.

27. M., "Dar Manjelab-e Fahsha," *Mard-e Emruz,* 10 August 1945, 5, 7; and Mohandes Hasan Saʾebi, "Shahr-e Favahesh," *Mard-e Emruz,* 10 December 1945, 6, 10 April 1946, 6.

28. Dr. M. Nezhad, "Lozum-e Favahesh dar Ejtemaʿ," *Mard-e Emruz,* 3 November 1944, 3.

29. *Baba Shamal,* 28 April 1943, 7.

30. *Baba Shamal,* 12 May 1943, cover.

31. Tahereh Yazdanfarr, "Zan va Zendagani," *Eqdam,* 9 May 1942, 2.

32. Farangis Mazandarani, "Zan va Zendagani," *Eqdam,* 12 May 1942, 3.

33. Ibid. The editor's note was "Men can also respond to women." Soon, a male worker at the Ministry of Post, Telegraph, and Telephone did respond. He cited the Koranic injunction that men were guardians over women to justify the way of things, but conceded that men needed to provide better examples. The editor noted that "Religion is the best guide for humanity and refiner of morals." See Sayyed Morteza ʿAliqoli, "Zan va Zendagani," *Eqdam,* 17 May 1942, 3.

34. The expression is *beh kodam saz-e shoma be-raqsim* or "to which *saz* of yours we should dance."

35. Puran Hajilu, "Zan va Zendagani," *Eqdam,* 30 May 1942, 3.

36. M. H. F., "Zan va Zendagani, *Eqdam,* 4 June 1942, 3.

37. Khaleh Kukumeh, "Haqq-e Ray-e Khanomha va Taʿlimat-e Ejbari," *Baba Shamal,* 29 December 1943, 8.

38. "Zanha va Haqq-e Ray," *Baba Shamal,* 17 February 1944, 4.

39. Lady M. S., "Taraqqi-ye Zanan Basteh be-Azadi-ye Iran Ast," *Mardom,* 6 February 1944, 2.

40. Moghissi, 94–95.

41. Maryam Firuz, *Khaterat-e Maryam Firuz (Farmanfarmaian),* 42–43.

42. Ibid., 69–70.

43. Dr. Keshavarz, *Mozakarat,* 14: 834. In her pro-Pahlavi memoirs, Badr al-Moluk Bamdad also remembered the images of Girl Scouts, women athletes, women factory workers, and women pilots-in-training as proof of the "success" of the Women's Awakening. See Badr al-Moluk Bamdad, *From Darkness Into Light: Women's Emancipation in Iran,* trans. F. R. C. Bagley, 100.

44. Moghissi, 94–95.

45. *Mozakarat,* 14: 965–68; and "Akhbar-e Majles," *Ruznameh-e Rasmi-ye Keshvar-e Shahanshahi-ye Iran* 17 (2 March 1944): 113.

46. "Gozaresh Az Komisiyon-e Eslah-e Qanun-e Entekhabat be-Majles-e Shura-ye Melli," *Ruznameh-e Rasmi-ye Keshvar-e Shahanshahi-ye Iran* 32 and 33 (19 and 26 March 1945).

47. "Gozaresh (Part 1)," 184.

48. Ibid., 186.

49. This issue was raised by Mr. Ardalan during the discussion of another bill. Unfortunately, his specific comments were not recorded. See "Kholaseh-e Jalaseh-e 194," *Ruznameh-e Rasmi-ye Keshvar-e Shahanshahi-ye Iran* 2, no. 319 (15 March 1946): 1136.

50. Abrahamian, 230.

51. *Mozakarat,* 15: 2019–21.

52. Sadiqeh Dowlatabadi, "Vatan va Ma," *Zaban-e Zanan* 24, no. 8 (December 1944): 7.

53. Sadiqeh Dowlatabadi, "Hess-e Ehtiyaj," *Zaban-e Zanan* 25, no. 1 (March 1945): 27.

54. Sadiqeh Dowlatabadi, "Be-Yad-e 17 Day," *Zaban-e Zanan* 25, no. 1 (March 1945): 5.

55. "Za'f-e Mashrutiyat-e Ma," *Zaban-e Zanan* 25, no. 3 (June 1945): 17.

56. Ibid.

57. Ahmad Kasravi, *Khwaharan va Dokhtaran-e Ma,* 4. The first edition was printed in 1323 (1944/45). Parts of this book were published in Kasravi's magazine *Payman* (The Promise) on 22 March 1935, on the eve of the first efforts of the Pahlavi state to encourage unveiling. The periodical—like Kasravi himself—was controversial. It appeared irregularly and, in 1941, was published as *Parcham* (The Flag), Sadr-Hashemi, 2:3–7. See also Carol Regan's English summary of this work in *Women and the Family in Iran,* 60–78.

58. Ibid., 30.

59. Ibid., 32.

60. Ibid., 34.

61. Kasravi frequently coined his own words and expressions, which he felt were more Persian. From the context the word *baya* seems to mean "nature" or "temperament."

62. Ibid., 24–25.

63. "Agar keh Zan Vakil-e Mellat Shavad," *Atesh,* 17 April 1946, 4. A women's magazine entitled *Banu* had also started a similar contest in 1945, but unfortunately no issues were available at the time of this study.

64. Ibid.

65. Ibid.

66. Dr. Maryam Mir Hadi, "Agar Zan Vakil-e Mellat Shavad: Movafeq,"

Atesh, 27 April 1946, 4. See also Afsar Sadqadar, "Agar Zan Vakil-e Mellat Shavad: Movafeq," *Atesh,* 4 May 1946, 4.

67. Ibid.

68. M. B., "Agar Zan Vakil-e Mellat Shavad: Mokhalef," *Atesh,* 27 April 1946, 4.

69. Moluk Fannizadeh, "Agar Zan Vakil-e Mellat Shavad: Mokhalef," *Atesh,* 22 June 1946, 4.

70. This threat was reiterated by an anonymous woman under the rubric of this same discussion. Although she was addressing the issue of misogyny in public discourse rather than the right to vote per se, she warned that the Women's Party might have to complain to the UN Security Council if current trends continued. See J. N., "Agar Zan Vakil-e Mellat Shavad: Movafeq—Aqayan, Movazeb Bashid Zanan be-Shura-ye Amniyat Shekayat Nakonand," *Atesh,* 22 June 1946, 4.

71. The phrase she used was *dowreh-e vahshat va hayvaniyat,* a rather similar rhetorical device to the Muslim use of the term *jaheliyat,* or "ignorance," to refer to pre-Islamic times. See Afsar Sadqadar, "Agar Zan Vakil-e Mellat Shavad: Movafeq," *Atesh,* 4 May 1946, 4.

72. "Mosahebeh ba Banu Doktor Fatemeh Rezazadeh Sayyah, Ostad-e Daneshgah," *'Alam-e Zanan,* June/July 1944, 13; and "Mosahebeh ba Banu Doktor Iran A'lam, Ra'is-e Servis-e Zayeshgah-e Tehran," *'Alam-e Zanan,* November/December 1944, 13, 32.

73. "Pishraft-e Zanan dar Englestan," *'Alam-e Zanan,* July/August 1944, 13, 32.

74. "Khanom-e Ayrin Vard [Irene Ward], Namayandeh-e Parleman-e Englestan dar Tehran," *Mihan Parastan,* 25 December 1943, 1; Badr al-Moluk Bamdad, "Zanan-e Iran va Ayandeh-e Anha, Chand Kalameh ba Khanom-e Vard," *Mihan Parastan,* 28 December 1943, 2, 4; and "Sokhanrani-ye Khanom-e Vard," *Mihan Parastan,* 8 January 1944, 3. The last item was actually a translation of a speech given by Ms. Ward on Tehran radio.

75. In her oral-history narrative, Moloud Khanlary saw the Women's Party and the Tudeh Party as one and the same—a fact obviously doubted by her interviewer. However, the overlap of some personalities at Tudeh events, Women's Party events, and events held at the Society for Soviet-Iranian Friendship points to a very fluid system of political affiliation in the 1940s, one in which family relations could play as important a part as ideological agreement. See Khanlary, tape 4, pages 1–6 of transcript.

76. *Atesh,* 24 December 1946, 1, 4.

77. Ahmad, "Agar Zan Vakil-e Mellat Shavad: Movafeq," *Atesh,* 18 May 1946, 4.

78. See also, Sadqadar, 4, and Afshar Qasemlu, "Agar Zan Vakil-e Mellat Shavad—Pasokh-e 3," *Atesh,* 4 November 1946, 2, 3.

79. Habib Allah Shamluli, "Man ba Entekhab Shodan-e Zanan Mokhalefam," *Atesh,* 22 October 1946, 4.

80. Ibid.

81. Fatemeh Sayyah, "Zan va Entekhabat Dar Iran," in *Naqd va Sayyahat,* 144. The article originally appeared in *Ayandeh* in August 1945.

82. Ibid., 146.

83. Sayyah, "Khanom, Agar beh Majles-e Shura-ye Melli Raftid, Cheh Kh^wahid Kard?" in *Naqd va Sayyahat,* 149. The article was part of an essay contest by a magazine called *Banu* (Lady) and originally appeared in December 1946.

84. Saffiyeh Firuz, 1984, 755–89 on the tape counter.

85. Mehrangiz Dowlatshahi, tape 3, pages 5–6 of transcript.

86. Safiyyeh Firuz, 892–905 on tape counter.

87. Ibid., 826 on tape counter.

88. Ibid., 727–35 on tape counter.

89. Ibid., 864–68 on tape counter.

90. Ibid., 996–1004 on tape counter.

91. Ibid., 717–25 and 835–55 on tape counter. She did not say where these attacks occurred.

92. Sisters of the king, Mohammad Reza Shah.

93. KVF, document 138. Regarding the subsequent investigation of the incident that led to arrests of several men by 16 October 1943, see also documents 139–41.

94. Copies of *Nahzat-e Melli, Baba Shamal, Khorshid-e Iran,* and *Tehran-e Mosavvar* were not available for the time of this incident.

95. "Telegraf-e Shahri," *Kushesh,* 30 August 1943, 2.

96. Mohammad Amanpur, "Payam beh Banovan-e Iran," *Mardan-e Kar* 165, 30 August 1943, 1.

97. Ibid.

98. Anonymous, "Ay Kash Mottafeqin Nabudand va Shoma Ma ra Riz Riz Mikardid: Aya Shoma In Chador va Chakhchur-bazi ra Hejab-e Eslami Minamid?" *Iran-e Ma,* 24 August 1943, 1.

99. "Shoma Shaqalan keh dar Kamal-e Pasti be-Zanha-ye Mosalman va Najib Towhin Mikonid be-Dast Ma Shadidan Mojazat Kh^wahid Shod," *Iran-e Ma,* 29 August 1943, 1. A translation of a work by the Egyptian writer Towfiq al-Hakim in support of women was published under the title "Seyasat va Ejtema', Zendeh-bad Zan . . . !!" in the same issue, 1, 4.

100. Seyamak, "Maqam-e Zan Dar Jame' eh," *Mehr-e Iran,* 29 August 1943, 1.

101. Majid Movaqqar, "Ghowgha-ye Hejab! Ya Atesh-e Nefaq-e Dakheli," *Mehr-e Iran* 31 August 1943, 1.

102. S. Khatemi Saravi, "Hejab-e Haqiqi ' Effat va ' Esmat Ast," *Mehr-e Iran,* 2 September 1943, 4.

103. *Atesh,* 14 December 1946, 4.

104. For a specific explication of its views on the state, see Manuchehr 'Ala'i, "Bahs-e Ejtema' i—Dowlat," *Parcham-e Eslam,* 29 May 1946, 4. For more on the rise of political Islamic revivalism in Iran from 1941 to 1953, see Houchang

Chehabi, *Iranian Politics and Religious Modernism: The Liberation Movement of Iran Under the Shah and Khomeini*, 103–39; and Fakhreddin Azimi, "The Fada'iyan-e Islam: Fanaticism, Politics and Terror," in *From Nationalism to Revolutionary Islam*, ed. Said Amir Arjomand. See also Amin, "Selling and Saving 'Mother Iran': Gender and the Iranian Press in the 1940's."

105. "Vaqe'eh-e Khorasan: ' Addad-e Haqiqi-ye Maqtulin—Dalil-e Haqiqi-ye Nahzat-e Khorasan—Qahramanan-e In Dastan-e Haqiqi va Tarikhi—Hamleh-e Shabaneh-e Qoshun—Aramgah-e Shohada—Mosahebeh ba Jenab-e Aqa-ye Novvab Ehtesham Razavi," *Parcham-e Eslam*, 15 May 1946, 3.

106. Sayyed Kamal al-Din Nurbakhsh, "Nekah," *Parcham-e Eslam*, 19 October 1946, 4.

107. Dr. Faqihi Shirazi, "Moshahedat-e Ma Yek Ruz-e Jom' eh," *Parcham-e Eslam*, 9 May 1946, 1.

108. Manuchehr 'Ala'i, "Sinema, Ya Bozorgtarin 'Amel-e Fesad-e Akhlaq," *Parcham-e Eslam*, 9 May 1946, 1, 4.

109. "Mod-Parasti," *Parcham-e Eslam*, 5 June 1946, 1.

110. Ibid.

111. F. Shakibi, "Ta'limat-e Qor'an Motabeq ba Fetrat-e Bashar Ast," *Parcham-e Eslam*, 20 November 1946, 3.

112. Ibid.

113. F. Shakibi, "Ta'limat-e Qor'an dar Zan-e Jame' eh-e Eslami," *Parcham-e Eslam*, 27 November 1946, 3, 11 November 1946, 3, 4, and 18 December 1946, 3.

114. Mohammad Meftah, "Mozarrat-e Kashf-e Hejab az Noqteh-e Nazar-e Ejtema' va Mafased-e An," *Parcham-e Eslam*, 27 November 1946, 2.

Chapter 9. The Legacy of the Women's Awakening

1. Soroush quoted in Ziba Mir-Hosseini, *Gender and Islam: The Religious Debate in Contemporary Iran*, 224.

2. Moghissi, 41.

3. Guity Nashat, "Women in Pre-Revolutionary Iran," in *Women and Revolution in Iran*, ed. Guity Nashat, 28–29.

4. Erika Friedl, *Children of Deh Koh*.

5. The site address is www.salamiran.org. Of course, the propaganda of the Islamic Republic, like the propaganda of the Women's Awakening, masks the complexity of debate within Iranian society and many of the difficulties women continue to face there. For recent studies see Ziba Mir-Hosseini, *Gender and Islam*, and also the documentary *Talaq: Divorce Iranian Style*, directed by Ziba Mir-Hosseini and Kim Longinotto.

6. The site address is www.salamiran.org/Women/General/index.html

7. The site address is www.salamiran.org/Women_And_Family.html

8. The site address is www.salamiran.org/Women/General/Women_And _Islam.html

Bibliography

Author's note: In parentheses, I have indicated the locations of the Iranian periodicals used for this study. LOC indicates the Library of Congress, from which microfilms of the periodicals can be purchased. MEDOC indicates the Middle East Documentation Project at the University of Chicago from which microfilms of periodicals can be purchased (www.lib.uchicago.edu/e/su/mideast/CatIntro.html). In addition, the Foundation for Iranian Studies has a catalogue of its oral history collection on-line (www.fis-iran.org). The Harvard Iran Oral History Project has begun to publish edited transcripts as memoirs (www.ibexpub.com/ibexiohp.html). However, in all but one case I used the IOHP transcripts made available to the collection at the University of Chicago. Two women's magazines indicated below are available at Princeton University.

Abadi, Sho'leh. "Mirza Fath 'Ali Akhundzadeh va Mas'aleh-e Zanan." *Nimeh-e Digar* 17 (Winter 1371 [1992–93]): 29–37.

Abrahamian, Ervand. *Iran: Between Two Revolutions.* Princeton, N.J.: Princeton University Press, 1982.

Abu Torabiyan, Husayn. *Matbu'at-i Irani.* Tehran: Entesharat-e Ettela'at, 1366.

Adamiyat, Feraydun. "Seh Maktub-e Mirza Fath'Ali." *Yaghma* 19, no. 7 (Mehr and Aban 1345 [1966]): 362–67.

———. "Seh Maktub va Sad Khetabeh-e Mirza Aqa Khan." *Yaghma* 19, no. 8 (Mehr and Aban 1345 [1966]): 423–28.

———. *Andishah-ha-ye Mirza Aqa Khan.* Saarbrucken, Germany: Entesharat-e Navid, 1992.

Adamiyat, Feraydun, and Homa Nateq. *Afkar-e Ejtema'i, Seyasi va Eqtesadi dar Asar Montasher Nashodeh-e Dowran-e Qajar.* Tehran: Agah, 1356 [1977/78].

Afary, Janet. *The Iranian Constitutional Revolution, 1906–11: Grassroots Democracy, Social Democracy, and the Origins of Feminism.* New York: Columbia University Press, 1996.

Aflak. Tehran. MEDOC.

Akhavi, Shahrough. *Religion and Politics in Contemporary Iran: Clergy State Relations in the Pahlavi Period.* Albany: State University of New York Press, 1980.

Akhtar. Istanbul. MEDOC.

Akhundzadeh, Mirza Fath'Ali. *Maktubat-e Mirza Fath 'Ali Akhundzadeh*. Edited and introduced by M. Sobhdam. N.p.: Mard-e Emruz, 1364 [1985].

'Alam-e Nesvan. Tehran. Princeton.

'Alam-e Zanan. Tehran. Princeton.

Alamuti, Dr. Mostafa. *Iran Dar 'Asr-e Pahlavi*. 18 vols. London: n.p., 1988.

Al-e Ahmad, Jalal. "The Joyous Celebration." In *Modern Persian Short Stories*, edited by Minoo Southgate, 19–33. New York: Three Continents Press, 1980.

Algar, Hamid. *Mirza Malkum Khan: A Study in the History of Iranian Modernism*. Berkeley: University of California Press, 1973.

al-Tabari, Muhammed ibn Jarir. *Tafsir al Tabari, Jami' al-Bayan 'an Ta'wil Ay al-Qur'an*. Edited by Mahmud Muhammad Shakir. Cairo: Dar al-Ma'arif bi-Misr, 1954.

Amanat, Abbas. *Resurrection and Renewal: The Making of the Babi Movement in Iran, 1844–1850*. Ithaca: Cornell University Press, 1989.

———. "The Downfall of Mirza Taqi Khan Amir Kabir." *International Journal of Middle Eastern Studies* 23, no. 4 (November 1991): 577–99.

Amin, Camron Michael. "'The Attentions of the Great Father': Riza Shah, 'the Woman Question,' and the Iranian Press, 1910–1946." Ph.D. diss., University of Chicago, 1996.

———. "Propaganda and Remembrance: Gender, Education and 'the Women's Awakening' of 1936." *Iranian Studies* 32, no. 3 (Summer 1999 [2000]): 351–86.

———. "Selling and Saving 'Mother Iran': Gender and the Iranian Press in the 1940's." *International Journal of Middle East Studies* 33, no. 3 (August 2001): 335–61.

Amin, Qasim. *The Liberation of Women*. Translated by Samiha Sidhom Peterson. 1899; reprint, Cairo: American University of Cairo Press, 1992.

Amir-Mokri, Cyrus. "Redefining Iran's Constitutional Revolution." Ph.D. diss., University of Chicago, 1992.

'Aqa'ed al-Nesa va Mir'at al-Bolha: Du Resaleh-e Enteqadi dar Farhang-e Tudeh. Edited by Mahmud Ketra'i. Tehran: Tahuri, n.d.

Arfa, Hassan [Hasan Arfa']. *Under Five Shahs*. London: John Murray, 1964.

Armaghan. Tehran. University of Chicago.

Aryanpur, Yahya. *Az Saba ta Nima*. 2 vols. Tehran: Jibi, 1354 [1975–76].

Asnad-e Matbu'at (1286–1320 h.s.). 2 vols. Edited by Kaveh Bayat and Mas'ud Kuhestani Nezhad. Tehran: Entesharat-e Asnad-e Melli-ye Iran, 1372.

Asnad-e Matbu'at-e Iran (1320–1332 h.s.). Vol. 1. Tehran: Entesharat-e Sazman-e Asnad-e Melli-ye Iran, 1374.

Astarabadi, Bibi Khanom. *Ma'ayeb al-Rejal*. Edited and introduced by Afsaneh Najmabadi. Chicago: Midland Press, 1992.

Atesh. Tehran. LOC.

Ayalon, Ami. *The Press in the Arab Middle East*. New York: Oxford University Press, 1995.

Baba Shamal. Tehran. MEDOC.

Babayan, Kathryn. "The Safavid Synthesis: From Qezelbash Islam to Imamite Shi'ism." *Iranian Studies* 27, nos. 1–4 (1994): 135–61.

———. "The *'Aqa'id al-Nisa'*: A Glimpse at Safavid Women in Local Isfahani Culture." In *Women and the Medieval Islamic World,* edited by Gavin R. G. Hambly, 349–81. New York: St. Martin's Press, 1998.

Badran, Margot. *Feminists, Islam and Nation: Gender and the Making of Modern Egypt.* Princeton, N.J.: Princeton University Press, 1995.

Bahar va Adab-e Farsi. Vol. 1. Edited by Mohammad Golbon. Tehran: Sahami, 1351 [1972 or 1973].

Bakhash, Shaul. *Iran, Monarchy, Bureaucracy, and Reform under the Qajars, 1858–1896.* London: Ithaca Press for the Middle East Centre, St. Antony's College, 1978.

Bamdad, Badr al-Moluk. *From Darkness into Light: Women's Emancipation in Iran.* Translated by F.R.C. Bagley. Hicksville, N.Y.: Exposition Press, 1977.

Bamdad, Mehdi. *Sharh-e Hal-e Rejal-e Iran.* 6 vols. Tehran: Zovvar, 1347 [1968].

Banani, Amin. *The Modernization of Iran.* Stanford: Stanford University Press, 1961.

Baron, Beth. *The Women's Awakening in Egypt: Culture, Society, and the Press.* New Haven: Yale University Press, 1994.

Bassari, Tal'at. *Zandokht: Pishahang-e Nahzat-e Azadi-ye Banovan-e Iran.* Tehran: Tahuri, 1345 [1966–67].

Beck, Lois. *The Qashqa'i of Iran.* New Haven: Yale University Press, 1986.

Behnud, Mas'ud. *In Seh Zan: Ashraf Pahlavi, Maryam Firuz, Iran Taymurtash.* 3d ed. Tehran: Nashr-e 'Elm, 1375 [1996–97].

Bolkosky, Sidney. "Interviewing Victims Who Survived: Listening for the Silences that Strike." *Annals of Scholarship* 4, no. 2 (Winter 1987): 33–51.

———. "Of Parchment and Ink: Varieties of Survivor Religious Responses to the Holocaust." *Journal of Holocaust Education* 6, no. 2 (Autumn 1997): 1–35.

Book in the Islamic World, The. Edited by George N. Atiyeh. Albany: State University of New York, 1995.

British Documents on Foreign Affairs—Reports and Papers From the Foreign Office Confidential Print. Part 2, From the First to the Second World War. Series B, Turkey, Iran, and the Middle East, 1918–1939. Edited by Robin Bidwell. 35 vols. Frederick, Md.: University Publications of America, 1985–.

Brooks, Geraldine. *Nine Parts of Desire: The Hidden World of Islamic Women.* New York: Anchor Books, 1995.

Browne, E. G. *The Press and Poetry of Modern Persia.* Cambridge: Cambridge University Press, 1914.

Cambridge History of Iran. Edited by Peter Avery, Gavin Hambly, and Charles Melville. Vol. 7. Cambridge: Cambridge University Press, 1991.

Chaqueri, Cosroe. *Conditions of the Working Class in Iran: A Documentary History.* Tehran: Antidote Publications, 1989.

————. *The Soviet Socialist Republic of Iran, 1920–21: Birth of the Trauma*. Pittsburgh: University of Pittsburgh Press, 1995.

Chaqueri, Cosroe, and D. Bozorg. *Asnad-e Tarikhi: Junbesh-e Kargari, Susiyal Dimukrasi, va Kumunisti-i Iran*. Florence, Italy: Mazdak, 1970. MEDOC.

Chehabi, Houchang E. *Iranian Politics and Religious Modernism: The Liberation Movement of Iran Under the Shah and Khomeini*. Ithaca: Cornell University Press, 1990.

————. "Staging the Emperor's New Clothes: Dress Codes and Nation-Building Under Reza Shah." *Iranian Studies* 26, nos. 3–4 (Summer/Fall 1993): 209–33.

Chehrah-e Matbu'at-e Mo'aser-e Iran. Tehran: Press Agent, 1973.

Clawson, Patrick. "Knitting Iran Together: The Land Transport Revolution, 1920–1940." *Iranian Studies* 26, nos. 3–4 (Summer/Fall 1993): 235–50.

Cole, Juan R. I. "Marking Boundaries, Marking Time: The Iranian Past and the Construction of the Self by Qajar Thinkers." *Iranian Studies* 29, nos. 1–2 (Winter/Spring 1996 [1997]): 36–56.

————. *Modernity and the Millennium: The Genesis of the Baha'i Faith in the Nineteenth-Century Middle East*. New York: Columbia University Press, 1998.

Confidential U.S. State Department Central Files. Iran, 1945–1949 [microform]: Internal Affairs. Frederick, Md.: University Publications of America, 1985.

Danesh. Tehran. MEDOC.

Daneshkadeh. Tehran. MEDOC.

Daneshvar, Simin. *Savushun: A Novel about Modern Iran*. Translated by M. R. Shanoonparvar. Washington, D.C.: Mage, 1990.

Da'vat al-Eslam. Bombay. MEDOC.

Delrish, Boshra. *Zan dar Dowreh-e Qajar*. Tehran: Howzeh-e Honari-ye Sazman-e Tablighat-e Eslami, 1375 [1996–97].

Douglas, Allen, and Fedwa Malti-Douglas. *Arab Comic Strips: Politics of an Emerging Mass Culture*. Bloomington: Indiana University Press, 1994.

Dowlatabadi, Sadiqeh. *Sadiqeh Dowlatabadi: Nameh-ha va Neveshteh-ha va Yad-ha*. Compiled and introduced by Mahdukht San'ti and Afsaneh Najmabadi. 3 vols. New York: A. Najmabadi, 1998.

Eisenstein, Elizabeth L. *The Printing Revolution in Early Modern Europe*. Cambridge: Cambridge University Press, 1983.

Ekhtiar, Maryam Dorreh. "The Dar al-Funun: Educational Reform and Cultural Development in Qajar Iran." Ph.D. diss., New York University, 1994.

Elwell-Sutton, L. P. "The Iranian Press, 1941–1947." *Iran* 4 (1968): 65–105.

Encyclopaedia of Islam: The New Edition. Edited by H.A.R. Gibb, J. H. Kramers, E. Levi-Provençal, and J. Schacht. London: Luzac & Co., 1960.

Encyclopaedia Iranica. Edited by Ehsan Yarsharter. London and New York: Routledge and Kegan Paul, 1987.

Eqdam. Tehran. MEDOC.

Eslamiyeh, Mostafa. *Reza Khan Maksim*. Tehran: Agah, 1372 [1993–94].

Essad-bey, Mohammed, Paul Maerker Branden, and Elsa Branden. *Reza Shah*. London: Hutchinson & Company, 1938.

Ettehadiyeh, Mansureh. *Maramnamehha va Nezamnamehha-ye Ahzab-e Seyasi-e Iran dar Dowreh-e Dovvom-e Majles-e Shura-ye Melli*. Tehran: Nashr-e Tarikh-e Iran, 1361.

Ettela'at. Tehran. University of Chicago and University of Michigan–Ann Arbor.

Faghfoory, Mohammad. "The Impact of Modernization on the Ulama in Iran, 1925–1941." *Iranian Studies* 26, nos. 3–4 (Summer/Fall 1993): 277–312.

Fallaci, Oriana. *Interview with History*. Translated by John Shapely. Boston: Houghton Mifflin Company, 1977.

Farman Farmaian, Sattareh. *Daughter of Persia*. New York: Anchor Books, 1992.

Feminism and Islam. Edited by Mai Yamani. New York: New York University Press, 1996.

Findley, Carter Vaughn. "A Ottoman Occidentalist in Europe: Ahemed Midhat Meets Madame Gülnar." *American Historical Review* 103, no. 1 (February 1998): 15–49.

Firuz, Maryam. *Khatorat-E Maryam Firuz* (Farman farma'iyan). Tehran: E Helaz'at, 1373 [1994–95].

Fleischmann, Ellen. "Crossing Boundaries of History: Exploring Oral History in Researching Palestinian Women in the Mandate Period." *Women's History Review* 5, no. 2 (1996): 351–71.

Floor, Willem M. *Ettehadiyah-ha-yi Kargari va Qanun-e Kar dar Iran, 1900–1941*. Tehran: Tus, 1992.

Floor, Willem M., and Abu al-Qasim Sirri. *Sana'ti Shudan-e Iran va shuresh-e Shaykh Ahmad Madani, 1900–1925*. Tehran: Tus, 1992.

Fowziyah, Malekeh-e Ghamghin: Tarjomeh az Majalleh-e al-Maw'id (Chap-e Bayrut). Tehran: Dastan: 1373 [1994/95].

Fraser, J. B. *Narrative of the Residence of the Persian Princes in London in 1835 and 1836*. Vol. 1. London: R. Bentley, 1838.

Friedl, Erika. *Children of Deh Koh*. Syracuse: Syracuse University Press, 1997.

From Nationalism to Revolutionary Islam Edited by Said Amir Arjomand. Albany: State University of New York Press, 1984.

Ghani, Cyrus. *Iran and the Rise of Reza Shah: From Qajar Collapse to Pahlavi Power*. London: I. B. Tauris, 1998.

Gheissari, Ali. "The Poetry and Politics of Farrokhi Yazdi." *Iranian Studies* 26, nos. 1–2 (Winter/Spring 1993): 33–50.

Gitlin, Todd. *The Whole World Is Watching: Mass Media in the Making and Unmaking of the New Left*. Berkeley: University of California Press, 1980.

Goffman, Erving. *Frame Analysis*. 2d ed. Boston: Northeastern University Press, 1986.

Habl al-Matin. Calcutta. MEDOC.

Haeri, Shahla. *Law of Desire: Temporary Marriage in Shi'i Iran*. Syracuse: Syracuse University Press, 1989.

Hakimi, Mahmud. *Dastanha'i Az 'Asr-e Reza Shah*. 3d ed. Tehran: Qalam, 1374 [1995–96].

Hekmat. Cairo. MEDOC.

Honar va Adabiyat: Goft va Shonud ba Parviz Natel Khanlari va Simin Daneshvar. Babol, Iran: Ketabsara-ye Babol, 1366.

Hourani, Albert. *Arabic Thought in the Liberal Age, 1798–1939*. Cambridge: Cambridge University Press, 1983.

Iran-e Bastan. Tehran. MEDOC.

Iran-e Emruz. Tehran. MEDOC.

Iran-e Ma. Tehran. LOC.

Iran-e Now. Tehran. MEDOC.

Iranshahr. Berlin. MEDOC.

Iran under the Pahlavis. Edited by George Lenczowski. Stanford: Hoover Institution Press, 1978.

Islam and Revolution: Writings and Declarations of Imam Khomeini, translated and annotated by Hamid Algar. Berkeley: Mizan Press, 1981.

Jamalzadeh, Mohammad Ali. *Once Upon a Time*. Translated by Heshmat Moayyad and Paul Sprachman. New York: Bibliotheca Persica, 1985.

Javadi, Hasan. *Satire in Persian Literature*. Rutherford, N.J.: Fairleigh Dickinson University Press, 1988.

Kar, Mehrangiz, and Shahla Lahiji. *Shenakht-e Hoviyat-e Zan-e Irani dar Gostareh-e Pish-e Tarikh va Tarikh*. Tehran: Raushangaran, 1371 [1993].

Kasravi, Ahmad. *Kh^w ahafan va Dolzhtavan-e Ma*. Bethesda, Md.: Ketab forushi-ye Iran, 1992.

Kaveh. Berlin. MEDOC.

Keddie, Nikkie R. *Iran Religion, Politics, and Society: Collected Essays*. London: Frank Cass, 1980.

———. *An Islamic Response to Imperialism: Political and Religious Writings of Sayyid Jamal ad-Din "al-Afghani."* Berkeley: University of California Press, 1983.

Kermani, Mirza Aqa Khan. "Arshiv: Bakhshha'i az *Sad Khetabeh*-e Mirza Aqa Khan Kermani." *Nimeh-e Digar* 9 (Spring 1989): 99–112.

———. *Mirza Aqa Khan Kermani, Namehha-ye Tab 'id*. Edited and introduced by Homa Nateq and Mohammad Firuz. Cologne: Ufuq, 1368 [1989].

Khalq. Tehran.

Khatami, Mohammad. "On the Virtues of the West." *Time*, 19 January 1998, 36.

Khoshunat va Farhang: Asnad-e Mahramaneh-e Kashf-e Hejab (1313–1322). Tehran: Entesharat-e Sazman-e Asnad-e Melli-ye Iran, 1371 [1992–93].

Kh^w andamir, Ghiyas al-Din. *Habib al-Siyar*. Edited by Jalal al-Din Homa'i. 4 vols. Tehran: Khayyam, 1333 [1954].

Knörzner, J. E. *Ali Dashti's "Prison Days": Life Under Reza Shah*. Costa Mesa, Calif.: Mazda and Bibliotheca Persica, 1994.

Kohen, Go'el. *Tarikh-e Sansur Dar Matbu'at-e Iran.* 2 vols. Tehran: Agah, 1360 and 1363.

Kushesh. Tehran. MEDOC.

Ladjevardi, Habib. *Reference Guide to the Iranian Oral History Collection.* Cambridge: Harvard University Center for Middle East Studies, 1988.

Lewis, Bernard. *The Emergence of Modern Turkey.* Oxford: Oxford University Press, 1968.

Losensky, Paul E. "'Welcoming Fighani': Imitation, Influence, and Literary Change in the Persian *Ghazal,* 1480–1680." Ph.D. diss., University of Chicago, 1993.

Machiavelli, Niccolò. *The Prince.* Translated by George Bull. London: Penguin, 1999.

Mahmud al-Sadati, Ahmad. *Rida Shah Bahlawi: Nahdat Iran al-Hadith.* Cairo: Al-Maktaba Al-Nahda Al-Misriyya, 1939.

Makki, Hosayn. *Modarres Qahraman-e Azadi.* Tehran: Bongah-e Tarjomeh va Nashr-e Ketab, 1358 [1979–80].

———. *Tarikh-e Bist Saleh-e Iran.* 8 vols. Tehran: Nashr-e Nasher, 1363 [1984–85].

Mansur, Rowshanak. "Chehreh-e Zan dar Jarayed-e Mashrutiyat," *Nimeh-e Digar* 1, no. 1 (Spring 1363 [1984]): 11–30.

Mardan-e Kar. Tehran. LOC.

Mard-e Emruz. Tehran. MEDOC.

Mardom. Tehran. MEDOC.

Mas'ud, Mohammad. *Golha'i keh dar Jahanam Miruyad.* Tehran: 'Ali Akbar 'Elmi Publishers, 1337 [1958–59].

———. *Tafrihat-e Shab.* 7th ed. Tehran: 'Elmi, n.d.

Matthee, Rudi. "Transforming Dangerous Nomads into Useful Artisans, Technicians, Agriculturalists: Education in the Reza Shah Period." *Iranian Studies* 26, nos. 3–4 (Summer/Fall 1993): 313–36.

Mehr. Tehran. MEDOC.

Mehrabi, Mo'in al-Din. *Qorrat al-'Ayn: Sha'ereh-e Azadikhʷah va Melli-ye Iran.* 2d ed. Cologne: Ruyesh, 1990.

Mehregan. Tehran. MEDOC.

Melman, Billie. *Women's Orients: English Women and the Middle East, 1718–1918.* Ann Arbor: University of Michigan Press, 1992.

Menashri, David. *Education and the Making of Modern Iran.* Ithaca: Cornell University Press, 1992.

Mihan Parastan. Tehran. LOC.

Ministry of Culture. *Salnameh va Amar 1315/16 and 1316/17—Part 2.* Tehran: Sherekat-e Sahami-ye Chap, 1317 [1938–39]. MEDOC and University of Michigan–Ann Arbor.

———. *Salnameh va Amar, 1319–22—Part 2.* Tehran: Sherekat-e Sahami-ye Chap, 1322 [1943–44] MEDOC.

———. *Salnameh va Amar-e Vezarat-e Farhang-e Dowlat-e Shahanshahi-ye Iran, 1322/23–1326/27* [1943-48]. Tehran: Sherekat-e Sahami-ye Chap, 1327. MEDOC and University of Michigan–Ann Arbor.

Mir-Hosseini, Ziba. *Gender and Islam: The Religious Debate in Contemporary Iran.* Princeton: Princeton University Press, 1999.

Mir-Hosseini, Ziba, and Kim Longinotto. *Talaq: Divorce Iranian Style.* Iranian Films, 1998.

Mirza, Rezaqoli. *Safarnameh-e Rezaqoli Mirza Naveh-e Fath ʿAli Shah.* Edited by Asghar Farmanfarmaʾi Qajar. Tehran: Entesharat-e Daneshgah-e Tehran, 1347 [1968–69].

Modarres. 2 vols. Tehran: Bonyad-e Tarikh-e Enqilab-e Eslami-ye Iran, n.d.

Modern Middle East, The. Edited by Albert Hourani, Philip S. Khoury, and Mary C. Wilson. Berkeley: University of California Press, 1993.

Moghissi, Haideh. *Populism and Feminism in Iran: Women's Struggle in a Male-Defined Revolutionary Movement.* New York: St. Martin's Press, 1994.

Moin, Baqer. *Khomeini: Life of the Ayatollah.* New York: St. Martin's Press, 1999.

Monshi, Eskandar Beyg. *History of Shah ʿAbbas the Great.* Vol. 1. Translated by Roger M. Savory. Boulder, Colo.: Westview, 1978.

Mosse, George L. *Nationalism and Sexuality: Middle-Class Morality and Sexual Norms in Modern Europe.* Madison: University of Wisconsin Press, 1985.

Moʿtazed, Khosrow. *Fowziyeh: Hekayat-e Talkhkami, Qesseh-e Jodaʾyi.* 2 vols. Tehran: Alborz, 1372 [1993–94].

Nafisi, Saʿid. *Tarikh-e Moʿaser-e Iran: Az Kudeta-ye Sevvom-e Esfand Mah ta Bist va Chaharom-e Shahrivar, 1320 (Tarikh-e Shahriyar Shahanshah Reza Pahlavi).* Tehran: Foroughi, 1345 [1966].

Nahid. Tehran. MEDOC.

Najmabadi, Afsaneh. "A Different Voice: Taj os-Saltaneh." In *Women's Autobiographies in Contemporary Iran,* edited by Afsaneh Najmabadi, 10–20. Cambridge: Harvard University Press, 1990.

———. "Zanha-yi Millat: Women or Wives of the Nation?" *Iranian Studies* 26, nos. 1–2 (Winter/Spring 1993): 65–71.

———. "Veiled Discourse and Unveiled Bodies." *Feminist Studies* 19, no. 3 (Fall 1993): 487–518.

———. *The Story of the Daughters of Quchan: Gender and National Memory in Iranian History.* Syracuse: Syracuse University Press, 1998.

———. "Crafting an Educated Housewife in Iran." In *Remaking Women: Feminism and Modernity in the Middle East,* edited by Lila Abu-Lughod, 91–125. Princeton: Princeton University Press, 1998.

———. "(Un)Veiling Feminism." *Social Text* 18, no. 3 (2000): 29–45.

Origins of Arab Nationalism. Edited by Rashid Khalidi, Lisa Anderson, Muhammad Muslih, and Reeva S. Simon. New York: Columbia University Press, 1991.

Ostad Malek, Fatemeh. *Hejab va Kashf-e Hejab dar Iran.* Tehran: Moʾassaseh-e Matbuʿati-ye ʿAteʾi, 1367 [1988–89].

Pahlavi, Mohammad Reza. *Mission for My Country*. London: McGraw-Hill, 1961.

Paidar, Parvin. *Women and the Political Process in Twentieth-Century Iran*. Cambridge: Cambridge University Press, 1995.

Pakravan, Fatemeh. *Memoirs of Fatemeh Pakravan, Wife of General Hassan Pakravan, Army Officer, Chief of State Intelligence and Security Organization, Cabinet Minister, and Diplomat*. Edited by Habib Ladjevardi. Cambridge: Iranian Oral History Project, Center for Middle Eastern Studies, Harvard University, 1998.

Parcham-e Eslam. Tehran. LOC.

Parvaresh. Cairo. MEDOC.

Parvin, Nassereddin. "The Sources of Historiography of the Iranian Press." *Iran Nameh* 26, nos. 2–3 (Spring/Summer 1998): 191–210.

Paykar. Berlin.

Peirce, Leslie. *The Imperial Harem: Women and Sovereignty in the Ottoman Empire*. New York: Oxford University Press, 1993.

Perry, John. "Language Reform in Turkey and Iran." *International Journal of Middle East Studies* 17 (1985): 295–309.

Qajar Iran. Edited by E. Bosworth and C. Hillenbrand. Edinburgh: Edinburgh University Press, 1983.

Qanun. London. MEDOC.

Rasayel, E'lamiyehha, Maktubat, va Ruznameh-e Shaykh-e Shahid Fazlollah Nuri. Vol. 1. Edited by Mohammad Torkaman. Tehran: Mo'assaseh-ye Khadamat-e Farhangi-ye Rasa, 1362.

Reconstructing Gender in the Middle East. Edited by Fatma Müge Göçek and Shiva Balaghi. New York: Columbia University Press, 1994.

Records of the Department of State Relating to Internal Affairs of Persia, 1910–1929. Microform. Washington, D.C.: National Archives, National Archives and Records Service, General Services Administration, 1968.

Regan, Carol. "Summary of Ahmad Kasravi's Our Sisters and Daughters." In *Women and the Family in Iran*, edited by A. Fathi, 60–78. Leiden: E. J. Brill, 1985.

Remaking Women: Feminism, Modernity, and the Middle East. Edited by Lila Abu-Lughod. Princeton: Princeton University Press, 1998.

Reza Shah: Khaterat-e Solayman Behbudi, Shams Pahlavi, 'Ali Izadi. Edited by Gholamhosayn Mirza Saleh. Tehran: Tarh-e Now, 1372 [1993].

Ruznameh-e Khaterat-e E'temad Al-Saltaneh, Vazir-e Enteba'at dar Avakher Dowreh-e Naseri, 1292–1313 Hejri-Qamari. 2d printing. Edited and annotated by Iraj Afshar. Tehran: Amir Kabir, 1350 [1971–72].

Ruznameh-e Rasmi-ye Keshvar-e Shahanshahi-ye Iran, Mozakarat-e Majles. Tehran. MEDOC.

Sadeq Hedayat: An Anthology Edited by Ehsan Yarshater. Boulder, Colo.: Westview, 1979.

Sadr-Hashemi, Mohammad. *Tarikh-e Jarayed va Majallat-e Iran*. 2d ed. 4 vols. Isfahan: Kamal, 1363.

Sahlins, Marshall. *Islands of History*. Chicago: University of Chicago Press, 1985.

Salnameh-e Daneshsara-ye 'Ali 1315/16 va 1316/17. Tehran: Chapkhaneh-e Rowshna'i, 1317 [1938–39]. MEDOC.

Sanasarian, Eliz. *The Women's Rights Movement in Iran: Mutiny, Appeasement, and Repression from 1900 to Khomeini*. New York: Praeger, 1982.

Sarmad, Gholam'ali. *E'zam-e Mohassal beh Kharej az Keshvar dar Dowreh-e Qajar*. Tehran: Chap va Nashr-e Bonyad, 1372 [1993–/94].

Sayigh, Rosemary. "Engendered Exile: Palestinian Camp Women Tell Their Lives." *Oral History* 25, no. 2 (Autumn 1997): 39–48.

Sayyah, Fatemeh. *Naqd va Sayyahat: Majmu'eh-e Maqalat va Taqrirat Doktor Fatemeh Sayyah*. Edited by Mohammad Golbon. Tehran: Tus, 1354.

Schrager, Samuel. "What is Social in Oral History?" *International Journal of Oral History* 4, no. 2 (June 1983): 76–98.

Schudson, Michael. *Discovering the News: A Social History of American Newspapers*. New York: Basic Books, 1978.

Scott, Joan Wallach. *Gender and the Politics of History*. New York: Columbia University Press, 1988.

Setareh-e Iran. Tehran. MEDOC.

Shafaq-e Sorkh. Tehran. MEDOC.

Sharq. Tehran. MEDOC.

Shaw, Stanford J., and Ezel Kural Shaw. *History of the Ottoman Empire and Modern Turkey*. Vol. 2. Cambridge: Cambridge University Press, 1977.

Shaykh al-Eslami, Pari. *Zanan-e Ruznameh-Negar va Andishmand-e Iran*. Tehran: Zarrin, 1351 [1972–73].

Sheehan, Vincent. *The New Persia*. New York: Century Co., 1927.

Shifteh, Nasr Allah. *Zendegi-nameh va Mobarrazat-e Seyasi-e Mohammad Mas'ud, Modir-e Ruznameh-e Mard-e Emruz*. Tehran: Aftab-e Haqiqat, 1363.

Shirazi, Mohammad Mirza Saleh. *Majmu'eh-e Safarnamehha-ye Mirza Saleh Shirazi*. Edited by Gholamhosayn Mirza Saleh. Tehran: Nashr-e Tarikh-e Iran, 1364 [1985–86].

Shokufeh. Tehran.

Smith, Dorothy. *The Everyday World as Problematic: A Feminist Sociology*. Boston: Northeastern University Press, 1987.

Sorayya. Cairo. MEDOC.

Southgate, Minoo, ed. *Modern Persian Short Stories*. New York: Three Continents Press, 1980.

Spooner, Brian. *Suppressed Persian: An Anthology of Forbidden Literature*. Costa Mesa, Calif.: Mazda Publishers, 1995.

State Department, U.S. *See* Comfidential U.S. State Department Central Files, Iran; Records of the Department of State Relating to Internal Affairs or Persia.

Stories from Iran: A Chicago Anthology. Edited by Heshmat Moayyad. Washington, D.C.: Mage Publishers, 1992.

Stowasser, Barbara Freyer. *Women in the Qur'an, Traditions, and Interpretation.* Oxford: Oxford University Press, 1994.

Sur-e Esrafil. Tehran. MEDOC.

Szuppe, Maria. "La participation des femmes de la famille royale à l'exercice du pouvoir en Iran safavide au XVIe siècle." *Studia Iranica* 23 (1994): 211–58.

Taqi Saravi, Mohammad Fathollah Ibn Mohammad. *Tarikh-e Mohammadi, "Ahsan Al-Tavarikh."* Edited by Gholamreza Tabataba'i Majd. Tehran: Amir Kabir, 1371 [1992–93].

Tavakoli-Targhi, Mohamad. "Imagining Western Women: Occidentalism and Euro-eroticism." *Radical America* 24 (July/September 1990 [1993]): 72–87.

Tuchman, Gaye. *Making News: A Study in the Construction of Reality.* New York: Free Press, 1978.

Tufan. Tehran. MEDOC.

Vaqaye'-e Ettefaqiyeh. Tehran. MEDOC.

Vaqe'eh-e Kashf-e Hejab: Asnad-e Montasher Nashodeh. Edited by Mortaza Ja'fari, Soghra Esma'ilzadeh, and Ma'sumeh Farshchi. Tehran: Sazman-e Madarek-e Farhangi-e Eslami and Mo'assaseh-e Pezhuhesh va Motala'at-e Farhangi, 1371 [1992–93].

Wilber, Donald N. *Riza Shah Pahlavi: The Resurrection and Reconstruction of Iran, 1978–1944.* Hicksville, N.Y.: Exposition Press, 1975.

Women and the Family in Iran. Edited by A. Fathi. Leiden: E. J. Brill, 1985.

Women and Revolution in Iran. Edited by Guity Nashat. Boulder, Colo.: Westview, 1983.

Women and the Medieval Islamic World. Edited by Gavin R. G. Hambly. New York: St. Martin's Press, 1998.

Women in Middle Eastern History. Edited by Nikki Keddie and Beth Baron. New Haven and London: Yale University Press, 1991.

Women in the Muslim World. Edited by Lois Beck and Nikki Keddie. 3d ed. Cambridge: Harvard University Press, 1980.

Women's Autobiographies in Contemporary Iran. Edited by Afsaneh Najmabadi. Cambridge: Harvard University Press, 1990.

www.salamiran.org

Zaban-e Zanan. Tehran. MEDOC.

Zabih, Sepehr. *The Communist Movement in Iran.* Berkeley: University of California Press, 1966.

Zirinsky, Michael P. "Presbyterian Missionaries and American Relations with Pahlavi Iran." *Iranian Journal of International Affairs* 1, no. 1 (Spring 1989): 71–86.

———. "Imperial Power and Dictatorship: Britain and the Rise of Reza Shah, 1921–1926." *International Journal of Middle East Studies* 24 (November 1992): 639–63.

———. "A Panacea for the Ills of the Country: American Presbyterian Education in Inter-War Iran." *Iranian Studies* 26, nos. 1–2 (Winter/Spring 1993): 119–37.

———. "Render unto Caesar the Things Which Are Caesar's: American Presbyterian Educators and Reza Shah." *Iranian Studies* 26, nos. 3–4 (Summer/Fall 1993): 337–40.

Zonis, Marvin. *Majestic Failure*. Chicago: University of Chicago Press, 1991.

Index

Abadi, Sho'leh, 27
Adamiyat, Fereydun, 262n40
Afary, Janet, 2
Afghans, 82, 85, 88–89, 100, 108
Afkhami, Gen. 'Abd al-Reza, 196
Aflak, 73
Afshar, Mastureh, 192–96
Afshars, 16
Akhavi, Shahrough, 111
Akhtar, 31, 49
Akhundzadeh, Mirza Fath 'Ali, 6, 8, 25–28,
   30, 34, 50, 78, 91, 115, 145, 262n40
Al-Afghani (Asadabadi), Jamal al-Din, 31,
   33–34
'Alam-e Nesvan, 8, 60–63, 123–126, 150,
   157, 168–69, 178
'Alam-e Zanan, 211, 216
'Ali ibn Abi Talib, first Shi'ah *imam*,
   246–47
Amanollah Khan, 81
American La France and Foamite Corpora-
   tion, 104
'Amid, Maryam. *See* Mozzayen al-Saltaneh
Amin, Mohammad, 213
Amin, Na'imeh, 142, 148, 151, 213
Amin, Qasim, 36, 79, 83, 91, 192
Amir Kabir, Mirza Taqi Khan, 20–21, 145
Amirteymour, Mohammad Ebrahim, 87–
   88, 104–7, 122
Anglo-Persian (Anglo-Iranian) Oil Com-
   pany, 84, 174
Anglo-Persian Treaty of 1919, 42, 110
'Aqa'ed al-Nesa (Kolsum Naneh), 17, 23
Aqa-ye Nakhostin. *See* Delshad Khanom
Arabs, 29, 58, 66, 279n19, 291n8
'Arefnameh, 69–70, 92
Arfa', Hasan, 84–85, 89, 105–6, 111

Arfa', Ibrahim, 104–6
Arfa', Reza Arfa' al-Dowleh, 104
Armenians, 58
Ashraf al-Saltaneh, 'Ezzat al-Molk, 24
Asadi, Mohammad Valikhan, 86, 108–9,
   273n34
Astarabadi, Bibi Khanom, 8, 35–36, 46,
   55, 81, 92, 141, 224
Atatürk, Mustafa Kemal, 84–85
Atesh, 232–36
Azad, Sayf, 171, 208
Azerbaijan, 17, 50, 63, 181

Baba Shamal, 222–26
Babism, 17, 20, 30, 67, 258n22
Badran, Margot, 11
Baha'ism, 17, 31, 152, 258n22
Baha'o'llah, Mirza Hosayn 'Ali Nuri, 31
Bahar, Malek al-Sho'ara, 98, 159, 261n27
Bahlul. *See* Shaykh Bahlul
Balaghi, Shiva, 258n23
Bamdad, Badr al-Moluk, 296n43
Banani, Amin, 255–56n1
Basri, Tal'at, 3
bazgasht-e adabi (the "literary return"),
   25, 261n27
Beauty contests, 208, 212
Bethel American School for Girls, 60–62,
   95, 100, 150, 152–53, 164–65, 200
Bidari-ye Ma, 226
Bidari-ye Zanan (Women's Awakening,
   communist), 74
Butler, N. M., 101–2

Caucasus, 59, 239
Chador (full-length veil), 23, 83, 90, 100,
   178, 210–11, 241

Chehabi, Houshang, 6
CiXi, Empress Dowager, 23
Communism, 10, 12, 15, 49, 63, 74, 81,
    154, 200, 213, 245. *See also* Tudeh
    Party
"Companionate" marriage, 114, 135–41
Comte, Auguste, 201–2
Constitutional Revolution, 2–6, 8, 37, 47,
    49, 145
Courtship, 114–26, 133–34
"Cultural scheme," 258n25

Dabbagh, Hosayn. *See* Sorousch, ('Abd al-
    Karim
Dabbaj, Amireh, 260n12
Damascus, 189–90
Danesh, 8, 40, 42–6, 49, 56–57, 59–60,
    91, 96, 97, 114, 117–18, 126, 141,
    207–8
Daneshsara, 83, 94–97
Daneshsara-ye 'Ali ("high college"). *See*
    University of Tehran
Daneshvar, Simin, 7–8
"Dangerous" women, 15, 205–14
Dar al-Fonun, 23, 145, 283n4
Dar al-Mo'allamat, 42, 60, 283–84n11
Dashti, 'Ali, 108–9
"Daughters of Quchan," 37, 108
Dehkhoda, 'Ali Akbar, 56, 68, 159
Delshad, Khanom, 124–25
Democrat Party, 226, 237–38
Doolittle, Jane Elizabeth, 61–62, 95–96,
    124–25, 153–54
Dowlatabadi, Sadiqeh, 42, 63, 82, 119–22,
    146, 174–77, 219, 229–31, 269n60
Dowlatshahi, Gholam 'Ali Mojallal al-
    Dowleh, 115–17
Dowlatshahi, Mehrangiz, 7, 83, 115–17,
    148–49, 151–54, 159–61, 164–65, 184,
    237
Dowlatshahi, Mohammad 'Ali Moshkat
    al-Dowleh, 83–84, 115–17
Dowlatshahi, Sadiqeh (Qodsiyeh), 8, 11,
    174–78, 200, 212, 232
Dowlatshahi (Pahlavi), 'Esmat Taj al-
    Moluk, 115–17
Dowshan Tepe Airfield, 176–77

Ebtehaj-Samii, Nayereh, 139–40
Ecolé Franco-Persan, 146
Education, 142–65. *See also* Teachers;
    Women's Awakening
—elementary, 90, 145–49, 151–52
—secondary, 66, 146–48, 150–55, 163–64
—university and postsecondary, 146–48,
    151, 154–65
'Effatiyeh School, 146
Egypt, 31, 83, 135–39, 145, 190–92, 195,
    239, 272n5, 282nn78, 86
Electoral Law, 38–40, 197
Employment (for women), in medicine and
    typing, 165–89. *See also* Office work;
    Teachers; Women; Women's Awakening
England, 42, 49–57, 64, 88–89, 108, 113,
    117–18, 153, 234
Eqdam, 220–224
Esfandyari, Hajj Mohtashem al-Saltaneh,
    90, 92–93
Eskandari, Mohtaram, 74, 81, 272n5
Eskandari, Solayman, 74
ESKI (Labor Union), 184, 226
Estifa, Fakhri, 220, 223
E'temad al-Saltaneh, Mirza Hasan, 24,
    261n22
E'tesami, Parvin, 98
Ettela'at, 62, 85, 93–94, 96, 98, 132, 155–
    159, 190–197, 206
Europe, 29–30, 58, 65–66, 198, 217, 240
"Euro-American example," 48, 50–67, 71,
    76–77, 79, 115–22, 165–72, 205, 212,
    224

Fakhr al-Dowleh, 221
Farmanfarma, 'Abd al-Hosayn, 110
Farmanfarma, Hasan 'Ali, 53–54
Farmanfarma, Hosayn 'Ali, 53–54
Farmanfarmaian, Firuz Nosrat al-Dowleh,
    110
Farmanfarmaian, Mohammad Vali, minis-
    ter of labor, 182
Farmanfarmaian (Farman Farmaian),
    Sattareh, 110, 152–53, 155, 200–201,
    225
Farmanfarmaian (Firuz), Maryam, 225–28
Farrokh, Jamileh, 153

Farrokhi. *See* Yazdi
Feda'iyan-e Eslam, 242–45
Firuz, Maryam. *See* Farmanfarmaian, Maryam
Firuz, Saffiyeh, 139–40, 200, 234, 236, 238
Firuzeh, 212
Flight school. *See* Dowshan Tepe; Women pilots
Forughi, Mohammad 'Ali Zoka al-Molk, 38–39, 109, 133, 170
Foucault, Michel, 103, 251
Fowziyeh (Egyptian princess, first wife of Mohammad Reza Pahlavi), 5, 14, 114, 134–39, 282nn78, 83, 86; wedding of, 134–37; divorce of, 138–39
"Frame analysis," 258n25
France, 118, 157, 168, 177–79, 209, 284n25
Frasier, James Baille, 54
Fundamental Law of Education (1911), 145

Garighozalou, Ebrahim Khan, 82
Garighozalou, Naghi Khan, 82
Georgia, 17, 259–60n2
Germany, 56, 63, 117–18, 157, 159, 168, 170–73, 177, 209, 237
Ghani, Cyrus 5
Gibson, Thomas, 201
Girl Scouts, 94, 200–201
Göçek, Fatma Müge, 258n23
Golanabad (Battle of), 89
Golestan, Ebrahim, 71
Gowharshad Mosque, 8, 86–90, 100, 105–11, 157, 242

Hadashian, Heshmat, 169
Haeri, Shahla, 10–11
Hajilu, Puran, 224
Hamadan, 99
Hamadeh, Nur, 191, 194–95
Hart, Charles C., 82, 102, 127–29, 133, 135, 170
Hashemi-Ha'eri, 'A. 'A., 191–96
Hasht Behesht, 30
Hat Law: (1935), 86, (1928 and 1935) 110, 112–13

Hayat-e 'Elmiyeh, 39, 265n96
Haydari, Zohreh, 169–71, 289n120
Haydeh Khanom, 153
Hedayat, Rezaqoli Mirza, 53–55, 206
Hedayat, Sadeq, 71
Hejazi, Mohammad, 72, 204
Hekmat, 'Ali Asghar Khan, 83–85, 285n36
Helyat al-Mottaqin, 18
Hollywood, 15, 208–9
Homayun, Batul, 93
"Honor killing," 280–81n59
Hosam, Pari Khanom, 94
Hosayn, Third Shi'ah *imam*, 107

İönü, İsmet, 85, 198
International Women's Congress (Istanbul, 1935), 93
India, 100
Iraj Mirza, 69–70, 78–79, 93
Iran-e Bastan, 171–73, 208
Iran-e Emruz, 172–76, 178, 199, 201–4
Iran-e Ma, 240–41
Iran-e Now, 40, 49, 58–63, 67, 224
Iranshahr, 63, 91, 119–22, 126, 171, 210
Iraq, 60, 191
Islamic Republic, 2, 15–16, 39, 71, 79, 87, 162, 226, 251–53, 256n13, 300n5
Islamic Revolution, 2, 107, 211

Jam, Mahmud, 99
Jamalzadeh, Mohammad 'Ali, 65, 68, 78
Jamalzadeh, Zhazhi, 65–67
Jam'iyat-e Ershad al-Nesvan, 60
Japan, 56–57, 168, 232, 289n35
Jews, 58, 279n19, 284n28
Joan D'Arc School, 151, 181
Journal de Teheran, 85

Kamrooz-Atabai, Badry, 159
Kandiyoti, Deniz, 114
Kanun-e Banovan. See Women's Society
Kashf al-Asrar, 112–13
Kasravi, Ahmad, 230–32, 245, 297n57
Kaveh, 63–67, 91, 96, 122
Kazemzadeh, Hosayn, 119
Kemal, Namik, 31

Kermani, Mirza Aqa Khan (Mirza 'Abd al-Hosayn Khan), 25, 27–32, 34, 35–36, 43, 50, 78, 145, 236, 279n19
Keshavaraz, Fereydun, 228
Khalesi, Ayatollahzadeh Mehdi, 122–23, 149–50, 153
Khalili, 'Abbas, 220
Khalq, 73–77
Khanlari, Moloud, 151, 159, 298n75
Khatami, Mohammad, 3
Khayr al-Nesa Begom (Mahd-e 'Olya), 19, 20
Khayrat Hesan, 23
Khomeini, Ayatollah Ruhollah, 112–13
Khorshid-e Iran, 240
Khuri, Hanineh, 190–92
Khʷajehnuri, Ebrahim, 81
Khʷajehnuri, 'Effat, 132, 196
Khʷansari, Mohammad Ebn Hosayn, 18
Kolsum Naneh. *See* 'Aqa'ed al-Nesa'
Koran (Qur'an), 12, 20, 26, 29, 35, 38, 40–41, 46, 242–44, 255n1, 265nn111, 112, 269n33, 288n103
Kushesh, 208–9, 217–19, 224, 240

Labor history, 295n5
Ladjevardi, Habib, 10, 160, 259n33
Lahuti, 70
Lebanon, 193–95
Linday, Sir Henry Bethune, 53
London, 30, 52
Loraine, Percy, 272n15

Ma'ayeb al-Rejal, 35–37
Machiavellli, Niccolò, 103
Majles. *See* Parliament
Majlesi, Mohammad Baqer, 18
Makki, Hosayn, 4, 111–13
Malak al-Zaman, 123
Malcom, Sir John, 52
Male backlash, against women office workers, 217–26, 231–32, 250
Male guardianship defined, 12
Mansur, Rowshanak, 32
Mardan-e Kar, 240–41
Mard-e Emruz, 221–22, 243
Mardom, 112, 225–26

Marmon-Harrington, Inc., 104–5
Marriage Laws:
—of 1931, 7, 9, 14, 110, 114, 126–32, 196, 247; passing of, 127–29; enforcement of, 130–32
—of 1937, 7, 132–34
Marriage versus higher education, 155–59, 205–6
Mashhad, 6, 13, 24, 86–90, 100, 101, 105, 155, 210, 273n34
Mas'ud, Mohammad, 3, 7, 71–73, 111–12, 221, 243, 245, 285n36
Mas'udi, 'Abbas, 85, 190–92
Matbu'i, Iraj , 88–89, 106
Mazandarani, Farangis, 223–24
Mehr-e A'in School, 153
Mehregan, 99, 134–35, 208–9, 212
Mehr-e Iran, 111, 240–42
Menashri, David, 146–47
Mihan-Parastan, 234
Mill, John Stuart, 201–2
Millspaugh, Arthur Chester, 109, 221
Ministry of Health, 179
Ministry of Labor, 181–83
Mir Hadi, Maryam, 232–33
Mir-Hosseini, Ziba, 300n5
Mirza Malkam Khan, 8, 21, 31, 32–36, 64, 78, 91, 125
Missionaries: Bah'i), 150; Presbyterian, 40, 149–50, 284n25
Moayyed-Sabeti, Parvin, 100–101, 210, 276–77n99
Modarres, Sayyed Hasan, 39–40, 170, 264n93
Modern Iranian womanhood defined, 12
Moghissi, Haideh, 249
Mossadeq, Mohammad, 3, 177, 180–81, 229
Movaqar, Majid, 99–111
Mozayyen al-Saltaneh, Maryma 'Amid, 40, 58
Muhammad, Prophet, 26, 58, 242–43, 246, 252, 284n28, 288n103
Murad, Fatimah, 192

Naficy, Habib, 182
Naficy, Ozma Adl, 151, 181–84

Naficy, Sa'id, 151

Nahid, 73–79, 270–71n96

Nahid, Mirza Ebrahim Khan, 73

Nahj al-Balaghah, 246

Nahzat-e Banovan. See Women's Awakening Project

Nahzat-e Melli, 240

Najmabadi, Afsaneh, xii, 6, 35, 224, 245, 291n8

Najmiyeh Hospital, 180–81

Nameh-e Banovan, 63

Namus School, 146

Nashat, Guity, 249

National Bank Hospital, 180

Nosrat al-Dowleh, Mirza Malkam Khan. *See* Mirza Malkam Khan

Nowzad, Ahmad Khan, 125

Nurbakhsh School, 153–54

Nurbakhshiyan Society, 100, 210–11

Nuri, Shaykh Fazlollah, 149, 284n28

Office work, 167–71, 174, 177, 181–84, 216–22

'Olama (clerics), 18, 87–88, 109–10, 130–31, 239–42

Organization of Public Enlightenment (*sazman-e parvaresh-e afkar-e 'omumi*), 239, 259n26, 281–82n77

Ottoman Empire, 13, 117–18, 145, 148, 283–84n11

Owrang, Zahir al-Eslam, 194–94, 291n8

Pahlavi, Ashraf, 137, 183, 234–35

Pahlavi, Mohammad Reza, 5, 13–14, 84, 102, 114, 134–39, 200, 234, 240, 292n29

Pahlavi, Reza, 1–5, 13–15, 37, 46, 49, 63, 73–75, 78, 80–96, 103–13, 115–17, 126, 132, 146–47, 174, 177–78, 184, 189–90, 195, 197, 217, 219, 221, 228, 252, 292n29

Pahlavi, Shams, 196

Pahlavi Dynasty, 25, 46–47, 114, 246–53

Paidar, Parvin, 126–27, 249

Pakravan, Fatemeh, 178–81

Parcham-e Eslam, 242–44

Parliament, 37–42, 55, 63, 74, 78, 97,

107, 109, 124, 127, 148–49, 224, 228–32, 236–37, 264n93, 265n95

Parsa, Fakhr Afaq, 269n60

Patriotic Women's League (*jami'at nesvan-e vatankhʷah*), 74, 81, 192–96, 248

Payk-e Sa'adat-e Nesvan, 78

Persian Cossack Brigade, 46

Pishehvari, Ja'far, 183

Polygyny, 26–28, 35–36, 45–46, 115, 117

Press as a source, 9–10

Prostitution, 222, 267n19

Qajar, 'Abbas Mirza, 50

Qajar, 'Ezzat al-Molk, Ashraf al-Saltaneh, 24

Qajar, Fath 'Ali Shah, 21, 53

Qajar, Malek Jan Khanom, 21

Qajar, Naser al-Din, 21, 31, 35, 67, 124, 284n25

Qajar, Vosuq al-Dowleh (Prince), 46, 98–99

Qajar Dynasty, 2, 5, 13, 17, 20–22, 25, 31, 32, 37, 46–47, 142, 145, 259–60n2

Qane', Mas'ud, 103

Qanun, 8, 31–34, 64, 96, 125, 234

Qavam, Ahmad, 109, 138, 226, 228–29, 237, 239–40

Qezelbash (qizilbash), 16, 18–19

Qommi, Ayatollah Hajj Aqa Hosayn, 86, 239–42

Qorrat al-'Ayn, Fatemeh Zarrin Taj, 6, 8, 17, 20–21, 23, 257–58n22

Queen Victoria, 23, 56

Queen Wilhelmina, 23

Renewalism, 17, 25, 37, 46–48, 63, 78, 114

Renewal Party, 46, 63, 67, 73, 207

Revivalism, Islamic, 242–46; 97–98; in Pahlavi propaganda, 248–53

Romania, 56

Ruhi, Shaykh Ahmad, 30–31

Russia, 13, 37, 56–57, 59, 64, 83, 108, 113, 118, 149, 170–71, 200

Saba, Badr al-Moluk, 3, 119–22

Saberi, Pari, 161–62

Sa'di, 30, 51
Sad Khetabeh (Hundred Sermons), 27–32, 262n40
Safavi, Pari Khanom, 19
Safavi, Shah 'Abbas I, 19
Safavi, Shah Esma'il, 259–60nn2, 12
Safavi, Shah Esma'il II, 19
Safavi, Shah Soltan Hosayn, 18
Safavi, Shah Tahmasb I, 19
Safavid Dynasty, 15–21
Sahlins, Marshall, 258n25
Salam Iran, 238, 249
Sami'ian, 'Effat, 168
Sanna'i, Mahmud, 202–3
Sanssarian, Eliz, 4
Saudi Arabia, 195
SAVAK, 180
Savushun, 153
Sayyah, Fatemeh, 4, 7, 146, 163, 199–200, 201–2, 233, 236–37
Scott, Joan Wallach, 258n23
Second Congress of Eastern Women (1932), 6, 8, 14, 83, 189–97, 247–48
Seh Maktub (The Three Letters), 5, 6, 26, 262n40
Sepehr, Mirza Mohammad Taqi Lisan al-Molk, 20
Setareh-e Iran, 60, 78, 122–23
Setareh-e Sobh, 73
"Seventeenth of Day," 80, 94–96, 101
Shafaq, Rezazadeh, 169
Shafaq-e Sorkh, 63, 71, 81, 122, 153–54, 168
Shanehchi, Mohammad, 107–8
Sharaf, 23
Sharafat, 23
Shaykh Bahlul, 88, 273n34
Shaykh al-Eslami, Pari, 3
Sheehan, Vincent, 108, 255n2, 289n120
Shi'ism, Sevener (Esma'ili), 26
Shi'ism, Twelver, 17–18, 20, 29, 39, 255n1
Shirazi, Dr. 'Abd al-Karim Faqihi Shirazi, 242–45
Shirazi, Mirza Saleh, 50–53, 55
Shirazi, Sayyed Mohammad, 17
Shirazi, Zandokht, 12, 237
Shokufeh, 8, 40, 49, 57–60, 91, 96, 126, 146, 165–68, 172, 207

Smith, Dorothy, 250n23
Social Democrat Party, 145–46
Socialist Party, 46, 49, 63, 73–74
Sorayya, 37
Soroush, 'Abd al-Karim, 246–47
Sur-e Esrafil, 49, 55–63, 224
Syria, 189–90, 195

Tabataba'i, Sayyed Mostafa, 119–22
Tabataba'i, Sayyed Zia al-Din, 109
Ta'dib al-Nesvan, 34–38
Tafrihat-e Shab, 71–73
Tahrir al-Mar'ah, 36
al-Tahtawi, Rifa' Rifa'a, 31
Taleqani, Ayatollah , 107
Taqizaeh, Sayyed Hasan, 63–64, 170
Tarbiyat, Hajer, 93, 158, 244
Tarbiyat School, 152, 174
Tavakoli, Mohammad, 2, 55
Tehran-e Mosavvar, 240
Tehrani, Shaykh 'Abdollah Masih, 103
Teymourtache, Hasan, 83, 115
Teymourtache, Iran, 83, 272n11
Tobacco Concession of 1890, 31
"Traditional womanhood," 22–23, 48, 67–79
TransIranian Railroad, 46, 113
Tudeh Party, 8, 74, 112, 151, 225–26, 234, 238, 245, 298n75
Tufan, 73–74, 78
Turcomanchai, Treaty of, 17
Turkey, Republic of, 13, 84–85, 104, 195, 197–98, 239
Turks, 24, 59
Tusi, Maryam, xii, 10, 142–44, 148–49, 152, 154, 159, 161–63, 212–13
Typing, 93, 168–70, 217–19

United Aircraft Exports Corporation, 104
United Nations, 233, 298n70
United Women's Organization, 83
University of Tehran, 142–65; clubs, 159–60, 283n4

Vakil al-Ra'aya, Hajj Shaykh Mohammad Taqi, 38, 264n93
Vaqaye'-e Ettefaqiyeh, 22–23
Vauxhall Gardens, 52

Vazir Khan-e Lankoran, 26
Vaziri, Afzal, 81
Veil, 1–15, 57–8, 69–70, 75–77, 80–113,
144–45, 255n1. *See also Chador*
—attacks on unveiled women, 103, 239
—attacks on veiled women, 102. *See also*
Women's Awakening
Vokala-ye Morafe'eh, 26–27

Ward, Irene, 234
Wilson, Woodrow, 66
"Woman question," 16, 21, 25–47, 174
Women:
—in medicine: doctors, 60, 142–44, 148,
154, 168, 212–13; hospital administrators, 178–80; nurses, 165–68, 180–81
—as pilots, 155, 169, 175–78, 290n140
—as teachers, 180, 186–88. *See also* Education
—as telegraph operators, 274n60
Women's Awakening Project (*nahzat-e
banovan*), 1–15, 74, 79, 80–113, 141,
189–90, 215–16, 228, 230–31, 239–40,
243, 245–53
—and education, 142–44, 146–47, 158–65
—and employment, 165–88, 204. *See also*
Office work; Typing; Women in medicine; Women as teachers
—and propaganda, 90–99, 161, 172–76,
200–205, 207, 243
—and social etiquette, 101–3, 105–7, 160,
207, 212–13
—and unveiling enforcement, 99–101,
103, 105–13
—and women's athleticism, 64, 156, 171,

173, 251–52; conflation with glamorous
beauty, 207–9
Women's Committee (*tashkilat-e zanan*), 8,
228–28, 238
Women's Council (*shura-ye zanan*), 8, 234,
236, 238, 298n70
Women's Party (*hezb-e zanan*). *See*
Women's Council
Women's Society (*kanun-e banovan*), 8,
85–86, 93–96, 98–99, 158, 161–62,
219, 239, 248
Women's suffrage, 14, 197–200, 248–50,
252; in Denmark, 56; in Great Britain,
56, 234; in Turkey, 197–98; in the
United States, 199–200
—in Iran: discussed in parliament, 37–42,
127, 197, 234; campaign in the 1940s,
225–39
World War II, 215, 217

Yazdanfarr, Tahereh, 223
Yazdi, Mirza Mohammad Farrokhi, 72–
73, 271n97

Zaban-e Zanan, 42, 63, 119, 219–20,
229–31
Zanan, 122
Zanjan, 234–35
Zarghami, General, 105
Zarkesh, 'Abbas, 119–22
Zand Dynasty, 16
Zoroastrian School, 151–52, 164, 279n19
Zoroastrianism, 58
Zulu, 117–18
Zur-khaneh (traditional gymnasium), 156

Camron Michael Amin has published articles in *Iranian Studies* and the *International Journal of Middle East Studies*. He is an assistant professor of Middle Eastern history at the University of Michigan–Dearborn and serves as the project director for the Modern Middle East Sourcebook Project.